OUT OF WORK

A Study of Unemployment

FRANCES A. KELLOR

Arno Press & The New York Times
NEW YORK   1971

Reprint Edition 1971 by Arno Press Inc.

Reprinted from a copy in
The University of Illinois Library

LC# 71—137172
ISBN 0—405—03111—4

POVERTY, U.S.A.: THE HISTORICAL RECORD
ISBN for complete set: 0-405-03090-8

Manufactured in the United States of America

OUT OF WORK

A STUDY OF UNEMPLOYMENT

BY

FRANCES A. KELLOR

AUTHOR OF "EXPERIMENTAL SOCIOLOGY," "ATHLETIC GAMES IN
THE EDUCATION OF WOMEN," AND EDITOR OF THE
"IMMIGRANTS IN AMERICA REVIEW," ETC.

G. P. PUTNAM'S SONS

NEW YORK AND LONDON

The Knickerbocker Press

1915

The Knickerbocker Press, New York

TO

A. M.

A CITIZEN OF THE WORLD'S HEART

PREFACE

THE extraordinary conditions of unemployment prevailing in the winter of 1914 and 1915, and the little real progress made in the organization of the labor market since 1904, the date of the first appearance of *Out of Work*, have led me to revise the data published at that time in order to make it describe accurately the unemployment situation of the present, and the remedial measures now undertaken or projected. I hope this presentation may serve in some way to bring about a coördination of the work now being done, to stimulate new activities, and to focus attention upon unemployment as a national problem, looking toward the adoption of a governmental policy.

In the preparation of the data and its formulation, I am especially indebted to my collaborator, Esther Everett Lape, and to the Committee for Immigrants in America. The Committee has not only unreservedly placed its resources at my disposal but has created a division on employment in charge of a counsel which stands ready to furnish further data and to consult with and advise all organizations and persons who may wish to take up the practical measures, hereinafter

outlined, for the purpose of alleviating distress
and preventing unemployment.

Through the sympathetic interest and generos-
ity of Mrs. Willard Straight many of the practical
measures outlined have already been put into
operation and a station has been opened for the
distribution of the unemployed from New York
City. I hope this beginning will in a short time
lead the government to assume the work of distribution as well as other responsibilities in relation to this great human and industrial problem.

FRANCES A. KELLOR.

January 29, 1915,
95 MADISON AVENUE, NEW YORK CITY.

CONTENTS

CHAPTER I

CHAPTER II

Contents

Contents

Contents

PAGE

mittees—Functions—Opportunities for aid from
civic organizations and individual citizens—Long-
time or preventive program—Securing of accurate
information covering industries and workers—
Study of labor-market facilities, of emergency
measures—Establishment of Federal clearing-house
system—Abolition of state agencies below standard
—Strengthening of existing city agencies and creation
of new ones—Coöperation of private and civic
agencies, in separating employables and unemployables—Federal regulation of agencies doing interstate business—Uniform state and municipal laws
regulating private agencies—Regularization of
industry—Developing coöperation between employers and employees—The Protocol—Regularizing and planning of government work—Reorganization of civil-service laws—Direction of children into
industry—Unemployment-insurance experiments.

APPENDICES

Out of Work

CHAPTER I

UNEMPLOYMENT IN AMERICA

WAR has torn Europe asunder, shattered industrial activity and prosperity, destroyed industrial peace, and halted social insurance and other industrial welfare measures. Its first immediate effect in America has been stagnation of business, disturbance of credit and an enormous increase in unemployment, especially among skilled and professional workers. There are thousands of dollars and hundreds of organizations for relief in this immediate crisis, but practically no agency for steadying the labor market, and at the same time providing work. Unemployment is not yet regarded as one of the factors that must be taken into account in the problem of industrial organization, and no adequate provisions have therefore been made for its representation, such as credit has in the banking system, and treasury department, investments in the stock exchange and capital in boards of trade. It is not strange therefore that the present intensification of unemployment is being met merely by increasing relief measures.

Prosperous America has steadily and obstinately refused to admit that it has a genuine unemployment problem, chargeable against industry. Publications establishing this fact have been frowned upon as harmful to business. Protest meetings and public discussion have received little encouragement. The unshakable belief of the American in the prosperity of his country and the prevalent delusion that every man willing to work can find steady work have prevented him from taking stock. The ease with which workmen have been drafted from foreign countries and the indifference which has permitted them to return to their home industries in slack seasons to spend their earnings have prevented industry from noting certain very important industrial changes, such for instance as the entrance of women and children into industry, covering losses in wages and in regularity of work for male earners and blinding many to both the growth and cost of unemployment. It follows that upon the subject of unemployment in this country, research is limited, knowledge circumscribed, and literature local or indefinite; the remedies, if there are any, are inadequate and antiquated. In a country where there is a commission or civic committee or trade organization dealing with every other social problem, the wilderness of unemployment has remained unexplored, its waste has gone unchecked, its causes remained obscure.

America's persistent refusal to face existing conditions is partly due to certain illusions which exist in the popular mind:

"Any man who really wants a job can get one of some kind." The implication is that every man in a bread-line is aged, infirm, deficient, or a shirker. There is complete disregard of the fact that many fields of work are highly specialized and the standards exacting. Why, it is asked, for instance, should not every man shovel snow, provided the snow is obliging enough to come at a critical time, and in sufficient quantity to warrant equipping all the waiting thousands with snow shovels? In the winter of 1913–14 one county superintendent of the poor in New York State, somewhat distrusting the old tradition that any man out of work should be able to do anything that could be called work, asked for a physical examination of thirty men who were detailed to go "out on the road." The physician that made the examination certified that twelve of the men were unfitted for the work in their present condition, and that six others were organically unfitted for that particular work at any time. Another answer is found in a study of 2000 unemployed men in the Municipal Lodging House in New York City in the winter of 1913–14. Far from being incapacitated by age, they were in the very prime of life, thirty-six years being the average age.

Five per cent. of them were under twenty-one years of age, and only 127 were over sixty years. Only twelve per cent. showed actual evidence of defective mentality; forty per cent. were skilled workmen. The superintendent of the lodging house summarizes the investigation thus:

> About thirty-five per cent. of these homeless men are unemployable. This included habitual loafers, the confirmed beggars, those physically disabled, the mentally deficient, the infirm from age, and those handicapped by the loss of a member. The remaining sixty-five per cent. are employable—willing and able to work. More than half of these are skilled and, *evidently, are reserve labor out of place and out of season.*

"You can always get work on a farm." This popular theory ignores the seasonal and isolated nature of farm labor, the growth of manufacture, and the differences in wage rates. It minimizes the fact that it is often impossible for the laborer to pay for transportation to the places where farm work exists. It ignores the more obvious fact that there is no farm work in winter. The theory is as little tenable as the dictum "Anybody can raise chickens," the fallacy of which now perhaps needs no comment.

"But so far as the women are concerned—any girl can get housework!" This is based on the knowledge that good houseworkers are in demand, but ignores the fact that factory workers are often no more fitted to do housework than housewives

who know nothing about housework are fitted to
direct them. In times of industrial depression,
moreover, the first economies are practised within
households. During the winter of 1914 many
housewives did their own work or reduced their
staff; and a considerable number of unemployed
women were household workers, set adrift in this
way for the first time in many years.

Finally there is the triumphant "Stop immigration." The advocates of this remedy for unemployment apparently do not know that although
the highly skilled trades engage few immigrants
in New York State, sixteen per cent. were reported by the unions as unemployed in 1913. Of
the already mentioned 2000 cases at the Municipal
Lodging House in New York City, about forty
had been in the United States less than three
years, while only nine per cent. had been in the
city less than one year. The *average* time of
residence in New York City proved to be thirty-
two years and four months. Certainly these
were native sons. Moreover, the forty per cent.
of skilled workmen at least had not been displaced
by immigrants. And, on the other hand, the
ranks of "hoboes" include few recent immigrants;
rarely do they beg at the back doors of American
homes.

Is there a genuine unemployment problem inherent in our industrial life, of sufficient importance
to be dealt with by business, labor, and government, or is there simply an increasing body of

vagrants for the police to handle, and of unemployables for whom charity should furnish relief?

Such questioning as this is formulated more clearly by the rude shock this country has received in the European war and by the subsequent realization of America's dependence upon international markets. Just as a shirt-waist factory fire was a sad prerequisite for fire prevention laws, a *Titanic* disaster a tragic preface to safety on the sea, a holocaust at Calumet and a massacre at Ludlow heartrending antecedents to a more authoritative knowledge of labor conditions, so, it seems, may the present war be a tragic agent for arousing America to the menace of unemployment. Before it, unemployed men had invaded churches, asking for shelter and work; babies had clamored for places in bread-lines; armies of men had started out to march to Washington to register a protest, and men had been shot down in hop-field riots. None of these things, however, served to focus public attention upon unemployment as an *industrial* evil. The employed, from the vantage point of a job, and the employer, secure in his investment, have held placidly to the old tradition that there was plenty of work. Even the unemployed, tramping the streets for jobs, have cherished the traditional faith of a new country famed for prosperity, and had their fears lulled to sleep by the first temporary job. The "won't works," feeling secure in America's generous but not too inquiring liberality and lax regulations of vagrancy, escaped both work and discipline. The men on the firing line who urged action were regarded not as prophets but as agitators.

But so many "steady jobs" have been lost that the most complacent believer in prosperity is abandoning his belief that unemployment is a matter of morality rather than of industry. When, for instance, he read in the newspaper one morning in the winter of 1913–14 that 325,000 men were out of work in New York City alone, he may have felt some annoyance at the perpetrator of statistics so disturbing and at the shiftlessness, if not the immorality, of those that furnished any reason for being included in that count; but he found less satisfaction or peace of mind than formerly in so expressing his opinion. Somewhere lurked the fear for his own job and family.

Close upon these revelations followed others which further threatened his complacency. Nightly the New York City Municipal Lodging House was overtaxed to double its capacity, and the city's icy piers overcrowded with sleepers, even the Morgue opened that the homeless living might sleep beside the unknown dead. There were new faces every night; it was a shifting crowd. Where they slept on the other nights, and what moves they made to find a corner or to find work is a question answered only by the resourcefulness of the individual sufferers and the incidental kindness of citizens more fortunate than they. Settlements served as lodging-houses though they had nothing better to offer than newspapers for sheets and floors for beds.

"Swept out with the sawdust in the morning," laconically answered one man when asked where he was living. While city authorities and civic societies debate whether unemployment is a relief or an industrial matter, and whether shelter without a work test will pauperize the homeless, the back rooms of saloons are the actual refuge for many. Fourteen hundred and twenty-six unemployed and homeless men were found sleeping in *ninety-four* saloons during one investigation in the winter of 1913–14 in New York City. The man that has a nickel gets a drink, a free lunch, and a spot on the floor in the sawdust; and perhaps this is the best nickel's worth and the cheapest, warmest, surest, and cleanest guarantee against freezing in many cities to-day. If he has no nickel the saloon-keeper checks up his promise of future patronage,—a promise he is pretty certain to keep. Moreover, the saloon-keeper knows the contractors, the city officials, and the head waiters, and can manipulate more jobs than the best employment agency in existence. He is ready to listen to a tale of woe, to make a small loan, to provide food—in short, he is a genuine, if interested, friend of the "down and out" man. It is grimly significant that in 1913–14 the New York State Excise Department found it necessary to deal with this subject at some length. It made recommendations for relief including the establishment of municipal lodging-houses, at the same time emphasizing the point that until such lodging-houses are adequately established, it is futile to call for the closing of the saloons to the homeless.

One reason for the popularity of the saloon as a lodging-place is found in the answer of one of the men in the bread-line, to a question as to where he expected to sleep:

Saloon for mine [said he], I've been staying at some of the Missions, but you see, most of them want you to get converted every night before you get a bed, and those that whoop up the penitence most are on the preferred list for pew seats. I don't know but what the saloon's a bit more honest with God—for me. And then it's handier—you can make connections better.

For it's a funny system, this,—you can't get both a bed and meal together in this town. You can't hit the bread-line until midnight and every bed is gone at 9:30, and the Mills Hotels beds are gone at 3:30 in the afternoon, and then at five in the morning,— and that's pretty late,—you have to get in line and start answering "ads" or get left.

The eager, silent, shivering line waiting in the still dark winter dawn outside every newspaper office in the city for the advertisement sheet, hot from the press, is certainly not recruited from slothful sleepers. "If I could tell you," one of these men said, "how often I have got down here early and the thousands of miles I have tramped answering advertisements, only to find hundreds of men in line or turned away before me, you'd get some idea of what this disorganized advertising business means to us. Also you'd know how much I want a job!"

"I left the Bowery bread-line at one in the morning," said one man, "and walked up to 125th Street so I could get a newspaper up there early and find a job in that vicinity, and so get ahead of the fellow that waited in Park Row and then had to hoof it uptown." One opportunist in the newspaper line made the brilliant discovery that by paying one of the pressmen a quarter he could get advance sheets of advertisements, and get out to the job before the rest of the line got their papers. It is characteristic of our wasteful methods that in periods of unemployment hundreds of men answer each promising advertisement and there is no way to stop the stream which may keep up for days. Few advertisers know how to state their requirements, and only after spending time and carfare do applicants learn that an important requirement has been forgotten. Desperation, hunger, cold, and the bitter consciousness of dependent families, lead men to tramp long distances in the hope that they can do work for which under other conditions they would know they are not qualified. Men capable in times of employment are weak, improperly clothed, and the very want in their faces makes an unfavorable impression upon men who would hire them under other conditions.

Sometimes [said one man], I walked all night in
the hope of seeing "DISHWASHER WANTED" in a window
somewhere. I've done that twenty nights since the
middle of December [this was February]. Sometimes I got converted and got a bed and a meal ticket.
Once—in the day time—I actually landed a dishwasher's job for the next day. I couldn't get a bed
that night until 1 A.M., but I left a call for five in the
morning, and I woke—at nine. I jacked them up
at the lodging-house office, for I was pretty sore at
losing out on the first nibble for four months. But
they said they had called me three times and couldn't
get me waked up. Forty hours without sleep and
food had left me so exhausted that I actually couldn't
cinch a job when I got it.

A few men told of trying employment agencies.
Few of these, however, are free, and those that
are free are usually limited in their scope and in
the variety of occupations with which they are
concerned. In private agencies, the man with
the fee is on the preferred list and the man without
the price of bed or breakfast is on the waiting list.
"The only place a man can get a job in this town,"
said one of the pier sleepers, "is at an agency
where you have to pay ten per cent. of your first
month's wages, and I haven't even the car fare to
get there."

These are the stories of individuals. Their
significance lies in the fact that they are typical
of a widespread condition. The gatherings of the
unemployed in which these men were found were

not the isolated experiences of a few winter nights or confined to a few centers. Night after night it was that nearly two thousand besieged the Lodging House in New York City, that 1400 lay on the city's ferry-boats packed together like sardines in quarters where the odor from the dirty, restless men made sleep well-nigh impossible. Probably few of these that saw in their newspapers at breakfast the cartoonist's sketch of the "Wreck-reation" pier knew that six hundred nightly stretched out there for rest. Only the very early risers saw them coming every morning from the piers, docks, stables, and back saloon doors, brushing off the sawdust and hurrying stiffly off. More stiffly still came farm-hands waiting for spring jobs, whom a benevolent employment agent allowed to stay in his waiting-room all night—250 of them at one well-known agency—standing up, however, since to lie or sit down would mean turning someone out in the cold.

Through the day, making a sorry pretense at merging in the life of the city, the army kept in motion, tramping toward the job with which they never caught up, or, exhausted, crowding the park square benches, courting the pale winter sun, or standing in the aisles in a free reading-room—seizing any excuse for indoor shelter anywhere. But the night was all their own. Sharply defined from the well-ordered citizens possessing a home and a job, they maintained their separate vigil while the city slept. Somewhere in the city

many of these men had families—but unemployed
men cannot pay rent for a home.   In eviction
cases unemployment has so frequently been the
reason for non-payment of rent that in New York
City a committee to deal with such cases has
been formed by some of the justices before whom
such cases come.

And what of the silent sufferers?   Women did
not stand in bread-lines or frequent municipal
lodging-houses, stations, and saloons.   Men that
had homes often gave up their beds, families
"doubled up" and untold sacrifices were made
that hundreds of unemployed women might be
kept off the streets.   The statement was not
infrequently heard from a working girl: "My sheet
costs me $1.50 a month," meaning that she paid
this for the privilege of sleeping with one or more
children or with other women.   This helped the
family in distress and helped her tide over the
slack season.   Women that had not worked before
silently took the places of men that could not find
work.   Lonely, elderly women sat in their little
lodging-house rooms and wondered whether they
would be allowed to stay there for one night more,
and if the morrow's tramping would bring forth
the work as yet unsighted.   In New York down
in a little crowded room on Washington Square,
women stood in line and besieged a little sewing-
room started by the Conference on Unemployment
Among Women for the chance to earn enough
food to enable them to gain sufficient strength to

hunt for work, and sufficiently decent clothing to make themselves prepossessing candidates for it.

Hundreds of children, withdrawn from school by the sharp urge of poverty, formed what was practically a baby's bread-line.   One of the newspapers started a fund and distributed bread from two until four in the afternoon.   Before the doors were opened the children heckled the policemen that held them in line, and when the door opened the inside of the shop looked like a miniature football scrimmage.   Many of these were babies of from four to ten years of age, too young to go to school, but old enough to forage for family supplies!

The scrimmages elsewhere were not always so harmless.   In New York City the Industrial Workers of the World advanced upon the churches in an appeal—or rather a demand—for aid, shelter, and work.   Some of the churches closed their doors in fear, others did not think that the demand came within the province of the church, while others opened their doors, feeling that the call was a just one.   The leader of the church invasions is now serving a year in prison, but there is as yet no church report which deals with the unemployment situation in New York so effectively as does that of the State Excise Commissioner.

From the Atlantic to the Pacific the situation was the same, however various its manifestations. While the young leader of the Industrial Workers of the World was being sentenced in New York,

Chicago was quelling a riot and California was dealing with an "army of the unemployed." Fifteen hundred to two thousand men constituting this army demanded from the Governor transportation to Utah on their way to make a protest at Washington. They were dispersed by the militia. By what route did the honest men seeking jobs get into this group?

In Wheatland, California, a hop-grower, in order to get pickers at the lowest possible wage, advertised alluringly throughout California and even in Nevada. Within four days about 3000 people arrived at the ranch—1500 more pickers than the number of drying ovens made possible. On a low, unshaded hill they camped together, workers and non-workers, made up of aliens, typical Western American casual and migratory workers, a few American "hoboes," and many American families of the better middle class for whom the hop and fruit seasons often furnished a "country vacation." At least one half of the campers were destitute. Many of the 1500 for whom there was no work had spent their last cent to get to the ranch and had now no choice but to camp there, waiting for a chance to get in a stray half-day's work, or possibly to succeed workers who, from time to time, left in disgust. The living conditions of the camp soon made it unfit for habitation. There were nine toilets for nearly three thousand people, there was no provision for removing garbage, the wells were often pumped dry by the time the sun rose, and the campers had either to go to town for water, or to distant wells among the ranch buildings. However, a glass of water could be obtained by those who bought stew, and the boss's brother had secured a lemonade concession! Into this group of famished, idle, dissatisfied men and women came the Industrial Workers of the World. The climax was a riot in which four people were killed.

These localized manifestations of unemployment in various parts of the country were but the most spectacular signs of a really prevailing condition. Had it been possible to take a bird's-eye view of the industrial map of this country, there would have been disclosed a less obvious, but more constant and more sinister manifestation in the straggling, confused, and disorganized lines of casual and seasonal workers ceaselessly picking their way over the face of the United States. More than riots, more than armies marching on to Washington are these lines of the temporarily employed a constant index to a prevailing national situation. Some of them are always hunting the elusive steady job; some are merely trying perpetually to fit their equipment successively to various seasonal trades. Sometimes they have worked out a fairly definite circuit, from factory to cranberry bog, from labor camp to ice camp or to the home country in winter and back in the spring. Or, lacking such a scheme of rotation, they simply move on and on in a jagged line, which starts from the steamship dock for the foreigner and from the freight-yard of the city for the native, and covers from spring to spring the camp, the mine, the factory, the saloon, the municipal lodging-house, the hospital, and not infrequently the jail.

From the beginning of this country's history the "mover on" from the Atlantic coast to the western frontier has been a dramatic figure. He is a manifestation of an eternal type, we are reminded, and is not a recent economic product. But it is not merely a spirit of adventure, not merely the impulsion of restless feet that drives many a steady workman "laid off" in a railroad shop or factory from one town to another, seeking an opening in another factory in his trade, in another railroad shop, or failing that, in allied industries such as machine shops or steel works. Meanwhile, as his entry into a town and an opening in his trade there usually fail to coincide, the only possible thing to do seems to be to move on; and move on he does until it becomes a habit and he is classed with the "drifters" of the earth. It is undoubtedly true that nowhere else in the world is there so much ground covered in the blind pursuit of work as there is in these United States.

After a continued experience of this sort, the drifter is likely enough to adopt one of three courses; he may take to roving as his normal routine and eventually degenerate into "hoboism"; or take account of stock and decide on a new pro-

2

fession, the journeyman tailor, painter, or mechanic becoming a timber cutter in the northwest, or a worker in the lignite mines and cement fields of Texas, or any sort of hand in a thriving factory in the newest town he has struck. From one point of view this adaption to things as they are may be morally most commendable; from an economic point of view, and too often from a human one also, it merely indexes a waste of abilities diverted from their normal exercise. Lastly, the seasonal or casual worker that fails to make a sufficient number of connections with the varieties of work he can do may easily become one of the visionaries of the earth, that people the "boomed towns" of our prairies; or that vainly urge the arid acres of our foothills to yield their increase; or that follow in the wake of every new development, almost anticipating the report of a new discovery of oil in Oklahoma, or the establishment of a new factory in Texas.

The answer to the question, "Who are the unemployed?" may vary at different times; but in America no matter how many other factors are comprised in the answer these two will always be prominent: the casual worker who is left to bear the burden of unorganized industry, and the migratory worker who is a thoroughly important asset as he goes from State to State moving the nation's crops but who must make his own arrangements for much of the year as best he can.

It is peculiarly American that recognition of the unemployment problem in this country will be dependent upon proving that its volume is great. *How much* unemployment is there?

It is peculiarly American also that there is no satisfactory answer to this question. This was made most humiliatingly apparent in the winter of 1914 when all over the country people were asking: How many are out of work? Who are the unemployed? What is the matter with America that hundreds of thousands of unskilled workers have to find jobs or *change jobs annually?* Why are cities congested in winter and farms idle in summer? Why do children ready for work crowd certain employments and end their lives in blind alley trades having no industrial future? Why are operators turned away in the sewing trades when homes are being abandoned for the apartment hotel because there are no servants? Why in non-perishable goods trades must skilled workers look forward to long months of idleness or leave their homes and families to find other work?

Upon this question, suddenly become acute, as to the extent of unemployment in America, the records of the nation and states are comparatively silent. Because this country cannot afford to publish the census returns of 1910 upon the subject of unemployment, the latest comprehensive data is fourteen years old. Imagine the Department of Agriculture's furnishing crop reports so antiquated! We have for our guidance only estimates that are local, haphazard, or out of date. They establish little, but they imply much.

The 1900 Federal census shows that 22.3 per cent. of all persons having gainful occupations were not working, either at their particular occupation or at any other, at some time during the census year. Over 2,600,000 men and nearly 500,000 women were out of work from four to six months, and over 500,000 men were out of work seven months or over. The report on unemployment summarizes its tables as follows, showing the number of persons unemployed in various occupations:

It appears that approximately four persons out of five who claimed gainful occupations were continuously employed throughout the census year, while the fifth person was idle for a period varying from one to twelve months.

In 1901 the Federal Bureau of Labor made an investigation into the cost of living of 25,440 families of workmen or persons on salaries of not over $1200 a year distributed over the United States. The report shows that about half—49.81 per cent. —of the 24,402 heads of families were idle for part of the year.

The Geological Survey reports on coal mining from 1890 to 1910 show that workmen in bituminous mines lost from 22 to 43 per cent. of their working time annually, and workmen in anthracite mines from 23.7 to 50 per cent. disregarding the year 1902, when the great strike took place.

The Wainwright Commission in New York State, appointed in 1909 to inquire into the question of employers' liability and other matters, said in its report on employment:

There are no statistics available from which to compute the actual number of those without work. From the evidence before us we can say with certainty only this: That there are at all times able-bodied wage-earners out of work in every city of the state; that the number varies from month to month and from year to year; that it grows larger during the winter and during the years of industrial depression, and reaches tremendous proportions every fifteen or twenty years. A conservative estimate would be that in ordinary years of business activity the least number out of work is three per cent. of the wage-earners regularly employed in the industries of the State, while during the winter months the number would rise to 8 or 10 per cent. In a year of business depression like 1908 the number out of work ranges from 15 to 40 per cent. These estimates do not include all the unemployed. Over and above the percentages here given are the beggars, tramps, and vagrants, who have entirely dropped out of our industries.

Significant in this connection are the figures for union labor. The New York State Department of Labor collected reports each month during the ten years 1901–1911 from organized workmen, averaging in number 99,069 each month. It was found that the average number unemployed each month was 14,146 or 18.1 per cent. These men, it is to be remembered, were organized skilled workmen—not unskilled casual laborers.

Official bulletins published by the Commissioner of Labor of New York State show that the percentage of unemployment among union workmen was greater in the fiscal year from September 30, 1912, to September 30, 1913, than in any other year since 1896, with the single exception of 1908. 16.1 per cent. of the union men reporting to the department were idle on September 30, 1913. Through the winter this percentage rose steadily. On December 31, 1913, it was 38.8 per cent. The percentage of unemployed from July to December was 22.7 per cent.—nearly equal to that in 1908, when it was 22.9 per cent. Ninety-two per cent. of this enforced idleness was due to lack of work, and only 2 per cent. to labor disputes. These returns represent 300 different trades or branches of trades. The increase in unemployment was especially heavy in the building and clothing trades, which are also the two largest groups with union membership.

These are the figures for New York State. In New York City the percentage was even higher— 45.5 per cent. at the end of December, 1913. As two-thirds of the union members in the building industry and over 90 per cent. of the members in the clothing trades live in New York City, the

number of unemployed in the city reached a very
high mark. The activities of various unions in
the matter of furnishing relief were unusual. The
six unions of Jewish bakers on the East Side assessed
each of their members who was working one
dollar a week toward a fund for unemployed
members. At least one, and probably a number
of the garment trades, assessed their members
five per cent. of the weekly wage to be devoted to
the same purpose. The organizer of the United
Hebrew Trades estimated that about 75,000 men
were idle on the East Side, including several thousand in the seasonal trades who were habitually
idle at this time.

Manifestly with national data fourteen years
old, with State data limited to skilled workmen
in unions, with municipal records consisting of
reports from miscellaneous lodging-houses, missions, bread-lines, and relief organizations, and with
no records available from the industries themselves,
no trustworthy statement can be made of either
the volume of unemployment or of the area over
which it is spread, to say nothing of its nature
and causes.

In these circumstances, estimates placing the
number of unemployed high have naturally been
eagerly denied in some quarters. This is true
of the already mentioned estimate of 325,000
unemployed in New York City alone in the winter
of 1913–14. As a result of the discussion that
ensued, and the allegation by rival party papers

that the present administration was the cause of
the prevailing unemployment, the Federal Industrial Relations Commission, a temporary body
appointed by the President to ascertain the causes
of industrial unrest, decided to test the reliability
of these figures by a census of the unemployed.

Apparently without consulting the government experts who formulate schedules and make
a business of gathering statistics, the Commission
asked the chiefs of police in cities to have the
captain of each district fill out the following
schedule and return it to the Commission:

1.   How many unemployed men do you estimate
there were in your precinct on March 3, 1914?

2.   How many are residents of your precinct?

3.   How many are skilled workmen?

4.   How many are foreigners?

5.   How many of the unemployed in your precinct
do you believe are honestly hunting work?

6.   How many of the unemployed in your precinct
do you believe find odd jobs in your precinct?

7.   Where do the unemployed men, who have no
homes in your territory, sleep at night?

8.   In your experience does unemployment increase the amount of crime?

As this census is typical of the hurried, ill-
advised way in which much of our investigation
is done, and as it is likely to be given considerable
current political value, as the latest data, it is
well to call attention to certain characteristics
of the inquiry:

So far as is ascertainable no uniform instructions accompanied this schedule. What were the common denominators of "estimate?" Did they include a house to house canvass; did they include employment agencies and lodging-places; did this take account of wage-earning children, and what was done to verify the information? To what extent were rumors and guesses included?

The reports do not indicate that there was any common understanding among the enumerators as to the terms used. Did unemployment include men with a few days' work each week and those doing odd jobs or piece-work? What trades were covered by "skilled workmen" and was the record in each case based on previous training and profession or the last position held, or neither? Did the term foreigner include the naturalized alien or not? To illustrate from some of the returns:

In one report on 1000 unemployed, 800 are recorded as skilled workmen, but 900 are recorded as foreigners—an unusually high percentage of skilled workmen among foreigners. On the question of the amount of unemployment, the exclusion of women, of whom there are over 8,000,000 wage-earners in the United States would invalidate this report as an accurate statement of the unemployment situation in this country. It is also difficult to comprehend just how the captain counted the thousands of men who sleep in saloons at night and tramp the street by day looking for

work, or sleep in employment agencies, outbuild-
ings, and in the by-ways of cities where no records
are kept. One report says in answer to question 7,
"150 have homes in this section, 70 in other sections and 50 in public lodging-places about the
city." Were the 120 counted twice? If not, by
what process was duplication avoided? In another report one captain says *ninety-eight* per
cent. are residents of his precinct, but replies
under question 7 that *all* live in their own homes
in his precinct. Two per cent. are lost somewhere
between "residents" and "homes." On the
question "How many of the unemployed in
your precinct do you believe find odd jobs in your
precinct?" one captain replied: "None, except
the forty-five who would not work." If this is a
fair sample of the replies, the publication of the
data will be awaited with interest.

As a result of this canvass New York City
estimates were reduced from 325,000 to 96,000
and a public statement was issued to that effect.
This is one of the illustrations of the influence of
political expediency upon statistics.

Some of the states have made studies or kept
records of placements by public agencies. These
at best give information for but a small locality,
and it is difficult to ascertain their accuracy. For
instance, the Massachusetts Committee to Investigate Employment Agencies reported that it
had investigated 666 cases that the public employment agency had recorded as "hired" and had

found that from 14 to 36 per cent. of them were not hired. This is a considerable percentage of error in so vital a matter.

If there have been negligence and carelessness in gathering data on unemployment, there has been more than indifference to the necessity for defining the subject, and for distinguishing the employable from the unemployable. Yet it is difficult to see how any estimate of numbers, or any generalizations as to extent or causes of unemployment can proceed upon a basis that does not sharply differentiate these two classes. The first presents an industrial problem. It includes those unemployed persons able and willing to work, those who are ready to enter industry for the first time, the victims of maladjustment who may seldom actually join the ranks of the unemployed but who are constantly in process of change from industry to industry or who are engaged in seasonal or casual work, those who are under-employed, the short-time men who accept reduction in hours and pay rather than be thrown out entirely, etc. These constitute a constant unemployed group with which we are here concerned.

The second class, the unemployables, presents primarily a relief problem. They cannot be made a charge upon industry, nor can the problem be solved by organized business. Whenever this has been attempted in any large measure, it has tended to disorganize the labor market, to lower the efficiency of the industry and to bring about

endless controversy. Typical of this class are
vagrants that will not work, persons incapacitated
for work by old age or illness (not due to industrial
accidents and diseases) the handicapped such as
cripples, defectives, mothers that must keep their
children with them daily while they work, con-
victs, girls and boys on parole, and those that are
inefficient or defective for some non-removable
cause. These are temporarily or permanently
out of the normal industrial field. Many are
capable of some form of work, but require special
organizations or personal arrangement to adjust
this. Some are defectives and require institutional
care. Some are physically unfit and need to be
brought up to a better standard, while others
require relief. Obviously this group requires a
different examination and treatment from that
contemplated here.

The initiation both of immediate and long-time
programs of constructive action is the primary
purpose of this book. Some limitation, therefore,
must be set upon so unwieldy a subject as unemployment. So far as practicable, it is treated as
a problem of industry, and limited to those who
are able and willing to work.

Even within this field, exceptions occur. First,
it refers primarily to those that work for wages.
Any pronouncements concerning the professional
class for which there is a complete lack of data,
will be highly speculative. Obviously also those
on a strike cannot be included, because other

issues are involved and the unemployment is not involuntary.

Unemployment, then, as here used, is involuntary idleness, not due to refusal to accept a wage-rate lower, or conditions less favorable than those in which the workman is habitually employed, or those obtaining by reason of existing agreements between associations of employers and employees; or, failing such agreement, than those generally recognized in the district by good employers. In other words, the workman involuntarily idle who refuses work in which he is customarily employed because of the lower wage-rate or less favorable conditions is not by this act transferred to the unemployable class.

Since America has taken neither the trouble nor the expense to determine the extent and nature of its unemployment problem, it follows that the causes of unemployment must be wholly speculative so far as this country is concerned. There is a long list of so-called popular or unpopular explanations, as you please, which include: monopoly of land, the prevailing wage-system, politics, and loss of business confidence, "psychological" depression, the tariff, convict labor, patent laws, immigration, minimum wage, child labor, mechanical inventions, entrance of women into industry, trusts and labor organizations. Advocates are many who claim that any one of these, or a combination of them will explain the prevalence of unemployment. The International Conference on Unemployment, in the course of its three years' investigations, has been presented by its members with a number of different theories upon which there is as yet little agreement. America has not contributed much to the formulation of these theories, and there is still to be set forth for this country an analysis of conditions which will establish indisputably the causes of unemployment.

There is much more agreement as to the social effects of unemployment; results rather than causes, indeed, have claimed our attention. It is admitted that casual labor is one of the most direct routes to vagrancy and pauperism because the habit of regular work is easily lost, and with it are lost self-respect and confidence, so that when opportunity comes the workman may not be employable; that uncertainty of income demoralizes housekeeping methods and standards of living and leads to shiftlessness and misery; that a feast or a famine is a ruinous existence; that children brought up in such surroundings are stunted, undernourished, inadequately clothed, morally weak, and do not have the opportunity to enter trades with a promise of a future in them; that vice and immorality increase with unemployment; that the wearying search for labor day after day destroys the moral fibre; that periods of unemployment impair technical skill; that precariousness of employment leads to intemperance and gambling; that a large expenditure in prosperous times does not compensate for the privations and depression

of unfavorable times and is not conducive to
habits of thrift; that the dread of losing a job
impairs efficiency and destroys happiness; that
the sense of being useless and thrown out of the
routine of life is a shock which leads to rapid deterioration, and that a succession of jobs gradually blunts fidelity, zeal, and disinterested effort.
Aside from these obvious results of unemployment,
the cost to industry in the waste of men through
lost time and maladjustment and deterioration,
in the loss of skill and in cost of supervision are
beyond calculation at this time.   To communities
the cost is not less.   No community can safely
carry large numbers of unemployed men and
women deprived of normal activities and therefore
susceptible to harmful influences, and unable
without their earnings to maintain a decent standard of living for themselves and their families.
Mr. Sidney Webb, speaking of conditions in England, says that while casual laborers and their
families constitute one-tenth of the population,
they are responsible for four-fifths of the problems
with which the health officers have to deal.

The European war has intensified very greatly
the problem of unemployment, has increased its
range of variation, and is testing to the utmost
America's capacity for adjustment.   The lack of
raw materials, the stopping of exports, the falling
off of the shipping trade have challenged American
industry in many directions.   Again rumors are
rife as to just what is the extent of the present

unemployment. Five hundred thousand are reported to be out of work in the Pittsburg district, the same number in New York City. What the figures for these sections and others really are, nobody knows. But so pressing are the local manifestations in many places that recognition is not lacking that, whatever the numbers may be, they are great. For the first time there is a general tendency among municipalities to provide public works. Everywhere relief agencies are combining. Two cardinal facts stand out in the present situation: first that there is undoubted need for immediate relief measures on a large scale; and secondly that the rapid transition from a normal immigration to a dearth and then to a probably enormous increase, and the transition from feverish activity in some industries to stagnation in others require a peculiar mobility in labor and a flexible organization of the labor market not characteristic of America.

By the present situation, therefore, as well as by signs evident long before it we are forced to these conclusions: America has an unemployment problem, industrial in its nature. The problem is without definition. Government, business, and the average citizen have, within recent years, been forced to recognize it. There is but little data by which to gauge its character or extent. Its causes are obscure, its remedies inadequate. Confusion exists between the provinces of relief and philanthropy on the one hand, and industrial organization and regulation on the other. A study of unemployment which will point remedies by an adequate interpretation of effects and therefore an analysis of causes has never been begun. It is now indicated more urgently than ever.

3

CHAPTER II

ON a morning in January, 1914, Cooper Union in New York City held one of the most appealing audiences in its history. A curiously heterogeneous crowd of women and girls, department-store girls, stenographers, operators, seamstresses, scrub women, young and old women of all races and all temperaments, drifted into that meeting, united only by their common lot of ceaselessly and vainly hunting work. It included girls laid off in the shops on Christmas Eve for "a short holiday," who, in the dead of winter, had found no other work; women in whose trades the slack season had begun; women whose husbands had been idle all winter and who were ready to do anything to keep the little family together; widows with babies to support; and young girls who had become the breadwinners of the family.

Such public manifestations of unemployment among women are rare. Unemployed women elude enumeration even more than unemployed men. Scattered and to a degree sheltered as they are, a mass-meeting in which a resolution like the

34

following was adopted, is indeed significant of conditions in this country:

Whereas thousands of working women and young girls who are dependent upon themselves for support are idle—we, the unemployed women and girls in mass-meeting assembled do hereby call upon the city and state authorities to provide us with work—we emphatically protest against our enforced idleness.

No social or economic change of the last fifty years has been more important than that relating to the employment of women. The simple solution of idleness by finding domestic service for girls has become a very complex problem. Two things have materially changed the situation: Many, in fact, most industries have been taken outside the home. Dyeing, weaving, spinning, preserving meats and vegetables, making bedding and clothing, which were formerly done by each household, are now done in mills and factories; and the general tendency is to have all work done outside the home. "Home work" has come in most instances to mean the same thing as sweat-shop work, done under conditions detrimental to the workers and dangerous to the community.

The other significant change is the increasing opportunities for women in professional, commercial, mercantile, and industrial fields. The entire working force of certain trades is recruited from among women and girls. Whether a "woman's place is in the home or not," one fact stands out tooclearly for much dispute to-day; that a woman's place is where she can find work to support herself and those dependent upon her; and that that place no longer is, for many millions of women, in the home; it is in the office, the factory, the department store, and the mill.

There is no accurate or comprehensive data upon the amount or the kind of unemployment among women. It is usually assumed that women have some one to whom to turn in times of distress. To verify this and to be sure that the home conditions were right, the homes of some forty women admitted to a temporary sewing-room in New York City to tide them over, were visited, and it was found that in over one-half of them, women were the family wage-earners with children and others dependent upon them, while nearly all of the others were living alone or were solely dependent upon their own efforts. This is a local but a typical illustration; these conditions among wage-earning women or women deprived of the family wage-earners, are far more prevalent than it is generally believed.

In the absence of more complete data concerning unemployed women, the extent and the character of unemployment among women can be better estimated inferentially from the present character and conditions of women's work. There is perhaps no field which has received less scientific study than women's position in industry, and especially the irregularity of women's employ-

ment.   It is true that for many years a tendency
toward protective legislation for women workers
has shown itself.   This is not to be ignored; but
it probably owes its present strength more to a
public health movement than to any general
appreciation of the industrial position of women.

It will surprise many to learn that of the wage-
earners of New York State, 983,686, or about
one-third, are women; and that in the whole
country there are over eight million wage-earning
women, and the proportion is correspondingly
great in other industrial states.   According to the
13th census more than one-half of the workers in
the textile, bookbinding and glove-making trades
were women, and one-third of the workers in
professional service, canning, and clerical occupations were women.   In all branches of work,
excepting such occupations as military service,
trainmen, etc., women are found largely engaged.
There are now even fifty-five policewomen in the
country.

The Federal Senate Commission in reporting
its inquiry concerning women and children in
industry threw very considerable new light upon
the industrial position of women.   The inquiry
covered seventeen states and twenty-three industries.   In twelve of the twenty-three industries, women formed one-half or over one-half
of the workers.   The twelve industries included
canning and preserving (vegetables and fruits),
the cigar-box trade, the manufacture of cigarettes,

of cigars, and confectionery, of hosiery and knit goods, paper boxes, shirts and overalls, tobacco and snuff. In all the other trades, except core-making, women formed at least one-fourth of the number.

If so many women are employed in the industries of the country, the converse of the proposition is also likely to be true—many of them are frequently unemployed.

Moreover certain characteristic features of women's industrial position as compared with men's indicate that unemployment among women is not only more detrimental when it does occur, but also more constantly impending. There is nothing in the organization of these various trades to indicate that in the matter of regularity and permanency of employment, women are favored more than men. On the other hand, there is evidence that the discharge or laying off of women is more lightly undertaken by industry on the assumption that they are not breadwinners with families dependent upon them. Protests by unemployed women also find less expression in political and organized action and therefore have less compelling weight in industry. "On the whole," says the Senate Report, previously quoted, "the strongest impression left by the study of this group of between 50,000 and 60,000 women and girls is the absolute haphazard and unstandardized character of the industrial world as known to them."

In the first place, many of the trades in which women most largely engage are peculiarly subject to seasonal variations. This is notably true of all the sewing trades, and of the canning and preserving of fruits and vegetables. In canning, for instance, in addition to all the ordinary hazards such as the risk of breakdown in machinery, common to all industries, and the difficulty of securing an adequate labor supply at the proper time, the work varies according to the weather, the condition of the soil, the pests and blights peculiar to vegetables, especially toward the close of the harvesting season, and lastly the difficulty of enforcing contracts with farmers (when canners do not control the land) as to time of planting and harvesting. Oyster canning depends, among other things, upon the weather, the supply, and the time of arrival of the boats.

It is unquestionably true that these and other industries are creating a vagrant type of working women and are establishing the migratory home. The families that work in canneries and cranberry bogs, for instance, frequently live in city tenements during the winter in idleness or engaged in casual labor. When spring comes, the family moves to the cannery, taking the children out of school during the school year and out of reach of the truant officer. Here they live in conditions of congestion, bad sanitation, and long hours, giving the children little or no care. They return to the city in the fall too late for the child to catch

up with his class in school which has been in session
from two to six weeks. The gypsy caravan is
being replaced by the cannery caravan. It bodes
ill to the welfare of the children in it, to constant
and decent standards of living, to regular employment and to steady and adequate incomes. No-
madic families have little opportunity to become
attached to any community and to participate
in its social, religious, and cultural life.

Other trades in which women are engaged are
highly seasonal. In artificial flower making in
Paris it has been estimated that less that one-
fourth of the employees are employed all the year
round and that sixty-five per cent. of them do not
work at all during from one to seven months in
the year. In New York the trade is little less
variable. In a typical shop the number employed
in the high season is 5000, and in the dull season
less than 1000. Some of the "florists" transfer
in dull seasons to the feather trade, but if they
cannot do that they are indeed unfortunate, for
the work of flower making is not conducive to skill
in any other trade. In the paper-box industry in
Philadelphia, twenty-five employers stated that
one-fourth of the entire force of girls in their
establishments are regularly dismissed after Christmas. Of forty-five firms in the same business only
five are busy throughout the year. In the bookbinding trade in the same city one-eighth of the
women have not steady employment throughout
the year. Clothing catalogues in early spring and

autumn, patent medicine almanacs in time for
winter colds and bronchitis, annual reports and
bank statements for the first of the year, seed
catalogues in the spring,—these, with theatre and
concert programs throughout the winter, and
telephone directories quarterly, seem to guarantee
at least a sufficient succession of seasonal work
to protect these workers from a high degree of
unemployment. But as a matter of fact in the
magazine binderies twelve days often make a
working month, and even in the larger and better
organized businesses, the period of depression is
regularly recurrent. In the winter of 1913, the
waist and dressmakers' business season in New
York City did not begin until the end of February
and ended in May. The millinery trade has a
similar history, the millinery year being at best
only seven or eight months long. Confectionery
is distinctly a seasonal trade.

It is undeniably true that industrial unrest is
increasing among women, and that agitation and
protest are finding able leaders and a sympathetic
hearing. It would be of interest to know how
much of the root and justification of this lies in
the seasonal employment of women, involving
long periods of idleness without any of the comforts and even the necessities of life and with
little to do but agitate. May it not be that just
as our neglect of immigrants and our isolation of
them in camps and industrial communities with
no opportunities for education and recreation

have furnished an ideal laboratory for I. W. W. cultures, so our indifference to how women live during periods of unemployment may be the cause of many of the social problems which we are vainly trying to solve by inadequate methods and with limited understanding.

Nowhere is the lack of standardization in women's work more evident than in the hours and wages that prevail in the various industries. There seems to be a fairly constant relation between seasonal work and overtime, home-work and under-employment. The wages paid women do not cover unemployed periods, the dovetailing of work being considered the solution—the responsibility for it resting upon the worker. Within recent years there is evidence of increasing public concern in this subject, of which the agitation for minimum wages for women is an illustration. An analysis of such local studies as have been made would indicate that, roughly speaking, there are three groups, those that earn under $6 a week, those that earn $6 on an average, and those that earn between $6 and $10. During the busy season, artificial flower makers make about $6 per week. In New York City, 97 per cent. of the workers, on whom this inquiry was based, lived with their families; there were, however, no "pin money" workers among them. In the bookbinding industry, three-fourths of the women were found to receive less than $400 a year and the average was $300. In oyster canneries, the

investigators found that 99.4 per cent. of the
women earned under $6 and not one woman in
the whole group earned so much as $8.   In the
confectionery business, it was found that one-
sixth of the women earned under $4, more than
half under $6, and only eight per cent. reached
or passed $10.   Among the cigarette makers, one-
third earned less than $6, and in the cracker facto-
ries one-half earned less than $6.   In the clock and
watch industry, work requiring judgment and
accuracy, and therefore akin to a skilled trade,
only one woman in twenty was found to reach or
pass $10 a week.

The investigations made by the Industrial
Commission of Ohio in 1913 into the rate of wages
in mercantile establishments in that State showed
that the prevailing rate for women was $6 to $8.
Either the $6 or $7 rate predominated in every
one of the large cities and groups of smaller cities
and towns in the State.   If the living wage be
put at $8, fifty-two per cent. were getting less
than enough to live on; if at $7, thirty-five per
cent.; if at $6, twenty-one per cent.   For girls
under eighteen the prevailing wage was $3 to $5.
Seventy per cent. were getting less than $5, forty-
seven per cent. less than $4, and seventeen per
cent. less than $3.   In 1906, a normal year in
Ohio in the paper-box trade, eighty-five days were
lost and the average pay was $3 to $5 per week.
Speaking of some of the conditions a report of the
Consumers' League of Cleveland says:

A girl of 17 works 10 hours per day, regularly, and 12 hours for several weeks at a corner staying machine, that will cut off or crush her fingers if she is not continuously careful. Pay $7.

A girl of 15 stands at a machine gluing boxes 12½ hours twice a week for two months, other days, 10 hours. Pay $3.50. She complains that her feet are calloused from standing and she suffers from backache.

A girl of 14 stands 9½ hours a day fitting and gluing partitions into tiny boxes by hand. Pay averages $2.50. The rate is 20 cents for 1000 boxes. Each box has two partitions.

A girl of 15 makes thumb-holes at a machine 10 hours per day. The work causes a special strain on the fingers and tends to produce inflammation and callouses. Pay $3.50.

The Bureau of Labor's investigation of the payrolls of twenty-six large department stores in New York, Chicago, Philadelphia, and Boston, disclosed a weekly average of $7.93 a week, as compared with $7.21 for all stores large and small in these cities. "Average" figures in this case really tell a more benign story than would a citing of the numbers of these workers whose lower wage needs very considerable aid to bring it up to the average. Telephone operators after two years of service average $8 a week; but this, again, is practically a skilled trade, or at least a sharply exacting one, requiring training and experience.

The relation of the efficiency of women workers

to the present organization of industry is a fundamental question. It is contended that opportunities in industry are available to women exactly because they are unskilled and unorganized, and that women will rapidly be displaced when they become too efficient. On the other hand, it must be clear that any trade requiring dexterity and steadiness and interest will be less well served by women who are underfed and underworked part of the year, badly fed and overworked the rest of the year; depressed and exhausted looking for jobs some months and buoyant and sure of life other months; or who have the steadying association of busy minds and happy hearts some days and walk among the "down and outs" and castoffs of society other days.

On the whole, no characteristic of women's work is more notable than the little skill required. It is true that in trade and transportation, a comparatively skilled group, the number of women is increasing, but it is still relatively small. In the Pittsburg Survey, it was shown that of twenty-two thousand women workers in all trades, skilled workers or women with a handicraft together formed only three per cent. Time after time in the Senate Commission's analysis of twenty-three industries, occurs the note "Speed and a certain amount of dexterity, but no skill are required." Even in the trades in which men and women work side by side, there is a clean-cut division of labor, the less skilled and more monotonous processes

being in every instance in charge of women.
The very monotony of the work often destroys
any high degree of skill, and the small fragment of
the process given to each worker intensifies this
danger. In the neckwear factory the woman turns,
or makes the point, *or* tacks, *or* presses, *or* labels,
but never does all of these. It is very generally
true of women's industrial work that it requires
little or no skill and furnishes no opportunity to
acquire it.

One striking phase of the irregular conditions
that often accompany women's work has received
little attention from any source. "Home-work"
in the tenement is familiar and has been condemned
to a considerable degree by public opinion, though
not largely prohibited. There is another form of
home-work, by which the manufacturer tries by
misrepresentation and fraud to get his work done.
The home-workers are the handicapped, the unskilled, the "genteel," the misfits, the hard-driven
mother, often in small towns, reached by alluring
advertisements. The following letter tells its
own story, and a careful examination of advertisements in daily and so-called home papers indicates
that this kind of imposition is widespread:

Finding it necessary to help somehow to improve
the conditions of our home budget, which has sadly
diminished on account of my husband's lack of steady
work, I decided to find some employment myself.
Having three school children, the only thing I could
do was home-work, so I set out looking for it.

An ad. in a Long Island paper called for women to sew on buttons. With glad heart I went, for what could I do better? Well, I waited in the office for about one hour when a young woman approached me asking had I my reference. No. I was sorry not to have any with me as the ad. did not mention any such thing. "You have to have one," she said, "from your butcher, grocer, or landlord just to show that you are an honest woman and we can trust you with our buttons."

Two hours later I was back with the written assurance of all three above-mentioned persons that they had known me long, and the proprietor of the "button works" could sleep at ease although I had the buttons home. After making a satisfactory sample I was told the price was two cents for a gross; no thread supplied. Bewildered, I made some mental multiplication, but I could not think of more than sixty cents for thirty gross of buttons. Of this I subtracted five cents for cotton and thirty cents for car fare, which left a total of 25 cents' earnings.

However, I was elated at being of some help, and set to work as soon as I reached home. It took me one whole week to mount the 4320 buttons, and when I delivered them, using my last five cents for car fare, I was told that only ten gross were mounted properly; that all I could get was 30 cents, and would I call next Saturday.

My next experience was neckties. I made four samples for a firm in Broome Street, which took from 9 o'clock in the morning until 3 o'clock in the afternoon. Then when the fourth bow was finished a pimply-faced young woman approached me with outstretched hand. "One dollar deposit, please,"

she chirped, and I not having any dollar of which I did
not know how to dispose, left this "home-work"
place, and also my day's work to its benefit.

No. 3: I furnished a sample, received 75 cents'
worth of work, and on delivery fifteen cents was taken
off for a bow for which I did not get any material,
being accused of theft, although not directly.

All a woman can earn at home is $1 to $2 weekly
at the most, while she has to call for and deliver the
work, spend a half-day every time making samples,
and cannot get her money before the regular pay-day.
Something ought to be done for these poor women
whom care of children prevents leaving the house to
earn something when the husband is out of work.

The question generally arises why women
have not managed to obtain some degree of
standardization by organization such as men
workers have. A significant reason is their
lack of skill already cited. By economic pressure they have been forced into industry and
because they were not skilled they could not command as high wages as men. A man who has
spent three or four years in becoming a skilled
artisan can be replaced in many trades by a woman, or even a child—who has learned what levers
to pull and when to shut off the power. The result
has been that women's attempts to organize have
been met with hostility from all sides—especially
from the employers. The first thing a union
does is naturally to ask for better conditions—
for higher wages, or shorter hours. This destroys

the value many employers set on women's labor—its cheapness. Union after union that has been founded among women had been fought to its destruction as soon as it became effective. The canning departments of the Chicago packing-houses, the Commercial Telegraph Union, the tobacco trade, the shirt-waist factories at Troy, the Chicago waitresses, all furnish examples of this. The present determination of department-store owners that women clerks shall not be organized is another example of the same attitude. Practically the only trades where manufacturers do not object to having the women workers organized are those where the sale of the manufactured article is helped by the union label.

Another thing that has kept women from organizing effectively is the opposition of union men to the presence of women in many trades. Workmen have vibrated between two attitudes—they have endeavored to exclude women from their trades and their trade unions; and yet in some cases they have seen that the harm to themselves lies not in the mere presence of women in the trade, but in the fact that the women are unorganized and can be more easily exploited. Occasionally women have fought their way in, and a sharp contest has shown men that women could not be excluded, and that if they were to be in the work, they had better be in the union. In 1869, the women printers had formed strong organizations and forced their way into the International Typo-

4

graphical Union. Where unions have admitted women to the union, the evil results of competition have been eliminated, and during the past few years the opposition has been gradually disappearing until now women are welcomed in many unions. In the International Typographical Union and the International Cigar-makers Union, for instance, women are on exactly the same footing as men with reference to benefits and all union privileges.

Trade organization does not assume the importance nor hold the promise of solving serious problems of unemployment and under-employment to the degree among women that it does among men. The home is still the group to which most women tie and the family is the largest social unit that their loyalty embraces. But women are coming more and more to recognize that certain trades are women's trades, and to take an interest in their organization for women rather than for themselves. The organization of women as a means of securing standards in women's work presents peculiar difficulties: when the standards of the large number of incoming working women are considered, as well as the vast numbers engaged in domestic and personal service and home-work, it is evident that hand in hand with trade organization must go a broad program of industrial education, vocational guidance, and education of the general public to the dangers of irregular employment among women.

It is a popular fallacy that unemployment among women is a modern development, a manifestation of feminism perhaps, due to the sex unrest that is characteristic of this age. The history of women in industry in the United States does not bear out this plausible conclusion. On the contrary, it confronts it in two ways with an emphatic denial; from the beginning of this country's history, large percentages of the nation's population of women have worked under conditions even less standardized than those under which they work at present. And always they have trembled on the verge of unemployment. With the invention of machinery controlling the principal industrial operations, the individual homework changed first to the contract system and from that to the factory system; the increasing development of machinery, with the sub-divisions of processes, resulted in the use of cheap unskilled labor—into which women are drafted.

Their wages have always been low, and their work uncertain. In 1836, it was stated that women shoe binders in Philadelphia were so poorly paid that if they had children their wages were barely sufficient to give them a scanty supply of the commonest food and raiment, even when fully employed; and that they were frequently employed only part of the time, and sometimes wholly unemployed, particularly in the dreary season of the winter. In those cases they suffered intense distress and were actually reduced to pauperism.

The New York *Tribune* found a similar situation
in New York in 1845—"a most deplorable degree
of servitude, privation, and misery among this
helpless and dependent class of people," including
"hundreds and thousands" of many kinds of
workers—shoe binders, artificial flower makers,
straw-braiders, who "drudge on in miserably
cooped-up, ill-ventilated cellars and garrets, pining
away heart-broken, in want, disease, and wretched-
ness. They find that by working from fifteen to
eighteen hours a day they cannot possibly earn more
than from $1 to $3 a week, and this, *deducting the
time they are out of employment every year*, will
barely serve to furnish them the scantiest and
poorest food"—(New York *Daily Tribune*, August
19, 1845. During the Civil War men's wages
rose 100 per cent., but women's rose only about
20 per cent., and in some trades even fell, although
food and fuel increased in price.

In all trades, women have always suffered
as much, perhaps even more, than men from
unemployment. The census of 1890 showed
that 12.7 per cent. of all women engaged in gainful
operations were out of work during some part of
the census year. By 1900 the percentage had
risen to 23.3. The unfortunate hazards that
dominate the industrial life of women are well
illustrated in the history of the group of sewing
trades, one of the traditional trades into which
women who do not know how to do anything else
have always drifted. The result has been a steady

over-supply of labor.   For over a century the percentage of workers without steady employment
has been large.   Grim protests and pathetic appeals
have been made for many years.   Matthew
Carey's pathetic crusade against low wages in
Philadelphia shows that from 1828 on there was
a high degree of unemployment among sewing
women, and even when employment was constant,
they worked sixteen hours a day to make $1.25 a
week.   Conditions in New York were as bad; the
women were sweated by a contract and sub-
contract system, and their wages forced down to
what the contractors could have the work done
for in almshouses.   Matthew Carey sums up the
situation thus:

A skillful woman, constantly employed, working
early and late, could not make more than nine shirts
a week, which would bring her 90 cents; she could not
get a room for less than 50 cents, which left her 40
cents, or less than 6 cents a day for food, clothing,
fuel, light for her night sewing, and other necessities.
Many of them were not skilful, some were superan-
nuated, or sick, or had sick husbands, or had children
to take care of, while a large number could not get
more than two or three days' work a week.

When the Civil War came, it made the situation
of these women even more hopeless, for their
ranks were swollen by the great number of "war
widows," with no training, no commercial experience, nothing, in fact, but a very immediate need.

There were 25,000 of these widows in Boston alone. The situation of the tailoresses and sewers became so intolerable that a committee was sent to interview President Lincoln, to tell him that the "women making the soldiers' uniforms were being bled to death."

The popular theory that housework is a solution of all unemployment among women is no longer tenable and does not lift the burden from the conscience of society. This assumption betrays as great ignorance of economics as it does of human nature, or better perhaps, of human limitations. The amount of household work itself has been greatly reduced by the changes in family living and by inventions. Horace Greeley's comment in 1846 is not yet untimely: "When nine-tenths of the Yankee girls prefer to encounter the stunning din, the imperfect ventilation, monotonous labor, and excessive hours of a cotton factory in preference to doing housework, be sure the latter is not yet what it should be."

There is no similar occupation which as a whole is so disorganized in the matter of hours, free time, freedom in use of leisure time, methods and equipment for work, amount and kind of labor, and in the environment in which the work is done, as is domestic service. The abruptness with which household employees are dismissed (it often occurs that a girl is told to leave before night and is therefore both homeless and jobless) is a great drawback. When in this connection are considered the additional disadvantages of social stigma, class prejudices, lack of education and social opportunities, little prospect of promotion, etc., the preference for organized routine work, however hard, becomes understandable, and such advantages as higher wages and a home lose their potency with the girl choosing an occupation.

A description of the social effects of unemployment among women would include all the aspects that have been noted for men—deterioration in skill and employability, loss of physical competence and of moral courage. If women are sometimes more sheltered, they are at all times handicapped by not being able to take advantage of even the few resources provided for unemployed men. Such emergency measures as wood piles, rock piles, snow shovelling, etc., are not open to unemployed women, and the increased interest in sewing rooms due to the war situation indicates how little the critical need of unemployed women has been considered before. Emergency shelters are almost generally not open to women. A short time ago one of the cities of the country placed before its council these facts: first, that there were a number of unemployed women in the town, homeless or likely to be homeless; secondly, that there was no place in the town to which they could go for a night's shelter except the city jail, when they would have to be arraigned the following morning. The instance is typical. And Municipal Lodging

Houses, where they exist at all, are in most places
not suitable for women.

Within the last few years there have been a
number of local and desultory investigations into
the connection between the social evil and women's
unemployment. Because so little is known of
women's unemployment, it is not to be expected that the connection has been established.
Throughout the industrial history of the United
States, however, the idea has persisted that there
is a very vital relation between vice, low wages,
and unemployment. So far back as 1846, "agents
of debauchery" were circulating tales of ease and
luxury among the 600 shirt makers in New York
City—among young and friendless orphans, or
widows with helpless children, who were making
shirts for four cents a piece, as one of them said
"sewing with a double thread a shroud as well as
a shirt." In 1845 the Female Industrial Association reported that the scarcity of work and low
rates of pay had "driven many virtuous females
to courses which might otherwise have been
avoided." Temptations that fall lightly upon the
girl with change in her pocket-book, with an
obligation to be at her post the next day, with a
duty to perform, with the certainty that she can
afford a modest frolic, may be the ruin of the
despondent girl out of a job. It is of no avail to
say that girls at such times may seek the shelter
of their homes and friends even if they have them.
They have acquired the desire to work regularly,

and the standards of a regular income, and are economic factors which the industry of this country can little afford to permit to deteriorate. It is impossible to evade the conclusion that increase in prostitution goes hand in hand with increase in unemployment.

In volume, therefore, unemployment among women is less serious than among men. In effect it is more serious, and its increase carries with it social and economic dangers, not only to industry, but to the home and the community. Any attempted solution concerned only with unemployment as it relates to men will fail, for unemployment among women is inherent in the peculiarly general conditions of women's work—lack of standards in the work, lack of organization and solidarity in the workers. Any study of the industrial position of women discloses at once that very vital causes of unemployment, lack of equipment in workers, lack of regularity in work, are here involved, and in a degree that necessitates particular attention to the organization of women's work before unemployment among women is even susceptible to the same remedies as is unemployment among men.

CHAPTER III

CHILDREN AND THE LABOR MARKET

THERE is no more important subject in America to-day than the entrance of children into industry. For the purposes of this discussion, child workers will include those between the ages of fourteen and twenty-one, who, in an industrial sense, if in no other, are certainly still children.

These workers are related to unemployment first, because they form a constant source of cheap labor by means of which the increase of machine processes has been more and more capable of displacing adult labor.

Secondly, by flooding the market with untrained workers set upon no particular line of work and destined to shift from one job to another in blind attempts toward adjustment, they add greatly to the instability of the general market.

Thirdly, they form the nucleus of the unemployed and unemployables of the next generation by engaging in work which is unfitted to their immature physiques and which often within a few years destroys their physical fitness for constant sustained work.

Finally, many such young workers, because

they either fail to connect with opportunities for general or industrial training, or deliberately or ignorantly cut themselves off from any opportunities that do exist, remain in the ranks of the unskilled, the low skilled, and casual labor, and thus become the most promising candidates for future unemployment.

Two movements in this country have been concerned with children in industry—an anti-child labor movement which has been in existence for a number of years, and has achieved some notable results in legislation and public opinion, and various agitations throughout the country for industrial training and vocational guidance, initiated sometimes by industry itself, sometimes by civic organizations, and of late years more and more by the public-school system.   But the anti-child labor movement has little to do with workers past the sixteen years' limit; as yet, indeed, it has very little to do with children past fourteen years of age.   Its point of view is rather the protection of childhood and of society, secured by minimum legislative standards for child labor, than the direct connection between children and the labor market including the whole problem of employment and unemployment.

It must be admitted, however, that all attempts to improve the industrial condition of children are dependent upon the settlement of the minimum age at which children may enter industry without detriment to themselves or to industry.

For some years now there has been a noticeable attempt in this country to reduce the number of inefficient young workers and amend the conditions of children's work by increasing facilities for trade training. But the facilities are still very few. And in the course of the movement to increase them, two things have become clear: first, that the causes of the disorganization attending children's work go deeper than the lack of training facilities; and secondly, that these facilities cannot be intelligently provided until other causes are also known and dealt with. These other causes are intricate; they concern industry, the public educational system, and the attitude which parents, employers, and the public generally take toward children's work.

By mere force of numbers, children, including all those under twenty-one years, are a very considerable factor in the labor market. And in spite of the convictions both of child labor and vocational guidance experts that there is no place in industry, as at present organized, for workers under sixteen years, the labor market now contains many thousands of such children. The Thirteenth Census of the United States (1910) shows that 16.6 per cent. of all the boys in the country between the ages of ten and thirteen were working, and 8 per cent. of the girls; of those between fourteen and fifteen, 41.4 per cent., more than two-fifths, of the boys and 19.8 per cent. or one-fifth of the girls were employed. These figures, of course, take no account of the wholesale evasion of the child-labor law in various states. The Federal Senate Investigation into the condition of women and children in industry found that in its New England group of states 50 per cent. of the establishments visited were violating the child-labor laws; and in the Southern states 74 per cent. of the establishments were violating them.

These estimates, moreover, take no account of "home-work." Investigations conducted in New York City tenements in 1911–12 gave results which showed that of 41 families in the nut industry, 9 families had no children. In the remaining 32 families there were 91 children from three to sixteen years old; of these 77 were found at work. In the same investigation 69 out of 72 children between the ages of four and sixteen were found working at brush making; 35 out of 35 between four and sixteen were working on dolls' clothes. An intensive study of artificial flower making made by the Russell Sage Foundation disclosed the fact that 49 per cent. of the home-workers among the "florists" were children under sixteen years, and 37 per cent. of them were children under fourteen.

So much for the younger group. As to the older, the Thirteenth Census showed that of all the boys in the country between the ages of sixteen and twenty-one, 79.2 per cent. or four-fifths were at work; of all the girls between these ages, 39.9 per cent. or two-fifths were workers.

Children are found in practically all industries in which there are unskilled processes suited to their capacities, or machines which they are capable of tending. These are largely the unskilled and the low-wage industries. In some of them the factor of children's work has apparently come to be fundamental. The Federal Senate Commission's Investigation into women and children wage-earners throws some light upon the extent to which children form the labor force of various industries. In the cotton textile industry in Mississippi 23.8 per cent. of all the employees were found to be children under sixteen. In South Carolina 22.9 per cent. were children. In the glass works covered by its investigation the Senate Commission found that 10 per cent. of the employees were children. For the silk industry the percentage was almost the same. In the cracker and biscuit factories investigated from 25 to 29% of the workers were children. In cigarette making the percentage was also considerable—about 20 per cent. In oyster canning in 1905 children formed 22.9 per cent. of the total number of employees. By another investigation of 147,651 workers in the mine regions, 24,023 were reported to be children, boys from eight years old and up. It is significant that in these coal regions children even have their unions. More local studies confirm the implication of these figures. In the vegetable canneries of New York State the Factory Investigating Commission found that 942 children under four-

teen years were regularly at work; 141 of them were
under ten years. Studies of industries in Massachusetts in 1913 showed that over 5 per cent. of the
shoe workers were children under seventeen, over
16 per cent. of the silk mill workers. It is plain
that many industries having discovered that children's work is readily available and easily controlled, have made it an organized part of the trade.

What do children gain from these industries
in the way of money, training, and industrial
development?

A government report estimated the average
weekly wage of child workers at $3.46. The Fed-
eral Bureau of Labor reports the wages of children
between twelve and fourteen years in a South
Carolina cotton mill as between $3.54 and $5.04
weekly. The Federal Senate Commission gives
the average wage of children in the glass works it
investigated as from $4 to $6; in the silk industry
children's wages ranged from less than $2 to $5, a
majority earning $3. Apprentices in corset fac-
tories begin at about $3.50 a week. In some of
the semi-skilled trades the beginning wage is somewhat higher. Beginners in dressmaking and millinery receive from $4 to $6. In the telegraph
business young workers begin at $3.50 a week;
in the telephone business at $6. Slightly skilled
office assistants received from $4 to $7 a week, but
the first figure is the more usual. A careful
investigation of the wages of 622 working children in an industrial center in Massachusetts

showed that 374 of them received less than $5, 146 above $5.50, 93 from $5 to $5.50 and 9 no wages at all.

The most significant fact about children's wages, however, is that while they are certainly low enough, they are often *not* low as compared with the wages of adults in the same trade. In the same South Carolina mill that pays children from $3.54 to $5.04 a week, doffers of twenty years and over receive $2.52 a week. This is an extreme case, but the tendency is a general one. Wage progression is not the rule in the industries most largely employing juveniles, and the maximum may often be reached within a few months.

A recent investigation by the Federal Bureau of Labor showed that of a number of children under sixteen who left school to go to work, 90 per cent. entered industries in which the wages of adults were $10 a week or less. The road to be covered is very short indeed, and the trade in fact is, merely from the point of view of wage, a "blind alley trade." A summary of the wage advances possible and usual in some of these unskilled trades reads like a conspiracy against youth. The wage prospect is bright enough at the beginning, comparing only too favorably with the first wage offered the young apprentice in a skilled trade; it sometimes progresses for a brief space sufficiently to satisfy buoyant youth, and then suddenly stops. And the children that have so eagerly grasped the opportunity find themselves bound fast to a stationary wage, not only contributing all their present energies, but by an insidious one-sided contract also relinquishing the hope of wage advancement that fairly belongs to every young workman.

A Massachusetts investigation showed that in the textile industry (which was found to employ 43 per cent. of the child workers included in the 1913 study) the children that had been at work six years got less increase than those that had been at work one year.   Over 43 per cent. of one of the groups studied were, after one year, still at the beginning wage.   For many other jobs filled by children the rule is the same: no wage advance at all over an attractive first offer.

The result is inevitable: the longer children stay in such occupations, the more steadily their earning power decreases, the more surely they have started upon an industrial decline.   The Douglas Commission in Massachusetts estimated that boys of fourteen entering such employments—the only kind they can get at a possible wage at fourteen—at $200 a year, reach their maximum earning power ($640 a year) at the age of thirty-five, and at sixty years have fallen back to an earning power of $200 a year.   On the other hand the Commission held that a boy entering employment at eighteen, with the four years' additional training, earns $550 a year, reaches a maximum of $1365 a year at the age of forty-five, and at sixty-five is still able to earn $1000 a year. The beginner at fourteen is, at eighteen, earning $290 a year, or $160 a year less than the amount at which the boy at eighteen begins work. At the age of forty-five, the beginner of fourteen is earning only $545, or $150 less than the beginner at eighteen receives for his first year's work. These are difficult points to establish by figures, but the tendency is obvious.

Exceedingly long hours are the rule in these trades. The fact that these industries most largely employing children are the less standardized presages irregular work, long hours, and overtime, as well as the home-work already mentioned. In the distinctly seasonal industries, especially in fruit and vegetable canning, where the work is done under heavy pressure, according to the time of ripening and the supply, children are sure to feel all the effects of the rush season. The hours in the canneries average well above sixty a week. In oyster canning the work often extends for both children and adults from twelve to thirteen hours a day, beginning at 4 A.M. In the silk mills of New Jersey the number of hours for children has been limited to fifty-five a week. The utmost that agitations against long hours for children have been able to do is to make a fifty-four to sixty-hour week prevail in most sections of the country, while in the South a working week of from sixty to sixty-six hours is still common. Of 622 working children in Massachusetts, 50 per cent. had a ten-hour day, 11.6 per cent. had an eleven-hour day, and 2.1 per cent. had a twelve-hour day.   The usual time for beginning work is 6.30 or 7 A.M.

In every direction lack of opportunity to advance characterizes the work of children.   They have no opportunity to increase their earning power, no opportunity to increase their efficiency. If they chance upon an opportunity outside the factory or shop they scarcely have time or energy to embrace it.   In the industries themselves, there is little suggestion of any real skill or of opportunities for developing it.   In most of them the maximum amount of industrial development possible to a task is reached quite as soon as the maximum wage, or sooner.   In a Massachusetts investigation, 97 per cent. of the children who began to work at from fourteen to sixteen years of age were found in trades requiring little or no skill, and developing none.   Of 13,740 working children in Philadelphia distributed among various trades only 3 per cent., again, were in trades that could possibly be called skilled.

When the trade is in any sense skilled, it is not likely that the processes in which children are used are related at all to those requiring skill.   In the factories the work of the girls has very little relation to manufacture; when it is not running errands it is boning corsets, folding waists and shirts, doffing in the textile mills, "finishing," *i.e.*, snipping threads, in the clothing factories, or, in the box factories, putting pasteboard sheets into the machine.   Clothing factories report that the

rougher work in the needle trades is no preparation for the finer operations, and may, indeed,
be an obstacle to developing higher skill. In the
glass works the mold boys, the clearing-off boys,
the snapping-up boys, the machine boys keep
strictly to their respective processes, and learn
no other. In the 184 separate jobs of the shoe
trade, there is no reciprocity. In the short seam
at the back of the heel of a shoe two sharply
differentiated jobs are represented.

Over and over again it is demonstrated that
progression from unskilled to skilled processes, or
even from one process to another is almost impossible. A few of the more enterprising or more
daring children may watch their chance, "steal a
trade," and then go to another factory to "bluff
the job" there. A study of 200 women in Boston
and 109 women in Worcester in one of the highly
skilled trades revealed only four workers who
began their career in the unskilled trades. The
point of view of the hiring industries includes
little idea of children's future industrial efficiency,
or a use of them later for any more complex or
developing processes than those at which they
began. Of 406 occupations in which 406 children
in New York City began their working life so soon
as it was possible for them to secure employment
certificates, 21 occupations offered an opportunity
to work under some supervision; 30 offered an
opportunity to learn one process of the trade; 41
offered a chance to pick up training; while 314

offered no opportunity whatever for training.   In
Massachusetts it was found that after one year
in a certain trade, 46 per cent. of the children were
engaged in so-called skilled processes, and 54
per cent. in unskilled.   To learn the "skilled"
processes would have required very little time or
ability.   Even so, after these same children had
worked for six years in the trade, those in the skilled
processes numbered 58 per cent., those in the unskilled 42 per cent.   *Only 4 per cent., that is, advanced from unskilled to skilled processes during
the six years.*

Such a body in the labor market causes the
displacement of adult laborers.   There can be
little doubt that a considerable percentage of the
unemployment of the last ten years has been due to
this.   In Chicago the trade unions' reports to the
Mayor's Commission on Unemployment in 1914
as to the causes and remedies for unemployment
are significant.   "Too many young and incom-
petent workers" is a cause sent in by one union;
the same thing differently phrased occurs in the
reports of others.   Among the suggestions as to
how to abolish unemployment are the following:
"Children under sixteen should not be permitted
to work"; "We believe there should be some
regulation of the schools that are at present turning out hundreds and thousands of young men
and women, unequal for work—flooding the
market, lowering wages as well as standards of
work."

Up to this time we have been chiefly concerned in ascertaining how much the occupations of children offer them in the way of satisfaction or of industrial opportunity. It is important to ask, also, what do the children bring to the occupation? What is the equipment of the thousands of children yearly initiated into the industries of the United States?

So far as equipment consists of manual dexterity, physical fitness, and endurance, the question is not susceptible of an accurate answer. But if the amount of public-school instruction may constitute a rough guage of general training, the answer furnished to this inquiry is startling.

In the schools of the country at large, from 40 per cent. to 50 per cent. of the children in the elementary schools are eliminated before they have finished the grades. Most of these children either go to work or drift about looking for it. The amount of school training possessed by the average child worker is easily inferred from the following study of a class in the elementary schools of New York City: in a single year it contained 86,000 pupils. In the graduating year of that class, i.e. at the eighth grade, there were left 48,000. Of these 41,000 qualified for high-school entrance. Only 23,000 of these entered high-school, and only 4,079 of them finished the high-school course. The conclusion is that in New York City alone more than 40,000 children leave the public schools every year without completing the primary grades. A Massachusetts study showed that 70 per cent. of 40,000 working children between the ages of fourteen and seventeen leave school in the seventh grade or lower; 21.4 per cent. leave at the sixth grade, 43.6 per cent. below the seventh grade, and only 3.9 per cent. go beyond the grammar grades.

The fourteenth birthday is the common milestone marking the beginning of the work life of children. What is the training of the average child of fourteen in American public schools? At the very best, if he begins his school life, as comparatively few do, at six years of age, is promoted regularly and suffers no handicaps, such as the removal of his parents to other cities, etc., he can have finished the eighth grade and can be ready to enter the high school at the age of fourteen. The maximum training possible to him at the eighth grade in the present public-school system includes the elementary branches of the preliminary "arts" course—geography, history, arithmetic, English, in addition to a bit of "nature study" in some places and possibly physical training. In cities where the public-school system is more extensively developed, the girls are taught sewing and the boys some form of shop work.

But this training has very little reference to the mass of child workers for two reasons: a great many of them do not reach the eighth grade; and when the prospective workers leave they are not so far along in the grades as they should be. Not long ago a study was made of thirteen-year-old boys in seventy-eight American cities. *They were found to be scattered in every grade from the kindergarten to the high school. One-half of them were in the sixth grade or below.* A study of 1573 child workers in the candy, shoe, and textile industries in Massachusetts showed that 81.7 per cent. were retarded one year or more. Any one familiar with public-school records knows that the thousands of children that yearly enter American industry at the age of fourteen have only the most elementary training and no vocational instruction.

The public education system of America has no graver challenge than this. There is no implication here that it has not recognized the challenge. If all the child workers left school to work unwillingly, forsaking school out of sheer necessity, departments of society and government other than the department of education might be chiefly concerned. Undoubtedly there is a considerable percentage of children forced to work by grim poverty at home, the under- or over-employment of their parents; but over and over again it has been shown that actual economic pressure is not *in a majority of cases* the chief reason for children's going to work. Of the 40,000 workers in Massachusetts between the ages of fourteen and seventeen, it was found that 65 per cent. *could* give all their time to school rather than work; 35 per cent. could not. In Worcester fully 50 per cent. of the girl workers investigated had not gone to work because of actual poverty. In Cincinnati a study of 134 child workers showed that only 32 were forced to leave school because their earnings were needed at home. The rest of them preferred uncertain employment to school routine. A very large percentage of children go to work at fourteen, or shortly thereafter, because they hate school, are intensely bored by it, or are failing in their work and consequently not being promoted with their classes. Given these facts, youthful impatience and arrogance, and parental ignorance and short-sightedness do the rest. The boy is sent to the factory, the girl to the "Commercial Institute" which guarantees to turn her out a stenographer at the end of six months.

Children do not choose their "vocations"; they blunder into them. They want *a* job. One is about as good as another. If it is not, the advantage is likely to be reckoned solely in terms of a quarter or a half dollar more salary, or of nearness to home. It rarely occurs to them to *choose*, and if it did they have no basis of information from which to make a choice. They know nothing about the industries of their community, and nothing about comparative conditions and prospects in the various industries. A report of the Federal Commissioner of Labor shows that 550 out of 622, or 88.7 per cent., gave the following reasons for their "choice" of work: (1) Worked for parents, 29; (2) Took first position offered, 313;

(3) Went where friends or relatives worked, 192; (4) Wanted something near home, 16. Seventy-two out of the 622, or 11.3 per cent. may be said really to have had some principle of choice: (1) Wanted to learn trade or skilled profession, 27; (2) Attracted by high wages, 11; (3) Attracted by desirable work, 31; (4) Set up in business by father, 3.

Sometimes the parent is the autocrat. Far more often parents are merely helpless and perplexed spectators, sometimes suspecting that something is wrong, usually powerless to right it. The following instance reported from Cleveland is typical:

Margaret is fifteen years old. She is an only child and came to Cleveland two years ago with her father and mother. The father is a motorman and is able to keep the home for his family. Margaret is tired of school and has been well pleased with work as cash girl in one of our large department stores. The father says Margaret might go to school if she wished to do so. On the day before I visited the home Margaret had returned from work at about eight o'clock at night, and had failed to account for her tardiness. The incident had caused a little uneasiness, and the father expressed a wish that Margaret had stayed in school. I asked if he could not persuade her to go back. Before he answered, the recollection of a recent struggle came across his face and he said, "I'd hate to try."

The results of the arrogance of the young people and the ignorance and shortsightedness and helplessness of parents can hardly be attributed to the public schools.   But within the public school itself for years has been growing a criticism of the inability of the school to hold the pupils, and a conviction that it is the business of the school to reach and develop all of the energies of the child. There is food for thought in the fact that so many of the very children that go to work because they hate school *like* work—with its long hours, and its monotonous round.   Aside from their satisfaction in an independent "income," they like the sense of accomplishment replacing that of failure at school. A great majority of factory children in Chicago vigorously declared for work rather than for school, maintaining that you can "do things" in a factory. It seemed better to keep the wheels moving and to see the thread coming through than to write "Make hay while the sun shines" ten times every day and be no nearer to making it.   A few years later when the industrial grind has borne down the buoyancy of youth, and left the young worker sophisticated and indifferent, he realizes, usually with a pitiful hopelessness, how many are his handicaps.   In the textile industry, for instance, in an investigation made in Massachusetts 54.1 per cent. expressed an eager wish for vocational training either for the mill or for some trade outside the mill; of the candy workers, 48 per cent. wanted to learn some trade *outside the confectionery estab-lishments*, where the monotony and limitation of the work is marked.

The supply of children has seemed inexhaustible and therefore the *means* of getting them work have never been organized in this country. Given a great demand for workers in many unskilled processes, and given thousands of children ready to take "the first job that offers," and an organized labor market for children becomes quite unnecessary. Brothers and friends speak to foremen—and the young friend or brother is at the machine the next day. If he has his working papers he needs no other voucher. Those that do not secure their jobs through friends or relatives depend upon signs in windows or newspaper advertisements. The newspaper is the child's agency *par excellence*. Regular agencies have little interest in finding children work in mills, factories, stores, etc., because this is easily arranged without their mediation and because the wages paid are too low to provide a profitable percentage fee. In the skilled trades, for instance, commercial agencies that deal with high-grade workers usually exclude the inefficient child workers, leaving them to the agencies which combine placement with some form of training, as business institutes and typewriter agencies. In New York City there is a civic employment agency established for the purpose of placing boys and girls in factories. A small fee is charged, investigations are made of conditions, and every effort made to start the child right or advance him. Some children's societies instruct their

agents to assist children in getting work but the
work is not organized as part of the labor market
and very few of the thousands of workers come into
contact with such agencies.

It is a natural consequence of the manner of
"choosing" and the methods of securing their
jobs that children shift frequently from one
position to another. This is one of the most
serious aspects of children's employment; the
practice not only increases periods of unemployment, but also leads directly to satisfaction with
casual work. Occupations lightly chosen may be
as lightly resigned for others. Having reached
the maximum wage and the maximum development in one mill, the boys and girls reason that
they can hardly hurt their prospects by changing
to another. Even if the new positions offer only
a change of scene, there is some stimulus in that.
At any rate, change they do. The report on
children in connection with the employment
bureaus of the Boards of Trade in England
showed that it was very unusual for a boy to pass
through fewer than six places between the ages
of fourteen and twenty-one. For the American
boy and girl the situation is the same. It has been
estimated that eight or nine jobs within a few
years is not a high estimate for children in some
kinds of work and in some communities. It is
naturally in the most monotonous industries
that the greatest amount of shifting occurs. The
Federal Commissioner of Labor in noting this

condition in 1910 cites 213 boys and girls who had made 318 changes of employers, 254 changing to a different industry also. Other reports suggest more startling figures. In a recent New York City survey, 79 boys had jobs as follows: (1) 38 had had 38; (2) 20 had had 40; (3) 12 had had 36; (4) 6 had had 29; (5) 3 had had 6; making a total of 150 jobs. Reports of individual firms are even more significant. A paper-goods firm reports that in a year it takes on 250 learners, fifty per cent. of whom "do not stay long enough to give either themselves or the work a fair trial." A biscuit factory (in which the maximum wage is reached in two months) reports that although the regular force consists of about 150 girl workers at any one time, from 400 to 500 learners pass through in a year staying a few months each. The superintendent of a large corset factory in Worcester reported that one-half of the young workers get discouraged and quit before they reach the point of maximum speed. A rubber factory employing 1600 reported 4500 on its pay-roll for the year. A jewelry factory in Somerville, Mass., reports that 5 out of every 6 of the young workers leave in a year. The reasons for this shifting may vary greatly in different plants; the fact remains that the boys and girls do shift, and that the waste and cost to both industry and child are enormous.

With most untrained, unequipped workers, periods of unemployment are early taken for granted as a normal condition of their industrial

life. Of 700 children in Cincinnati, 50 per cent.
of the girls and 60 per cent. of the boys worked 52
weeks in a year; 10 per cent. of the boys were
unemployed for 12 weeks or more, and 10 per
cent. of the girls were unemployed for one-half
the time, or more. In Philadelphia 21,000 boys
and girls, the majority of whom were of compulsory
school age, were found to be not at school and not
employed. It is a safe inference that those not
employed in "home-work" were drifting around
hunting work or were in transit from one position
to another. The same Massachusetts survey
that found 40,000 regularly employed in the state
found also that there were 35,000 boys and girls
between the ages of fourteen and seventeen not
in school, *and employed intermittently or not at all*.
No doubt some of this unemployment was voluntary; but the conditions of the trades most largely
using children predicate for the workers a certain
amount of unemployment. A study of textile
workers in Fall River and New Bedford showed
that 9.4 per cent. of the boys and 33.9 per cent.
of the girls lost several months in a year. In the
study made at the New York City Municipal
Lodging House in 1914 of 2000 adult unemployed,
50 per cent. had left school before they were
fourteen; 46 per cent. had had no business or
trade training of any kind; most of them though
not of the unemployable class had been subject
to periods of unemployment throughout their
lives.

What opportunities does this country offer its youth to get the industrial training which so many of its beginners in industry lack, and which is plainly so often responsible for unemployment?

There is first, the apprenticeship system. With the introduction of machinery and the specialization of processes, apprenticeship in its original form has almost disappeared. The passing of some features of it, as indenture for periods longer than learning the trade really required, and exactions often covered by the personal nature of the contract, are not to be regretted. In a modern form an apprenticeship system is now to be found in a considerable number of industries throughout the country. In some of these "apprenticeship" dwindles into the most perfunctory instruction in a single process, and is little more than a means of securing cheap child labor. Its meaning is certainly variously interpreted.

In sample mounting, for instance, girl "apprentices" taken on at about $3.50 a week in the busy season, have an opportunity to become in good time *bona fide* mounters or labelers. In the perfumery trade, girl apprentices begin by labeling the cheapest goods, then the better grades, learning to cap and ribbon. All these firms take learners, at from $3.50 to $4.50 a week. In two seasons they reach an average wage of from $6 to $7. This is of course a kind of apprenticeship. The boy apprentices in the perfumery trade usually begin as errand boys in office or shipping room. It is only in the more highly organized industries and the powerful railroads and corporations that there exists an apprenticeship system which involves any agreement to teach the whole trade and which can be said to furnish industrial training. The following are typical of the most liberal apprenticeship systems now in operation:

An electrical company in Buffalo accepts for trial periods any grammar school graduate over fifteen. If he is found promising, a regular apprenticeship contract is signed by the firm, the apprentice, and the parents. The rate of pay is 10 cents an hour for the first year, 12 cents for the second, 14 cents for the third, and 16½ cents for the fourth. Also there is a cash bonus of $100 when the course is satisfactorily completed.

A printing company in Chicago accepts any boys of fourteen, pays them 5.4 cents an hour for the first year, 6.6 cents an hour for the second year, and the third year 10 cents, with an increase of two cents per hour after every subsequent six months.

A large electrical company in Pittsburg has a trial period of six months. If the probationer is accepted he receives a wage scale progressing from 11 cents an hour for the first year to 18 cents an hour the fourth, with a gratuity of $100 at the end.

On the whole, the existing apprenticeship systems in the country differ very widely, as to wage rates, methods of instruction, and general

6

scheme.   Sometimes companies build up apprenticeship systems in connection with outside schools.
A Massachusetts shoe company runs classes which
alternate weekly between the shops of the company where they work on piece-work and the
industrial school of the village where they receive
special training in drawing, shop mathematics,
business science, civics, and economics.   A firm
near Pittsburg has apprentices working under
a yearly contract, receiving regular wages, and
for nine hours a week attending a school run by
a Y. M. C. A. supported by the company.   At
the end of their apprenticeship the workers receive
a bonus of $150.

A survey of apprenticeship systems now in
existence leads to the conclusion that certain plants
are, within their own confines, working them out
intensively, here experimenting with a bonus
system to stimulate the development of workers,
there working out graduated lines of employment
with fixed conditions of promotion.   But they
reach only a few and are rather a mark of development of their respective industries and companies
than an evidence of the extension of vocational
training to untrained youth.   In Wisconsin in
1911 the legislature adopted a comprehensive
scheme of industrial education, at the same time
enacting an apprenticeship law, the enforcement of
which was entrusted to the Industrial Commission.

The chief difficulties relating to the apprenticeship system are the impracticability of it for the

smaller industries which are unable to maintain a
high grade of instruction covering all the processes
of a trade and continuing through several years,
and to pay the apprentices throughout this period.
The second difficulty is that apprentices leave to
enter other trades where the pay is higher but
the opportunities for learning not so great.

There can be little question that for highly
skilled trades some apprenticeship in the shop
itself, quite aside from any trade school training,
will probably always be necessary.   But there is
a great deal of question as to how the present
apprenticeship system with its lack of standardization, lack of supervision, and of any relation to
academic as well as industrial training, and most
of all, with its independence of compulsory education can be offered as a solution for the lack of
preparation of children for industry, and the disorganization consequent upon this.

From the employer's side also has sprung a very
recent experiment in industrial training, the corporation school.   This again is an "efficiency"
movement.   It reaches few workers under seventeen, and most of those it reaches, while inadequately trained, have had some little industrial
or business opportunity.   Recently a number of
corporations maintaining schools have combined
into a national association, and the articles of this
association express a keen recognition of the urgent
need for industrial education throughout the
country.   It believes that the public schools fail

to provide fundamental general training, which the corporation must therefore supply, in the interests of efficiency; and that every job in a company, whether it be that of salesman or advertiser or what not, is really a complex process involving, for real efficiency, varied information, and varied points of view, all of which can be learned more quickly and effectively from organized instruction in a number of allied subjects than from time and experience in the one job. The corporation school maintains that business has its science, in which workers may be systematically instructed. An automobile company, for instance, puts its salesmen through their "laboratory work," placing them in the factory to investigate the construction of new models of which they must have a definite technical knowledge.

The actual amount of time given to instruction does not seem to be great. In some corporations, the course covers three years, but an ambitious member may cover it in his first year if he so desires. Sometimes the work takes the form of lectures by experts, averaging about an hour and a half a week. The student is required to submit a *précis* of it the next week. Economics, business organization, accounting, money problems, investment and speculation, insurance, real estate, advertising, selling and buying, commercial law—these are some of the courses required. Advertising, selling and buying, as a group division for one job, are subdivided into the principles of psychology, factors in distribution, the relation between expense and profits, etc., etc. The whole scheme is an analysis of business requirements, and an attempt to develop them constructively. The theory upon which these corporation schools are based leads also to a practical policy in at least some of the corporations, a policy significant in the history of business, an organized system of noting the *general* capacities of employees as well as their usefulness in their specific jobs. A large electrical company in New York City, a member of the association, has a well-defined adjustment system, a policy of never dismissing a young man on account of inefficiency in certain lines of work. He is not only invited but encouraged to try other lines, and is provided with the training necessary in the new work. Not long ago a young man was on the verge of leaving, because of his inability to carry a certain kind of work. He was prevailed upon to stay, sent to the "training class," and is now an assistant manager. The corporation school goes upon the theory that every employee is an investment, to be conserved so long as there is any possibility of its turning out well.

Among general industrial schools there are several distinct kinds; those run as private businesses for profit; those run by philanthropies; those run by public education institutions. Some of these teach definite trades including both theory and practice; some of the more highly organized teach several trades; some of them are simply "manual training" schools giving training in manual work rather for the purpose of directing pupils toward trades than of fitting them for immediate entrance into any trade in particular. Some, notably among the public schools, put the chief emphasis upon academic work and others include very little or no academic work. In addition to the manual, the technical, and the trade schools, both day and evening, there are the agricultural schools, the commercial schools, the arts and crafts schools, which often include some form of industrial training, and the correspondence schools run as private businesses, which attempt to give instruction in the theory of trades by correspondence. Of these schools, which it is impossible to survey here, it may be said that, taken altogether, they reach only a small percentage of the young workers of this country, and a large percentage of those they do reach have already started out to work.

In his twenty-fifth report in 1910 the Federal Commissioner of Labor cited the fact that the matter of industrial education had up to that time received *far more attention from philanthropies and private businesses in America than from any other source.* A public policy for industrial education, either identified with or in very close relation with the regular public school system, is the only institution that has scope and power sufficient to deal with the conditions set forth in this chapter.

Up to this time the states have moved slowly. Within the last twelve years some states have appointed special commissions for the study of industrial education, with a view to its introduction wholly or partly at public expense. Eight states have enacted special legislation for the maintenance of public industrial training. Four states have established systems of industrial training apart from the public-school system. In New York it is an integral part of the public-school system. The Massachusetts provisions are typical of the "State Aid" system. Where a city or town furnishes building and equipment, the state will bear one-half the cost of maintenance. As a result thirty-five different cities and towns have some form of state aided vocational schools; 11 have all-day vocational schools, with 9 lines of trade training for boys, and 4 for girls; 3 have part-time schools; 35 have evening courses. It must be added that these schools have dealt with only about 1500 in the day schools, 300 in the part-time schools, and 6000 in the evening courses.

Public industrial education has long been the subject of experiments. For years it was regarded as a promising sign that vocational courses were introduced into high schools, and that finally manual training high schools and later a few trade schools were established. But considerably before the high school age, many of the real "manual workers" have left. Most of the vocational courses and schools require an eighth-grade certificate for entrance. Such schools have no point of contact with the thousand of workers described as leaving before they reach the seventh grade. The fact is that at the present time public industrial education, so far as it exists at all, does not offer any preliminary training to the vast army of children who by every tradition are bound for industry. The future shoemakers, weavers, electricians, tinsmiths, plumbers, masons, saddlers, sales-people, etc., are not taught in the public schools. It was pointed out recently that in an expensive technical high school in one of the smaller cities of the country 650 children were happily engaged in learning, for purposes of general culture, things of which they would make no use, while at the same time 7400 other children between fourteen and fifteen years of age in the same city were entering upon jobs to which they brought no training—and which would bring them none.

This realization has lead to a movement for fitting supplemental education into the working life of such children. Immediately, however, it appears that if the public educational system is to follow this "continuation school" plan, the young workers must either be instructed at night, or the coöperation of the employer obtained. In some places children that go to work at fourteen are already required to attend night school until they are sixteen. But it is an open secret that the law works badly, and that educational measures forced at night upon young undeveloped minds and bodies exhausted by the day's work have little promise of industrial betterment even when the law can be enforced. It refers in most places, moreover, only to those children who at the age of fourteen are still illiterate. The night high schools in a few cases offer instruction in various trades, but again for young workers these night school opportunities are dearly bought. The ambitious and the more physically fit boys and girls between fifteen and twenty will attempt them. But even the task of making up in night schools for the deficiencies of their common school education are great, and when to this is added a study of trades the undertaking is formidable indeed. Besides, night schools, alas, are few, and trade training in them more infrequent still.

There have been a very few scattered experiments in the *day* continuation school in this country, wherein, by the coöperation of employers and local public school systems, a certain amount of public school instruction is given in the factory or establishment each week, or pupils are required to attend school elsewhere for part of the day. Sometimes the instruction is general and academic only, sometimes it has definite relation to the trade. As yet it has been more favored in the department store than in the shop or factory, for the obvious reason that dull times of the day are the rule in the former, while every minute in the latter has its value in cents and in production. In Massachusetts part-time courses exist now in candy-making, printing, salesmanship, office work, pattern-making, machine work, draughting, iron-moulding, tin-smithing, saw-making, bricklaying, carpentry, textiles; and they have been arranged for in electrical work, shipwrighting, shipfitting, ship-caulking, cabinet-making, plumbing, blacksmithing, copper-smithing, steamfitting, boilermaking and riveting, and sheet-iron working. The continuation school for apprentices in Cincinnati was at first an employers' movement, and was later taken over by the public-school system. The central public school plan has been in operation there for four years, and is reported to be satisfactory to all concerned. In Wisconsin attendance at continuation schools is required for all children between fourteen and sixteen. Homogeneous groups are made up according to the groups represented, and the five hours' work is divided into one-half devoted to English, hygiene, etc., and the other half to vocational training.

In this transition stage of industrial training some provision for *part-time* training for young people during the day seems necessary. For the less fortunate young workers driven to work too early by poverty, some such scheme may always be needed. But the drawbacks to the plan as a permanent policy are obvious. They include the difficulty of managing the trade training of groups which though small may represent a number of miscellaneous trades, and the difficulty of making sure, in any such plans, of the principles of compulsory attendance and practical control.   This does not modify the present need for the development of part-time courses in the all-day vocational schools.

A more constructive attempt than the day continuation school, at least in its present stage of development in America, is a readjustment of the ancient public school scheme *from the beginning*, as evinced in the public school at Gary, Indiana. Because of its courageous renunciation of an iron-bound tradition and its definite relation to the equipment of children for industry by a system of "prevocational training" the scheme of the Gary School may be set forth here somewhat fully.

The Gary School is really a "plant" run on the same scientific principles of efficient management as any working plant.   It requires that the materials of the curriculum be sufficiently various to meet the needs of every class of individuals and that the course of study be sufficiently flexible so that the individual can be given just the things he needs.

The system provides (1) classrooms and libraries where the child can study books and recite from books; (2) playgrounds, gymnasiums, and swimming pools where the child can play and secure a general physical training; (3) shops, gardens, drawing-rooms, and laboratories where the child can work and learn to do efficiently many things by doing them; (4) an auditorium where by lectures, recitals, dramatization, phonographs, player pianos, stereopticon lantern and motion pictures, the visual and auditory education of the child may be efficiently looked after. The new school arranges the classes so that different sets of children are in the four separate departments at different times. In this way four times as many children are accommodated.

But more important is the fact that children want to go to such a school every day in the year and ten hours a day. The school provides a real life so that the child wants to educate himself at the very moment that he has the opportunity. The curse of the public schools is the lock-step of the grades. But in Gary every month the pupils file up and down the grades. The children go as they grow, subject by subject, month by month. Attendance in shop classes begins in the fourth grade. The teachers are specialists; grade teachers teach the three Rs and special teachers the special subjects. The work is interesting because the teacher knows what he is teaching and the children stay at school because they like it.

The school hours at Gary are from 8:30 until 4 and 5. Each child must spend four hours in school and may spend eight. Play and work are alternated during the day. The course is twelve years, thus doing away with any formal distinction between grade schools and high schools and making easy and natural the transition from one to the other. The last four years, specifically, are

the high school years which include the trade
classes. Sixteen trades are taught. The instructors are overalled workmen, experts, and members
of their respective trade unions. When the boys
reach the third year in high school they elect
cabinet-making, printing, or painting, etc., and
enter a regular apprenticeship. If, when they leave
school, they enter the trade they elected, the time
spent in the school work is counted off from their
apprenticeship. High school girls may study,
under an expert teacher, stenography, typewriting,
professional bookkeeping, or may enter the printing shop.

The superintendent of the Gary Public Schools
has formed a close association with the employers
of Gary. Occasionally he invites a group of
bankers, or lawyers, or merchants, or builders, to
visit the Emerson School. In this way he has
awakened in the business community a wonderful
spirit of coöperation with the work of the school.
A certain number of jobs are permanently at the
disposal of the superintendent of schools. When
a boy gets ready to leave school, there is an apprenticeship or at least a job waiting for him in the
superintendent's office. When a high school girl
completes the commercial course, there is an office
position waiting for her.

When the restless spirit of youth impels a four-
teen-year-old child to leave school, the superintendent says to him: "All right, we will give you a job.
You try work for three months. At the end of that

time you will have earned some money and perhaps you will feel like coming back to school again for a while." Usually the child returns to school. Since the job is at the disposal of the superintendent, the child can retain it no longer than the superintendent thinks best for him. Then he recalls the child and gives the job to another restless spirit.

In the evenings the schools are at the disposal of adults and older children. The buildings are open until 10 P.M. There are classes in languages, printing, commercial chemistry, mechanical drawing and drafting, sign painting and lettering, cabinet work, machine shop work, forge shop work, moulding and foundry work, sheet metal work, electrical practice, and others, each taught by experts. The library is open, the laboratories, manual training shops, and gymnasiums are available. And so soon as application is made for new classes, the classes are formed. It is to be added that the cost per capita is not higher than that of the conventional school system.

There is one group of child workers which has not even a ceremonial relation with the public-school system of this country or, except by an unusual chance, with any opportunities to increase industrial efficiency. These are the immigrant children arriving in this country at or after the age of fourteen, and flocking at once to mill, factory, and sweatshop. With many immigrant

children *under* fourteen indeed, the public schools
do not make connections.   Perhaps at the time of
arrival the children are twelve or thirteen years
old.   If parents do not send them to school, the
compulsory education department, unless it has
taken the trouble to secure from the immigration
authorities the names of children manifested to a
particular locality, does not know that they are
in the country.   And the children either go to work
at once, engage in home-work, or drift around for a
year or two.   If the parents go to work in the
canneries, in the rural communities, as they so
largely do, the children go too, working in sheds
in states where they are forbidden to work in the
canneries proper, and not going to school for the
simple reason that there are no schools to attend.
When they are fourteen, they go to work in earnest.
The parents have little to say about it—the children have become to them the interpreters of
America; if they do have anything to say, they
know nothing of industrial conditions and it
probably seems to them that it is well for the boy
or girl to begin early to work out a future in
American industry.

   If we confine the young immigrant workers to
those fourteen or over upon arrival, we are dealing
with a large factor in American industry.   One
needs only to stand at 6 o'clock upon a New York
City street in the factory sections and watch the
tide of workers moving eastward to know how
large a body of these workers is made up of im-

migrants between the ages of fifteen and twenty. In twenty-eight states, including the states of heavy immigration, there were by the 1910 census 855,973 foreign-born white persons between the ages of fifteen and twenty. 11.5 per cent. of these were in school.

They accept whatever they can get, trustfully, upon almost any conditions. The boys become bootblacks and flower peddlers, working under the padrone, who perhaps paid their passage, for sixteen and sometimes even eighteen hours a day, and are entirely in the padrone's hands as to living and wage conditions. With no knowledge of the industrial conditions, and with no guidance, the boy fitted to be a general laborer naturally accepts the suggestion that he become a waiter, and on the other hand the Greek peasant buys a pushcart. Immigrant girls, falling in with the general belief that immigration—without discrimination—is the answer to the American domestic servant problem, make domestic service at least their first job, a sort of preparatory industry from which those fitted for other work do not always escape. Little girls under the age limit for working papers drudge in private households where the truant officer rarely looks. The work of many young immigrants in this country bears little relation to their capacities, equipment, or previous training. Skillful needle workers are found at mangling machines in laundries, fine embroiderers in bakeries, skilled dressmakers making harness, and bookkeepers and typewriters doing unskilled needle work in the shops.

In addition to their ignorance of American industry, they are handicapped by their ignorance of English. Only a few are reached by night schools, and, again, the younger ones are unfit for the strain of night work. In New York City in the winter of 1913–14 a continuation class run by the department of education in a white-goods factory had as its object making literate in English forty young girls of different nationalities, all ignorant of English. The firm estimated that the acquisition of English with the resulting increased facility in understanding instructions and explanations of processes resulted in a gain of about 25 per cent. in industrial efficiency.

This was merely a matter of literacy. The interest of foreign-born workers in the industrial training they rarely attain to is a matter of record. A large electrical company reports: "Every Polish boy on our force is up on his work. The majority of boys behind in apprenticeship work are the sons of American fathers." When in Buffalo a few years ago the vocational school system was extended by establishing one in the Polish section, the local interest in it was startling, and the registration of students record breaking. Here temporary quarters were established for a school giving instruction in carpentry, cabinet-making, electrical construction, and machine shop practice.

The idea was so popular that the first year over

three hundred boys were given this form of training and more than three hundred were on the waiting list.

Clearly, the safeguarding of young people's industrial futures is a far greater and more complex task than creating facilities for industrial education, important as this is. Out of this realization has sprung up in various places throughout the country a movement toward vocational guidance, the scientific direction of young people into industry in accordance with their abilities and capacities determined as accurately as may be by preliminary experiments in various trades as well as by other methods; in accordance also with the future opportunities in the various trades, and finally, with the state of the current labor market, the need or the over-supply of workmen in any given trade at a given time.

Few movements in this country at this time have the social or economic significance of these vocational guidance efforts. They represent an attempt to put education, as a public institution, into a direct relation both with the needs of the individuals which are its proper charges and with the industrial standards with which up to this time neither education nor any other institution or body has had much concern, and over which there has never been any general supervision.

It is true that, taking the country as a whole, the vocational guidance movement is still in its infancy. The hopeful signs for its continuance and effectiveness are the very different sources of interest in it. Business men, chambers of commerce, mayors of cities have made it their active concern, and have in some cases furthered—and financed—movements begun in their communities. The significance of this is in the first place that "business" recognizes—as it has marked opportunity to do—the viciousness of the present conditions under which young people enter industry; and in the second that vocational guidance should not be permitted to become an academic movement.

In the long run it is not the direct concern of business to see that every child has a fair opportunity to fit himself for work in the world; it *is* the concern of a public educational system to do this. It is, indeed, inherent in the very idea of a public educational system. But this will be an exceedingly complex task, touching upon provinces which are not only new to educational departments, but with which in the present state of affairs, these departments are hardly equipped to deal. In the adaptation of a public educational system to industrial conditions, industry and civic bodies must coöperate if the best results are to be secured both for the young workers and for industry.

According to a recent Federal Bureau of Education report, vocational guidance has eleven aspects: (1) the investigation of occupations; (2) the study of vocational schools and courses; (3) the study of

individuals to discover their vocational tendencies;
(4) the giving of vocational information; (5)
provision for talks and lectures on vocational
subjects; (6) the publication of vocational pamphlets; (7) the correlation of vocational work with
work in English; (8) the direct teaching of occupations; (9) placement; (10) the following up of those
placed; (11) the providing of scholarships for the
gifted and needy.

In several cities either under the auspices of the
departments of education or otherwise, promising fundamental work has been done, notably in
connection with surveys of occupations, and
studies of vocational schools and courses already
open to students in the respective state or community. In Boston extensive surveys of these
two situations were made several years ago, and
the returns analyzed. In Cincinnati it was decided
that the enormity of the task would require a five-
year survey, and this survey has now been carried
on for more than three years. In Philadelphia and
New York vocational guidance committees authorized by the boards of education have been at
work for several years. In New York a number of
pamphlets containing vocational information have
been issued. The work in that city has lately
received a new impulse in the warm interest of
officials high in the city's government. In Washington a vocational guidance movement is operating
under the encouragement of business. And in
Buffalo the work has been definitely undertaken

by the Chamber of Commerce who last year
engaged an expert in vocational guidance to
organize the work for them and to make intensive
studies of certain trades and put these studies into
serviceable form for young people.

The first aspect of the vocational guidance
program as outlined, *i.e.*, giving exact information about the various trades, involves researches that have never been accurately made.
The already mentioned children's agency for
factory work in New York City, and the Consumers' League in certain places, have made some
studies of industry from the point of view of their
suitability for children. As yet, however, these
studies do not purport to be general or exhaustive.
To study *accurately* the conditions of even the
"constant occupations" of any particular community needs no small amount of industrial
knowledge and observation. For the purpose of
vocational guidance it is necessary to find out,
about any given industry, for what processes in it
children may be trained, what qualities or what
degree of strength the work requires, what are the
probable effects of the particular work upon health,
what are the moral conditions, whether employment in the trade is constant or seasonal and to
what degrees, and especially, what are the opportunities both as to wage and training. Such data
must of course be constantly revised to meet
changing conditions.

That such community studies of industry are

necessary to the success of any system of industrial training cannot be doubted. Even the circulation among young people of accurate information about various industries, in a form in which the boys and girls could see the applicability to their choice of vocation would be of inestimable value. With this work alone organized and in operation, the number of children in blind alley trades would be appreciably lessened even if the facilities for industrial training were not greater than they are now.

The second phase of vocational guidance work, a study of the already existing opportunities for trade and industrial training in the separate communities is obviously a prerequisite for that extension of facilities for vocational training which must follow in the wake of the vocational guidance movement. For this extension the vocational guidance movement must furnish impulse and direction. In the larger towns and cities it is probable that few people have any opportunity to gain comprehensive and exact information about even those trade schools and courses offered in their own town, exactly what is offered in them, and what returns may be expected from the preparation they give. The Henry Street Settlement in New York recently published a directory giving all the trades and vocations taught in the day or evening schools of greater New York, the price of tuition if any tuition is charged and other necessary details. Such an educational directory seems a very simple thing; as a matter of fact it is most infrequent. In the instance mentioned it served a double purpose: to instruct the children where to look for training; and to instruct the citizens of New York how few and inadequate opportunities for industrial training there are in the greatest industrial center in the country. When all this information is compiled by discriminating investigators and made public under the authority of the public-school system the ground will have been cleared for a more discriminating extension of facilities for industrial training.

The third aim of vocational guidance, the study of individuals to discover their vocational tendencies is a very difficult matter. But when information about trades is obtainable, when parents, children, and the public generally are informed in this respect, and when the means of trade training are available, the young workers themselves will do a good deal toward making clear their own vocational tendencies. This study of individuals and the studies of the trades are interdependent. This is recognized in the Cincinnati Survey, where, for instance, an expert in psychology has been employed to study every detail of shoe-making. The difficulty offered by such studies and the need of expert knowledge for the making of them is indicated in a recent instance in New York. A philanthropic agent concerned with the placement of children in work guaranteed not to be detrimental to them, after a study of diamond polishing, directed that it be placed upon the white list. Learning of this, a social worker who had happened to come into contact with a number of girl workers in this trade and had noticed the unusual amount of illness and break-downs among them, herself investigated the trade and systematically questioned the workers. She learned that so far as hours, wages, and decent conditions of work were concerned, the trade did indeed compare not unfavorably with other industries entered by young girls in the community. But the power of attention necessary to hold the stone in just the right position, the constant danger of losing it, the strain that resulted from knowing how slight a wavering of attention could lead to catastrophe was a severe daily strain that many of the girls were physically not equipped to endure. What was needed to insure success in this operation was not "skill" in the industrial sense at all, but a condition of nerve and physical organization which "experience" cannot be depended upon to produce. Fairly simple tests would have indicated those that had the requisite qualities and could safely be directed to the work.

The fourth, fifth, and sixth aspects of vocational guidance, the giving of vocational information and talks, and the publication of vocational pamphlets, represent the campaign for the education not only of the children, but of parents, the general public, and industry as well. It is probable that the development of all the other work depends on the effectiveness with which this campaign can be

accomplished. It will be the means of securing
several things which are prerequisites to the abolition of the conditions which now surround working
children: the intelligent coöperation of tax-payers,
and a greater standardization of those industries
that employ children in one or more of their
processes.

It is often pointed out that the actual teaching of
trades within public schools and correlation of this
trade training with English and other subjects
present great difficulties. This is true, but the
difficulties, however great, are not insuperable.
The owner of a shoe factory in Lynn, who, as a
member of the board of education, is interested in
an industrial school now being contemplated by
the board, was asked: "Could you find within your
own factory able workmen who would also make
good instructors?" He weighed the question for
some minutes and then answered: "*Yes, I should
have to select them with great care, but they exist.*"
That is the sum and substance of the matter;
teachers of trades will have to be sought carefully,
but they exist. And textbooks, where they can
be made to serve, can also be made, perhaps by
the coöperation of academic and trade instructors.
Greater difficulties than these will lie in getting
effective training early enough to those children
that are forced by poverty to go to work as soon
as the law allows them; and in keeping a careful
balance between academic and trade training.

As the foregoing lines of vocational guidance

activities become more and more developed, the relation between industry and a system of public industrial training will become more and more close and coöperative. With the growth of public employment agencies, both state and municipal, now on the increase in this country, and with the possibility of a Federally supervised system of employment exchanges now pending, the possibilities of effective coöperation between such agencies and the vocational guidance committees of the departments of education are at once apparent. Of the twenty states in this country that provide for state employment agencies, two, Wisconsin and New York, now recognize the importance of differentiating the children's problem from that of other candidates for work, and provide for advisory committees of parents and employers for looking after their interests in juvenile departments. It is one of the chief businesses of public employment agencies to accumulate and circulate information about trade conditions. Vocational guidance bureaus will need their coöperation, and they in turn will need the information about industry which the vocational committees will have gathered from a more highly specialized point of view, with direct relation to youthful workers. In England the Board of Trade Employment Exchange in its work with children keeps in direct and close relation to the educational authorities who attend to the personal side of the work. In Birmingham, for instance, the public labor exchanges receive and register applications from children under seventeen, and also from employers, then endeavor to place the applicants in the positions best suited to them. This work is in charge of an officer who has in his possession the child's school report, a report from the school medical officer, and from the school care committee "helper." In these school care committees members assigned as "helpers" to a small number of children keep in touch with them for about three years. There is also a Central Care Committee consisting of six members of the Education Commission, four representatives of teachers, three of employers, three of workmen, four social workers, school medical officers and others. Through these relations, the exchanges become far more than placement agencies. Through their efforts, firms are induced to promote their own boys instead of discharging them and taking in men from outside. One exchange has started a school for unemployed boys.

Some such follow-up work is recognized as necessary in America and is set down as the tenth aspect in vocational guidance work. Follow-up work will really be less a matter of sentiment and paternalism than an administrative function quite necessary for the successful carrying out of the other lines of vocational guidance work, a system of checks both upon the workers and the form of work. The eleventh aspect, the provision of scholarships for the gifted and needy,

introduces no new principle into American
education.

The most significant contribution to the subject
of vocational education and vocational guidance is
contained in the recently published report of the
Federal Commission on National Aid to Vocational
Education[1] and the bill providing for its recommendations. As a general survey of the present
need of vocational education this report is indispensable to students of the subject. It does not in
any sense remove the necessity for accurate local
studies both of industries and facilities for trade
training. What it very definitely does do is to
explain why and wherein a *policy* for industrial
education in this country cannot be left to states
and municipalities, but must be a Federal responsibility, with the granting of Federal aid to
all-day, part-time, and evening vocational schools
of less than college grade, for persons over fourteen.
An amount equal to that supplied by the Federal
government is to be supplied by the state or the
community. The conditions governing the Federal
grants recognize state and community differences;
appropriations for salaries of teachers of trade and
industrial subjects are to be allotted to the states
in proportion to their urban population; the
agricultural appropriations are to be in accordance
with the rural population.

We have elsewhere in this discussion shown the
difficulty of securing satisfactory teachers in voca-

[1] H. R. Document 1004; in 2 volumes, 1914.

tional subjects. A significant recommendation by
the Commission is national grants for the training
of teachers, on the principle that "the economic
differences among the states and the migratory
character of teachers justifies the nation's aid in
training them."

The report in detail deserves study. The significance of its recommendations can hardly be
overestimated. It reformulates the educational
policy of this country, relating it to industry, to
society, and to individual efficiency in a manner
never before attempted and long sorely needed.

*It has been demonstrated that there are in industry
large numbers of untrained workers between the ages
of fourteen and twenty-one, displacing adult workers
and destined, many of them, by the conditions of their
work and their equipment, to become themselves the
unemployed and the unemployable of the next generation. It is submitted generally that there is no place
in industry for children between the ages of fourteen
and sixteen, but they are at work in large numbers.
A general raising of the minimum working age from
fourteen to sixteen is certainly desirable, but the situation cannot be remedied thus at one stroke by legislation. The real answer lies in adapting the system of
public education to the varying capacities and tendencies of boys and girls; and in providing industrial
training at a sufficiently early age to make it profitable
to those that by reason of poverty or capacity are
destined for early entrance into industry. A system
of public industrial training, instituted not merely as*

an adjunct to secondary education, but as an integral part of elementary education as well, is the crying need of this country to-day. It cannot be left merely to wealthy cities to work out individual plans for themselves. The rural districts and the immigrant population must be provided for also. In changing the present conditions of juvenile work, industry also must have a part. Indeed, a standardization of the conditions under which children work must result when throughout the country an industrial education policy becomes a permanent part of the system of public education.

Vocational guidance should be given every possible encouragement along practical lines within the public school system and in public agencies under the direction of special committees of experts acting in an advisory capacity. Children of working age constitute a legitimate part of the labor market organization. The training and placement of child workers, therefore, belong respectively to the public school system and the public agency, the two constituting a governmental responsibility.

CHAPTER IV

IMMIGRATION AND UNEMPLOYMENT

THERE is an increasing tendency in this country to ascribe social and industrial disorders to the immigrant. This is an easy way to explain overcrowding of cities, wretched housing conditions, increase in crime and in the number of "public charges," and political and social discontent that crystallizes in such organizations as the Industrial Workers of the World. It is as a part of this general theory that immigration is held to be the explanation of unemployment. There are many who believe that if immigration were permanently stopped, unemployment as a problem of any considerable intensity would disappear.

There is no doubt whatever that immigration adds to our liabilities just as it adds to our assets. It brings certain benefits and it intensifies some of our social and industrial difficulties. To the immigrant as an element of confusion, we have given a good deal of apprehensive attention; to him as a contribution, we have given very little thought beyond recognizing his capacity for hard labor. So insistent has been our demand that he build our subways and roads and aqueducts, work in our mills, mines, or foundries that we have not inquired what equipment he has, what degree of thrift and invention, what savings to invest in America, to say nothing of what spiritual capacities, what traditions of art and literature.

It is only occasionally that we recall that the law of admission requires that he have a sound body and some money, that each adult immigrant is worth at least $1000—the cost of rearing a child to the age of production—and that it is consumption as well as production that maintains our markets. That immigrants are not larger consumers and better investors than they are is partly the fault of our educational and assimilative processes which as yet operate chiefly to make the alien a producer.

As to how largely he *is* a producer, even to one prepared in some measure for the results, the findings of the Federal Immigration Commission in this regard are astounding. From the figures given, one is led to conclude that the principal industries of the nation are dependent upon immigrant labor for their continuance. The iron and steel manufacturing of our country employs 86,089 workers, of whom 57.7 per cent. are foreign born, while a good many others are the children of foreign-born parents. Germans, Irish, English, Slovaks, Poles, Magyars, and Croatians—all sink their common native differences in favor of the common denominator "iron and steel worker." The slaughtering and meat-packing industry includes 43,502 workers, 60.7 per cent. of whom are

foreign born. In bituminous coal mining, out of
88,368 workers, 61.9 per cent. are immigrants. In
the woolen and worsted manufacturing industry
61.9 per cent. again of 23,388 employees are foreign
born. Cotton goods manufacturing scores 68.7
per cent. out of 66,800 employees; clothing manufacturing scores higher with 72.2 per cent. foreign-
born employees out of 19,502; while the high-water
mark is reached in sugar refining where, out of
5826 workers, 83.3 per cent. are foreign born. In
every industry of importance there is evinced a
startling dependence upon foreign-born workers.
It is impossible to discuss any aspect of industrial
life without taking into account the immigrant
factor. So large an industrial factor cannot help
having an important connection with employment
conditions generally, and with unemployment.
Just what the connection is, this country has never
determined. There are many assumptions, but
little data. Only when it is really known rather
than assumed why the immigrant figures so largely
in American industry, under what conditions he
gets his work and does it, what standards he imposes and what standards are imposed upon him,
will there be any adequate basis for formulating
the relation of immigration to unemployment in
America.

Every adult immigrant that lands on our shores
is at least temporarily in the unemployed class.
He may have the address of an employer or the
assurance of a job, but until the tools are in his

hands he is a prey to the influences, fears, and mis-
haps which befall every working man or woman out
of a job. Even when there are friends or relatives
to help him face the dangers or to offer a share of
their homes, he does not feel that he has a firm
grip on life until he is earning a wage. He does
not begin his industrial life—nor for that matter
any phase of his life in America—on equal terms
with the American born. Eager to work, and to a
degree able, he has nevertheless handicaps which,
if not met, cannot fail to prove fatal to his success.
He does not know the industrial game. He has
little conception of the rules by which it is conducted. And his education is left to instructors
who exploit him, teach him the wrong moves, or
assign him to a position on the field which gives
him no conception of the game as a whole, or of
the general theory and scheme of American industrial life.

The chief concern of the immigrant is to find a
job; the concern of America should be to give him
the right job—neither above nor below his capabilities—a job that will fit him into American industrial life at the point most economic both to
him and to industry. The immigrant presents a
peculiar need. He has not grown up in our industrial or educational system. He is more often
than not face to face with a great industrial mechanism entirely foreign to his experience or training.

He reaches Ellis Island, the greatest market-
place for unskilled labor in the world,—and the

least organized. From it the Greek boy pursues his way undisturbed to the padrone's gang in the shoe-shining parlor, the tailor goes to the mine, the peasant to the factory and pushcart, the scholar to the hotel kitchen and dining-rooms, and the craftsman to the farm. Among women it is no better: a girl of nineteen who had graduated from the gymnasium and was a bookkeeper and type-writer was found sewing in a shop where she made $4 a week; a girl who had always made her living by fine embroidery was found working as a baker earning $4 a week; a trained dressmaker was found making harness in a leather shop for $5 a week— her sore hands, used to skillful adjustments not to stiff leather, told her story. Several skilled needle workers were found at a mangling machine in a laundry. A girl who had been a lithographer in Russia was working as a sleevemaker for $4.50 yer week after she had been here for almost a year. The instances typify a general situation. General housework is considered the inevitable first job for most immigrant women whether skilled or un-skilled; and many never escape from it. America makes no attempt to ascertain the qualifications and fitness of these men and women; they in turn know nothing of the conditions and opportunities in the various trades. The results could not be other than they are.

The only step ever taken by the government in this direction was the establishment of the Division of Information in the Federal Bureau of Labor.

From its beginning in 1907 it has been exceedingly limited in its powers and appropriations. As a vocational service bureau upon any adequate scale it has been a failure. At this time, however, the work of the Division is being enlarged and centers are being opened in eighteen cities.

The determining factors in the choice of an immigrant's first work in America to-day are the occupations of his friends or relatives, the orders on the books of the employment agent or banker to whom he comes, and the help of chance street and saloon acquaintances. His aptitude, training, experience, and qualities other than physical strength, have little influence upon the decision. Local studies have repeatedly shown that the history of immigrant workmen in this country is not a history of intelligent placement, but of the most ruthless waste of energy, ability, and aptitude to be found in modern life. Failure to make the right connections in the first place is likely to mean, with the immigrant workman, a complete history of wrong connections. The following story is only typical:

The 3rd October, 1912, I arrived with S. S. *Noordam* at Hoboken and had about $20 in my pocket. I stay in Hoboken two weeks looking for a position as office clerk not knowing that there were more jobs as that for me. I never heard in my country about dish-washer, janitor, and other positions as waiter and many others were not in my way because I never had any experience about them.

After my money was spent I left Hoboken and went as given in a newspaper to Park Row to an office where they sent men out in this State for farmers and the reason that the manager was a Dutchman found a good place in my heart that I could get some advice around there. He told me he had a job for $12 a month and I get it. Well I took it, he paid my fare to Erieville, about forty miles from Syracuse (N. Y.) and arrived following day at the farmer. After working for three weeks the farmer told me that that kind of work was nothing for me and that I had to go. He give me $2.13 being $9.00—$6.87 fare what he paid for me when I was send to him. The money being $2.13 was not enough to go beg to New York and was the only way for me to go to Syracuse for $0.87. In Syracuse, a small town, was no work at all. I stay there for three months and sleep in the station or walk outside in the snow and cold night. At last I work in a lunchroom as dishwasher for $5.00 a week, meals free.

In the same time a friend of me was working Morris Plains (N. J.) Hospital, and wrote me a letter that I must come to him because he could give me a position for $20.00 a month in the laundry. The reason that he was a countryman from me and friend in my town I listened to him and came two days later for $6.78 in Morris Plains. He had send me $6.00 for fare. In all the time being four months I had my trunk with clothes in Hoboken at a hotel, Hudson Street, for his keeping. I had to pay every months $1.25, so that I must pay him for four months $5.00—The manager heard that I was working, wrote me a letter that he would not be any longer responsible for my trunk and ordered me to take the trunk away and told me in two days. I was in Morris Plains just about one month

and pay day was a few days later. There my clothes
were from fine quality and I would not lose them. I
must quit my job for to get money. I received about
$18.00—I paid my friend his $6.00 and the hotel-
keeper $5.00—for the train $0.78—$11.78, so that
when I was in New York I had $6.00—in my pocket.
I took my trunk and took it with me to my room
Hudson Street, where I was only one week, and till this
day my trunk was left in that room and never saw her
again. I went in the Bowery because people told me,
it was in February, I could get if I had no money
always something to eat down there, and from that
time the miserable life was beginning. After a few
weeks the Bowery Mission gave me a position as writer
addresses in Barclay Street where I work one and one
half months. They had no work more and I had to quit.
I went to Hoboken one night and got a job as bartender in Hudson Street. I must work there eighteen
hours a day for $5.00 a week. I get up 9 A.M. and has
as my first duty to clean the bar and rooms what tooks
about five or six hours and in the same time bartender.
At 3 o'clock P.M. the manager comes down and then I
am a waiter. But don't supposed that I could sit
down for a rest. No if he could not find more work to
do, then he ordered me to play the piano, and many
times that I did that from 3 P.M. till 11 P.M. while he
had told me that the afternoon was for me to take a
walk. And when I was playing I had to keep music
all the time he only found that we had to take a rest in
bed after 3 A.M. when I was finished. Once he did not
understand me right and became so mad that, so he
always did with his customers, took his police stick
and would hit me. I found it the best way to beat it
and not asking for my money went out and to New

York where I got a job as orderly in a Hospital. There I work three weeks as orderly and after that the sister gives me a porter job what only tooks one week. After that the sister came in the morning and told me that she heard I wasn't a Catholic and there I had money enough made I could look for another job. Before she hired me she told me that the salary was $12.00 a month. I went down the office with her and thinking to get $12.00 I received $4.50, and told me that it was all the money she got.

After that I was discusted and after paying $2.00 I was shipped to Venango about sixty miles from Buffalo to work as laborer at the railroad. There I came to the recovering that I had to do with a bunch of thieves. I work one and one half months and quit with $8.25 left. The commissary man where a man buy his stuff, so as meals, clothes, etc., was a big thief, and he steal from us Americans and other men all he could get. He steal the money before my face and as I told it him then I have to be very quite because he did not care to kill me. From there I went for $2.90 to Cleveland, Ohio, and paid at an agency $2.00—that was all the money I had for a job in West Virginia with a tie treating plant at $1.75 a day. I arrived and was surprised to hear that it was piece-work and there were no jobs for $1.75. I had to take it and work one month. I made about between $.75 and $1.00 a day and had to pay $.60 for meals. I went after one month to the railroad who was laying a new track in the neighborhood. They took me as laborer and in the hope that there were no thieves there, started the laborer job again. But the railroad is worse as the N. Y. roads. The commissary man was all right sometime he took some dimes more but he did it not so often as his partner in Venango Erie railroad. Now was it the railroad who did not pay me $9.00 and I found it after three months' work better to go to New York when they lay us off and came first in Philadelphia bought clothes there and walk from Philadelphia without one penny in New York's Bowery after six months' work and all kind of experiences.

The amount of social and industrial waste due to our lack of intelligently devised and operated machinery for guiding immigrant labor into activities for which it has been trained has never been estimated. The possibility of drawing intelligently and directly on foreign countries for the kind of labor needed instead of leaving the supplying of it to steamship agents, to whom all immigrants with passage money look alike, is still a far distant dream.

Most Americans see in our immigration problem simply a question of restriction or non-restriction: Shall immigrants be admitted or not? If admitted, under what limitations and with what qualifications? So bitter has been the strife that we have been unable to get any concerted action upon what to do with the immigrant after his admission. We are admitting a million immigrants a year and are officially utterly indifferent to what becomes of them after admission. We have refused to see that any intelligent policy of restriction would depend upon a thorough study of the immigrant's relation to American institutions, his use or abuse of them, and upon the establishment of the fact that his failure to use them with profit to himself and to America alike has not been due to America's actually keeping them out of his reach while nominally proffering them. Any attempt to develop a domestic policy of protection, distribution, and assimilation leads to the charge that it will increase immigration; it has been impossible to obtain in any but two states[1] more than investigative bodies[2] and the formulation of legislation.

More and more within the last few years, with the general increase of unemployment in this country, the restriction agitation has focussed upon the question of employment. It will be of service to indicate upon what basis the agitation rests. At the outset it must be said that on this critical point of the alien's relation to American employment and unemployment, there is no trustworthy information to prove our contentions either way, and we ought to make it our chief concern to get this information at once. If the aliens are the chief cause of unemployment, and we have reached the point where this country has a population greater than it can support in comfort, and can educate, then certainly immigration should be restricted, but we want to determine this by fair and just means and not by race prejudice or by the presentation of isolated local or misleading statistics.

The ways in which immigrants are conceived to

---

[1] New York and California have immigration *bureaus*.

[2] New Jersey, Rhode Island, and Massachusetts have had Immigration *Commissions*.

cause directly or to influence unemployment are the following: (1) They displace American workmen; (2) by flocking to cities and factories immigrants overstimulate industry, cause over-production and unemployment, while agriculture correspondingly loses; (3) the heavy male immigration, composed chiefly of single men, "birds of passage," who have come here simply to work for a time and earn money and then return to the old country, are a serious element of confusion in the labor market; (4) immigrants actively lower the standard of living, and consequently wage-rates; and, further, chiefly by strike-breaking, they prevent the improvement of American standards and of American industrial conditions.

(1) An analysis of such data as is available shows that immigrants do displace Americans in certain industries, but the data does not show that these same displaced Americans are unemployed or employed at a lower wage-rate, or that they would have stayed in this industry, or that they would return to it, if it were to be abandoned by the immigrants. This may be the case; but the evidence is not so conclusive as that which establishes the displacement of Americans. It is analogous to the statement that the introduction of machinery has caused unemployment; when we attempt to find the men displaced most of them appear to be employed in other industries, many of which have been virtually created by such inventions.

Even so great a pessimist over the future of America, as influenced by immigration, as Professor E. A. Ross, says:

Does the man the immigrant displaced rise or sink? The theory that the immigrant pushes him up is not without some color of truth.   In Cleveland the American, German, and Bohemian iron-mill workers displaced within the last fifteen years seem to have been reabsorbed into other growing industries. They are engineers and firemen, bricklayers, carpenters, slaters, structural ironworkers, steamfitters, plumbers, and printers. Leaving pick and wheelbarrow to Italian and Slav, the Irish are now meter-readers, wire-stringers, conductors, motormen, porters, janitors, caretakers, night-watchmen and elevator-men. I find no sign that either the displaced workman or his sons have suffered from the advent of the Pole and Magyar. Some may have migrated, but certainly those left have easier work and better pay. It is as though the alien tide has passed beneath them and lifted them up. On the other hand, in Pittsburg and vicinity the new immigration has been like a flood sweeping away the jobs, homes, and standards of great numbers, and obliging them to save themselves by accepting poorer occupations or fleeing to the West.

It is to be noted that he fails to point out any "poorer occupation" into which the American born in Pittsburg have gone, and the effect upon the prevailing rate of wages, to correspond with the specific enumeration of the upward tendency where wage-rates and conditions are known.

It is said that if the aliens were withdrawn the
American born would re-enter their occupations.
There seems to be no data to support this contention. When organized labor had the law passed
in New York prohibiting aliens from working on
public contracts, a desperate effort was made to
secure American workmen for the New York City
aqueduct. These camps present none of the
features of the average foreigner's camps. They
are as clean and sanitary as the American workman's home, and there is an eight-hour day. It
was impossible to find native workmen, although
many men were working as teamsters and in
factories at less wages. Another effort was recently
made to enforce the law with reference to the
New York subway work, with a like result. In
short, there is a fundamental reason why labor
and capital have ignored this law, or made spasmodic, half-hearted attempts to enforce it; trench
digging has a social stigma not put upon it by the
immigrant but by the American. It is in the same
class with domestic service and no one has yet
alleged that its social stigma was created by the
immigrant woman. If American workmen could
not be found to work on the New York aqueduct
under excellent conditions, when aliens were prevented by law from "displacing" them, is it to
be assumed that the vast number of aliens in the
Western mines, for instance, are usurping the
native American's right to work?

(2) It would be hard indeed to prove *by what*

methods immigrants have found it possible to over-stimulate industry to the detriment of agriculture. The following statement, from Professor Ross, exemplifies the only kind of data upon which such a contention has apparently been based, as yet:

Among us there is one American white farmer for fourteen American whites, one Scandinavian farmer for eight Scandinavians, one German farmer for eleven Germans, one Irish farmer for forty Irish; but it takes 130 Poles, Hungarians, or Italians in this country to furnish one farmer. Failing to contribute their due quota to the production of food, these late-comers have ruptured the equilibrium between field and mill, and made the high cost of living a burning question. Just as the homestead policy overstimulated the growth of farms, the new immigration has overstimulated the growth of factories.

Most Americans would be unwilling to advocate restriction upon a conclusion of this kind. It completely disregards the thousands of immigrant farm-hands who annually harvest these crops, recruits from the ranks of casual labor, because the farming industry does not offer *the regularity of employment that the factory does* and so cannot compete with it. Furthermore, there could not have been at Professor Ross's disposal, the data which shows that far from overstimulating the growth of factories, peasants upon arrival have been prevented from going to farms crying out for their help, by the *better organization of industry,* which maintains agencies to direct these men to factories and away from farms. Neither does the advent of immigrants explain why several hundred thousand American farmers have removed to Canada, nor why the American boy is deserting the farm. All of the conditions in which immigrants play a part are far too complex to be explained by one set of data or by any one line of reasoning.

(3) "Birds of passage" and the increase in male immigration undoubtedly contribute to the instability of the labor market and have an important relation to unemployment. Much publicity is given to such statistics as those showing that between June 30, 1913, and May 31, 1914, 1,254,-548 aliens entered the country; during the same eleven months, 288,469 immigrants returned to the old countries. In the six years following the panic of 1907 over three million immigrants sailed eastward again. These are indeed significant figures, but they may be significant in more than one direction. The fallacy of the American position lies in assuming that, excepting the few returning home for visits, all the others eastward bound were returning as a part of a preconceived plan, because they had never intended to stay.

There is no proof of this. It is true that from June 30, 1913, to May 31, 1914, of the 808,144 men entering the country, only 307,367 were married. It is also true, in a general way, that unmarried workmen, having no local ties, would naturally

move more readily from place to place if the pros-
pcct seems slightly better somewhere else, and
more readily return to Europe in a season of industrial depression. The real question is whether
large numbers of them come here intending to do
just those things.

Some of them do; it is probably, however, a
comparatively small percentage. Many men do
not bring their families, confidently meaning to
send for them later when they can afford to do so.
A powerful influence, not of the immigrant's
making, encourages him to leave his family at
home; the family man is not wanted in casual and
seasonal labor industries; no provision is made for
his family, and he is told so. The employer wel-
comes the family of the steady laborer as it steadies
that market, but the reverse is true for the seasonal
laborer. The family man greatly increases the
difficulties of housing and makes a community life
necessary. Moreover, most of the camps of the
small mining and manufacturing towns to which
immigrants go to work have no facilities for recreation, education, or religious observance. Even
the most hopeful immigrant may well hesitate to
take his family to places where they will be shut
off from all civilizing influences.

"Every immigrant comes here to make money."
This is the last word of the immigration posi-
tivist. But along with the intention—and the
immediate need—of making money, nine out of
ten immigrants cherish the hope of a new and

better home, a freer air, hope of a brighter future in all spiritual ways for themselves and their children. The average American is not in a position to deny that these two ideals are compatible and sometimes interdependent. America permits him to realize the first if he can—since industry needs him—but offers him little opportunity to realize the second.

(4) An analysis of living conditions does show that the standard of living among immigrants is lower than that of Americans in the same industry, but it does not clearly appear that there is a deterioration of the American standard due to the presence of immigrants. Investigations of camps show repeatedly American quarters of one grade and immigrants' quarters of another; foreign families living in one group, Americans in another. Small industrial communities show the isolated foreign colony with a different standard of comforts and sanitation. How much of this is due to the immigrants' ignorance, and inability to change it and how much is due to the race prejudice of American workmen and the cupidity of padrone and employers who are interested in the immigrant for profit, is not known. Mr. Ross points to a typical Western town of 26,000 inhabitants, 10,000 of them immigrants, in which he gives a picture of vice, intemperance, and bad housing and living conditions due to the immigrants. This picture is chiefly disquieting because of its overthrow of our ideal of majority

rule. There was a safe margin of 6000 Americans to establish any standard they chose. One is tempted to think that here, as in many other places, the American population quite definitely ignored or isolated the immigrants, permitting them to work all day with Americans at the mills or factories where they were needed, and then encouraging or compelling them to spend all the rest of their time in their own corner of the town, in Little Italy or Hungary Hollow, and to encroach no more than necessary upon the respectable streets and schools and churches and recreations of the American section. Such a situation illustrates a sufficiently familiar American policy, a policy of internal restriction. Lawrence and Calumet and Ludlow are the products of it.

If the above story is typical, immigration should be restricted to prevent the American from exploiting the alien—a temptation he seems unable to withstand otherwise. There is abundant proof, however, that the immigrants' standard rises just in proportion as he is organized, educated, and associates freely with Americans whose standard he thus learns. If the American believed that the immigrant is good enough for his standard of living, then no power could prevent his having it. Let the American railroad build bunk houses alike for American and immigrant, and the immigrants will rejoice to live in them just as they now leave the places in disgust whenever they can.

At the time of entering this country immigrants

9

are, very generally, fairly stable workmen inclined to settle down at one occupation and do their best. The fact that after a few years many of them have found their way into the migratory class, drifting from camp to camp, from industry to industry, is, as has been suggested, sometimes accounted for by their entrance upon work for which they are not fitted and which they cannot stand. How largely their industrial descent is due to the actual standards of living forced upon them in certain industries it is hard to tell.

It is known that American employers have established and maintain conditions in which the newly arrived immigrant has no choice and against which he can make no protest. What are these conditions which *immigrants do not make but find awaiting them on arrival*, and which are so vitally affecting regularity of employment, causing maintenance of large reserves of labor, and unsettling the labor market? Speaking from personal experience in labor camps, Raymond Robins says:

Let me present some details for your consideration. The lumber industry is one of the ancient trades. In the old days the logger was, in his rough, uncouth way, a splendid type of the pioneer. He went forth from his cabin to the forest to fell trees in the timber strip and returned at night to his home and family. It was from such conditions that the men and women came forth to lead the industry and government of the West. From such a home came Lincoln! What are the conditions to-day in the great lumber camps of

the West and South? Let me describe one in which I
worked. We slept in bunks four tiers deep, one rack
on each side and two in the center of a big tent. When
called for dinner, we washed our hands and faces, if
the habit still lingered, at a trough of running water.
Then, lined up in front of the hash tent, we waited for
the bar to go down. In we rushed, each man grabbing
whatever he could reach and then covering his plate
with his hands looked about to see if he had missed
anything. At night, we slept in our clothes minus
coat and shoes. We did this because our clothes, wet
with sweat, protected us from the other inhabitants of
our bunks. One night the tent leaked just above my
bunk, and I got up. A light was shining in the foreman's cabin. I went over and found him wrestling
with some accounts. I told him I was some shark at
figures myself and asked if I might help him. He con-
sented, and after I had straightened out his muddle,
we lighted our pipes and had a talk. Some men from
the nearby settlement had been at the camp that day
asking for work. We were short of hands, yet they
were sent away. I asked this foreman why he did
not hire these men. He said that the company preferred men like us that were shipped out from the city.
Pressed for the reason, he said, laconically, "you fel-
lows don't kick about the hours or the wages or the
grub. When you get fired you leave camp. If you get
killed, the company don't have to pay."

Every man but two that I talked with in that camp
seemed to be interested in just three things: whiskey,
women, and the gamblers' trance. They were all
waiting to get a stake large enough to have a "good
time" in the red-light district of Chicago, Seattle, or
San Francisco.

Railroading and boating are very much the same. The surfacing of the tracks on the great railroads of this country is now done by homeless men shipped out from the great cities. The men in the boats on the great lakes belong in the main to the hopeless human waste of the casual labor group. Only the captain, the mates, and the engineers have survived as a real craft. All the others are roustabouts, industrial human drift, half vagabond, half criminal. Fed on rancid food, sleeping in lousy forecastles, and working irregular hours, they average one trip to a booze, or one booze to a trip, just as you please to put it. You can find similar conditions at the foundation of the steel and iron industry. I have worked as a common laborer, wheeling in the yards at the South Chicago Steel Works. When I left my work at night, I went to sleep in bunks that were still warm from the man who had gone to take my place in the next shift. For seven days, those bunks were never cold. I was told that they had not been cold for nine months.

Still, you say, "the farming class is yet sound and pure." Never were you more mistaken. The development of machinery in agriculture and the specialization in farming has abolished the class of agricultural common laborers that used to live upon the soil. The seasonal needs of the farm are now supplied by the homeless casual labor group of the great cities. Read any newspaper during the harvest season and note the cry for labor that comes up from the farms. How long will that employment last? Six weeks at the most, and if you do not leave the locality so soon as the season is over, you will be "vagged" by the sheriff and made to work on the county roads. I know, for I have been there. When the farms of a country are

put on an anti-social casual labor basis, it is time for
men and women concerned with the moral issues of
civilization to think and act.

Continuing his statement of the results of this
camp life upon cities in winter Mr. Robins says:

When this group with whom I have intimate personal acquaintance returns to the city, they return
with more or less money. Many of them remain for
four or five months, absolutely without any of the
natural associations or friendships, living as men in
their bunk houses. It is even true of the bonanza
farms; and in the great bunk houses on the bonanza
farms of the West you can find some of the worst
instances of what I am relating to you to-night. They
go back to the great city, and to what part? Away to
the quarters of my friend, Hinky Dink; in the lodging-
houses of that region of the city they frequently take
lodgings a week or two months, pay for all in advance,
and then with what money they have in their pockets
they go out and have a good time. They always wind
up at the bawdy houses if they do not wind up in jail.
The resources in the pockets of these men divorced
from social obligations and community relations, is
very great. I estimate it,—although I make no claim
for the accuracy of my estimate,—at something over
four million dollars in money, which comes into the
city of Chicago every year from the pockets of the
casual labor group, varying in amounts for each person
from three or four dollars to seven and eight hundred
dollars. I have known one case of nine hundred dollars,
never more. These men in nearly every case have been

divorced from social responsibilities in some way, not a few have become embittered, depraved, and are no longer contemplating anything in the future.

There has been a tendency on the part of certain central reserve labor cities like New York to deny residence and refuse help in winter to these camp and summer laborers. It is pertinent to ask in this connection, where is the "home" of the man who in the spring is sent out from the city to build roads and dig ditches and construct aqueducts, and repair railroads? Where can he go when these works close in the fall? What argument will be used to get men on farms in the spring and summer if they lose their residence and are treated as "hoboes" when the farmer does not want them in winter? If the unskilled workman is to lose the benefits of his city residence by doing this work in the summer, what arguments will be used to get him to do this work hereafter?

It may be said that these conditions are isolated. In New York State alone (which is not primarily a camp state) there are during the summer in busy seasons between two and three thousand camps and small industrial communities where the conditions among immigrants form a striking contrast to those among Americans. The highway camps operated by contractors on state work, are among the worst, as the following descriptions taken from reports of the chief investigator of the Bureau of Industries and Immigration show:

Camps on public works are devoid of any Americanizing influences. With two exceptions there are no amusements or recreations other than the saloon, no educational facilities, and no religious influences. Most of them have no regulations and are remote from town authorities and are therefore a law unto themselves. Where aliens live in nearby towns they are usually in boarding-houses run by their countrymen. In the minority of camps (outside the aqueduct) are laborers with families employed, as unattached men are generally preferred. Excepting in the aqueduct camps, these men are crowded into the barest shanties, hovels, or barns, with no sanitary provisions, and none of the decencies of life, to say nothing of the comforts. These quarters provide bunk space only, and here laborers must keep their clothes, supplies of food, and all other possessions. They usually cook for themselves, do their own laundry work, and in every respect the life is the simplest camp life. The greed or cupidity of the bosses crowds them into quarters which soon become so vermin and germ ridden that they prefer to sleep out of doors.

The majority of the contractors believe that the only way they can obtain or keep laborers is through a padrone. Statistics show that fully one-third of the men obtained in this way shift from one place to another—not a very satisfactory result in justification for such a vicious method. In return for furnishing laborers, from each of whom the padrone collects a fee of from $1 to $5, he is given the privilege of housing the men and furnishing them with provisions. Since his greatest profit is made on these two items, it is no wonder that laborers were found housed in tiers in horse stalls in stables, in condemned houses, in hovels, and in old wooden shacks. In one such building, where the only way to reach their sleeping quarters was by means of rickety stairs, a notice was posted by the contractor to the effect that the men used the stairs at their own risk! Where the men worked in shifts, the rude bunks frequently served daily for two or three sets of men. For such accommodations each man paid $1 a month. The prices charged for his food were higher than in the city, and the quality of that inspected by this Bureau was rarely good and it was frequently kept in basements, barns, and in out-buildings. If a laborer bought his supplies elsewhere he usually lost his job. Some of the laborers testified that they bought the padrone's food, threw away what they could not eat, and then bought the remainder in the village nearby.

These conditions do not prevail for Americans. The contractor usually puts up their houses for them and often has them taken care of. Even the barns used for the teams are erected by the contractors, and in many highway camps these were better than the quarters furnished to the alien workmen. The Americans buy where they please and often have a dining club. The contractor apparently takes no interest of any kind in the alien, but he assumes this for the American. The alien cannot protest or even bring his grievance to the foreman or contractor, as can the American, but is turned back to the padrone. The testimony of dozens of men taken in these camps shows them to be dissatisfied and discontented; they feel they are being exploited; and the prevailing conditions are creating restless workers, who change from one employer to another, and who have a spirit of retaliation and of ruthless disregard of the rights of others.

The system of paying wages in use by the majority of contractors is a direct temptation to the padrone to graft. The usual method is for the timekeeper to turn in to the bookkeeper the time worked and the rate paid. The padrone turns in his charges, and without any checking up whatever, these are deducted from the pay envelopes. A few of the contractors require tickets to be turned in, and at least one requires that each slip turned in shall be signed by the employee. Wherever this method prevails, the Bureau has had no complaints. The usual method, however, is to enter in a book the amounts of the purchases, which book the employee keeps. But the contractor never asks for these books. A number of such books turned in to the Bureau and checked up with the company's charges showed discrepancies of from $1 to $3 bi-weekly.

The alien employee always goes by number, never by name, and his identity is established by a brass check. This is a source of grafting by boarding-house keepers and bankers, who get possession of the checks, especially of discharged men with small balances due. Another matter which causes great hardship is the practice of sending discharged employees to the city office to collect their wages, instead of paying them at the works. As an illustration of a frequent hardship—one group of fourteen Austrians arrived in the city on a Tuesday and were told they would not be paid until Saturday. They were penniless, and as some had offers of immediate jobs outside the city, they were placed in a philanthropic home for the night and the company was induced to settle the next day. Such business methods are often due to mere thoughtlessness on the part of the company, but they entail great hardship and show the need of the protection of alien workmen.

In many camps it is the custom to deduct fees for hospital or medical service. Where the service is adequate, the charge of from twenty-five cents to sixty cents per month may not be exorbitant, but it has become the subject of much abuse. These sums are often deducted on the merest pretext of medical service. In one camp where some one hundred men were employed, a regular charge of fifteen cents a week was made and the service consisted of calling a local physician when necessary. The income was thus about $60 per month and the calls of the physician averaged about three monthly. These charges are the cause of much dissatisfaction, since the padrone who offers the job does not notify the men that they have to pay hospital fees, or that they require certain supplies before they can work. In order to sleep they must have blankets; in order to work, boots and shoes of a certain kind; they have no knowledge of the prices or often of the necessities themselves when they leave the city for the job, and are ill prepared to make some of the necessary purchases. It is not unusual, where a number go together, for one or two to work for a few days in order to lend the others money to buy the necessary articles needed before they can work.

The labor and living conditions of the men employed in labor camps by private industries are nearly as bad, as is evidenced in the Bureau's investigation of railroad camps:

Of all the wretched living conditions in this great State to-day these in the railroad camps surpass anything investigated by the Bureau. Nowhere else has been found such an absolute disregard for comfort, health, morality, and justice. The graft permitted by these two great railroads through the padroni is almost unbelievable, did not the testimony of these men, taken in camp after camp, amply prove it. Boiled down to its tersest expression this is the practice of one of the roads which obtains its men through a widely known padrone in New York City:

(1) Every charge made by the padrone,—who is not an employee nor a director of this line,—is deducted by the railroad employees before the wages are paid, upon the sole statement of the padrone. Absolutely no proof whatever is required from the employees that they have received any equivalent for the sum deducted.

(2) It is the custom in some of the camps for this company to deduct from $1 to $3 every two weeks for supplies. It makes no difference, these employees testify, *whether they buy supplies or not*, that amount is regularly taken out, and if they object they are dismissed on the order of the padrone. The men, therefore, ordinarily buy up to the amount demanded and then purchase elsewhere. *No man may work for this road unless he pays the price set, and one result is an unsettled labor market*, since the men are not subjected to these conditions on all roads and in all industries.

(3) If the food is "rotten" or the men do not receive all they order, no refund or adjustment is ever made and the prices in this padrone's camps are higher than at any similar place in the state. The quality of the food furnished, and the conditions under which it is kept in box cars, merit the attention of the health authorities.

(4)   This company also deducts $1 per week, before paying the wages, for shack rent. The shacks are of two kinds, old box cars unfit for any other use and small sheds made out of pieces of tin and wood which the employees pick up along the line. Although some of these camps have been in existence from three to eight years, they have never been cleaned and are so filthy or vermin ridden that the men have built huts outside or sleep out of doors. If they refuse the pay the $1 is deducted *just the same, regardless of where they sleep*, or they are discharged on the order of the padrone to the road. The result is that men who *want to live decently pay two rents or are dismissed.*

(5)   The men get for this $1 rent space for a bunk in one of these filthy cars, no place to cook except out of doors, and in winter they have to keep their food in their bunks and put a stove in the middle of the car. There are no sanitary provisions whatever for men who have been faithful in the road's service for many years. Although the camps adjoin public highways, the beasts of the jungle have better sanitary and bathing facilities than are afforded in the quarters where the men must live to hold their jobs.

(6)   The employment fee charged by this padrone is from $1 to $3. No man can go to work for this road unless he gets a brass check from the padrone, and for this the road deducts the amount the padrone asks. This is the interesting point: In at least one of these camps, a foreman testified that he went to New York and hired twenty men who in no way came from this padrone's agency, *but the fee for each was deducted, although the men never saw the padrone or his representative.* Men who apply to the foreman on the section and are hired by him pay their toll just the same.

Whenever men are changed from one gang to another a new fee is asked. A new check means a new fee, and the padrone is the sole judge of when they shall go or stay. Good men who are needed are dismissed by the foreman upon the order of the padrone, without any reason being given therefor, and the toll in fees is sometimes as high as $9 a year for positions.

This survey of the conditions imposed upon immigrants by industries and by communities explains how immigrant workmen become an easily manipulated body, and suggests the origin of the charge that immigrants are used both to prevent and to break strikes. They undoubtedly are; so are Americans with much greater opportunity to know the issues concerned. When college boys engage in strike breaking as a lark, what can be expected of the peasant who has either never heard of a union at all, or who has heard of it as the one thing in America that will surely cost him his job, or lead to his deportation, if he becomes connected with it.

Immigrants engaged to break strikes are frequently not told when engaged that a strike is in progress and all sorts of devices are used to keep them in ignorance of it. Immigrants have refused to work on arrival at industries where strikes were in progress. In other words they have organized their own protests against conditions. The history of the Colorado mine struggle, lasting throughout years and brought to wide notice by the recent crisis there, brought to light, among other things, one very significant fact: every force of immigrant workmen there has reached its climax in its protest against conditions within ten years after arrival. These successive revolts by different groups, after years of helpless endurance, have only one significance: left wholly to themselves, with little help in education or organization, these immigrant workmen not only attain in ten years to a desire for the American standard of living, but are prepared to starve and die for it.

The immigrant workman has not only to accept the conditions imposed upon him by employers and industries; his employment conditions are also subject in many cases to legislative provision. Various states and cities, in the effort to protect the rights of American workmen, have established certain legal discriminations against aliens. These, in addition to hastening his political corruption, have often hampered his securing employment even when his services were needed. Against these he has made little complaint, doubtless believing them to be an American practice which he did not understand. The extent to which unemployment among aliens is caused or increased by statutes or ordinances restricting the alien's right to follow certain callings or occupations or limiting his right to hold property is not dreamed of by those who carelessly talk of "lazy foreigners." An analysis of laws regulating the status of aliens in the United States shows that many of the occupations open to men without capital are closed to him. Eight states, for instance, specifically forbid his being employed on public works, the one thing to which unskilled immigrants naturally turn. Yet Arizona, Massachusetts, New York, New Jersey, Louisiana, Pennsylvania, Wyoming, and Idaho expressly prohibit his doing this work. Many municipalities supplement these state laws by ordinances of the same nature. In Butte, Montana, aliens are barred from public work and only resident voters can be employed by the city on day wages; in Quincy, Illinois, the employment of aliens in any capacity is forbidden; in Pueblo, Colorado, aliens cannot be employed in any capacity by the city; in Dayton, Ohio, aliens cannot be employed by the city on public works, although a city contractor may employ them; in Baltimore, Maryland, contractors are required by law to employ only registered voters, when possible, on city contracts.

Other cities report that there are no ordinances discriminating against aliens, but that "the Commissioner of Public Works has a rule of his own," not to employ them, or that there is no ordinance, but that "any administration that employed them would be short-lived."

Add to these discriminations—already sufficiently extensive—the fact that in eight states and over two hundred cities, aliens are shut out from work by civil-service laws, which in many cases cover not only high-grade work, but general labor as well,—and the extent to which the alien is handicapped in his struggle to become self-supporting grows more clear.

Licenses for various occupations are in many cases given only to citizens or declarants. In some cases these prohibitions are imposed by a state law, as in Ohio, where an alien cannot hold a liquor license; in Georgia he cannot obtain a peddler's license; and in Michigan an alien cannot obtain a barber's license. Usually, however, these discriminations are local. The following are examples of callings closed to aliens by these local regulations:

Niagara Falls, New York,—Peddler, hackman, vender; Portland, Oregon,—Junk dealer; Taunton, Massachusetts,—Junk dealer or second-hand dealer; Buffalo, New York,—Stationary engineer, pawnbroker; Fitchburg, Massachusetts,—Public cartman, truckman, hackman, expressman, drivers, junk dealer, dealer in second-hand articles, hawker, peddler, vender, ticket speculator, coal scalper, common shows, shooting galleries, bowling alleys, billiard tables, dirt carts, exterior hoists and stands within stoop lines under the trains of the elevated railroad (news stands and bootblacks).

One of the inevitable results of passing laws that do not represent the will of the people is that they are not only violated but are used for "graft." Fruit peddlers and flower peddlers in New York City, for instance, work in many cases in defiance of the law. Unable to secure licenses on account of the citizenship requirement, they work without them. When they are arrested the boss pays a fine and placidly sets his boys to work again, and has the protection of the district policeman in this proceeding. The alien naturally comes to regard with contempt what he thinks is an unjustifiable law; and Americans come to regard the alien as a born lawbreaker. It is of course impossible for the alien who goes from city to city or state to state even to know these laws; their variety and contradiction make it wholly impossible for him to know whether he is violating the law or not and the contractor therefore finds him an easy pawn in the game.

In the passage of recent social insurance legislation we are putting a premium upon immigrant labor, for which some economist will hold the alien responsible in the future. Under the workmen's compensation laws in at least two states, an alien's beneficiaries, if non-resident, may not benefit. In two other states, Connecticut and Kansas, they are discriminated against in the amount they are entitled to receive; by the Connecticut law nonresident beneficiaries are given only half as much as residents, and by the Kansas law the maximum payment to them is $750, whereas a resident beneficiary may receive from $1200 to $3600. The Nebraska and New York laws, and the laws for the Canal Zone and for employees on railroads engaged in interstate commerce provide, in the case of payment in a lump sum instead of in installments through a series of years, that payments to non-resident beneficiaries shall be less than those to residents—whether the residents be citizens or aliens.

The two immediate problems before America are to organize the labor market in order to increase the mobility of labor and decrease mal-adjustment; and to regularize industry in order to lessen casual labor and to meet the evils of seasonal employment. The immigrant increases the difficulties of both. The present system of distribution through the padrone, dependence upon bankers for communication with his family at home, remoteness from American institutions, language, and customs, will have to be fundamentally changed before the immigrant can be freed and his labor directed where it can be used to the best advantage for him and the country alike.

So long as industry can draw unsparingly upon an inexhaustible supply of labor, there will be little incentive for it to undertake regularization and other measures tending to conservation. But there are evidences that the methods of industry are already proving its undoing in this respect. Tales of the labor camps and of peonage in the South are diverting immigrants to South America or elsewhere. America is getting a bad name. It is no longer the country with streets paved with gold, but the land where men are driven with whip,

lash, and gun, and housed with vermin and rats.
Agriculture is becoming organized, and the greed
of industry for every newly arrived immigrant is to
suffer serious competition; the adoption of social
insurance against sickness and unemployment,
etc., are making the home country seem more
desirable than the risks in the American venture.

*In the absence of any policy or machinery for the
distribution and assimilation of the adult immigrant,
and of any attempt to direct immigrants into industry
in accordance with their abilities and training, we do
not know whether our reserve of immigrant labor is
larger than the country should carry or not. Farms
are deserted; seasonal labor cries for more hands at
certain seasons, cities are crowded in winter. Is the
remedy less supply or better use of it? It is not clear
whether all interests would be better served by a policy
of domestic regulation or by a policy of exclusion.
Statistics and other data bearing pon the immigrant's relation to unemployment are incomplete
and contradictory.*

*It is clear, however, that recent immigrants are
more and more segregated in colonies, that secular
schools are increasing faster than public schools,
that foreign customs and habits and traditions are
being preserved rather than blended with American
ideals and concepts.*

*The United States should therefore take steps to
determine which races are not only assimilable, but
desire assimilation and which are not. We have
already determined that certain races are not and*

doubtless others should be added, but this is not primarily a question of unemployment. We need to determine what is this country's need of immigrant labor, and to insist upon a living wage, which shall be spent largely in this country. And when that is determined we need to know whether we wish continually to have in this country a large number of resident aliens contributing to American industry but entirely shut off from American society and American ideals, and unable therefore to comply with American standards. Only on the basis of such information can the immigrant's responsibility for unemployment be established or refuted.

CHAPTER V

HOW AMERICA MARKETS ITS LABOR

THE Federal government maintains a department to develop agriculture and facilitate the marketing of crops. Most of the states have similar departments and make considerable grants to agricultural colleges, granges, and other institutions for education along such lines. Foreign. consuls report on markets, and no small part of their interest is devoted to discovering and utilizing industrial opportunities for America. Municipalities maintain free markets and facilitate the marketing of produce. Business has combined, cöoperated, systematized, experimented, invented, and investigated until it has a fairly good system. There is waste and friction and loss, but the subject commands the best intelligence and organization is being perfected.

The labor market presents an entirely different situation. It has long been contended that labor is not a commodity and that each individual should dispose of his own. Under this system, we have seen unemployment grow, the helpless unemployed exploited from coast to coast; and we are coming to realize that the individual can no longer bear the burden of finding a job. The organization of industry is so far-reaching that the individual workman can not acquire the information necessary to guide him in a course of action which will assure him of steady employment at the work he can do best. Able, willing, and even skilled, he cannot find work. Yet he is left to do it. Moreover, many thousands of children under our best laws offer their labor for sale at fourteen years of age, and in many states and in some occupations much younger. Thousands of arriving immigrants annually flood our markets with the raw material of common labor. Women enter the industrial field at most points without direction. Nationally, the government has no official knowledge of this market, and does little to regulate or supplement it. A few states have bureaus for directing labor but their efforts are largely local.

In a recent survey of New York City, where the situation is typical, more than 1000 employment centers were engaged in furnishing jobs. Eight hundred of these were private employment agencies, with no central clearing house of any kind— all reaching the same sources of supply, with little or no knowledge of the activities of the others; and with no obligation to report to any governmental authority. There were more than two hundred philanthropic, civic, benevolent, racial, and religious organizations engaged in the same work, with a similar disregard for each other's activities and methods. There were some one hundred bankers, steamship ticket agents, and others who acted as padroni or the "steerers" of padroni. There were all the newspapers carrying "want ads," self-constituted employment exchanges. There was the New York State agricultural bureau and an immigration bureau and a branch office of the Federal Division of Information. Each trade union of any efficiency had its local labor center for its members; each industrial establishment had its waiting list or hung signs in its windows for help as the demand varied, thus keeping its own group of hangers-on at the door instead of drawing upon a common reserve. Three different organizations were studying unemployment, unknown to each other, and some relief organizations were adding employment work to their regular work. It was not possible to ascertain the number of saloons that were hunting jobs for their patrons—but the number was in the hundreds. About five hundred churches were giving attention to some phase of unemployment. Since the war, indeed, a new committee has appeared each day, equipped with enthusiasm, good intentions, and funds, to add to the general demoralization of the market. One astute observer on the Pacific Coast writes:

Our unemployment situation is serious and amusing too. If you can imagine about ten committees of perfectly good intentioned people each trying to run the matter independently of the other and each hav-

ing in mind getting CREDIT for its special group and
scarcely one of them having practical ideas for administration, you will get an idea of the situation. You
will wonder at the effect on the unemployed. They
seem to enjoy the situation and being in the limelight.

In brief we have on the one hand a confused
body of labor, ranging from the unemployables
including the defectives, the dependents, the
vagrants and the "won't works," to the handicapped who can work only under special conditions,
and to the employables, skilled and unskilled. In
the problem here presented are included all the
difficulties of seasonal, casual, and professional
work, as well as of children and alien workers.

On the other hand we have the means of handling this miscellaneous body, employers' agencies, trade unions, newspaper advertising, private
business agencies, philanthropic and semi-philanthropic agencies, organized charities, religious and
racial bodies, civic committees, women's clubs—
a body of effort quite as indeterminate and disorganized as is the body of labor. Each selects its
field without reference to what is being done, or
what has been found to be a failure, without consideration of cost or of the necessity for intelligent
administration.

Out of this chaos of effort and administration,
there can be but one result. The unemployed bear
the burden of this disorganization. They pay the
many agency fees, pay for advertisements, car fare

to these various places, and they waste their vitality
and time in the needless wearying tramp day after
day in search for work, which a central clearing
house could have told them did not exist; they are
the sufferers from lack of shelter, food, and adequate
clothing. Industries, on their part, bear the burden in securing misfits and in limited output due
to a constantly shifting force.

When we turn to governmental activities we
find the same conditions. There is no Federal
organization for distribution other than the Division of Information for farm laborers, principally
aliens. Twenty-one states have public offices with
no uniform standards, with limited appropriations;
they suffer from political interference, and, with a
few exceptions, there is little interchange of information between offices in the same state and no
exchange between those of different states. Cities
that have municipal bureaus are grappling with
intercity, interstate and often international problems, with no supplemental Federal machinery;
while state departments of agriculture and immigration half-heartedly spend money to distribute
farm labor.

Regulation is in the same chaotic condition.
State and municipal laws governing private agencies have been written into statute books without
any understanding of the intricate matters involved, and without the support of a public
sufficiently educated in the subject to make these
laws enforceable. Although so large a part of the

distribution is interstate, there is no regulation of agencies doing an interstate business.

The regulation of fee agencies in states and cities and the establishment of governmental bureaus have not gone hand in hand; in fact, in some states they have had no reference to each other. Yet the establishment of any successful public agency, must depend either upon unexcelled advantages, or else upon a fair regulation of the field. The legislation in this country has reversed this position. Competition in the form of state agencies has been attempted in states where private agencies were not regulated at all. Many of these government agencies, established as a sop to labor, have become intrenched in the spoils system of party politics and have fallen into as deep disrepute as some private agencies, before the public has had the opportunity to comprehend their value or import.

In many states but little progress has been made since the law was enacted in 1847 in New York State to protect incoming aliens. An immigrant fund established by this law was to be used, among other things, to "aid in removing any of said persons from any part of this state to any part of this or any other state, or from this state, or in assisting them to procure employment, and thus prevent them from becoming a public charge." California has a separate provision authorizing the Immigration and Housing Commission to coöperate with employment bureaus and to devise and carry out suitable methods to relieve congestion and obviate unemployment. The law creating the New York State Bureau of Industries and Immigration gives that bureau similar powers of investigation. The Ohio Industrial Commission may investigate causes and devise remedies and may even provide employment to prevent distress. On the whole, however, the sum of the efforts of the various States in the direction of organizing the labor market is significantly slight.

The activities of business and of labor in this direction have not been more effective. It is true that industries have considered to a degree the possibility of steadying employment; there has been some discussion as to whether various industries can or shall combine so to dovetail their work that men may proceed directly from one industry to another; whether seasonal employment in certain industries can be diminished or regulated; whether farmers shall not coöperate with industry to secure nearby winter industries to take their laborers in the winter; whether some form of insurance cannot be worked out for skilled workmen. It is true that some industries have thus taken steps that show some recognition of the problem of unemployment; but the objective has not been a really general organization of the labor market. On this point there is no general policy or agreement among industries such as exists among them upon other business methods and enterprises. Different business organizations have coöperated,

for instance, to produce immigrant rates and
settlers rates, "crop cars," land excursions; but
the seasonal worker must either save enough for a
first-class fare from job to job or beat his way from
place to place. There have been all kinds of loan
funds, but, so far as has been ascertained, no such
funds are available for transportation. It is one
of the most urgent and most obvious difficulties in
the organization of the American labor market,
but it has never been met.

The activities of organized labor in the labor
market have been also restricted. Their employment activities have not proceeded from a general
realization of the need of a national organization
of the national labor market. In short, it has
become apparent that neither business nor labor
can organize or control it. A well-regulated neutral
labor market is the only answer.

In the following chapters is described in detail
the labor market as it is conducted in America
to-day, with a view to showing industry, labor, and
government the cost, waste, and total inadequacy
of the present system.

CHAPTER VI

GENERAL LABOR AGENCIES

THE distribution of unskilled labor is controlled by general labor agents. The employer on the one hand and, to a considerable degree, the trade union on the other, have tacitly agreed to this arrangement. These general agencies place and distribute contract laborers, general laborers, miners, lumbermen, brick makers, railroad hands, cattlemen, farm-hands, casual laborers, etc. They are of two kinds: the general labor agency which operates for a cash fee and confines its business to the exchange of labor, and the padroni who make a business of furnishing gangs of workmen, receiving in lieu of a fee, or in addition thereto, the privilege of housing and feeding employees whom they furnish.

The general labor agencies are numerous and well patronized by both native born and immigrants. Since most of the applicants for work are shipped out of cities, these agencies provide a significant means for relieving labor congestion. Many thousands of casual laborers might be homeless and idle charity seekers in cities if they were not sent out by these agencies to farms, mines, and other places where labor is needed. Their efficiency as distributing agents would be even greater if the dishonest agencies were regulated and the honest ones more adequately protected and encouraged than they now are.

Many of these agencies are much more than employment centers. Men flock to them by the hundreds in critical periods of unemployment, "hang around" the waiting-rooms all day, and if they are permitted, sleep on the floor at night. In a good many instances it is pretty generally known that no orders will come in for days, and are not expected; yet the men stay, finding shelter from the severe weather in the only place to which they feel they have a right to go.

In New York City in the winter of 1913–14 hundreds of unemployed men were constantly sheltered in these agencies. The report of a visitor to one of them follows:

Mr. B. (the employment agent) does not run a lodging-place but he allowed the men to stay over night in his place. One night an inspector called and found men sleeping on the bare floor. Two days later he received a letter that he must take out a license for keeping a lodging-house, and that he must not let lodgers sleep on the floor. The same night at closing time he ordered all the men to leave. But when a policeman standing near and some neighbors called him heartless he allowed the men to stay in. He did not charge the men anything. His place consisted of one-half the ground floor, four rooms, in which on

some nights he said 364 men were crowded, standing
up all night and so packed that it was impossible to
pass through.   In the morning a baker brings him
bread several days old for which he pays three cents a
loaf.   He breaks every loaf into four parts, but even
so there is not enough for one-tenth of his applicants.
The men fight for a piece, soak it in water and devour
it ravenously.   I went through the place, which is
barren of any furniture except a few wooden benches,
and counted 107 men in the place, most of them
standing as there was no place for them to sit down.
On account of the severe weather all the windows
were closed, and the foulness of the air was indeed
indescribable.   I approached a number of men whose
protruding cheek bones and red and strangely shining
eyes plainly showed their suffering, and spoke to them
in their native tongue.   In nearly all cases the men
had not had anything to eat for two or three weeks
and were keeping themselves alive on what they could
pick up from ash barrels.   They were all insufficiently
clad—not one man with an overcoat.   Mr. B. sent
several of the men who were sick to hospitals and
homes.

A survey of a number of these agencies indicates
the part they play in the life of the unemployed.
One, in the basement of a tenement, was a saloon
and restaurant, where the men smoked, talked, ate,
and drank.   At night they were allowed to sleep
on some rude benches.   Another, which advertised
"Employment for bakers and confectioners,"
was a bare room with a bar, one end being filled
with tables and chairs where the men played cards

and drank. Some so-called "hotels" often have a
combination office and saloon on the ground floor,
and the second and third floors are used for lodgers.
A trip through such a house showed men drinking
and playing cards all over the premises, and in
some places, where women were seen, the men
around said they "hang about to get the men's
money, and are favored and encouraged by the
house." In one of these there were card and
billiard tables at which several young men were
playing and groups were hanging about the windows and at the bar. Another was in a dark,
gloomy basement with a low ceiling, and filled with
wooden benches which at night were transformed
into rude bunks. This place was filled with
all kinds of indescribable baggage, and was dirty
and disorderly beyond description. There was no
eating-house, but employees brought in food, such
as cold meat, "street bacon," fruit, etc. Because
of the crowded condition, most of the "placing"
was done on the street, and benches were placed
along the sidewalk for the crowds that could not
get in. Another agency, with a hair-dressing store
in the basement below it, consisted of a large bare
room, filled with wooden benches and chairs.
Though women were waiting there, the proprietor
said he never did any business with women employers, and advised his callers not to get any such
help in his neighborhood. There is little reason to
doubt that some of these places are nothing more
than disreputable houses, and that the employ-

ment agency is the ruse by which patrons are attracted.

In some of the cities, certain types of employment have become almost the property of the saloonkeeper in collusion with the ward-boss. The "hotel help" used to be largely negroes and Americans. They are now largely foreigners, among them many Greeks. Certain headwaiters have made arrangements to get their employees at these saloons, an agreement profitable to both, and also to the politician who wants their vote if they have one. Only the patron of the saloon who is willing to spend or treat can get a job and that only through the saloon holding the contract. If the unemployed man patronizes the wrong saloon he cannot get the coveted hotel job. A less obvious arrangement exists between Italian saloon-keepers and contractors. The saloon agency has a grip upon the general labor situation which is very far-reaching in its consequences and which the laborer alone cannot break.

Agencies not in connection with saloons have a much better tone and more system. They usually occupy from two to four rooms, keep registries, and transact business in a space set apart by a railing from the general waiting-room, or in a separate room. The walls are frequently covered with maps, and the rooms are clean and well supplied with chairs. Occasionally intoxicated employees are seen, and the office is dirty, but the crowd of idle men is orderly and more or less free from the

11

sodden, disreputable "rounder" found in saloon
agencies.

Although farm labor is in the greatest demand,
so-called farmers' agencies are, without exception,
of the most inferior kind. In fact, the farmers'
labor market cannot be said to be organized even
to a small degree. Farm labor is, incongruously
enough, supplied from the cast-offs of other industries. A German man and woman, who were
found outside one such agency, said that they had
just landed and had been recommended to go there
by a man whom they met on the boat from Ellis
Island to the city. "The place seems no good to
me," said the man; "they advertise in country
places, and strange men come and pick the women
out like cattle and take them away." Both had
bundles and had been engaged to go to the country.

The farmer's proverbial difficulty in getting help
is certainly shown in the agencies maintained for
his benefit. There are twenty agencies run for
industry to one for farms; the former are better
manned, and the profits are higher, for the men
can be sent out in gangs. No one works in the
farmers' interest in the labor reserve cities except
some domestic agencies which handle gardeners
and small farm hands. The farmer needs to maintain his own organization because the kind of
"hands" he wants will not frequent the agency,
and as the farmer usually writes for help he himself
knows little about the conditions in such agencies.

Their methods are quite in keeping with their

general atmosphere. It would be misleading to say that the methods here summarized are characteristic of all general labor agencies. There are some notable exceptions to the general rule. The Atwood agency, in New York City, which handles large numbers of contract laborers and men for steamships, is an example of a labor agency run with efficiency and fairness. The regret, however, is that the better employment agencies should make so little effort to raise the character of the business as a whole, and that these descriptions should be so generally true. The employment agency business is not subject to the requirements and checks characteristic of most businesses, and although a well run agency requires integrity and business ability, owing to the excessive competition, the business of employment exchanges is not rated high in America. This is partly due to their miscellaneous, "anything to make a living" character.

Agencies have many sources of revenue. Where they run lodging-places and lodging is not free, the charge varies from twenty cents upward a night. The scheme in some cases is to keep a man out of employment until he has no more money for board. It is customary for employers to advance transportation, to be deducted later from the wages, but when the employee pays his own fare, or the agent advances it, the agent not infrequently charges a higher rate. Some agents refuse to allow the employees' baggage to be moved except by their own expressman. Some charge immigrants for sending money home to the old country and for changing money. One agent charged $5.02 for changing $105.02, and gave the man a worthless $100 bill. The money was recovered upon complaint to the authorities.

The chief income is from fees. In the more honest offices such employers as farmers pay $1 to $3 for each employee and the latter is charged nothing, although the farmer may later deduct $1 from his wages. Contractors and employers of large numbers of men frequently pay $1 to $2 each, while others get the entire fee from the employees. Fees for employers rarely exceed $4, and are quite uniform; but for the employee they are often limited only by law or by the amount he can pay. Men have paid $5, $10, $15 for positions varying from $1 to $2 a day, with no assurance of their permanence.

There are many misunderstood contracts, and many hardships to employees for which agencies cannot be held responsible. They are at best but a medium of exchange, and they cannot vouch for the competence and reliability of employees or for the honesty of employers. They are imposed upon by both. Worthless, unreliable men ask for positions and cause dissatisfaction when placed; orders come in from apparently reliable employers, and when the men arrive they find they have been hired as strike-breakers. Hours, wages, and work are misrepresented to the agent, and he in turn misrepresents them to the men. In many instances agents trust employers for fees and transportation, and are never paid. There is a desire on the part of employees to "do the agency" whenever possible and much bad faith is due to the desire of each to get ahead of the other.

But, granting all this, even honest agents work much hardship through carelessness and indifference in the pressure of business; the dishonest ones do this continually, making their living entirely by the "tricks of the trade." To attract men, some advertise on their cards "positions furnished free." Then, upon various pretexts, they charge from $2 to $5. Inside the agency the applicant finds the promises so alluring that he can hardly get out without paying something. In what is known as the "dollar office," chiefly located in the west, the manager obtains business chiefly by advertising. Every applicant is charged a dollar before any offer is made, though catchwords are thrown out about "good business," "orders," etc.; and when the dollar is secured nothing further is done. The agent lives on these dollars and the efforts he makes are confined to securing them. "There goes another d—— fool," said one proprietor as a man went out after laying down his dollar. "Well, we must make ice while the weather is cold; when it gets warm these suckers will look out for their own jobs." He boldly admitted that he made no attempt to get jobs, except by clipping advertisements. His contracts read, that "he (the employee) shall in no way hold the managers responsible for failure of service," and he advertised: "We are the helping hand of the public, and the all-seeing eye of your interests."

The transient agency is ordinarily simply an address at which mail is received. Attractive and unusual advertisements are inserted, and for further information applicants must send varying small sums. These agencies change addresses frequently to avoid detection by the postal authorities. This kind of business is usually lucrative, for the agents are shrewd advertisers. Typical transient offices spring up during periods of great demand for labor. For instance, they advertise for help for an exposition in a distant city, and furnish employees with addresses. After paying their fare, the men find when they arrive, that they are stranded, and that the city is crowded with similar disappointed people. In New York, after such an agency had in an incredibly short time collected about one thousand fees, it was notified that it must give a bond, and quietly decamped in the night with its proceeds. It is well known that other agencies depend for their existence upon strikes. One such opened an office in New York City and advertised for two hundred men for permanent work in Connecticut, to take the place of strikers on a street railway at high wages. Conspicuously lying about the office were newspaper accounts of the strike. The men reported and paid fees, and on the specified morning about 150, with their bags, gathered to receive the promised transportation. They were told: "The manager has received a telegram and gone to Philadelphia unexpectedly." His clerk had also disappeared.

There is little regard for the truth in some of the advertisements put forth to attract men, as witness the following:

Wanted—Farm-hands.—1000 laborers for railroad work in Iowa, Minnesota, Wisconsin, and Illinois; free fare. Men for Denver, Colorado, Wyoming, Kansas City, Minneapolis, and Omaha; cheap fares. Austrians, Greeks, and Italians for Indian Territory and Arkansas. 500 men for woods in Wisconsin; cheap fare. Molders and laborers for factory. Frame window makers, and help for all kinds of position.

Wanted—500 laborers for Railroad work in Missouri and Indiana; free fares. Marble cutters and carvers; no union. Porter who can speak German. We have positions for all classes of help.

Wanted—500 Railroad laborers, company and contract work; free fare; low rates to New Orleans and points South. Farm hands $25 to $30 per mo. and board. Good home for winter, also other jobs near city.

In addition to these advertisements, the agent's advertising cards read: "Wanted—500 laborers every day, highest wages, free fare, daily shipment"; and these are widely distributed throughout the year, regardless of demand or season.

Hundreds of men respond to these advertisements, and after paying a fee, usually $1, they are told by the agent that the transportation will come at any time, that they will be sent out before evening, and that they must "hang around within call"; and of course the saloon is most convenient. Naturally feeling cheerful at the prospect of a job, they spend money freely for drinks. By evening the transportation has not arrived, plausible excuses are given, and they are told to come the next day. This is kept up until the protest becomes vigorous, and then the dollar fee may or may not be returned; but in the meantime the saloon has taken in over its bar from $1 to $2 from each one.

Daily advertisements in newspapers, offering places to a number of men varying from one hundred up to one thousand, are frequently prospective and do not represent *bona fide* orders. Sometimes when an agency has filled a *bona fide* order for two hundred men, it does not scruple to keep the advertisement running, or to continue to send other men to the same places. When large manufacturers and contractors complain that these extra men are sent, as one agent explained, "We give them a rest and try others." In some cases, men are sent to firms from whom orders have been received years ago; and to others, because the agent has seen some newspaper account of a dearth of labor. Occasionally employers, or more often their foremen, lend themselves to these frauds, and for a small commission are quite willing to tell applicants, "The position has just been filled," when there were no vacancies at the time. It thus appears to the employee that the agency is honest but that he is too late; and the agency then has an excuse to retain the fee. One of the speakers before a labor congress, in commenting on this condition, said:

Another feature of modern industrialism which is proving a potent force in the disintegration of families, is the employment agency. It is the auction-block of the wage-system. While New York City is threatened with bread riots, while in Buffalo and in every industrial center in the state of New York factories are closed or running five hours per day, five days per week,—— Agency has a flaming sign, "4000 men wanted in New York state to work on railroads; good wages; free transportation." The men pay the employment office one dollar each. The railroads transport the 4000, its officials knowing at the time they want only 350. But the presence of the 4000 will make it easy to make their own terms with the 350 they want. The employment office has made $4000, and the railroad corporation has an overcrowded labor market as a menace to the refractory. The remainder of these men are a thousand miles from the homes they left buoyant with the hope of soon earning some money to send to the wife and babies. Out of work, away from home, they degenerate morally and physically until, in Chicago, there is another batch of deserted wives, in New York, another set of tramps. These victims are men who are out of work and want it."

This is further verified by the fact that an advertisement in a Chicago or Minneapolis paper asks for five hundred men for St. Louis, while a St. Louis paper of the same date is advertising for a thousand men wanted in Chicago or Minneapolis.

The character of work and of wages is often misrepresented. In one case five men were sent to work in a smelter. The contract called for employment at from $2.40 to $3 per day, and the return of the $12 fare if they remained thirty days. They were put to work as common laborers at $1 to $2 a day, ten hours' work; and when they demanded the terms of the contract they were discharged, and of course lost their fare, in accordance with the scheme. Another employee, with his countrymen, answered an advertisement in a German paper calling for men to go to Florida, to work in oyster canning factories. In giving his experience he said:

We started South in an emigrant car. In two days we were put off the car in a town in Mississippi. We were ordered into wagons and driven to an oyster cannery. There we were put to work "shucking" oysters at one cent a pound. The best we could make was fifty cents per day. We were shown a row of shanties, where we were told we could live, but that we would only have one room to eight persons. We had been promised furnished rooms. After enduring this for four days we threatened to go to the local authorities, and finally were sent back North.

When the agent who sent these men was arrested, twenty other homeless victims were found in his office, who had paid money for positions in Mexican mines and were waiting to be shipped.

In another instance, there were such frequent changes of men under some railway foremen that the officials investigated and found that they were in collusion with the agency, and had accepted men with the understanding that at the end of two weeks or a month they would be discharged and new ones taken. The foremen received forty per cent. of the fees for their part of this transaction. Contractors in league with agencies will sometimes not hire men directly, but send them to the agency first to pay a fee. Sometimes the men give the agency an order on their employer and the contractor sees that it is paid. Other contractors, not in league with agencies, have rake-offs, which they take as compensation for giving jobs to the men. This rake-off system, in whatever form, is one of the most serious problems of placing unskilled labor.

Not all the schemes are designed to defraud the employee. Occasionally agencies ask large industries to order men from them, especially when they employ a nationality in which the agency deals, for instance, Swedes. When the company refuses, they not only threaten, but sometimes deliberately send people out to cause dissatisfaction and induce the men to leave. In one case, an application was made for an injunction to prevent employment agents from carrying on this work. Advertising for partners has been found profitable. In one such instance several men were trapped and induced to put in small sums at various times during the year. Then they were forced out by misrepresentation as to the amount of the proceeds, or the methods were such that they were glad to withdraw, without insisting upon a return from their investment.

One practice is apparently peculiar to agencies that supply lumbermen: when the demand exceeds the supply, representatives from the camps come down, and with the aid of the agency men are made drunk and then sent up to the camps in box cars. When they wake up sober they are at the camp, penniless, and quite willing to work a while. Lumber camps are often imposed upon, too; for after ordering and paying for experienced men they are sometimes sent incapable workers.

Many frauds are practiced upon farmers. There are "rounders" who start out with the farmer and then desert him. A common practice is to get the farmer to advance both fees, and the employee agrees to have his fee taken out of his wages. Then he deserts at the earliest opportunity, and the agent gives him fifty cents out of the $3 for his share. Agents send out men not fitted for farm work, others whom they know will not remain, and others that have been induced to go by a misrepresentation of the kind and amount of work and wages. As the farmer usually advances the railway fare, he loses this in addition to the fee.

The contracts with the laborers are often barefaced frauds. One agency asks a $5 fee, and the contract reads:

If within——number of days we cannot secure you a position, upon surrender of the contract we will give you an especial advertisement in a leading morning paper in lieu of your fee.

Others state that the fee "is for the privileges of the office only," and their entire effort consists in clipping out advertisements and giving the addresses to applicants as a *bona fide* order from the firm. Of course they find the place filled, for others who have read these advertisements earlier in the morning have the advantage.

An agency which falls somewhere between the general labor office and the shipping agencies for sailors is that for shipping cattle helpers, etc. They obtain men by advertising and, in addition, have "pullers-in" to whom they pay $1 for every man brought in from the parks or elsewhere. All kinds of misrepresentations are made to ignorant foreigners about the nature of the passage, the possibilities of returning to the United States when they wish, and about railroad tickets to their homes when they arrive at European ports. Emphasis is placed upon the passage rather than upon the work to be done.

Upon the prosecution of some agencies in New York City, the following facts were brought out: That although the shipping companies furnish transportation free, the agencies charge the men "passage fees" ranging from $5 to $25; that although prompt sailings are advertised, the men, even when engaged by the agency, often find after being sent to the port of sailing that they have to wait days or weeks, paying their board at a place near the dock meantime; that misinformed men are often stranded without means of return; that they are told the work is light and the food good, and that instead they find the hours long, the work heavy, and their food only what the regular cattlemen leave; that they are often inhumanly treated and have undesirable places in which to sleep; and that some agencies refuse to let the men carry their baggage to the steamers, but make them bring it to the agency and charge from twenty-five cents to $1 for taking it down. The following is a typical advertisement for men:

Just a few dollars will provide you at our office a fast voyage to your old country on the best passenger boats doing some light work. Brotherly treatment. Passage from seven to nine days. Boats leave every other day to Hamburg, Bremen, Rotterdam, and Antwerp. All expenses covered. Try and write to us.

Here is an example of the "brotherly treatment" and easy work, as experienced by the investigator:

There were five of us, and when we obtained our
tickets we were taken to the office of a third agent
where nine more men joined us, and then we were all
taken to the Wall Street pier and there placed on a
boat bound for Fall River. The agent gave to every
one of us a ticket for this boat and a train ticket from
Fall River to Boston. The boat started at half-past
six. All of the fourteen men were sitting in one corner
of the smoking room, and, as we did not get any berths
to sleep in, we passed the whole night talking to each
other. I found out that five Hungarians paid $12 each
to one agent for their passage to Hamburg, but they
had no order to any agent in Liverpool, neither did
they have any tickets farther than Liverpool.

In Boston we were met by a man who took us and
some more men who came direct from the train to
another shipping agency which is rather a store than
an office, upon which were signs reading "Shipping
Agency" and "Cattlemen Wanted."

The agent told us that we should not leave the office
even for a minute because he expected a telegram
from the steamship company and then we must come
to the boat at once. In a time-table I found out that
no boat leaves that day and I did not mind the agent's
order not to leave the place.

In the evening of the same day, the agent told us
that the boat will leave early next morning, and to prevent our getting lost in town he recommended us to
a lodging house next door to his house where we had to
pay 25 cents each for the night. The agent's clerk, a
young man by the name of "Jack," came up to us and
told us that not all of our party, consisting of twenty-
eight men, can go with the next boat, and those who
do not wish to remain should pay him one dollar each

and he will see to it that they leave next morning by this early boat. Some of the men agreed to this and handed him the dollars, but I did not.

About six o'clock the next morning, October 17th, we were taken to the dock. Those who paid the one dollar to the clerk were not especially privileged as several of them were left behind.

We were shown to a cabin over the entrance of which was the inscription "Cattlemen's Cabin." It was a very small cabin with narrow passages between the berths. A table, which consisted of a board put on two poles, was fixed in the center of the room. The board of the table was lifted up, as it turns on hinges, and kept turned vertically all the time to allow more room to pass by, except during meals. Thirty-four "bunks" were fixed in around there and two cases of provisions. We placed our baggage in our berths. There were twenty-two men, eight of them Americans, the others Hebrews and Poles.

The boat started about 9 A.M. After we had arranged our baggage in our berths, every one of us expressed a strong wish to get something to eat. Four men entered our cabin and introduced themselves to us as our foremen. They were drunk and swore terribly and asked for whiskey and money. Half an hour later a supervisor came in and commanded us to go to work. Some of the men protested, asking for something to eat first, but the foremen drove us out of the cabin. Each foreman took five men to his section which consisted of more than two hundred cattle. Water pipes were drawn through the whole ship, but the openings were removed far from one another, and our work was to carry the filled buckets to our foreman who gave to each bull three buckets full of water. We worked till 1 P.M., when we got through with watering, and all dirty, tired, and hungry we came gladly back to the cabin hoping to get something to eat. A steward appeared and handed to us each a mug, a tin dish, a spoon, and a knife and fork. He also brought in two large dirty dishes and told us to go with him to the kitchen where we would get our dinner. Two of our men took up the dishes and went to the kitchen. A few minutes later they came back with full dishes. One dish contained some soup which looked like dirty dish water; the other contained a brownish black hot mess. They also brought twenty loaves of bread. All the men threw themselves eagerly on the food and began to eat, but in a few minutes they all stopped, and I could hear them swear and curse over the soup. Every one cut off a piece of the browny black matter in the other dish, but ate none of it and neither could we eat the bread because it was raw and sour.

The only things we could eat were potatoes in dresses. About fifteen minutes after dinner we were called to work again. We worked for several hours in succession, lifting heavy bales of hay which were hoisted by a block on the upper deck. At four o'clock we came back to the cabin and some of our men went to the kitchen expecting to get something to eat, and they brought down a kettle of hot but not boiled water and some rotten biscuits. There was neither tea nor coffee, but we all drank the hot water eagerly as it was. We found out later that sugar and luxurious "jam" was also sent to us, but our foremen took it away for themselves. At five we were again at work which consisted in carrying and dividing hay for the cattle. We worked till eight, then we got our supper; again soup, what the men called " ash, " and tea. No bread was given us.

After supper we had to work for two hours more. About half-past ten we got straw mattresses, pillows, and blankets and went to bed. Every day regularly we worked about sixteen hours a day.

Our foreman would curse while instructing us what to do. Those of the cattlemen who understood them and fulfilled their commands were their favorites, those who did not understand them were tortured severely. Among those unfortunate ones were four Jews. One gave some money to his foreman before he started to work and was well treated the first day, but on the following day was put to the hardest work. Another did not understand English, so he was beaten for not acting in accordance with his orders, but this only happened the first few days, after which he knew what to do and tried his best to work earnestly so the foreman stopped beating him.

One fellow was somewhat idiotic. He did not understand his orders and would not do them right even when he was shown what to do. The foreman beat him terribly and he would sit down and cry. He worked at the opposite end of the ship from where I was working so I never saw him at work, but at night he would come to his berth which was next to mine, and cry for hours.

When we landed in Liverpool, we were met by agents who took us over to their offices. I gave them the envelope which the agent had given me. He opened it in my presence and found in it three dollars and the card which is attached. He refused to give me a ticket to Hamburg, telling me that it costs $4.86, and he has no connection with the agent in New York.

He gave the three dollars and the advice back after
having made the statement in writing over his signature on the back of the advice.

This business is wholly interstate and international, and there is apparently no procedure at
the present time to fix the responsibility for these
conditions and no laws of protection.   It has been
proposed that the shippers conduct their own
agencies and, in coöperation with the transportation companies, establish standard conditions.
This is the only solution.   On account of the
cessation of cattle shipment from New York the
question is, temporarily, less important, but with
the increase in exports it will revive.

All seaport and large lake towns have shipping
agencies, for the purpose of supplying vessels with
employees.   Very little is known of these, for by
adroit methods and concealment of fees, they
avoid being licensed.   These shipping agencies
are usually located in or above saloons, and while
some have respectable offices, many are even worse
than the typical general labor office.   In one building the saloon was on the first floor, and the proprietor rented the attic to sailors for $1.50 a week
to sleep in as best they could.

The men who run these agencies are known
as shipping masters, and usually devote themselves to a particular line of work.   One, for instance, supplies trans-Atlantic steamships, another,
deep-water sailing vessels, and another, coasting

schooners. The usual fee charged is $2, which is paid by the boarding-house keeper, who gets a lien on the sailor's pay. For this fee and any board due, the sailor gives his note, and these amounts are deducted from his wages and paid by his employer. The agent, the boarding-house keeper, the saloon-keeper, and the runner for the boarding-house constitute a very effective combination. When a seaman finishes a trip the runner is waiting for him, takes him to a "good saloon" to spend his money, and then to the boarding-house. When he gets sufficiently in debt to the boarding-house keeper, that worthy gets him a berth and ships him out. Some of these boarding-houses are in league with immoral houses, which share profits with them. These boarding-houses ask $7 per week, and never charge for less than one week, even when the sailor is at the house less than one day.

When a sailor wishes to leave money before sailing, his recourse is to get in debt to the boarding-house keeper, and give him an assignment to cover this indebtedness and the amount for his family, which the keeper pays to them. It is to the boarding house-keeper's advantage to get him into debt, and he knows that pay is always forthcoming. Because of this system of shipping crews, and the alliance with saloons, American ports have a bad reputation; the masters say they never know what kind of crew they will have or how much premium they must pay boarding-house keepers.

The evidence that these agencies do collect fees from sailors is most conclusive. Investigators have been told the fee charged them would be $2 for furnishing licensed engineers. One affidavit shows that the sailor agreed that $1 should be deducted from his wages, and a receipt was given him stating this agreement. Another, who had signed no advance note, who had not stayed at a sailor's boarding-house, and was not in debt, had £4 deducted when he reached Liverpool as a fee for shipping him. His voyage was for three months at £6 a month. It is so difficult to prove that fees are charged that the following copies of affidavits are appended, selected from many:

I am a seaman and on——I was engaged as a fire-man to work on board the S. S.——at $25 a month by a shipping master named——who lives at No.——. At the time he engaged me he demanded two ($2) dollars as a shipping fee, and I went aboard said vessel and made the voyage to——and returned to ——and was discharged from the ship on April——, and the two ($2) dollars shipping fee was deducted from my wages by a man in the——Consul's office. I was refused payment of my wages until $2 was agreed by me to be deducted. I am acquainted with——, and to my knowledge he was a seaman on board the S. S.——and on the same voyage, and there was demanded of him a shipping fee of $2 in the—— Consulate.

I went to the boarding-house of——, in—— Street. When I had been in the house five or six days,——got me, through——, shipping agents, a job as fireman on the S. S.——. When I began work on the vessel, I left the house. I was engaged for a ——period of——days. When I finished, a note was given me by the engineer for my pay and this I took to the shipping office of——. I there signed the note, and gave it to Mr.——, who placed it on file. ——then gave me $2 saying that he had no more change and would give me the rest at the house. He never afterwards gave me a cent. According to—— reckoning, there was due me, at the rate of £4 5 s. a month, for which I worked, the sum of $15.82,—— therefore withheld from me $13.82. At that time I was only indebted to him $5 or $6 for five or six days' board. On Sunday, Nov.——, I made a demand on——for my clothes which were in his house. He refused to give them to me.

One boarding-house keeper's testimony shows the existing fee system between shipping masters and boarding-houses:

I brought six men to the S. S.——, bound for the ——, who signed on board and who made the voyage which was completed——. It was agreed by——, shipping masters for the said vessel, that $45 would be paid to——, for the said six men, to be deducted from the wages of the said six men, and $32.50 was paid and $12.50 was retained by—— as a shipping fee, and the said——refused to pay said $12.50 to the said——. This payment was made before the said voyage was begun.

The most significant thing about the general labor agencies is their limited knowledge of the labor market, and their crude ways of getting positions and workmen. There is little or no co-operation between them and no exchange of information. Sometimes two agencies located in different states will form a combine, for the purpose of covering their tracks and avoiding prosecution. When the New York agent has his colleague in Chicago make the contract for placement and accept the fee, it is very difficult to prosecute the New York agent for his share in the transaction, especially if the victim is somewhere else. Among the hundreds of such agencies existing throughout the country, there are no standards but a good deal of similarity; little coöperation but considerable connivance; great ignorance of the real demand for labor, but systematic manipulation of separate jobs and gangs. The cut-throat competition makes it doubtful whether these agencies can, under their present management, become efficient. Certainly to them cannot be entrusted the task of organizing the labor market. The question is how important a part shall they play in its work when organized.

In the present crisis, due to the European War, the efforts of so many competing but non-coöperative agencies are not merely unavailing; they become a menace. They accept fees when they know there are no positions, for they cannot exist otherwise; having no influence in the industrial world and touching it only at isolated points, they cannot place the unemployed to the best advantage for the man and society; antagonistic as they are to law and to civic agencies they cannot serve even as clearing houses for directing the unemployed to proper relief agencies. In the distribution of unskilled labor in a crisis they are without order, system, or resources; in the normal seasons of unemployment, they facilitate the placing of some laborers at great cost and with much waste.

The padroni, that most vicious anti-American institution among the foreign workmen to-day, still flourish. Their stronghold is in the labor camp, the general contractor is their backer, and the most arbitrary manifestations of their control are to be found among the Greek boys of the shoe-shining parlors and flower stores.

The padrone system grew up in America with the Italian, who thinks an intermediary is necessary to conduct any business outside the routine of life. Now it has become common also to the Slavs, Hungarians, Greeks, and other races. The padrone, who used only to deal with countrymen from his home town or province, now has a comprehensive system for getting all of his countrymen. He frequently has men on the other side who "drum up trade" and who consign laborers to him like so many bales of hay. He is frequently the only man they know in America, their only friend when they arrive, and they are to him so many shares of stock out of which he must squeeze the utmost profit. When the immigrant does not come addressed to his care he has runners and others who keep in touch with his fellow laborers or with friends and relatives who are expecting laborers, or who will, at his instigation, induce them to "come over." He gets copies of the ships' advices so he knows when and where they land, and he has many other methods by which he brings these laborers under his influence.

Several circumstances enable the padrone to control the laborer in this country. It works in this way: Sometimes the agent is himself a contractor or has a partner who is. But usually he arranges with the foreman, who is often a partner or ally, that instead of a fee for each man furnished, he shall have the privilege of housing and feeding the laborers. The employer is led to believe by his foremen that this is the best method and the only way that he can get or keep labor. The padrone not only controls the laborer's means of living but the necessities of life as well. In addition he bosses him, frequently acts as his banker, writes his home letters, and engineers many of his dealings. This system has grown out of the difficulty of directing large bodies of men who speak a foreign language and whose customs and habits are not understood by American foremen.

Why is the padrone of such great social as well as economic importance? The laborer knows no English, he has received his job from the padrone, has lived in his home country, buys his food from him, and the workman's pay envelope is opened and

the amount due the padrone is deducted before
the laborer receives it.   If he wants another job,
the padrone is the only one he knows who can
get it for him; and if he breaks away from the
padrone he may be blacklisted by numberless other
padroni and employers.   Such a system, while
bearing no ball and chain, is literal slavery, for it
not only keeps the men away from influences
which will Americanize them and lead to their
assimilation, but it controls their free will in all
aspects of their life.   The employer in many instances never comes to know the men, for they
have numbers not names, and when a particular
job is done they are passed on to another foreman
on another job.

The padroni are not usually men capable of
showing the immigrant American opportunities or
of instructing them in the requirements and principles of good citizenship.   In fact they prefer to
keep them ignorant—and docile.   Not infrequently
the foreman goes so far as to represent the employer or contractor as a vicious character without
human sympathies, so that no appeal will be made
to him.   The padrone system is an increasing
menace; within the past few years, great improvements have called into this country increased
numbers of workers who live temporarily in
shanties and then move on.   No agency contributes more to the disorganization of the labor
market and the deterioration of the labor supply.

There is a further social and political significance

in this system. With the padrone in full control, it
takes the immigrant a long time to learn that it is
not the padrone's favor that gives him the job but
the employer and the industries of America. This
position of fear and dependence makes the laborer
subject to frauds and abuses which give him a
poor return for all he puts into the work. In some
cases laborers pay each month a percentage or
regular fee to the employment agent (which de-
velops in a way the bribe idea), as they think, for
keeping their job against some other workmen,
although their labor is really in demand. One
immigrant in Chicago tells how he was charged a
fee of $5, worked a month, was discharged, and
then went back to the agent who charged him $5
more and sent him back the next day to the same
foreman and to the job he had just left. The State
of Washington, in its campaign for the abolition of
the payment of all fees for positions in 1914, stated
in the brief for its petition that one laborer who
secured work through the same employment agent
fourteen times was sent back to the same job each
time, paying $28 for the privilege of earning $120.
In another Western employment agency the men
are given tags or checks when they leave the
agency, which they surrender to the foreman when
they are employed. The foreman brings these
checks in to the agent at the end of each week and
gets forty per cent. of the fees the laborers have
paid.

The padrone practically sets the standard of

living. He builds the shanty or specifies the requirements and thus sets the standard of housing. He supplies the food and requires the men to furnish their own utensils and prepare their food and thus sets another standard. He robs them by short measure, illegitimate deductions from their pay, overcharging, etc., so that they have to save out of a *balance* instead of the *whole*. No amusements, no recreation, no opportunities for education are provided for this group of tired, badly housed, underfed, isolated men. There can be no steady workmen under such conditions. Even the humdrum, unimaginative peasant soon becomes a floater—since leaving one job for another is his only method of protest.

The intrenchment of the padrone is not wholly an industrial matter. It is a part of the old combination of business and politics when the contractor who got the job voted his men in favor of the party that secured him the contract and his padrone held the vote. In the breaking up of this alliance, the padrone, however, has survived. He is now reaping the reward for service. One of the best known of these padroni enjoys the distinction of being tacitly accepted as district leader for *both old parties* in his district, a difficult position which few men could hold. He was even the nominee on the Republican ticket for Congress in 1914.

The tolerance of the padrone is largely responsible for the existence of peonage in this country.

Peonage is defined by the United States Supreme Court to be "compulsory service based upon the indebtedness of the peon to the master. The basic fact is indebtedness." There is little difference between being held in slavery for debt and holding down a job through fear of the blacklist of the padrone to whom the immigrant owes money for passage and for camp supplies. Both are conditions of servitude incompatible with American institutions.

When rumors of the existence of peonage were first heard, the utmost skepticism prevailed. Americans would not believe that it could exist in America, and they insisted that the question of slavery was settled once for all. This is, however, what the Federal government found when it investigated the "rumors":

In the Raleigh Lumber Company of West Virginia a number of newly arrived Italian workmen were arrested upon warrants issued under the absconding debtor law. They were intimidated by an armed constable with a drawn pistol and all except five, who had money to pay their transportation charges, were confined in a box car. At the end of five days' confinement they submitted to going back to work. They were thereafter guarded while at work until an investigation by an agent[1] of the government led to their release.

In the Ritter Lumber Company, West Virginia, white workmen were held in peonage on railroad work

[1] Report of United States Department of Justice.

in the southern part of the State. They were guarded day and night by mountaineers and two of those who escaped were caught by a young railroad watchman named Hatfield who wounded one in the face by a blow with his pistol and tied the two with a rope and brought them back by train.[1]

Two white men of Seymour, Indiana, went to Vance, Mississippi, to work for a large stove company, as they supposed. When they reached Vance they were told they must go to the swamps to cut timber. When they demurred, the foreman had them arrested for securing transportation money under "false pretences." They were fined and had to work out their fine. They worked under armed guard at *15 cents per day*, this contract being made by the court officers.[2]

A statute in Maine makes it a crime for a person contracting to labor for a lumber company to receive goods, money, or transportation and then fail to work off the debt. According to the Federal Immigration Commission, the most complete system of peonage to be found in the United States exists in Maine.[3]

Because within late years paper mills have attracted men who formerly worked for the logging concerns, the lumber companies have been compelled to import laborers, largely foreigners from other states. Boston is the chief labor market for supplying them. The workers are often told that the lumber camps are only a few

[1] Report of United States Department of Justice.
[2] *Nineteenth Century*, vol. lxii.
[3] Report of Federal Immigration Commission, vol. ii.

miles from town to which they can frequently
return for amusement. They find when they
reach the end of their journey by rail that after
being driven a short distance into the forests
they must walk sixty or seventy miles into the
interior.

The Commission on Immigration found that
foreign laborers were restrained in every state
covered by its investigation, except Oklahoma and
Connecticut, under conditions which if substan-
tiated by legal evidence would constitute peonage
as defined by the Supreme Court. It found that
peonage cases in the South relating to immigrants
covered almost every industry, farming, lumbering,
logging, railroading, mining, factories, and construction work. It regarded as the chief causes of
peonage the practice of advancing fares and supplies to laborers, the operation of contract labor
laws, and misrepresentation made to laborers by
unscrupulous employment agents. In nearly all
of the Southern cases of peonage investigated, it
was pointed out that the laborers were the victims
of the misrepresentations of labor agents in New
York City as to conditions of work.

*The general labor agency is an inadequate, anti-
quated method of distributing labor, suited to the
village or local industry but wholly unable to meet the
conditions developed by interstate commerce, or to
understand the peculiar demands af our rapidly
developing industries. They are not in the hands
of men familiar with business or industry. Any*

*program for the organization of the labor market,
which includes the retention of general labor agencies, should provide first for their standardization,
increased efficiency, coöperation, and complete
regulation.*

*The padrone must go. There is no hope of reform-
ing him. His system is built on servitude and is
antagonistic to American ideals and institutions.
The agent who finds the unskilled workman a job
should be widely separated from the one who collects
his wages, feeds and houses him, and buys his return
ticket to his home country or banks his money there.
Indebtedness as a basis of control of employees, made
secure by employers' deducting sums from pay envelopes in favor of the padroni, is an anti-social
policy leading to industrial conflicts.*

*The general labor agent and the padrone block the
road to the organization of the labor market. They
retard education, knowing that when men are educated they escape the agency boss. So long as the
employer thinks the padrone is the only person to get
him his labor, inefficiency and disease due to bad
housing and food will prevail among his workmen; so
long as single men in large numbers are forced to live
alone under crowded and immoral conditions in
isolated places, the family social and moral ideal
cannot exist; so long as the padrone operates with
entire independence as he now does, the government
cannot distribute alien workmen because the particular agent into whose hands they fall may not have an
ally at the particular camp on the government's list.*

With a few notable exceptions, the general labor agency is an anti-social organization, with profit wrung out of exploitation as its most significant factor.

13

CHAPTER VII

DOMESTIC SERVICE AND INTELLIGENCE OFFICES

UP several iron steps, along two or three rambling halls, up a few more wooden steps—and here at last was the "intelligence office," in a small three-room apartment. The "office" proper was apparently a bare little kitchen with a table covered with a red and white cloth. The only visible attendant was a sallow slip of a girl with a red pigtail, with long thin arms and clawlike hands, washing dishes at the sink. When applied to for information she obligingly went out on the balcony to call her mother who was visiting in the street below, but who was induced to come in to see her clients.

A second was found in a basement salesroom, where second-hand clothing was piled around in dirty, disorderly heaps, with a living-room curtained off at the back. This so-called office was used as a bedroom at night. A third was a combination baggage- and living-room. The proprietor was an expressman and his wife ran the office. Any left-over baggage was piled in the office at night and utilized for beds or chairs, according to its adaptability. A fourth, literally covered with left-over bundles of waiting employees, had a table in one corner, which contained the remains of a meal, a "day-book," and advertising material. Over in another corner two flashily dressed girls were playing the piano and singing popular songs. In a fifth the proprietor was washing, and we discussed "servants" and "places" to the time of a rhythmic "rub, rub," through clouds of steam and soapy vapor, with an occasional flap of a wet cloth for variation. The sixth was the first floor of a little two-story corner house, in a two-room apartment where the husband worked as a carpenter in one room, while the wife conducted the office in the other. The two rooms were full of children; there was very little furniture, even for living purposes, and no records or system. The seventh was in a two-room apartment, with not a thing more than was required for living purposes. The front room was a bed- and sitting-room where the husband worked on a machine; the other a kitchen and bedroom, where the wife attended to the employment business.

One day, after wandering through a very dirty, disorderly building, an applicant for a job entered a small courtyard. A rough, good-natured Bohemian was washing clothes, and upon the steps sat his admiring wife and three children. When asked where the office was, he tapped himself, and smiling proudly, said, "Me the office; what you want? You want girl? I go out and find her." In another place it was a steaming kitchen, strung with lines of clothes. To meet her patrons a Slavish woman appeared from among the lines, washing in hand, and said: "No girls, me wash day; me open office get girl when wash done."

These are intelligence offices—so-called—in America. These are the forces which America trusts to deal with the unskilled immigrant in domestic service.

Altogether different from these is the aristocratic office located sometimes in or near the most fashionable part of the city, and fitted out with expensive furniture, and other equipment. The methods used here may be businesslike, simple, and above reproach, references scrupulously examined and care taken to see that only those servants are sent out who are capable of doing the work asked of them, and also of suiting the particular needs of the employer. The servant, as well as the employer, may be treated with courtesy and respect. In short, agencies for placing domestic servants vary as from pushcart to department store. In the intelligence office business, however, most of the trade is still transacted on the pushcart basis. And the connection between the two methods, between the squalid kitchen on First Avenue and the well-equipped office on Fifth Avenue is closer than one might think. Some girls work up in a surprisingly short time from one to the other; but many of them pass first of all through the kitchen agencies, and get their first place through the agent that deserts her wash-tub for the moment when they come in. Later, when they have learned English, got some American clothes, and know the ways of gas ranges, dumb-waiter shafts, and clothes lines on the roof, they may get to agencies of a better class.

In New York, of 313 offices which supply households, 120 are in tenements, 107 in apartments, 39 in residences, and 49 in business houses—a total of 266 which are a part of the family life and 227 which affect more than one family. This means that in 85 per cent. a large number of strangers, about whose character, life, and habits little is known, are brought into the daily life of the family, or are attracted to buildings where members of many families, especially mothers and daughters, must meet them.

To a less degree these conditions are true in other cities. Philadelphia, because of its many small houses, has 84 per cent. in private residences, about 10 per cent. in apartments, and about 3 per cent. each in tenement and business buildings. In Chicago about 81 per cent. are in buildings occupied by families. In Boston 73 per cent. are in business buildings and but 27 per cent. in residence buildings.

Even in small towns the situation is the same— or worse; for in a town of 5000 or 10,000 with few office buildings and only such stores as the needs of the population have brought into existence, the office is almost inevitably located in the little house or flat where the agent lives. And usually, by the nature of things, this house or tenement is in a run-down, perhaps an even suspicious region, over Jack's Oyster Café, or in the outskirts, or "Over on the other side of the railroad tracks." Yet through these pass the girls that go to live in the home of the school principal, the storekeeper, the minister, or the factory owner.

Intelligence offices may be roughly divided, according to the kind of servants they provide, into five classes. New York City furnishes interesting illustrations of the first four. In the first class come the racial offices which place mainly girls for general housework. A number of these, located in the lower part of the city, handle almost exclusively new arrivals—green girls altogether unused to American ways. In the upper part of the town are agencies for Swedish girls, for Danes, for Finns, for English—usually patronized by girls that have been in the country for some time. The second class, also located uptown, supply more accomplished servants for town and country homes. The third are hotel offices. The fourth handle only colored servants. The white agencies, however, usually handle any colored servants that apply to them. The fifth is the small town agency that handles anything and anybody.

These agencies tend to concentrate in certain neighborhoods. An agent opening a new office is likely to put it near some agency already in operation, on the theory that servants hunting for one will get into the other, and he also counts on attracting some of the loiterers. The effect of this concentration on standards of business hardly needs pointing out. Agents use various devices to get a servant to come into their agency, and frequently make promises that they are in no position to fulfil.

Their equipment furnishes a significant index to their methods. Some of the best have attractive furnishings in the way of desks, files, rugs, chairs, and a telephone. Sometimes the only equipment is a cheap day-book, a bottle of ink upon the kitchen table, and a pile of office cards upon the mantel. A parlor with an extra table for a desk and a dozen or more newspaper bundles of clothing constituted the fixtures of one office; and three bare rooms with no other furniture than a stove, beds, tables, and bundles describes another. About sixty per cent. have some equipment, those supplying chiefly hotel help being the best equipped and most businesslike, and resembling the mercantile agencies which are described later.

The remaining forty per cent. can be said to have practically no equipment nor system. The office is held in one room or all over the house, and addresses are written on any available scrap of paper—old envelopes, torn wrapping paper, the corner of a newspaper, or even upon a slate. When these memoranda are kept at all, they are found in various places—on the tables or chairs, or even under the bed. Chairs, beds, and tables are used to seat waiting applicants, and often there is not an extra article of furniture beyond that required by the family. In one, there were four chairs, a kitchen table, a telephone, a dressing-case, and a large cook stove—all in one room, and the wife was cooking while the husband wrote the addresses. The second room contained two beds and extra bedding which was evidently used in the kitchen at night. In one there was so obviously no place to sit down that the agent asked the employers not to wait and promised to send a girl. Occasionally, the proprietor's method is to take the employer out with him until he can pick up a girl, or she is left to entertain the children while he scours the neighboring tenements for help.

The success of any intelligence office depends on its ability to secure employees. For securing employers, advertising and recommendation by the patrons are adequate means; but to obtain a constant supply of employees other means have to be devised. The chief supply consists of immigrants, negroes imported from the South, and girls from out of town who are attracted to the city by promises of work. Many employees are attracted by legitimate methods, but many others must be sought. "Domestic servants" are not included in the contract labor clause of the immigration law, but that law does prohibit publishing or printing advertisements in any foreign country for the purpose of inducing aliens to come here upon promises of employment. To evade this, offices insert large and attractive advertisements in

Swedish, Hungarian, Jewish, Finnish, and other American-published papers; these are sent abroad in large quantities, and later the girls arrive with these clippings or with addresses found in this way.

Since the careful regulations at immigrant stations have been in effect, many office runners are "spotted" and can no longer get the girls out at will, for now they must satisfactorily prove that they are relatives of the persons to whom the immigrant is consigned. Immigrants are not discharged to male married relatives not accompanied by their wives. To evade such regulations, the agents send emissaries abroad who get acquainted with girls and send them over with the name of the office, or of some friend with whom the office works and who poses as a relative. Previously they have sent to this relative the name and description of the girl so that the two statements tally. Others have men who go back and forth on the ships, get acquainted with girls, and direct them to these offices. Cattle men on their return trips use their influence to direct both men and women to these offices and receive rewards. Steamship companies are their ablest allies. Although they maintain a careful supervision, they also have paid agents who drum up steerage passengers, and these agents include even school-teachers, postmasters, and priests. They reduce rates, and all of these things together help the office. These agencies frequently advance transportation and the girls repay the office at a fair rate of profit when they secure positions. Although steamship companies are prohibited from encouraging immigration by any means other than ordinary commercial letters, circular advertisements, or oral representatives giving the sailings, terms, and facilities, they extend many "courtesies" which increase the supply of domestic workers.

A number of negro offices import girls from the South. They have white agents in the large Southern cities whose business it is to corral girls from the country districts, bring them into the cities, and ship them to Northern offices. When the agent cannot get the transportation from the girl or her relatives, the offices furnish it, and the girl pays it back with considerable profit. A negro girl, for instance, was promised a position as nurse by an agent in Richmond, Virginia. She agreed to have $12.75 for her fare deducted from her wages, and all her personal effects were subject to the order of the New York office. When she arrived she was told there were no vacancies for nurses, and she must do general housework. She refused and the office still held her trunk. When she complained, the agent maintained: "She has worked us for a free passage north."

The migration of girls from small towns and rural districts is not so haphazard as it appears to be on first sight. Some offices have standing advertisements, which they run in the country newspapers, offering attractive work at good wages, but not necessarily appearing as advertisements from offices. Girls come to the city in answer to these and are met at the stations and taken to the lodging-houses run in connection with these offices. Others advertise in city papers and secure addresses which they follow up by mail or in person. Advertisements are answered by a surprisingly large number of girls in small towns who say they have never worked away from home.

In this way intelligence offices control the three main sources of supply for domestic servants. They have also devised various other ways of extending this influence. Many offices rely on cards, which they depend upon their patrons to distribute; a few issue announcements and circulars, and in all cities but Boston they use public signs and placards. Many immigrants and others say that they walk miles "just looking for these signs." These are sometimes misleading. One for instance reads "Industrial Home"; when questioned, the proprietor said it was an inducement to attract customers, and that she would like to train girls. When asked what she would teach them, she said: "Well, if they were cooks, I would expect to learn more than I taught." Some proprietors visit cheap lodging-houses and pay the keepers 50 cents or $1 for every girl they furnish; or they exchange, sending the girls there to board.

For the immigrant and negro the boarding-house is the crux of the whole situation, especially in such cities as New York and Philadelphia.

Other offices do not scruple to hold up girls on the street and induce them to come to the agency. A few have the endorsement of mission houses and pastors. Icemen, grocers, and marketmen are pressed into service. They are usually friends of the office keepers; so when they go into homes they become acquainted with girls, make them dissatisfied by telling them what the office will do, or what they have seen in other homes, and then, for a small commission, report to the office that at such addresses there are good girls. Later the agent makes their acquaintance, and the employers wonder why their girls have left. One Swedish office, notorious for taking away girls whom it has placed, urges them to attend church and advances the necessary money for clothes. In this way it secures an additional hold on the girl and the endorsement of the church for its work. Some place girls where there are other servants, with the understanding that they are to create dissatisfaction and secure their patronage for the office.

The methods, however, upon which offices chiefly rely are advertising and importation. The former is used more generally by the better-class offices and the latter by immigrant offices. Answering advertisements in newspapers is much more common than advertising and is, of course, cheaper. Some clip offers of places and give these to applicants, who often go only to find the places filled. Sometimes employees pay carfares for half a dozen such orders a day, not knowing they are

advertisements. Some offices run blind advertisements, and when applicants answer them they
find an employment office. Others do a mail-order
business and get their living from the small sums
they request by mail. Others run general advertisements from day to day, such as "Wanted,
chambermaids, cooks," etc., ending with some
attractive inducement. They may or may not
have these positions ready; the object is to attract
large numbers of girls, when they have no definite
orders, and secure registration fees. Thoughtful
employers who think they are placing their
employees by advertising "Lady leaving city
wishes to place maid" sometimes find they have
been caught by such an office.

That intelligence offices really do control the
available supply of servants almost any housekeeper can prove by her own experience. She
hires girl after girl sent by the office, presenting
different varieties of competence, but having a
certain similarity too, until at last she realizes the
truth of the French proverb: "The more you
change, the more you get the same thing," and
revolts. What can she do? She can advertise
and can specify very carefully what qualifications
the girl must possess—a Swede—let us say, between eighteen and thirty, able to cook and to iron.
No others need apply. For days she will have to
interview Irish, colored, German, and Finnish girls,
under eighteen or over thirty, who never did any
cooking, and who can wash, but not iron. Women

will come who want day's work, or women who want to bring three or four small children who, they guarantee, will "never be in the way." Occasionally, of course, a housekeeper and a servant who meet each other's needs are lucky enough to come together in this way, but not often. Sometimes, too, a housekeeper can get able servants through those she is already employing; but the chief supply is in the hands of the agents, who manipulate it as they see fit.

The real reason why they control the available supply of servants is not because they have studied the situation and developed business ability to deal with it. It is an unpopular field to which attaches much of the social stigma that characterizes household service. It is the last resort in business, the least organized of the labor markets, and is regarded with some contempt as women's work. It is the most difficult field in which to achieve success; the workers shift from country to town and from town to country; they try constantly to specialize so that the general houseworker, once the mainstay of the community, is fast disappearing, partly because servants have changed, but very largely because homes have changed too, and our present highly complicated standards of living have developed. Caste distinctions have grown up among servants to such a degree that an agency which advertises that it supplies girls for general housework risks limiting its supply.

This is a task worthy of the broadest intelligence and finest powers of organization, but it apparently attracts persons with but little of either. Investigation shows that a large percentage of intelligence offices are run by persons without business ability or training. It requires no capital and in many states no certificate of character. It is frequently a venture to cover other failures or to supplement inadequate incomes or replenish small losses. Or it is a side occupation, among women combining with washing, sewing, janitress work, or other unskilled labor; among men with keeping a saloon or small shop which the waiting employees can patronize, or running a steamship or railway agency where they can buy tickets.

Under such conditions it is difficult to estimate how well offices pay, for the competition is keen. On the whole, with a fair amount of energy and attention, they appear to yield good returns. Some deal with servants with such a poor quality of ability that they cannot possibly return a great profit, and many immigrant offices assert that they can scarcely pay expenses. The chief sources of income are fees, board and lodging, storage of baggage and express on it. It is not unusual to find agents who have retired and are living upon their profits; others are property holders, and some find it possible to close their offices for the summer and frequent popular resorts, or to go abroad to secure girls. On the other hand, many have a precarious existence maintained only by preying upon helpless unemployed women.

The fees charged may be a set price for each position filled, a percentage of the wages, a gift, or a subscription to the office "magazine." The amount of the employee's fee ranges from 50 cents to $2, averages about $1, and is good for one or more months. Employees, as a rule, receive but little attention unless they pay in advance, and in many offices they are not even permitted to wait, the attendants saying: "This place is crowded"; "All who ain't paid can get out"; "This is no day hotel." Unless prohibited by law, a registration or advance fee is charged. This is to cover incidental expenses, leaving the placement fee as clear profit. The latter is commonly a percentage fee, and is usually ten per cent. of the first month's wages. On such a basis it may reach $5. In rare instances the entire first week's salary is asked. Negro and immigrant offices, and occasionally others, have a gift system. Employers are repeatedly told that employees are charged nothing. The girls sent up to places, however, find that the office demands a gift, and upon its value depends the kind of position offered. This gift is money or any other valuable. The subterfuge has proved so profitable that several states have prohibited gifts. Some offices also make small loans to employees and receive valuable pledges. Under such circumstances, they are in no hurry to get a "greenie" work.

The length of time which an applicant must wait for a position after paying a fee varies with her

demands and her competence, with the season, and
with the inclination of the office to place her.
Sometimes she is sent out immediately, and again
she waits for days. If an applicant is fairly satisfactory and a position is not offered within three
days, it is usually safe to assume that the new
arrivals are receiving the plums. The office sometimes creates an impression of good intentions, by
sending an employee to a place which it knows
has already been filled. Even under such circumstances they put her at the end of the list where
she again waits her turn.

Almost all intelligence offices over-register and
over-promise. Even the most reputable seldom
turn away a patron. Most of them are willing to
accept the fee, and where employees are unwilling
to pay they make all kinds of extravagant promises.
In some instances they refuse orders, saying they
can barely supply their own trade; but they
rarely refuse an employee, even when she seems a
doubtful investment. The formula is, "Come
back in an hour," or "To-morrow, we will have
something for you."

Fees are good for various periods. Those good
for several months have some disadvantages. The
employer is told that the fee is good for two months,
and that she can have all the girls she wants until
one suits her. In answer to the question how many
girls were sent for one fee, the replies from employers indicate that one was the usual number,
though some say two, three, or even five. After

14

receiving one or two incompetents, employers are impatient and try elsewhere. Even granting that the office honestly tries to give satisfaction the first time, they may send a cook who for some reason cannot be kept, or who will not stay, and a demand is made for a second cook for the same fee. Now the office may do one of three things,— it may select another girl who will suit, but the chances are frequently against this. It has the fee, which is probably spent. It has forgotten the employer's particular request, and the supply of cooks is short. The agent reasons: why should she send the only good cook she has, when in line stands another employer whose three dollars have not yet been paid? The chances are that the cook goes to the one from whom the fee has not yet been collected. Secondly, it may delay. This is designed to tire out the employer and force her to go elsewhere, or to pay extra. The office does not fear losing a good patron, for she receives much the same treatment in others, and the demand so far exceeds the supply that it is rarely a question of enough employers. The third plan is more difficult to detect, but is not less common. These offices have a number of "hangers-on"—women who take places for a week or two to get a little money, and then spend it. These are useful. Even though they hold a place for only a few days, each one placed means a fee. After the first attempt to send a desirable girl, and sometimes at the beginning, the office sends these rounders, one

after another, and when an employer complains
the answer is, "We have sent so many girls—
there must be something wrong with the house,"
or, "The employer was too difficult to please."

A few agencies, chiefly those which supply
hotels and other large establishments, charge by
the season, the rate being $10 to $25. Others have
subscriptions or annual accounts. Some do not
charge large employers of help, such as hotels, for
the reasons that girls prefer to go there and hotels
advertise them. Some give a reduction when an
employer takes more than one employee, as two
maids for $5. In a number of these, fees depend
upon the degree of prosperity which an applicant
shows and upon the location of her home. Except
where regulated by law, there is no uniform standard. Fees are usually payable at the time of
leaving with the girl, or when she is sent to the
home and engaged.

The testimony of investigators and employers is
against the belief that offices refund any considerable proportion of fees except where the law is
rigidly enforced. When an applicant calls, the
office sometimes takes the address and promises to
send the fee by mail, hoping the applicant will not
reappear. Case after case arises of fees paid and
no satisfaction given, and women go repeatedly for
work or for a return of their money. In St. Louis
it appeared that two offices alone had "done" the
unemployed out of six thousand dollars in one year.
One of the most fashionable offices in New York

takes fees, and at the end of the week tells the girls it is their own fault that they have no positions for they are too homely; it refuses to refund the money, saying: "We cannot help the fad of employers in wanting good-looking waitresses."

The charging of advance fees is the most prolific source of fraud in what may otherwise be an honest transaction. The temptation to keep the fee at any cost, leads to the downfall of many an agent. This getting something for nothing is the beginning of the fabric of exploitation. First there is the explanation why this is justifiable, and the simplest friendly service comes to have a material value; then enter falsehoods, accusations, recriminations, personal abuse, and at the end of a few months the registration fee is the goal and common honesty is not the road by which it is reached.

American women have hitherto been singularly blind to the tribute they pay to this system. That it bears heavily upon servant girls they are willing to believe; that it sometimes entails inconvenience upon themselves they admit and lament. Yet they do not see that it is they, not the girls, who must, in the long run, pay a large part of the financial and moral cost of the present method of marketing domestic servants. The financial burden it entails, though far less important than the moral considerations involved, is sufficiently heavy. For instance, a girl is sent to a place upon the understanding that she will remain only until they send for her. One employer found that six

came to her with this understanding. One girl
said she had been placed ten times in one year,
netting the office twenty dollars in fees, for it
received a percentage of the wage each time, and a
neat sum for lodging until she was placed again.
If the employer who lost her returned to the same
office for other girls, there were additional fees.
This scheme is not often unattractive in the variety
it offers: "You can't save much," said one girl,
"but it's gay changing."

Fees good for a certain length of time encourage
short service. The employer discharges an employee more readily, and girls think they can
leave on slight provocation, for a new girl, or
position costs nothing. Such a system encourages
a bonus. When a fee is good for two months and
an employee is not secured, the employer is
tempted to add a small amount, just for a "little
special attention." Fees are really larger than
they seem; three dollars for three months appears
more of a bargain than two dollars for one employee; but it amounts to much the same thing
in the end, and is an adroit way of securing more
fees. A fee for each employee, to be refunded unless she remains a specified time, appears to work
less hardship.

The average housekeeper thinks that the wages
she has to pay her household workers depend on
the demand and supply. But the middleman is
just as important here as in other markets. This is
especially true where a percentage fee is charged.

Some agents never have an employee for just the wage an employer wishes to pay, but have plenty for fifty cents or one dollar higher, and the employer is made to feel "small" unless she yields. Offices are so largely wage brokers that many girls name no regular wage, but leave it to the office to get as much as it can. One employer says: "Unless you are quite decided as to what you wish to pay, you will find yourself paying more without realizing why." A few agents refuse to have anything to do with the question of wages, leaving it entirely to the parties to the contract, but many employees will only patronize agents willing to conduct the negotiations. This is one explanation of the high wages asked by newly arrived immigrant girls.

The disheartened housekeeper, who has trained girl after girl only to have her step out as soon as or even before her training in the ways of the household has been finished, knows the bitterness of her side of the problem. The servant has been shoved into one position after another, has had other standards forced upon her, and has paid the price for others' misdeeds until her own standards have become blurred and the keen edge of her honesty has been blunted; she too feels the intolerable wrong of the situation. Instead of the mutual confidences that should develop between the two, sullen disbelief or hostility grows up on both sides. This is one of the prices not set down in the schedule of fees, but none the less less vigor-

ously exacted, that the American home pays
to-day for the present method of dealing with
unemployment in domestic service.

The intelligence office is not only a business
agency, it is a social institution, dealing with
human beings in very intimate and critical ways;
on the one hand it supplies women to enter
intimately into home circles; on the other hand
the women for whom it gets work are often at
a crisis, without money, without homes, in grave
doubt of their ability to fit themselves at all into
the social and industrial scheme. Usually ignorant
and often without signal ability or specific training,
they may easily prove unequal to the stern challenge of being out of a job. Inarticulate, perhaps
sullen and apparently indifferent, timid in their
search for the first job, many of them go through a
period of spiritual upheaval which the uninitiated
observer never suspects. It is then that the agent
gets her strong hold upon the girl, as often by
kindness as by her services as agent. A girl's whole
moral point of view is weakened or strengthened,
according to the kind of office into which she gets.
The occasional good agent advises her to be faithful, honest, and hard working; the far more frequent one teaches her to be just the reverse; her
scruples are ridiculed, she is made fun of, and
coached to claim qualifications she does not
possess.

In the first place the actual treatment accorded
to the girls in these offices is important. Un-

doubtedly there are some offices in which they are accorded semi-courteous treatment. But, notoriously, this is not the rule. In the medium and best grade offices especially, the contrast between the treatment of "ladies" and of "servants" is most striking. Merely from the voice of the manager, an observer can tell whether she is in the "ladies'" or the "servants'" room. In the one it is modulated, polite, smooth, pleasing, courteous; in the other, rough, arrogant, and discourteous. This contrast in treatment must impress even the dullest employees. One of the most fashionable offices in New York makes its employees stand all day—"The room holds more," one girl said. Little thought or money is expended to make the employees' rooms either comfortable or healthful, and yet the girls wait all day, while at best the employers wait a few minutes or an hour. Employees cannot help contrasting the dirty, disorderly kitchen or uncomfortable back rooms where they are huddled together with the clean, comfortable parlor where they are taken to talk to employers.

In some agencies these girls are actually herded and treated like cattle. In one Swedish office, run by two young men, one guarded the door of the employees' room and by promises, threats, and actual force made it impossible for girls to get out without paying a fee. Swearing at employees who are restless or who demand their fees back is too common an occurrence to need mention. The means of maintaining order in some of the crowded offices is not only insulting, but brutal, and the best employees seeking housework for the first time will certainly not go there after one or two experiences. In a good office, a woman who insisted upon the refund of her fee was pushed out of the door and downstairs for "creating a disturbance," for she was encouraging others to demand their fees also. She said she had waited two weeks and had not even had an offer of a position. To insist upon "rights" after paying a fee is more often than not the signal for insolence and wrath, and employees are pretty sure to be ignored thereafter in the selection of positions. In one large office the male clerk came into the room and shouted out the positions wanted. When no one replied he then singled out girls. When asked why no one responded, a girl said: "Because he always answers us impudently, and picks out the ones he wants to have anyway." Sodden, uncomplaining, patient, submissive, must be the applicant's attitude, unless she responds to the familiarities and "jollying" of attendants. If there is not absolute brutality, there is discourtesy, noticeable lack of respectful address, "bossing," and contradictions. A girl fixes her wages; the office says, "Change it or get out"; another states the kind of work she wants; the office says, "Do something different"; another wants work in a private family; the office cajoles her into going into a hotel; another states she is twenty-five years old, and the office replies, "You are only twenty for our business." In other words, so far as it possibly can, it makes girls over to suit whatever position it has on hand; employees are forced, through such means, into places which they are not fitted to fill and into work in which they have no interest.

Far more grave, both in its effect upon servants and in its bearing upon the home, is the fact that an office often vouches for girls as respectable and honest, when it either knows nothing whatever about them, or else knows that they are dishonest and immoral. References, supposed to guard the employer and the honest servant, do not protect either. Offices have been known to change the text of references, to provide new ones, or to vouch for references which they have not seen. "She is all right," said one attendant to a patron, "we have seen her reference." So, in this case, they had, but the employer would have been surprised at the contents. They allow employees to use old references, changing the dates, and sometimes take especially valuable ones from waiting employees. An employer, when giving a written reference, never knows who will use it as a passport. Thoroughly respectable girls when they take new positions will lend, give away, or sell their references, trusting to get others from their new places. In few instances are references required from the employers; no questions are asked except about wages, hours, and address; and many do not require the last if a girl is taken at once. In the hurry of business they take little thought as to where the girl goes, and many are utterly indifferent, even when their suspicions are aroused, as when saloons, men's club-houses, etc., are specified in the request for help.

Concerning references for employees there are all shades of opinion. References are of two kinds —written and personal. Personal references are given directly by one employer to another through correspondence, telephone conversations, or visits. The written reference is ordinarily a letter carried by the employee, but it may be a statement returnable to the office by mail in answer to questions. These are called investigated references and are kept on file, but this method is used by but few offices. References may also be bonded, in which case the office receives a considerable fee for "making it good." This practice is, however, rare in unskilled trades.

The majority of offices detest bothering with them and use them only because so many employers insist. The best offices of all grades require them in some form, but are willing to take employees in the hope of persuading employers to accept them without these credentials. Of course, immigrant and negro offices cannot be expected to furnish them. They include among their reasons: "not asked," "nobody expects much of negroes," "we import girls and they bring none," "we don't care for patrons who want them," "too hard to get girls," and "can get places without them."

Investigation of references seems to be a proper function of the office, but it cannot be held fully responsible for failing to fulfill it.

Offices may well complain that they are imposed upon, for as a matter of fact the whole letter-reference system is a series of impositions, beginning with employers. They give references to get rid of girls, and refuse them in order to keep girls; they refuse them out of pique, and give them for purely sentimental reasons. Some employers refuse them on all grounds, insisting upon private interviews; some never refuse for any cause; some tell all the good points and are silent on the bad; others mention only deception or intemperance but not other faults; others refuse only when it is impossible to speak well of the employee; or they give them, but encourage personal interviews saying that they will state the truth in an interview but not in writing. Some think it their duty to tell faults only when questioned, and are careful not to over-praise. The only hope of remedy seems to lie in arousing employers to their sense of obligation and in securing uniformity of standards; in providing that employees remain at least three months before they are given a reference; that written references, in the shape of letters, carried by employees be abolished and some prescribed form adopted containing a description of the employee to prevent exchanges, and the essential questions to be answered; that personal references be encouraged, and that employers insist upon offices' using blanks returnable by mail.

An occasional office really endeavors to help its patrons, and to assist them to fit themselves into their work and life. Sometimes such agencies owe their origin to philanthropic impulses, as does one conducted for many years in Philadelphia; sometimes they are kept up from racial feeling, and sometimes they are simply business enterprises— conducted with system and consideration for the human side of the problem with which they deal. In the Philadelphia agency references are required from both employer and employee. Such an office endeavors to put girls where they will be safe, and will be decently treated, and where they can give good service to their employers. A girl passing through it learns to make the most of her present situation and is given a chance to establish herself in a way that gives her hope for the future. The employer gets a servant that has not been taught to lie and cheat, who is presumably healthy, who has not been exposed to temptations of various kinds, and who has not been taught to distrust and despise her employer. But agencies conducted on the mutual reference practice or even theory are rare as yet.

More insidious by far than the juggling with references are two other features of the intelligence office business which cannot help affecting a girl's standards—the noxious general atmosphere of many of the offices, and the conditions to which

girls are exposed in the lodging-houses run in
connection with many agencies. The frequent
proximity of intelligence offices to saloons has
already been mentioned. Often also they are
fairly surrounded by gambling-dens, fortune-tel-
lers, palmists, midwives, and other undesirable
"professions," which depend on them for patronage. These are often so prominently advertised that the offices may be easily overlooked.

The identification of an employment agency with
the family life of the proprietor, already mentioned,
is of doubtful value to either. Sometimes all the
applicants have to wait in one small, crowded
room, and not always in peace. On one occasion
investigators disguised as applicants were ushered
into a dark bedroom with unmade beds; a little
later they were moved to the kitchen to make room
for the proprietor, who was also the chambermaid,
and finally back into the bedroom, and out into
the hall to make room for the cook—again the
proprietor—who wished to get dinner. Early
morning visits reveal proprietors and lodgers in all
stages of dressing for the day, beds upturned, meals
being prepared, and altogether a social miscel-
laneousness not conducive to business relations.

Some of the employees' waiting-rooms are both
healthful and desirable, but many are dark, badly
ventilated, and crowded, are arranged with little
regard for comfort, and recognize no difference in
rank or education. Overcrowding is found in
almost every one at times, stairs, halls, and en-

trances—even the street, in immigrant offices—
receiving the overflow.   In one of these, this overflow of girls was lying out on a small iron balcony,
faces downward, peering into the fascinating street
below.   When one was wanted, the proprietor
went out, poked the pile with his foot, and one
disentangled herself and came in for inspection.

Where both men and women are supplied, there
are sometimes separate waiting-rooms, but many
offices are used as general meeting places for
making appointments or getting acquainted.
This means that men and women, regardless of
age, condition, or color are often crowded together
in small dark rooms.   In the winter many use
them for lounging places, and they are frequented
by many "rounders" seeking a good time rather
than places.   Some offices degenerate into mere
"hang-outs" where familiarities and demoralization of women are possible.   These conditions
are most demoralizing in immigrant and negro
offices; in the latter employees were found in bed
as late as ten to twelve o'clock A.M. and men were
waiting in these rooms or came in to ask them to
take positions.

Office lodging-houses are sometimes inferior to
the office with which they are connected.   In one
office the accommodations were two beds in a room
and four in a bed.   Six persons, some very sparing-
ly and others decently dressed, were cooking and
eating their suppers.   Each had brought in what
she had bought, and all were cooking and tasting

each other's food at the same time. No drinking or male visitors were allowed, as it "invariably leads to fighting." The beds were dirty and alive with vermin, and rates were $1.75 for lodging and breakfast, or $3.50 per week for full board.

Offices which do not lodge sometimes attempt to meet the demand by keeping in touch with boarding-places, which they recommend. Sometimes these are run by friends who send girls out of work to the office in exchange for lodgers. Sometimes the proprietors know nothing of the places they recommend, and sometimes they work in conjunction with what are called "working girls' homes," often of very doubtful character.

At present these lodging-houses seem to be a necessity, and there is need rather for their regulation and improvement than for their abolition. They accommodate such numbers of transients, especially women who are temporarily out of work and homeless, that if they were suddenly closed, hundreds, if not thousands, would be turned out nightly with no places to which their small means would admit them, or which their unfamiliarity with the city would enable them to patronize with safety. There are few places to which an employee can go for one or two nights, if she is suddenly turned away by an irate mistress, or leaves in anger. Municipal lodging-houses do not meet the need, for they are open to all women without discrimination, and the working girl temporarily out of employment needs something besides a "one night hang-out." In the reorganization of the American employment agency system, so imperatively needed, some provision will have to be made, both as a business matter and as a matter of common humanity, for the housing of domestic servants temporarily out of work.

Unemployment always carries one more danger for women than for men—the danger of being drawn or forced into an immoral life. The connection between intelligence offices and actual immorality is, unfortunately, not to be doubted. The situation has been greatly improved of late, owing to the passage of stringent laws, and the Federal white slave act. Yet even carefully drawn laws are of little avail; in New Jersey, for instance, the State Immigration Commission reported in the spring of 1914 that it found a large proportion of agencies willing to send girls to disorderly houses as servants, or to furnish them as inmates.

Indeed the business methods, the surroundings, and the frauds that have been described pale into insignificance beside the conscious, deliberate immorality of many offices and the traps which they set for their unwary and helpless victims. The bare fact is that while advertising honest work and while furnishing it to some, many agencies also degrade, debase, and ruin others, and later cast them out moral and physical wrecks. Not only are they robbed of their small earnings, herded like animals, and subjected to many indignities by proprietors, but they must submit to

15

association with and temptation by street-walkers and immoral men; not only must they lodge under conditions which rob them of their self-respect, but unsuspectingly they are sold into disreputable houses and held as prisoners.

It is no exaggeration to say that in many of the large centres, some agencies are not averse to sending women as employees to questionable places; a smaller number send them as inmates, obtaining their consent when possible. The best offices are so ignorant of the extent of this practice that when called upon to coöperate in reform measures, they refused to believe the charges until the contracts and affidavits were shown to them. Some offices, bearing every evidence of poverty, have insisted they would starve rather than furnish such houses, and have actually "kicked out" applicants for inmates for questionable houses. There is no question so pertinent among employers as, "Why cannot we secure servants?" The fact that offices receive from five dollars upward for girls furnished to disreputable houses, because the demand from these establishments is so great, and the evidence that many thousands of women are annually sent to these houses, supply one answer to this question.

No peonage among immigrant men is more binding than the slavery of the immigrant girl whose passage is prepaid by the office, or who comes from the country in answer to an advertisement and who is met by a runner—the essential factor in the system. One case typifies thousands. A country girl arrives in a city like Chicago, or a woman who does not know one word of English lands in complex, bewildering New York, straight from a peasant's home in Russia, Hungary, or Sweden. She comes consigned to friends or relatives whom the runner knows, and so he meets her with messages from them and wins her trust by his helpfulness. From that moment she is helpless. Her baggage is sent to the office or to a boarding-house in collusion with it, and there it is held, upon one pretext or another, if the girl shows any disposition to leave. The baggage of girls rescued from these places has sometimes been obtained only by a show of force or by the payment of pre-posterous charges for board and storage. Day by day the girl is paraded before employers; she goes out only under the strictest surveillance. After she is engaged and the fee is paid, the runner, still her faithful attendant, takes her to a new home. Not for one brief moment is she allowed to go to any place or to see any one without his approval. If she has fears she can tell no one, and too often she is sent to a place where all ears are deaf.

The methods used to secure girls for negro offices are equally shameful; where they are sent North by white agents the same system of slavery exists as in the case of immigrants, for the girls are met at the station or the wharf and kept at the offices until sold. They are often threatened until they accept positions in questionable places, and are frequently sent out without knowing the character of their destination. These negro girls are utterly unfitted to meet the conditions of a great city, for they usually have no friend but the employment agent.

As evidence of where some of them go, the superintendent of the Bedford Reformatory says: "Almost without exception the negro girls at my institution have been brought North by some employment agency." Unlike the white offices, the negro offices really believe they are bettering the conditions of these girls by giving them city life and advantages and the opportunity to mingle with whites.

Some offices advertised by prominent and alluring signs are simply disorderly houses, and the signs are used as a blind or ruse to attract girls. They are run chiefly in the daytime, lest at night they create suspicion. In some the girls are simply inmates under a proprietor who is in reality the madam; in others rooms are rented to the girls who pay a good price, and they can receive any one they wish or whom the madam sends. Girls out of work are induced to accept lodging in these by promises of employment. Sometimes offices are not disreputable houses, but permit street-walkers to lodge there and influence other lodgers. Other offices run their own mountain, seashore, and suburban disorderly houses and actually imprison girls who are unwilling to stay. One office sent three girls up to its own mountain house, assuring them they were going to take positions in a summer hotel. When they arrived they found themselves not only in a disreputable house, but prisoners. One of the girls made so much disturbance by crying and attempting to escape that the keeper beat her and threw her out. She was taken to a hospital, insane from her treatment and from fright. She died there, and a few days later another of the three escaped, also insane. The relatives, ignorant and poor, were powerless. They complained to the office-keeper, who insulted them and said: "The girls ask to be sent there and then make trouble." Their defense is always, "The girl went willingly."

Many offices that will not send a girl outright encourage and allow street-walkers and solicitors to frequent their offices, receiving from them gifts and large fees. They mingle with the girls, invite them out to lunch, make them presents, and induce them to accompany them to their homes. These painted, powdered, silk-gowned, jewelry-bedecked women are seen mingling with the bare-headed, booted peasants. They go out for walks in the parks and finally disappear with the girl and her little bundle. Still others refuse to send girls, but will refer employers to other offices which cater to this trade, thus assisting such work if not actually engaging in it.

Negro offices are so hopelessly immoral that some city authorities think it is useless to disturb them and argue that they do not affect the whites.

As a matter of fact they do, for some of their best patrons are whites, and they have many white girls. One white girl in Philadelphia was taken to an intelligence office by the colored cook in the house where she was holding her first position. She was told that the only position open was in a sporting house, where she need do nothing but have a good time and make money. Upon refusal, she was told she could go there and see how the white ladies fared, and if she did not change her mind it would not hurt her, and she could then go to another office and get a slave's job. They said they were "only sorry for poor white girls and tried to put them in the way of a good time." The negroes are not only more indifferent about the kind of place, but say frankly that they prefer to send girls to sporting houses. Negro offices supplying inmates for disorderly houses reflect the current thought among many city negroes that immorality between negroes and whites is a mark of distinction and is to be encouraged. So long as this is true, something more than legislation and inspection is required.

A far more insidious practice, and more difficult to remedy, is sending women to disorderly houses not as inmates but as employees. This means that the office, when challenged, has always a defense. Women, not all of them immoral, ask for such work because the duties are light and the pay better than in private houses. The office sends them willingly, the object often being through this gradual means to induce them to become inmates. One girl, whose case is typical, took a position as an employee in such a house. For a few days she was permitted to do her housework unmolested. She noticed that there were other girls in the house and many men, but was not suspicious. On the third day the mistress asked her to wear clothing more suitable to the house, saying: "You have worked long enough in street clothes and there are many men callers whom you must help entertain." No attempt was made to keep her when she declared that she would leave. Many agencies, even the best, fill applications from these houses and allege that women sent as employees are in no danger. But the life in such a house must either repel or tempt them to earn money more quickly and by less honest means than housework. The constant hammering upon their sensibilities by the things with which they come into contact must harden them, and they are continually exposed to persuasion. Even the more conscientious of the negro offices do not consider it wrong to send a girl into these places as an employee, although they acknowledge she may become both immoral and intemperate.

The connection between intelligence offices and disreputable houses will exist so long as the demand of these houses exceeds the supply and offices furnish convenient supply stations, and so long as the laws are inadequate and there is a "let-alone"

policy, for the chief aim of most cities where there
is regulation is to collect the license fee.   Even a
slight enforcement of law improves conditions.
Whenever an arrest is made or an office has trouble,
the others say for a while, "We must be careful";
"We are watched"; and "Our patrons must wait."
If the trouble lasted, many patrons would always wait.   Too much reliance has been placed
upon the free public agency to correct these
evils.

The work of intelligence offices must be considered from another point: the effect upon the
employer and her home.   Can employers afford
to accept household workers who come from such
dirty, disease-laden, vermin-infested, and immoral
places as many of these offices and lodging-houses
are?   Can they afford to accept women who associate with street-walkers and spend part of their
time in disreputable houses?   The employer may
get an employee from a good office, but she can
never be sure that she has not been the rounds.
Some girls would scorn an immigrant office, but
it must be remembered that the fashionable offices
supply the fashionable disreputable house, and
while the deterioration may be slower, it is equally
sure.   Certainly the grade of women in household
work can never be markedly raised so long as
workers are recruited from such sources.   That
these women take housework only when nothing
else offers is further shown by the fact that eighty
per cent. of the inmates of the workhouse on Black-

well's Island claim this, saying: "Oh, we do this when we are up against everything else."

The homes of America need the private intelligence office because of the personal interest which must be taken in the work under present conditions and because women workers need greater protection in this field. Their number can be reduced fifty per cent. without impairing their efficiency, and so long as the cut-throat competition continues they will be neither efficient nor reliable. They must be standardized and the dishonest, inefficient, and exploiting agents driven out. A few of these impair the integrity of the whole business, and the reputation of private employment agents cannot rise above them. The attitude of the public is that they are a necessary evil.

There stands out a small body of agents struggling desperately to give some of their own integrity and standards to the business and suffering hardships in their attempts. But they do not organize, they do not combine, they do not study the situation: they do not fight the foes of decency and the exploiters within their own ranks. When one is exposed, they defend themselves rather than aid the prosecution of those who bring into disrepute the whole business. The world knows the employment agent chiefly by the stories of exploitation in the newspapers. The agent who cares for the homeless, feeds the starving, comforts the discouraged, nurses the sick, and is first friend to the down and out man and woman and never has a complaint against her remains unknown. This must be so until these leaders arise and head a movement which will support fair legislation, devise and insist upon business standards, and develop coöperation among themselves. Suspicion, greed, and individualism block the way, and when government has found the way it will be too late, for even regular business to play any important part in the distribution of labor throughout this country.

To make intelligence offices efficient, clean, and reliable public service bureaus, foreign countries must coöperate and know more of the places to which their immigrants are going; cities and towns must watch to see who engage them and where they go in the city, and public opinion and patrons must insist upon honest work from every office. The employees must be given protection in looking for honest employment, and it must be assumed that they seek this. Those who prefer work in disreputable houses do not need an office, protected by a license from the city, to help them.

There is no evidence that intelligence offices as a class realize the crisis that they are facing in their business. They coöperate only to defeat legislation, combine only to combat public opinion, adopt new methods and honest policies only to increase profits. Such an unenlightened policy means self-destruction. One state has already passed a law prohibiting all fees within the state; regulations are becoming more stringent and free public agencies are multiplying.

Measures of relief for unemployed working women will be worked out through reaction against exploitation and extortion, through repression and regulation, through bitterness and hatred, because the business itself is doing nothing to establish standards, afford protection, develop efficiency or consider itself a public service amenable to public demands. Education seems possible only through regulation and it is to this method that government must sternly set its hand.

CHAPTER VIII

THE MARKETING OF SKILLED LABOR

NOWHERE is the consciousness of class more clearly defined than between skilled and unskilled labor in the labor market. A small degree of training or preparation, of skill or of experience bring the unemployed into a realm of exchange very different from that of unskilled labor. The differences between the agencies for skilled and unskilled labor are indeed so great that in some states the former have asked for separate legislation, establishing their status upon a different plane.

Skilled labor is marketed in three ways: in the organized trades, by trade unions, by employers' associations or directly by individual employers and employees. Organized workmen of course resort to other agencies, but these handle most of them, especially artisans.

Women being mostly unorganized find themselves in the hands of the private agency, but it is the private agency with standards, equipment, system, and with machinery for interstate distribution. These include agencies for teachers, librarians, nurses, theatrical performers, and office assistants, as clerks, stenographers, etc.

Competing with these to a considerable extent within the past few years are schools and institutions. The former include colleges, high schools and special schools endeavoring to place their students, and the latter such institutions as hospitals that concern themselves with the placement of nurses, etc.

Keen rivalry exists among these different agencies which have little coöperation with one another, with the result that the employee is frequently registered in all of them, paying numerous fees while employers are bombarded with requests from all of them, often for the same employee.

In the organized trades, one of the most important services rendered by unions is notifying members of opportunities for work. This phase of trade union service, however, has not received the attention it merits nor have the resources of such unions ever been developed to their full power. Local unions are often fairly effective in local work, but no widespread system of exchanging information or of distributing workmen from point to point has been undertaken by the various unions. Some of the unions have rendered excellent service by reporting unemployment and at least one state, New York, is dependent upon them for its statistics upon unemployment among skilled workmen.

Curiously enough, although skilled laborers are so much exploited by private agencies which are so frequently the base of operations in movements to secure strikebreakers, organized labor has been slow to initiate laws regulating such agencies or to compete with them effectively or to further the extension of government agencies. It is true that the unions have had a stupendous task facing them in the matter of hours, wages, and living conditions, but it would seem that they can delay little longer in the support of comprehensive and intelligent measures dealing with unemployment.

Where trade union organizations have attained sufficient power to compel the dependence of employers upon them, the employment work is on a sound basis; in other unions it is more or less incidental, being considered in many instances only an accommodation to members. Some unions have no employment bureaus at all; others have only a secretary who receives applications for workmen. The status of the unemployment work of trade unions is perhaps typically indicated by the findings of the Chicago Unemployment Commission. Of twenty-nine unions reporting, ten had employment bureaus. In one of these, manifestly a powerful union, a member was not allowed to look for work himself. Some powerful unions, including those among workers in the building trades, printers, firemen and engineers, and brewery workers have trade agreements whereby the unions agree to furnish men needed by contractors. Many of these contracts provide for the employment of non-union men if the unions are unable to furnish the men needed. It is an interesting commentary upon the attitude of organized labor toward the labor market that although it will insist upon the enforcement of alien labor laws forbidding aliens to work upon public contracts, it has few facilities for filling the places of the men so dismissed, and has opposed public agencies for unskilled workmen.

Since the activities of the bureaus of different unions vary so widely, it is to be expected that their methods will also differ greatly. These are, in general, haphazard. Often the employment work consists simply in having a loafing room at the union headquarters where the unemployed men come to play games and wait for telephone calls for workers. Some unions have bulletin boards on which jobs are posted, any men that wish being free to apply. Others have blackboards on which men write their names in the order in which they come in, and they are given opportunities in the same order. The standards by which candidates are selected by union bureaus, when they are selected at all, are chiefly seniority, priority of application, length of time out of work, and, finally, fitness.

Much of the efficiency of a trade union bureau depends on the initiative of the business agent, who may exercise a great deal of power. Since in most unions there is no well organized method of learning of positions, selecting applicants or keeping records, the business agent is really the important factor in the work. This necessarily localizes the employment work. Some unions attempt inter-communal work and issue weekly or monthly bulletins as to employment conditions in various places. Some have travelling members and provide for communication between secretaries in various places. Others go so far as to advance travelling expenses where positions are distant. In general, however, the work is local. An exception seems to exist in the seamen's union bureaus along the great lakes and seaboards. Once each week reports are exchanged among all union offices, as to the number of idle men, the chances for work, etc., so that the men may be more evenly distributed. When a number of men are needed suddenly and are not available locally, they are sent by the union from the nearest port. This situation is interesting in connection with the possibility and the problems of organizing casual laborers generally. In the Convention of 1913 Mr. Gompers urged that the American Federation of Labor should form a Department of Migratory Labor and organize under its control a system of employment agencies. This would seem to be the next most important matter before the trade union, but its success is somewhat dependent upon a more effective organization of the local work. It has not, as yet, received much support.

Employers, on their part, except along professional lines, have not permitted private agencies to monopolize the labor market. In view of the activity of private agencies, it is astonishing how few skilled workmen obtain positions through them. The great mass of factory workers, salesmen, and others, obtain their positions directly from employers or through free agencies, conducted by employers' associations. The latter have been developed to relieve their members of the responsibility of carrying on employment work separately and to make them independent of trade union bureaus and of employment agencies generally. They do not usually extend their services to employers outside the association. They are likely to be strongest in places where union organization is weak. In a strong union city like Chicago the bureau of the Chicago Employers' Association, although it receives applications and furnishes men at all times, is active only during strikes. In Detroit, on the other hand, where the unions are not so strong, the Employers' Association places each year from 75,000 to 80,000 wage-earners.

The bureaus of most employers' associations operate locally. The National Founders' Association of Chicago however reports that 95 per cent. of its workmen are sent out of the city. Sometimes local associations operate over wider territories during strikes. Even the most powerful of the local bureaus do not exclude other sources of supply and the members of the association do not depend altogether upon the ministrations of their own bureaus. In Detroit, for instance, the Employers' Association supplies only 52.9 per cent. of the employees engaged by its 190 members. In Providence the Metal Trades Association supplies 41.1 per cent. of the total number of workmen in the various plants; in Indianapolis the Employers' Association in conjunction with the Metal Trades Association supplies 39.8 per cent.

These bureaus investigate applicants carefully and file their records. Trade unions allege that they serve a double purpose, that a workman's pronounced activity in union affairs is sufficient ground for dismissal, and that he is thenceforth blacklisted by members of the employers' association. Unquestionably these employers' agencies are used as recruiting stations during strikes. On the other hand they deny that they discriminate against union men. The following extract from the charter of one of these associations whose chief business is the conduct of an employment bureau is typical:

A free labor bureau established by this association acts upon the fundamental principle that the labor bureaus shall be conducted in a broad and impartial manner, and shall be neutral ground where the workmen may express their complaints and present any difficulties in which they have been involved with employer or employees, and the employers shall recognize the right of the labor bureau to investigate the complaint. It is the aim of the labor bureau to assist in providing employers with satisfactory workmen and the workmen with satisfactory employment. There shall be no agreement to exclude any workman from employment.

Some of these agencies, however, freely admitted that one of their objects was to assist in maintaining an open shop. Bureaus which deny discrimination ask workmen upon application, whether or not they are union men. An instance is recorded of an employers' association which promised no discrimination, but required workmen to hand over their union cards. The union promptly issued duplicate cards to its members. The employers' association then required the men to sign a card "I am" or "I am not" a union man. The union instructed its members to sign "I am not." The employers' association then required men it hired to swear never to join a union so long as they were working in their trade in the localities covered by the association.

Many large firms, corporations, mining companies, etc., have organized their own employment departments with regular agents in charge. These are not to be confused with employers' associations. They have nothing to do with other firms, and coöperate with no other agencies. They have often been established to avoid dissensions between workmen and the foremen, and to discourage rake-offs, commissions, and understandings between foremen who hired men, and the employment agents, and to replace other unsatisfactory practices, such as hiring men at the doors. In one large mining company it was found that workmen not only paid individual foremen for jobs, but paid regular assessments to keep the job and to insure promotions to better jobs. The foremen that employ workmen without any check or supervision may become the greatest foe to security of employment and wield a very arbitrary power over the fortune of employees. Every firm using this method needs to provide a checking system and an easy way for men to present grievances to headquarters, without fear of dismissal. The ideal solution is the employment bureau in the general office of the business under one responsible person.

Government agencies, conducted by the various states and municipalities, are a comparatively negligible factor in the skilled labor market. Whether they will remain so is an open question. Wherever the union is strong, it is the controlling labor agent; where it is weak, the employer and the employers' association are more powerful. So far as the employee is concerned, neither agency is neutral ground; each stipulates conditions; each is antagonistic to the other, and each distrusts the other. The prospective employee is generally a bone of contention between them. Should the skilled labor market be narrowed down to these two contending forces, the employee might have to take sides in order to work at all.

It would seem the part of wisdom therefore that government should be giving some thought to the organization of a neutral ground. While labor and business may be left free to devise methods for placing and obtaining labor, it does not follow that every child beginning work, every employee and every skilled immigrant, for instance, should embrace or renounce unionism as a condition precedent to the right to work. The breaking up of the apprentice system has left a serious gap which has not yet been filled, and it is very doubtful whether either employers or trade union agencies can bridge it to the satisfaction of all concerned.

The professional classes in this country are fast in the grip of private agencies and it is a hard grip because here the agency business is highly organized. The greatest monopoly of all is found in the teachers' agencies, of which about five control the placement of most of the teachers throughout the country. Two conditions in this country favored these agencies until they now seem to be indispensable: the great numbers of young women yearly graduated from normal schools and colleges, trained from the cradle up to the idea of teaching as the one respectable, if not divinely fore-ordained, way for a woman to earn her living or to "bridge the gap" between school life and marriage; and the rapid extension of the public-school system and of the number of private schools and colleges in the more sparsely settled parts of the country. This necessitates distribution of teachers and makes teaching distinctly a migratory profession. Only a favored few can go back to the home town to teach; and in some cities even a beginner in the public schools must have three years' experience,—which she must get somewhere. A candidate has no alternative but to apply to an agency and accept a position, perhaps in a distant state, for $500 or $600, which will give her an opportunity to gain the "experience" demanded.

On the ground that they are not "common employment offices" teachers' agencies for years very generally escaped license fees and regulation, and in some places they still do. As a matter of fact they have all the characteristics of employment agencies as to purpose, organization, and methods.

There are two kinds of fees, collected solely from applicants for positions. The registration fee, usually called a subscription or a "consultation" fee, is rarely less than $2, is frequently $5, is good only for "office services," and is rarely refunded. It is good usually for one year, sometimes for two, and in a few instances is $5 and $10, good for a term of years. "Office services" include only the privileges of enrollment, of visiting the office, and of speaking to the clerks. In no instance is the registration fee considered payment for a position. Many thousands annually pay this fee, receiving only a receipt, and not always that, for it is only through a request for renewal of the fee that some applicants learn that the first payment was received.

Agencies claim that this high registration fee is necessary to keep away undesirable applicants, and to cover the outlay necessary to secure positions. It is not easy to substantiate the first contention because the most undesirable applicants can often best afford such a fee; and as to the matter of outlay, if a registration fee covers all expenses incident to obtaining positions, the large employment fee must be clear profit. There is evidence to show that in this field, as among the unskilled workmen, some teachers' agencies live almost entirely upon registration fees, filling but a few positions each year—just a sufficient number to give them a cover of respectability. Many teachers report: "I paid a registration fee, and never heard from it, except the request for renewal, at the end of the year, when they had 'something in view.'" So long as high registration fees are permitted, agencies will register applicants even when they know from their long waiting lists, or from the qualifications of the applicant, that they cannot offer them positions.

This advance fee is required before any application will be filed. There are other significant conditions. Some of the contracts read: "If a candidate secures a position in any way through us, even if it is one day after the two years expire, he must pay an additional membership fee." One agency charges $3 in the main office and then informs its candidates that it has ten branch offices, and advises them to register in each one, at $1 each, which is a "reduction of $2 from the regular fee." Thus, an agency which advertised that it covered the country required a registration fee of $13 to do it efficiently, as "each agency is independent, and the main office is not entitled to the services of any branch." In another, the charge is a $2 consultation fee for "advice only." In one case, after a teacher had paid this amount she was advised to "try some other line, as the demand for women teachers is very small this year."

Whenever a position is accepted, five per cent., and in a few instances ten per cent., of the entire first year's salary is due the agency. This is payable at once, or one-half at the end of the first month, and the entire sum within two months. It is never refunded, even if the position is lost, although the "agency agrees to use its influence to find another position." This is entirely a matter of its own conscience, however, for the temptation is to favor a new applicant whose percentage fee is not yet collected. There is no power to compel a return of fees, for the applicant has already agreed to these terms in writing. Teachers also pay a percentage on an increase of salary, within an agreed time, usually the first year, though it may occasionally extend to two years. Where board is included as part of the salary it is included in the percentage estimate and is rated at from $200 to $400 per year.

For substitute positions the charge varies from seven to ten per cent. of the wages for the entire time the position is held. Other provisions of contracts which favor the agency include the following: if an applicant has notice of a position not secured through the agency, she is required to return the agency's notice at once with the date of her prior information; otherwise it is understood that the teacher wishes the bureau's coöperation, and will pay the commission, though the agency may subsequently fill the position of which it notified her. If a teacher accepts a position from the agency, and subsequently gets a better one through other means, during the year, she pays a percentage on the increase in wages.

A contract seems to give an agency a lien on a teacher for at least one year, and sometimes for longer. It requires considerable skill to find any rights or protection for the teachers in these contracts. Many of them further require the teacher to give the agency any information about vacancies; "if, by any inadvertence," one contract reads, "a fellow teacher through some other means gets a vacancy existing in the same school, through the neglect of the teacher to notify said agency, she makes herself responsible for five per cent. of the salary of that teacher." Instead of paying a commission for such services, the agency says to the teacher: "For the privilege

of paying us $25 or $50 for a position, you must
also become an unpaid canvasser through whom we
may make other fees." And such an agency never
loses sight of a teacher. It sometimes uses threats
of removal to compel fulfillment of contract, and
when it has secured a teacher a position, and holds
her references, it is in a position to make good any
such threat. A hint of "later information" to a
school board can cause all kinds of trouble.

Teachers have found, when they have secured
positions through friends, that agencies to which
they have long belonged, and from which they
have never heard, suddenly develop a personal
interest, and appear with a chain of events to
show that they are officially responsible for the
position. If a teacher does not notify them that
she has a position they assume that she meant to
pay them; either way, therefore, she is reasonably
sure to pay something.

Most teachers' agencies advertise widely among
school officials and prospective teachers. During
their senior year, college students find their mail
boxes regularly filled with application blanks from
various agencies accompanied by pamphlets giving
a list of positions recently filled by the agency, and,
sometimes, a series of testimonial letters. Sometimes an agency makes a special bid for favor by
offering its services for a year to a particular
graduating class in a particular college, either free
or for twenty-five cents "to cover postage."
Young girls just out of school or college are fre-

quently sent to small schools in remote districts, about which little is known. The effect of such a system of distribution both upon teachers and upon educational standards has not been investigated.

There is no more important public service than that of directing teachers to public and private schools throughout the country. Whether the public school system of this country is content to leave this to a middleman having no connection with educational matters, frequently having little training for this work, is a pertinent question. Is it not possible to find some less wasteful and more efficient method in connection with the Federal Bureau of Education by which there could be a central registry, giving to the schools a better choice and better qualified teachers, and giving teachers more choice of climate, type of community, nature of educational work, etc.? Massachusetts and Minnesota have teachers' bureaus connected with the State Board of Education which charge a fee of $2 and place teachers throughout the school systems of the state. In these experiments lie suggestions for extension of the principle.

Colleges have for years been informal teachers' agencies. The larger colleges by their connections with managers of private schools and public school officials all over the country, and their ability to keep in touch with their alumnæ, often form very satisfactory clearing houses for teachers. More recently the work of finding employment for graduates and for undergraduates in the summer vacations has in most colleges been put upon a definite basis, and the work is now extended beyond teachers' registries. A good deal of the work is temporary in nature, ranging all the way from finding work for students as waitresses in summer hotels to securing them opportunities to aid in researches of various kinds. Many of the men's colleges have well-organized employment departments. The most interesting expression of this movement among women is an agency in New York City supported by nine women's colleges which has for its definite object securing work *other than teaching*. The purpose of this bureau as announced was "to investigate the present conditions of women's work, to *develop* new *opportunities*, and to secure positions for educated women in pursuits other than teaching." Within about twenty-one months the bureau filled over four hundred positions in at least sixty occupations, among which may be mentioned statisticians, investigators, bacteriologists, assistants to interior decorators, managers of employment agencies, farm managers, laundry overseers, interpreters, comptrollers, photographic printers, and —one chaffeuse! A research station is to be a permanent accompaniment of the bureau's work, and it is the aim to have this department endowed and in no sense dependent upon income from fees.

The fees include a $1 fee, payable at registration

and to be deducted from the first commission or returned upon request if no work is found, and a commission amounting to one week's salary; but whenever, in the case of temporary work, the week's salary is larger than 10 per cent. of earnings during the total period of employment only the percentage is collected. At first no fee was charged employers, but beginning last year a fee of $2 was charged in the case of temporary work and $5 in the case of permanent employment.

Among the informally stated conclusions of this bureau are the following: that the non-teaching occupations on the whole offer a better salary standard than does teaching, and advancement to the higher salary grades is more rapid; that college training, in contradicton of the reputed view of the business world, is in demand; *but that some form of supplementary technical training is almost indispensable to the successful placement of the average college graduate.* There is a suggestion that this last need could be met by more carefully planned work in college and by summer work of a more distinctly technical nature. All these recommendations have reference chiefly to the worker. In connection with the business world itself, it is stated that many positions could be more satisfactorily filled if the scope of them were extended, and if there were, so to speak, greater flexibility, more combinations of processes, and a resulting expansion of salaries in the interests of efficient and versatile workers.

The development of library work and training in this country within the last ten or fifteen years has created a labor market for librarians. The more elementary and miscellaneous forms of library work are sometimes handled by mercantile and sometimes by teachers' agencies; but for trained workers the really general and dependable agents are the library training schools. They make scrupulous efforts, in general, to fit the person to the position. They follow up their graduates and develop their opportunities for promotion. There is in existence an Association of Librarians which does some agency work, but as compared with the work of the schools, its activities are unimportant. In the states having library commissions, an interest is frequently taken by them in the placement of librarians through the state. This is notably true in New York, New Jersey, and Wisconsin.

From the point of view of the public or of the employer, a nurse's work is most frequently emergency work, and the call for workers admits of little delay. A telephone call and a few hours' waiting are the maximum trouble to which employers are willing to be put. From the point of view of the nurse herself a central registry is important. She is really "casual labor," and has little more opportunity than the ordinary casual laborer to control her own labor market. There are nurses' clubs which maintain free registries, and hospitals often secure engagements for their graduates, especially in the three months following graduation. Aside from these, there is a considerable number of nurses' agencies in all cities. They are usually run by private individuals in their homes. The only requisites are a license and a telephone, the former being not always required.

Registries are usually open to all types of nurses: the registered or hospital graduate; undergraduates, or those that have had some training; and practical nurses, or "handy women in sickness," having no hospital training but not averse as a rule to helping with the household work. The wages of these classes differ greatly; in New York City the graduate nurse's wages are now $28 a week, those of the undergraduate from $15 to $18, and those of practical nurses even less. Under the employment agency law in New York the nurses' registries may charge ten per cent. of the wages received, and this is the usual rate, sometimes with a registration fee in addition.[1] The agencies as a rule regard this commission as low, and those that maintain dormitories for nurses—a usual situation, due to the fact that many of the applicants have not homes in the city, often make large profits from their room rents. The usual charge is from $15 to $20 a month, without board. The rent continues when the nurse is on a case, even when her bed is occupied by another nurse.

In this way a room sometimes brings in $40 a

[1] Report of Commissioner of Licenses, 1913, p. 18.

month. The food, where board is supplied, is reported by nurses to be bad and expensive. This is the feature of the agencies most severely criticized by nurses.

Few professions need more urgently than nursing a better organization of their labor market, in an effective central registry system. The members of the large training schools in the city hospitals are very generally young and unsophisticated girls from small towns or remote sections of the country. Most of them, it seems, are entirely dependent upon their own resources. The strenuousness and the confining nature of their work during the three years of their training prevent them from learning the city, and peculiarly limit their *general* development in knowledge of the world, or in knowledge of even the general conditions in their own profession. If they want institutional positions, most of them have no idea where to apply, no conception of the range of the institutions throughout the country. Few adult workers are as little equipped to deal with employment conditions as are most of the graduates of the average training class; and this in spite of the fact that they have established their efficiency by practical experience.

In small towns, nurses are usually supplied by the domestic employment agencies or neighboring hospitals. The matter of supplying nurse-girls or attendants is usually met by local agencies, and is a subject much in need of investigation. It has long escaped the attention of truancy officers and child labor committees.

The business of supplying "artists" for the theaters is confined to a few large cities. In New York City alone in 1912–13, 112,900 contracts were approved by the Bureau of Licenses. The organization of vaudeville and moving-picture circuits has placed the theatrical business on a basis that is really national in scope. Many agencies not only secure the initial position for vaudeville performers, but have entire charge of the act during the season, and keep it moving from one to another of a chain of theaters, all of which are entirely in the hands of the agents. Probably no other employment agents have so arbitrary a power as the theatrical agents in the large vaudeville employment companies. It is left to them to inspect the act, to determine its worth, and to place it with reference to the desires of particular communities.

One such large agency, doing an interstate business with 147 theaters, rents three floors of a large office building at $5000 each, and in general is equipped and operated on a large scale throughout. To offset this, the "equipment" of a number of agencies in the large cities of the country is found to consist of a wooden bench, a table and telephone, and a printed name on a ground-glass door. The agents in charge of these are opportunists, who take advantage of the miscellaneousness of the theatrical business and the glamour of the stage which draws thousands of young people yearly from distant towns and villages.

The theatrical agency business now has very little to do with regular dramatic performers, and it is coming to have even less. Moving-picture actors also are as a rule engaged by employers directly. To vaudevilles and cabarets, however, agencies are indispensable, and in many instances constitute a necessary evil.

The usual fee allowed to theatrical agents is five per cent. of the salary for which the engagement calls. But, as a matter of fact, in New York City, where three-fourths of the theatrical engagements are made, what is referred to by performers as the "ten per cent. rake-off" is far more usual. The reason for this is that the five per cent. fees are collected by two sets of agents, only one of which, however, operates under the name of agent, and thus comes within the provisions of the employment agency law. The two-agent system is really the result of the performers' own protest against the agents selected by managers. The performers, not seeing their way clear to trusting their interests in the same hands, have insisted upon having their own agents who will protect their salaries. The manager's agent, having the strategic position, is able to collect his fee first; he insists upon the five per cent. allowed by law, refusing to acknowledge the claim of the performers' agent to the 2½ per cent. which the law allows to joint agents. In order to collect their fees, therefore, performers' agents have resorted to a simple expedient: they have constituted themselves business managers for performers, or "producers." They thus become principals, outside the scope of the agency law. The result of this in New York has been that while in 1911 there were[1] 158 theatrical agents under the supervision of the Commissioner of Licenses, in 1913 there were 69. The explanation of these figures is certainly not a decline in the booking business. Agents have simply become producers. The Commissioner of Licenses in New York City estimates that vaudeville performers pay to licensed agents about $500,000 a year in commissions, and about $300,000 to "producers."[1]

Whether he is dealing with one agent or with two, the performer is always at somebody's mercy. Even if other arrangements are satisfactory, he has often to bear in mind a clause in his contract that "the manager may terminate the contract if the act is unsatisfactory." He has no opportunity to judge for himself as to the employer's good faith or financial responsibility. It is true that in New York State the law requires agents to keep on file and exhibit statements signed and sworn to by them setting forth the facts as known to them about the responsibility and standing of each employer. But the employers of cabaret per-

[1] Report of Commissioner of Licenses, New York City, 1913, p. 11.

formers, for instance, usually restaurant and hotel-
keepers, are not likely to support very vigorously
investigations into their financial responsibility.
The success of some agents is dependent on keeping the market constantly in motion.   Some, by
getting applicants jobs and then charging illegal
percentages of salary, leave the performer so
impoverished that he soon abandons the job.
Recruits, constantly secured by rather extensive
advertising in Western and out-of-town papers,
become their successors.   In New York City every
year "roof gardens" are begun by speculators
entirely without capital.   They invite beginners to
make "three-night tryouts," at the end of which
time, the assumption is that the proper selections
will be made.   But it is possible to get many sets of
eager beginners, and thus to defer selections rather
indefinitely.   The agent that sends the performers
well knows that the discarded beginners are likely
to be too much engrossed by their own troubles to
demand legal redress, if indeed they know that
redress is possible.

Sometimes in the theatrical business the functions of agent and producers are really, as well as
apparently, merged, not always with the consent
of the law.   A. B. tells this experience:

I applied at L——'s theatrical agency for a job.
They asked me what I could do.   I told them I was a
Jewish comedian and wanted a partner.   They said,
"All right, we'll give you a contract and come around

to-morrow at four and we'll have a partner for you."
So I filled out a contract and they charged me 50 cents
for the typewriting. The next day I came around and
found a partner waiting. He didn't know a thing
about acting, but he'd also asked for a job as a partner
so they hitched him to me. He also paid 50 cents for
typewriting the contract. Well, they gave us an act.
It was the oldest, worst act you ever saw. Anyhow,
we bought our costumes—yes, we paid for them ourselves—and then they rehearsed us a couple of times.
They charged us each $5 for the coaching, and said
it had to pay for the hall. Then they gave us a tryout
at the Savoy. The house belonged to L—— and he'd
sit in a box and direct the hissing and applause. Our
act got over in spite of L—— and we expected he'd send
us on a tour of his houses. He was supposed to own
some in Jersey and Pennsylvania. But it wasn't so.
He didn't know what to do with us so he said our act
had to be revised and our costumes fixed over. So we
paid up some more money for the costumes. Then one
day I came around to the office and when I got to the
door I heard some one say, "We want our money back.
If you don't give it to us we'll take it by force." Then
L——'s voice said, "Sh—sh! Not so loud! The
others might hear." Well, shortly after this L——
was put out of business, and we were out of a job.
He's running one again now, but he's got a license.

One reason for the lack of standard and inefficiency in the employment business generally is
that almost anyone can be an agent. In the theatrical business, almost anyone may become an
employer. There are undoubtedly a number of

theatrical agencies operating upon sound business principles, but there are also many others that exercise an arbitrary power over both the professional and human fortunes of their applicants without either the responsibilities or resources commensurate with this power. Organizations of the performers themselves have at times attempted a solution of this situation, but they have not been successful. Some manager with power and insight is needed who will consider the performer before the contract. No uprising among the workers in this most precarious of professions will avail much without some such strong leader.

The furnishing of executive and technical help and especially of stenographers and typewriters to business houses and institutions is done in almost all cities through "mercantile" agencies. To a considerable degree, employers use newspaper advertisements to obtain such help, but since this is a more time-taking process, many employers prefer to delegate the work of "weeding out the undesirables" to outside parties.

A comparatively small class of mercantile agencies confine their work to applicants with a certain standard of skill, able to command in the general market salaries of over $1000 a year. These applicants are likely to be employed when they apply, are frequently sent to places outside the city or state, and are desirous of bettering their opportunities. Agencies that deal with them must in the nature of things make rather careful investigations, and they frequently have solicitors for investigating positions and employees. A typical fee schedule for such agencies is a $2 registration fee, and a commission amounting to ten per cent. of the first month's salary. Some of the positions are permanent. Some agencies simply specialize in this higher grade work, at the same time registering and placing ordinary office help. Others are "distinctly selective," evidently not wishing to have a "mixed reputation" or to have less distinguished candidates seen in their waiting-rooms.

The agencies that supply chiefly stenographers, typewriters, and ordinary clerical assistants are usually in office buildings and have a good business system. Many are, however, run on a rough- and-ready plan, making only superficial investigations, leaving it to the employer to carry the investigation farther if he so desires. He usually does not, leaving it to the applicant to "make good" or not in the day's work. Some of the agencies are for both men and women, others for women only. Of the sixty-three commercial agencies at present licensed in New York City, twenty-two are conducted by women and the majority of applicants for employment are women.

In all of these agencies, where not prohibited by law, a registration fee is charged varying from $1 to $5. In addition to the registration fee there is an employment fee, which is either the entire week's wages, or five per cent. of the first year's salary—whichever the agency prefers. If board is a part of the salary it is included in estimating the commission. Employment fees are not refunded even if a position is lost, and this is a greater hardship than in teachers' agencies, for annual contracts are seldom made.

Some offices, wishing to give the appearance of fairness, charge a large registration fee, and then say they will refund one-half if a position is not secured. Almost any agency could carry on business on these half-fees. Mercantile agencies know the tricks of sending men to places where no work exists, and of clipping advertisements and giving them out as *bona-fide* orders. By their fascinating advertisements, many young men and women are drawn into the city on promises of work, and in some instances, where they have refused to pay registration fees, they have been insolently dismissed.

Agencies which furnish women, especially stenographers and typewriters, are extremely careless where they send them. Many take but little trouble to ascertain if it is a reputable business house or office, and often send employees to places which they know to have bad reputations.

A great many stenographers and typewriters are placed by the employment bureaus maintained chiefly for advertising purposes by large typewriter companies. In New York City in one year about 100,000 candidates are thus placed. These bureaus are rarely licensed because they charge no fee. One advantage to the company is that the girls learn to use their machines, for they are given this opportunity while waiting and are often induced to purchase one, for the agency is usually in the salesroom. One firm insists that applicants placed shall use its machine, while another says in its contract that applicants are expected to notify it of any other vacancy and to recommend the office for repairing machines, etc. As a rule, however, the placement operations of these companies are conducted much more casually, and girls hunting jobs often visit several agencies quite impartially during the day. To be eligible to the waiting benches the girls must pass an examination. The report of 1913 of the Commissioner of Licenses in New York cites the statement of the manager of one of these typewriting companies that only about fifty per cent. of the applicants pass the test and are allowed to wait for calls. On the other hand stenographers state that they have never seen anyone rejected for failure to pass it. Those that have passed it once apparently never need to take it again, although they may not have kept up their typewriting and stenography at all during the intervals between their various applications.

The agent comes into the room and calls out the jobs, and the girls bid for them. If a girl takes a job and fails either to give satisfaction or fails to be satisfied herself she simply returns to the waiting-room the next day. No questions are asked. Several of the typewriter firms in New York City, notwithstanding the great number of placements, are considering giving up their agencies because of the expense and the general dissatisfaction with which they are regarded. Naturally enough, however, no one company is willing to start such a movement until it is known that the others will follow suit.

In this same class fall business colleges and institutes which conduct employment departments. Many such "colleges" prevent their pupils from falling into the hands of unscrupulous agencies. But unfortunately there are some who use the promise of employment to increase their roll, with the result that many are trained for business careers when they should be in kitchens and shops. Consequently, both employer and employee suffer. Sometimes in the rush season of big houses these colleges hurriedly train large numbers of pupils whom they attract by promises of work. The students are employed by these houses for only a few weeks, and after they have paid their money for tuition they often cannot get positions elsewhere. A few give the pupils experience in business houses while in training. Many business men look with favor upon reliable colleges, as they are a responsible reference. But such methods as advertising, "Special—Wanted, 100 men to fill our orders with downtown business houses," and then requiring applicants to take at least a month's training, regardless of previous qualifications, lay the agent open to the charge of making misleading statements, and holding out false promises.

A very usual complaint against business colleges on the part of business men is that they have no entrance requirements and that they open their courses to anyone that has the money. Hardly a town in the country is without its business "Institute," and within the last few years there has been a startling increase in the number of business schools whose pupils seem to be children in pigtails and short trousers recruited from public schools sometimes before they reach and usually before they finish the high school course. They can be taught the conventional spelling lists, to write notes accompanying the shipment of goods as "per your order," etc., and to attain respectable speed in typing and note-taking. But their business training has been in the nature of specific coaching and cramming rather than of training for responsible business positions. These schools are looked upon by many parents as a direct and practical answer to boys' and girls' lack of adaptation to school work. In many cases the boys and girls themselves have no particular interest in going. In other cases, the children seize upon it as a direct means of realizing their ambition to become wage-earners and contribute to the family income. The better class of business school has found four years by no means too long to supply training to pupils who at entrance have reached only the beginning of the high school course. Yet many schools offer courses of almost any length ranging from a few weeks to years, some of them even offering the seductive bait of "summer secretarial courses" covering a few weeks.

There is no branch of business which shows more enterprise and ingenuity than American newspapers. Some of them have proved themselves expert in the matter of securing advertisements. Few of them have paid attention to either organizing or safeguarding that part of the labor market which they handle. The post-office system of newspapers is the most wasteful and inefficient service in existence. Advertisements offering one job are answered by hundreds many days after their publication. Advertisers are not explicit in stating their requirements and the hundreds include the unfit as well as the fit, for hungry men and women out of work picture themselves as able to fill any job within their range of capabilities. Could newspapers know the thousands of miles men and women tramp uselessly and the hundreds of "last cents" expended upon the trail they lay daily, it would stimulate them to some means of organizing that end of the market. A few newspapers have attempted this by having employment bureaus which investigate the applications and handle the replies. These have been eminently satisfactory but not highly lucrative.

There has never been coöperation between the

real centers of employment and the newspapers. The only solution for the present waste and dishonesty is for each newspaper to conduct its own registry bureau from which all answers to advertisements can be cleared and in which will be kept a record of the positions filled or vacant. Such a registry should be an information bureau only and not the mediator between employer and employee nor the dispenser of jobs. There must come an end to miscellaneous haphazard advertising just as there must come an end to thousands of employment centers having no interest in each other, or in the general labor market.

The skilled labor market is primarily the province for business and labor to organize. Regulations and public agencies can do little more at this time than to educate, stimulate, and supplement such activities. It has infinitely more cross currents and undercurrents than the unskilled labor market; it must be the subject of conferences and of patient attempts to gather facts and to bring about understandings before any broad national action can be inaugurated.

CHAPTER IX

IT has been the firm belief of many who have attempted to relieve the hard lot of the unemployed that the establishment of philanthropic agencies would solve the problem, by substitution or competition. Whenever conditions have become intolerable and exploitation ·has pressed hardest, and suffering has reached the social surface, the community's response has been a new committee or bureau or experiment. As these spring up spontaneously or center about some leader of the moment, they are rarely constructive and many of them temporarily add to the chaos and to the duplication of effort, constituting an additional drain upon already over-taxed contributors.

The critical industrial period of the winter of 1913–14 brought forth the Religious Citizenship League as the result of the I. W. W. invasion of the churches; and the Conference on Unemployment among Women as the result of the mass meeting of unemployed women. The European War has multiplied the committees and organizations, some dealing with relief and others with employment, while some of the women's organizations, as the Vacation Committee of New York City, which has formed a Vacation War Relief Work Committee, the Emergency Aid Committee of Philadelphia, the Buffalo Red Cross War Relief Committee, the Women's Club of Chicago and a similar organization in Cincinnati, have very cleverly combined furnishing work and relief, by operating sewing-rooms for making war supplies. These are being started throughout the country and are relieving thousands of workers. It is difficult, of course, to secure the necessary funds for wages and materials. Among the men, no such practical remedy has been devised.

Since such movements have no place in the organized business system, it follows that the results must be and are pitifully small. Where one woman is reached hundreds go unaided. There is, however, the larger possibility that these movements will stimulate public interest and sympathy, and will open the hearts and minds of those needing no jobs to those that do need them. All of them are typically emergency measures, urgently necessary at times, certainly at the present time. But what is the vital relation of such movements to the *industrial* problem of unemployment? Do they help the employer to see and shoulder his own burden or does he lay it more lightly aside with his contribution and shorten seasons and retrench unnecessarily? Do the employment bureaus starting up here and there in response to

evidences of unusual stress lessen the burden upon
the unemployed or do they constitute one more
center upon which to spend car fare and fix
hope? Do they tend toward concentration of the
problem, economy of administration, and coöperation, or do they diffuse interest and focus effort
upon a new but futile point? Have they any
real comprehension of the problems, or do they
confound industrial and relief principles and policies? Do they strengthen or weaken government
responsibility?

There seems to be no doubt that philanthropic
organizations have a very broad field for their
efforts, but that they have also clearly defined
limitations. The field unquestionably at the
present time includes *every form of employment
work which has a relief aspect*, whether it be to
maintain unemployables, aid the handicapped who
require special services, or assist in restoring the
temporarily disabled person to the normal industrial field. It is also agreed that philanthropy must
support that pioneer work in unemployment which
includes the researches necessary to induce government, labor, and industry to assume their respective
shares of the solution of this problem. To what
extent philanthropy shall undertake to find work
for normal capable workers is debatable.

The organizations now occupying this field include racial, religious, charitable, and civic bodies.
Their work is based upon the special needs of
individuals, the fees being a secondary considera-

tion, since the organizations are rarely self-supporting or attempt to become so. Typical of the immigration group are immigration societies and homes, guide and transfer organizations, societies for the protection of women, and fraternal societies. The work of some of these organizations is considered so important that they receive subsidies from the home government, as in the case of the Italian Immigration Society in New York City. These have, of course, been largely handicapped since the war, leaving the alien unemployed even more helpless than they were before.

The most important of these racial societies are the immigrant homes under the direction of committees and frequently supported by churches. They have agents or missionaries at the most important ports, they lodge and protect immigrants intrusted to their care, and they usually have employment departments. They are also social centers. One has a mid-week and Sunday meeting to which all girls holding places are invited to come, and where they are urged to spend their evenings. Girls who are not ill enough to go to a hospital may come there and rest. Fifty cents a day is the charge for immigrants, and this includes board and lodging, storage of baggage, and the privilege of the laundry. In many instances the payment is not insisted upon, but girls are expected to pay it when able. In some other homes the charges are higher, and in one the rates are as high as $1.50 per day. There is no fee charged for positions as a rule. These homes require references from employers. Those signed by saloon-keepers are not accepted in one such home, and care is taken to protect the girls in all of them. Although established for one nationality, they frequently befriend immigrants of other nationalities.

It is impossible to put into such a brief description of immigrant homes any idea of their value when intelligently and honestly conducted. The helplessness of the unemployed immigrants gave rise to their establishment, and the personal, sympathetic, and friendly work which they do prevents many from going astray and gives them a refuge among strangers.

Some racial societies have become very effective distribution centers upon a broad scale. This has been accomplished by advancing transportation and making small loans, enabling the settler or employer to secure the necessary equipment for his work. The most extensively organized agencies of this kind in this country are the Jewish Agricultural and Industrial Aid Society and the Industrial Removal Office, for Jewish immigrants. The 1913 report of the Industrial Removal Office shows, however, that 72 per cent. of those "removed" during the year had been in New York City over three years. The fundamental activity of the society is rendering financial assistance in the form of loans to immigrant Jewish farmers throughout the United States. In connection with this form of work no effort was made to induce people to leave the city for farms, but in 1908 the society started a Farm Labor Department to secure farm positions for young men. In 1913 it sent 1117 out to work on farms. It has been part of the Farm Agency's work to keep in touch with the men it thus places. The activities of the Industrial Removal Office in shifting workers to more desirable openings elsewhere are marked by an imaginative insight into industrial philosophy and a scientific procedure remarkable in employment activities in America. It takes the whole country for its field, yet keeps its local operations definite. The largeness of its aim is not jeopardized by vagueness of administration. One of the most satisfying items in the 1913 report of this society is that out of 2473 wage-earners 2283 proved satisfactory. These figures are explained by the methods of the society's work. For every applicant they secure a record which, among other things, includes the language he speaks, his trade here and abroad, his unemployment record in the United States, his earnings, his social status and relatives in New York City and elsewhere in the United States. After a medical examination and a careful investigation of the record of his local conditions as stated by himself, he is sent to his destination where he is met by the local agent of the removal communities and work is found for him. In the whole scheme, the coöperation of interior committees with the home office is manifestly most important.

Not less significant than this distribution is the protection afforded Jewish immigrant girls by the Council of Jewish Women whose volunteer organization at the principal ports and in large cities annually finds employment for thousands of newly arrived immigrants.

In this connection may also be mentioned the Immigrant Guide and Transfer service in New York City which for a small fee delivers immigrants to their destination within the limits of the city, thereby safeguarding them from exploitation upon their arrival. Chicago and other cities which receive large numbers of immigrants also afford some such protection to the alien in transit to his work.

With the exception of the Jewish "Removal" and Agricultural Agency most of this racial employment activity is localized, its support is precarious, and it cannot develop a system which fulfills its promise. We therefore find that some races have excellent organizations in some cities, while others just as much in need have none; that there is, in fact, duplication in some and absence of effort in others; that some centers of comparatively little importance have organizations while more important points are neglected; that efficiency and economy mark the conduct of a bureau in one city while another bureau under the same organization in another city pursues its own course by different methods. There can be no question that at ports of entry and in the large reserve labor cities such organizations do not duplicate work and should be most effective if extended and co-ordinated. They are the only first friends that many aliens have and are the most effective competitors of the padroni. The regret is that they are not yet combined into some national system to protect the unemployed in their search for work across state boundaries and in the small industrial centers and rural communities throughout the country.

The unemployment activities of religious organizations originated in personal service to members of the parish. Their simplest expression is still seen in furnishing sewing to women, handicapped by age, physical disabilities, or home conditions; and their more ambitious accomplishments are the employment bureaus conducted in connection with institutional churches, run upon business principles and a fee basis, and social service committees. There is necessarily the greatest variety in this work. Many agencies are located in the parish or mission house, occasionally in charge of paid workers, but more often under a committee. Some are simply registries where names are left; others have agents in the field looking up patrons. Some limit their work to their own members, others are open to all. Some are for men, others for women, some require references, others do not; some are open for only part of the year. Frequently employment is but a small part

of relief or general welfare work and does not receive any special emphasis.   Most of such churches
maintain employment bureaus just as they maintain libraries and reading-rooms.   They do almost
no aggressive work in the way of advertising or of
studying the market.   Often they act simply as an
additional reference for an applicant, not taking
any very positive step to secure him a job, but
telephoning to a possible prospective employer as
to his capabilities and his need.   In a few instances
they serve in a valuable advisory capacity, furnishing data for civil service examinations, etc.
As a rule, however, they find their employers
chiefly among well-disposed church members.
Cften they do employment work for a special
group.   An instance of this is the association in
Episcopal churches doing missionary work for
wayward girls.   It is a part of the plan to secure
work, usually domestic service, for these and for
unmarried mothers with babies.

A not inconsiderable part of the church employment work is assisting "gentlewomen in
reduced circumstances."   There is no more
difficult task than providing for these helpless
women, who, without experience or the capabilities demanded by the modern industrial
world, find themselves unable to compete in the
regular labor market.   The church bureaus succeed
in this field as no other organization could and
render a most valuable and humane service.
Probably the most effective work among churches

to-day is the unorganized work which is done by deaconesses and visitors who go into neighborhoods and homes and not only find employment for individuals, but help the family in other ways.

Another type of religious organization dealing with employment includes the Volunteers of America and the Salvation Army. No organizations are brought more sharply than these into contact with the needs of their applicants and therefore more directly challenged to find them work. Their employment bureau is necessarily closely related to relief work. They find permanent as well as temporary jobs. They deal with the situation as they find it, by whatever means they can muster. In New York City alone the Salvation Army cares for seven hundred men at a time in its Industrial Homes. They deal with both skilled and unskilled labor, and are much more than a passive medium between men and jobs. The operations of these bureaus have the effectiveness of good intention and vigor but measure up to no conventional business standards. "We get along as best we can," said one manager of the Salvation Army bureau, "and get what fees we can, but never turn anyone away." This is not always true of all of their branches; hundreds of unemployed men have been turned from their doors at midnight with the thermometer at zero, because they did not have twenty cents for a bed when there were vacant beds in the house.

Under the management of religious associations
organized for the purpose, there are various seamen's homes or institutes in the seaport towns
open to the sailors of all nations. These have
shipping bureaus, some of which charge neither
sailors nor shipmasters for services rendered,
others of which charge employers only. One of
them in New York City ships from 1000 to
1200 men each month. In addition to the regular
shipping, temporary employment such as washing
down ships is often secured for the men.

The conditions of the seamen's life make such
employment centers an absolute necessity. Men
flock there for rest and recreation, and lodging can
rarely be given to all that apply. Beds cost from
fifteen to twenty-five cents a night. When a
request comes for men, those that happen to be
lodgers at the time have the first chance. The
bureaus are open to all seamen without discrimination. The only difficulty is that it is impossible
to get shipping for negroes, since ships do not carry
mixed crews. However, the reading-room, bank,
and chapel are open to all. There are special
funds for destitute and needy seamen, and dona-
tions of reading matter, knitted articles, comfort
bags, etc., are being constantly distributed. The
average attendance at one of these is 400 a day,
and jobs are secured for as many as 300 a month.

A summary of the employment work now being
done by churches shows that while the work is
often chiefly relief work and in most cases con-

nected with relief, or limited to a local situation, there is nevertheless discernible an increasing tendency to deal with unemployment as a general economic situation. The most notable illustration is the Inter-Church Committee on Unemployment of the New York City Federation of Churches. This Committee has an active paid secretary and staff engaged in finding out what the thousand churches in the Federation membership are doing, what they can do, and what they will do to meet this problem this winter. It will recommend to each church not only lines of work but standards of work.

Realizing that most churches in the towns and cities of the country will act individually, the Inter-Church Committee has formulated a program as to how individual churches may definitely deal with the unemployment in their communities. Each church is urged to have families or individuals in their church become personally responsible for needy families or individuals, after finding out the need; to print every week an announcement in the church calendar stating specifically that either a special committee or the regular church staff is prepared to serve those who need help, or those who need work, and to receive applications for workers from possible employers, and offers for general relief from any members of the church; to observe "Unemployment Sunday," as early in the winter as possible; to find jobs about the house, which are usually postponed until spring;

to find "left-over" jobs in the office, and to find repair jobs in the church; to urge employers of labor to continue operations as a *religious* duty; to influence employers to give part-time work to all rather than full-time work to a few; to help workingmen maintain a fair standard of wages; to coöperate with school teachers and get in touch with needy people through the public school; to make a supreme effort to assist families as such, keeping father, mother, and children at home; to coöperate with the recognized public and private charities and relief organizations; to provide shelter for the homeless man and woman.

As to the efficiency of church bureaus in finding work for employables, there is considerable difference of opinion. There is a mistaken idea that anyone can run an employment bureau. On the contrary, it requires expert business administration. Employees must be convinced that it is run without fear or favor; employers must be assured that sound business principles prevail in it, and that it has the dependability obtainable only by accurate attention to every significant detail. In few places will general good intention and fervor be less effective than in the management of an employment bureau. If it opens its registration list to all applicants for work, regardless of ability or of handicap, that fact must be made plain to employers. Too often employers patronize them from a sense of duty or of obligation, expecting to get not efficient and steady workers, but cheap help, and prepared to pay only for such. Church organizations, indeed philanthropic agencies in general, are rarely in a position to do any classifying that eliminates the inefficient and the handicapped. The more or less personal relation they usually bear to their applicants often makes it their first responsibility to *do what they can for any individual*, whose need and moral deserts are often much greater than his efficiency and training.

If church organizations and employment committees have in mind the education of their own members, an organized interest in unemployment will serve a valuable end, provided the burden upon the unemployed is not increased by this educational experiment. If, more actively, they have in mind caring for the unemployable as a matter of charity, finding employment for the disabled, the old, the infirm, and the handicapped, here again the churches have a situation with which they can deal very effectively. The field has never been fully covered, and it admits of much organization at the hands of far-sighted men and women.

But if the churches have in mind dealing with unemployment as an industrial matter; if they are to establish employment bureaus for normally capable men and women; if they are to attempt to stimulate employment in semi-paralyzed industrial organizations, and to assume the direction of children into industry, then they will but multiply the agencies of decentralization, retard the effective organization of the labor market, and in their zeal to deal with "cases" will discourage efforts to understand causes and prevent unemployment. We need now not more, but fewer centers of hope; not more stands for the peddling of jobs, but a few large clearing houses; not the competition of an increasing number of small committees and bureaus operating locally, but the coöperation of a few large centers with adequate scope and power. Every new agency opened in a reserve labor center increases the burden to the unemployed, gives them an additional place to call, thereby increasing their chance of missing a job and not increasing in any permanent or material way the volume of employment.

We shall never learn the causes nor adopt preventive measures, and we shall never adequately conserve human resources so long as a multitude of volunteer agencies cover the cost so willingly. It is doubtful whether the personal element which prevails in church agencies offsets the dangers. The normally capable person, willing to work, should be able to market that product through an efficient neutral clearing house which has the coöperation of organized labor and of organized business. The support of such agencies should be a definite charge against industry since they are an essential part of the machinery of production, whether it is collected in the form of taxes for government bureaus, or in standard fees or assessments. The normal laborer marketing his

labor power should be under no more obligations
to a subsidized organization of private individuals
than is the business man marketing his exports or
the farmer his products. If church organizations
would confine their work to relief matters and
throw the weight of their influence toward insisting that industry, labor, and government deal with
all phases of unemployment, except that concerning persons with handicaps not induced by industrial accidents and diseases, much of the confusion
and duplication and waste in the labor market
would disappear, and we should soon be on the
high road to dealing effectively with this problem.

One of the most perplexing of all unemployment
problems is that of placing the handicapped. Nor
is this a small part of the general employment problem, for if there is included under this heading all
those who need to work, but who would, for any
one of a variety of causes, be at a disadvantage
in the general labor market, the handicapped are
very many. Finding work for them may include
furnishing relief or training to meet the particular
disability, placing them in carefully chosen work
in regular industries, or creating special industries
adapted to their needs. All three methods are
being tried at the present time, but from the point
of view of the individual needs rather than of the
problem presented by the handicapped as a group
in the labor market.

Some years ago an employment bureau for the

handicapped, run by the Charity Organization Society in New York City, which has now been discontinued, thus classified 596 applicants for work:

The largest group among the new applicants was of those disabled by some crippling disease, generally rheumatism, numbering 125; 120 were convalescents; 94 were handicapped by age, 56 in the early stage of pulmonary tuberculosis, and 17 more were suffering from other forms of tuberculosis; 25 were partially blind, 2 totally blind; 20 had lost a hand; 17 a foot, and 2 more than one limb; 17 were mentally diseased and 4 were mentally defective; 13 were suffering from nervous diseases and 16 from diseases of the circulatory system; 9 were inebriates and 8 had a criminal record; 4 were defective in speech or hearing and there were 2 epileptics; a miscellaneous group included corpulency, hay fever, cancer, and loss of a singing voice; 4 had become unfitted for their previous employment and were not yet readjusted; and the remaining 33 had more than one handicap.

Among the occupations found for such handicapped persons, this bureau names domestic servants, factory workers, janitors and furnace men, and utility women, country laborers, clerks, porters, watchmen, newsdealers, slot-machine tenders, drivers, elevator and door men, attendants, job carpenters, manicurists, operators, printers, locksmiths, and cutters.

In a recent study of 100 handicapped men and

women in Cincinnati it was found that *less than 7
per cent.* had handicaps which were *obvious*, such
as the loss of a limb or an impaired special sense.
Persons suffering from heart disease constituted
the most numerous class and the rheumatic and
deformed were the second and third largest in
number.[1] Three-fourths of the men were breadwinners and a large percentage had others dependent upon them. Over one-half of them were under
forty-five years of age. It would be interesting
to know how many workers that pass as normal
really have handicaps quite as serious as the
loss of a limb, how many men and women have
bad hearts for instance, and, as a consequence,
fare badly at one kind of work, but do very well at
another. The Cincinnati study suggests possibilities of adjustment never worked out before
or proposed on any extensive scale.

Fitting these men and women into industry at
points where they can be of adequate service, and
where they will not increase their handicaps is no
light task. It involves medical advice, and a
careful study of various industries and processes
to determine their suitability for various kinds of
handicapped persons. And last, but far from
least, employers must be persuaded to give them a
chance to work; most employers need to be convinced that a request to give a handicapped man a

[1] A Study of the Handicapped, by the Council of Social Agencies in Conjunction with the Department of the Handicapped
of the Hospital Social Service Association.

chance in their business is not a plea to "make an exception" and a sacrifice in order to do a good deed. The demonstration that various industrial processes can be satisfactorily managed by handicapped workers, and a survey of the industrial field so that no possibility shall be omitted from the list of available occupations are the first business of the organizations that enter upon this work.

The Cincinnati Bureau has been very successful in this respect, not only in placing a considerable proportion of the handicapped but in the results obtained. Several shoe manufacturers reported that the handicapped workers were doing satisfactory work for them. A maker of automobiles reported that they could use men with one leg in a paint shop; another that he saw "no reason why handicapped men could not become skilled in some branches of motor car manufacturing." And handicapped men were found at work in the manufacture of woodworking machinery, tobacco, and flags, and in printing and lithographing, as well as in offices and factories.

There are other classes of workers that would suffer great hardship and industrial, if not moral, defeat were they to be thrown friendless and alone into the industrial battle which rages in the labor market of great cities. The following illustrate placement work for groups needing special assistance: one organization places unmarried mothers and babies at work in homes so that they may be kept together, and looks after dependent mothers and children, especially deserted wives and families. A study of 370 such women on the West Side of New York City showed that in every case the need to work was imperative. More than half of the women were widowed, deserted, separated from their husbands, or they were wives whose husbands were incapacitated or (a small percentage) idle. Seventy per cent. of the women were engaged in some form of domestic and personal service, chiefly outside the home. "Maintaining the home" for most of them must have been purely a matter of making every cent they could earn, for the women themselves had little time to be at home. Only 23 per cent. of them were in time-restricted industries. Most of them worked a full day from 7:30 A.M. to 6 P.M. A number worked at night from 11 P.M. to 7 A.M. In the 370 families 221 children were below school age. While their mothers were at work a fortunate few were in day nurseries, others were "looked after" by relatives or neighbors. In any large city these unskilled women upon whose work the welfare of the family depends are a considerable number in the general labor market. *There is no agency for many of them.* They hunt their own jobs blindly, depending chiefly on having a friend to say a word for them. Finding work for women in this condition cannot be adequately done by a general employment bureau, and it is doubtful if public agencies can do this work successfully.

Finding suitable employment for wayward girls

is an important need which is being met by probation officers and a very few organizations here and there. Similar work along preventive lines is at least as much needed. When some large department stores closed their doors in New York last winter, many new positions already waited the dismissed girls at the door. The coöperation of other department stores was obtained and they made places for many of the girls. Hitherto it has usually been the exploiter who saw the advantage of first meeting the dismissed girl. A woman's prison association coöperates with a home founded for inebriate women. They are sent there by the prison visitors, and must remain one month without drinking before their pay begins, or before they are placed in households. This agency and home conducts a laundry where the women are employed while on probation. They cannot leave without permission and if they come back intoxicated they are dismissed. The demand for household workers exceeds the supply even at this institution. There are prisoners' aid associations which help men and women discharged or paroled from prison. One other operates widely, covering the middle Western States. Its object is to secure employment for ex-prisoners, acting as a first friend. It extends the advantages of the parole law and the indeterminate sentence. It gets into correspondence with men in prisons and helps them when they are released on parole, and it has representatives who get acquainted with employers

and secure positions, and others who give their
time to investigating cases and looking out for
boys. Its work is peculiarly difficult, for many
employers will not take prisoners. Sometimes
fellow-workers refuse to associate with them, and
policemen report their history and they are discharged. Such associations have well-established
and well-equipped offices, and of course there are
no fees, though men are encouraged to return, when
convenient, the amounts actually expended for
them. A very few philanthropic agencies have
had as their chief object the direction of boys and
girls into industry. One agency in New York City
confines itself entirely to placing boys and girls in
factories, charging a nominal fee. Certain trades
and various processes of factory work are investigated for the purpose of determining their suitability for immature workers, and a certain amount
of "follow-up work" is done.

Interesting in this connection is the work for
children which has grown out of the Juvenile
Court. One such organization now finds positions
for children of both sexes from 14 to 21 years of
age, and most probation officers constitute themselves individual employment centers, realizing
that work is the best guarantee against breaking
parole.

It is impossible to classify all the various kinds
of employment work connected with general relief
or welfare activities. Settlements frequently have
employment agencies which are a very important

factor in neighborhood work. The bureau is usually in charge of one person whose duty it is to take the orders and look up employees. The demands are usually for women to go out for day's work, or as household employees. Many such applicants are placed each year. Some settlement employment departments coöperate with reliable agencies. A few which have large boys' clubs render a notable service in securing work for boys.

It will be observed that the salient features of the general labor market prevail even in the philanthropic employment bureaus. There is little coöperation, competition is keen, and many are interested in making a record or in gathering in their budget. There is at least as much waste and duplication as in the normal field; there is just as much need for system and clearing-house methods. There is less likelihood, however, that these changes will be as speedily accomplished, because of the indifference of both labor and industry to this phase of the work.

The most serious matter for regret, however, is that up to this time it has not been possible to secure coöperation between the various branches of the labor market. Private and public agencies are handling many who should be receiving the special assistance and care of the philanthropic group, thereby imperiling their own reputation for handling efficient workers and jeopardizing the health and working power of the applicants.

Philanthropies are placing workers who belong in the industrial branch and could be placed to much greater advantage by such agencies. It will never be possible to classify the employables and unemployables and the partly employable, a process wholly indispensable in an organized labor market, until some coördination between the two forms of employment activity is secured.

We have thus far been considering agencies which combine relief and employment. Some philanthropic agencies have attempted to eliminate the relief features and establish industrial departments and bureaus upon a competitive basis, with a fee system. The advantages in the competitive market are lower fees made possible by contributions, and a special clientele because of connection with churches, affiliated business concerns, etc.

The most familiar illustrations of this kind of agency are the industrial departments and employment bureaus of the Young Men's Christian Association and Young Women's Christian Association. An important feature of their work is vocational guidance. One manager says:

We do not try to handle the man who is down and out, but pay particular attention to the young man of good character and ability who is just starting his business life and needs help and advice. We only place men who prove to be all right after an investigation as to their character and ability. The business men of

our city call upon the Association for employees,
feeling that we are in touch with a good class of men
and they rely upon us to a large extent as to the
applicant's character and past record. We make a
businesslike arrangement with the young men, expecting them to pay a certain per cent. of their salary,
and while we do not plan to make money out of the
department we feel it should pay its own expenses.

The work of these agencies varies greatly. Some
give shelter and aid to all ages and nationalities,
others direct applicants to a "blue list" of lodging
places, while others accept no applicants unless a
fee is paid, and give no aid whatever. Some of
the Y. W. C. A. agencies do not handle domestic
servants, while others include them. This employment work is becoming a constant feature of
Christian Association work throughout the country, and thousands of young men and women are
placed yearly.

In their potential function of protecting young
workers, these bureaus may rank in importance
and service with immigrant agencies; from the
industrial point of view their importance is not
so clear. While they have greatly increased in
number and in size, the increase in private employment and public agencies has been relatively
greater, and there has been little or no decrease
in the number of padroni and other irresponsible
agents. This is true notwithstanding the fact
that they offer attractions other than employment. To what extent requirement for member-

ship is a help or a hindrance is not apparent. Wherever they have combined industrial training, as in their automobile schools, with employment work, they have supplemented existing agencies, and are making a distinct contribution both to efficiency and to placement.

On the other hand, many workers regard them with suspicion. It is a question whether they have in any way advanced the maintenance of neutrality in the labor market or hastened its organization. The proselyting which is carried on in some of them has created aversion in both business and labor circles. Some of the bureaus, moreover, have been charged with working in the interests of employers, especially where welfare work and educational work have been carried on in industries that also patronized their labor bureaus.

More and more, except in relief matters, public opinion is coming to demand that employment shall not be the bait held out for other activities, or be the tail to the kite of social welfare work, or be considered as a part of social service work, or as a means of increasing membership in organizations. The development of vocational guidance bureaus in the public-school system and of juvenile departments in public bureaus is a concrete expression of this growing belief.

Another experiment, possessing none of these industrial handicaps or social advantages, has recently been tried. This is the National Employment Exchange which has been in operation since

1909. Its purpose is stated as the establishment of

an organization covering all sections of the United States, so that it shall be in immediate and close touch with requirements for labor and employment wherever such exist, but its benefits should accrue primarily to the unemployed of the City of New York.

As yet no branches have been established outside New York City. It was part of the foundation principle of the enterprise to have agents circulating from place to place throughout the country establishing relations with employers, looking after the interests of the men placed, and learning when they would be free from engagements so that they could be transferred immediately to other places where they were needed. These plans could not be carried out at once, but in its development from year to year the scope of the bureau's operations has been gradually greatly widened, until now it covers a very considerable number of states and Porto Rico. Its record of placements on November 1, 1914, was 22,491 men and women. Although it charges fees, $2 for placing common laborers, $3 for mechanics, and the first week's salary, payable within six weeks, for clerks, etc., it has just become self-supporting. The announcement of incorporation contains a statement of the bureau's position as to fees.

In order to insure the success of this undertaking and its permanency, and in order to ultimately occupy a large field in the community, the exchange is to be run as a business and not as a charity. The purpose, however, is usefulness and the motive is philanthropic.

The bureau issues monthly a bulletin for employers which contains all essential facts, except the names, about the candidates it has to recommend at the time. It has a manual labor branch, a general mercantile bureau, and a technical department, which together pretty well cover the industrial field, except unskilled women's labor. It is to be noted that the bureau advertises as an exchange for employers "above the average" and for its mercantile branch adds: "We only list applicants of proved ability and integrity, a majority of whom are not out of work, but holding positions and seeking better opportunities."

There are also a number of civic bodies which while undertaking no actual work in placing unemployed men and women are definitely attacking the problem of unemployment. Since the outbreak of the war, the interest in unemployment on the part of such organizations as city clubs, boards of trade, and chambers of commerce has greatly increased, and has been evidenced by the calling of conferences, the appointment of joint committees in connection with the city council, and in other ways. Organizations like the American Association for Labor Legislation, and the Committee for Immigrants in America have done much by investigations, publications, conferences, and the proposal or stimulation of legislation to create public interest in the subject and to devise practical remedies. In the present crisis many organizations have very naturally concentrated their efforts on emergency measures; but some of them for years past have been working for such policies as state insurance, workmen's compensation, mothers' pensions, minimum wage, etc. Though sensing their own destruction as a result of the very accomplishment of their objects, they have through years been persistent in their efforts in these directions.

A survey of philanthropic agencies and of civic movements for the relief of unemployment shows that these efforts are absolutely essential for purposes of relief and temporary adjustment and for experiments. It also shows the great need of better organization and coördination. It is equally clear, however, that private philanthropic agencies do not succeed as middlemen between employer and employee. The employee distrusts or disparages them and resents charity; the employer expects favoritism or unreasonable service and does not regard them as a wholly businesslike medium. The task before these agencies is to define their field; to remove from the industrial branch all persons needing special service and help, and to turn back to it all other employees. One reason why public bureaus have not been more successful than they have is the lack of coöperation in these respects on the part of the very agencies that secured their establishment.

CHAPTER X

PUBLIC EMPLOYMENT OFFICES

IN the foregoing descriptions of unemployment conditions the twofold nature of the problem has become clear,—the need to conserve labor power by preventing the waste of health, money, time, efficiency, skill, and integrity of workers; and secondly, the need to increase work and thus permit the profitable expenditure of this working power. The first is the province of the labor agency, but beyond this it cannot go—it cannot create work. The second is the province of the employer, whether it be the individual, the state, or the corporation; the man with reserve in the form of capital must, under our prevailing industrial system, create the work.

Public employment offices have been created under a misapprehension on the part of the public that they could create jobs, whereas their general function is to collect and distribute information regarding situations and applicants for work. As a matter of fact, they first came into existence as a protest against the methods of private agencies, which they sought to drive out of business. Then the increasing congestion in cities and the cry of the farmers, especially in the West during harvest time, stimulated their development until now there is a National Division of Information for Immigrants, 20 state bureaus operating in about 50 cities, and at least 21 separate municipal bureaus. As many more cities are also conducting informal or temporary offices.

The Federal government maintains a national employment bureau for immigrants, chiefly farm laborers, known as the Division of Information of the Bureau of Immigration. This was established in July 1, 1907, "to promote a beneficial distribution of aliens admitted into the United States among the several states and territories desiring immigration."

The Division was also authorized to gather from the various state officials and other available sources

useful information regarding the resources, products and physical characteristics of each state and territory, and—publish such information in different languages and distribute the publications among *all admitted aliens who may ask for such information* at the immigrant stations of the United States and to such other persons as may desire the same.

States and territories are also authorized to appoint and maintain agents to represent them at the various immigrant stations and to "have access to aliens who have been admitted to the United States, for the purpose of presenting, either orally or in writing, the special inducements offered by such state or territory to aliens to settle therein."

To carry out the purpose of the law, offices were established at Washington and New York, and the active coöperation of the immigrant stations at Galveston and New Orleans was obtained in the work of distribution and in the direction of men to places of employment. During the fiscal year ended June 30, 1913, 19,891 applications for information were filed, while 5,025 immigrants were actually distributed. During the previous year (1912), 26,213 applications were filed, while 5,807 profited by the information given to the extent of securing definite employment. As men representing groups of from five to fifteen sought this information, the Division assumes that approximately 150,000 persons were benefited by the information given. The report of the Division for 1912 states:

As in former years the Division confined its efforts principally to directing applicants to agricultural opportunities, and the mechanics who applied for information were of the class that prefer to locate in country towns or villages where garden plots larger than the average city affords may be secured. In other words, they were seekers of homes where a plot of ground would aid in adding to the family income or help reduce the cost of living.

The one active office of the Division, the facilities of which are given little publicity and which is scarcely known to the thousands of unemployed, has devoted most of its resources to finding employment for farm and day laborers. In 1913, 1,920 farm and 2,482 day laborers or more than 87 per cent. of the total number sent out were thus distributed. Although the farm and day laborers were only a little more than one-half of the total number who applied for information, those placed in these occupations were about six-sevenths of the total distributed—little assistance having been apparently rendered to the other skilled or unskilled applicants.

Referring to the Division's work in the distribution of farm laborers, the Federal Immigration Commission found that:

The law of 1907 provided for the establishment of a division of information in the Bureau of Immigration the intent being that the division should disseminate among admitted immigrants information relative to opportunities for settlers in sections of the country apart from cities and purely industrial centers. It was hoped that the division could devise means of inaugurating a movement among immigrants which would eventually result in their more equitable distribution. The apparent result, however, does not indicate that the purpose of the law is being fulfilled. As conducted, the work of the division appears to be essentially that of an employment agency whose chief function is supplying individuals to meet individual demands for labor in industrial districts. It does not appear that persons thus distributed have, as a rule, been distributed with the purpose that they would become permanent settlers in the districts to which they went, but rather that a more or less temporary need of the employer and employee was supplied through this agency.[1]

To meet this criticism of its work, the Division in 1912 published bulletins in seven parts for different sections of the country, "giving information concerning opportunities open to those desirous of engaging in agriculture," on the resources, products, and physical characteristics of the various sections of the country.

The Division has had but small appropriations, has been unpopular from the start, and its abolition has been recommended several times. In the fear that immigration would be encouraged and laborers directed to places where there already was an over-supply of labor, its activities have been restricted and hampered. As a result only about 25,000 applicants of the "hundreds of thousands of men who have failed of success in our cities" and who "were brought up on the land" have availed themselves annually of the services of the Division, even though "many of these desire to take up land and are actually land hungry."

The Department of Labor created (March 4, 1913) by departmental order, established eighteen zones on September 1, 1914, "for the purposes of

[1] Report of Federal Immigration Commission, vol. i., p. 40.

facilitating the distribution of farm labor in the United States." The headquarters of the zones thus established are at Boston, Mass., New York City, Philadelphia, Penna., Baltimore, Md., Norfolk, Va., Jacksonville, Fla., New Orleans, La., Galveston, Texas, Cleveland, Ohio, Chicago, Ill., Minneapolis, Minn., St. Louis, Mo., Denver, Colo., Helena, Mont., Seattle, Wash., Portland, Ore., San Francisco, Cal., and Los Angeles, Cal. Each zone has from one to four sub-branches in as many different states—every state thus being represented. These are not yet in active operation and no report can be given on either the scope or the efficiency of the proposed new work. No additional appropriation or authorization has been given for this work.

Numerous attempts have been made to have the Federal government establish employment exchanges to organize the inter-city and interstate labor market along general lines and not merely with respect to immigration; but until this year the opposition of organized labor has made this impossible. Now, however, organized labor is coming to see that the government is more to be trusted than the private employment agent and that the states are not equal to the task.

Three separate propositions are before the government for its consideration at this time: the Murdock bill provides for the establishment of a bureau of employment in the Department of Labor, and, following the Wisconsin law and keeping in mind its signal success, has clothed the director with general powers to develop a system of free public bureaus, to establish labor market reports, to make the necessary investigations and regulations, and to establish an effective bureau of employment.

The MacDonald bill provides for the utilization of post-offices as employment bureaus. It provides briefly that every post-office in the country shall become a labor agency, that every postmaster shall be a labor broker, that the government shall appropriate $2,000,000 for this experiment, that a fee of 50 cents shall be charged for every application, excepting that for those receiving a wage rate of less than $1 per day services shall be free, and that transportation shall be furnished when funds are available. Under this plan 58,000 separate exchanges might be opened. A national employment bulletin is to be issued once a week and sold at ten cents a copy, except where the income of a person seeking employment is less than $1 a day when it shall be furnished free. In point of administration, it is proposed that the country be divided into zones of about 10,000 square miles each with a central post-office in each zone having jurisdiction over all the post-offices in that district. The system is to be under the jurisdiction of an inter-departmental commission of three members, two of whom shall be appointed by the Secretary of Labor and one by the Post-master-General.

20

This bill illustrates the kind of legislation this country may get, in the absence of information upon which to base a wise measure. It shows the dangers of too specific enactment and of imposing upon existing officials a veritable avalanche of unfamiliar business, with decentralized control,— dangers which the Murdock bill specifically avoids.

The success of any national system of employment exchanges depends upon four cardinal principles: (1) the recognition that the peculiar quality of the commodity of labor is not static but active, and that there is no parallel whatever between handling matter that can be sacked and crated, and handling men and women; (2) free service, in order that the agency may compete successfully with the 5000 or more established agencies which command the services of the best specialists in the country; (3) adequate regulation of the interstate business of competing private agencies; (4) a simple, yet thoroughgoing administrative scheme which will enable a highly centralized mechanism to deal effectively with the interstate problems of distribution of labor.

In what respects does the MacDonald bill meet these requirements? First, as to the handling of the labor supply: the appointment of postmasters, while many are in the classified lists, is still largely determined by political considerations; their duties are specified and will necessarily take precedence; the present equipment of post-offices is on the basis of handling matter; the development of the rural-delivery system and parcels-post is designed to diminish rather than to increase the number of people who frequent such offices. The fitness of existing postmasters to handle so difficult a problem as labor and of the present equipment and system to deal with increased numbers of inquiries and frequenters are matters for serious consideration.

The additional duties imposed on postmasters by the bill are to take applications, ascertain opportunities for work, collect fees, and determine whether a person shall pay a fee or be exempt under the $1 clause, post all applications and remove them when the job is filled or the person placed, notify the central office in the zone of all positions open or filled, advance transportation and check baggage to the employer as a guarantee that the man will arrive safely for the fund advanced, collect transportation funds from employers, and write a monthly report. Under this plan, from the central office in the zone each postmaster would receive a mass of reports which would have to be bulletined, and the central office would doubtless report these to all other sections of the country, a process involving additional work. In addition to this, there would be a mass of inquiries by mail dealing with every phase of unemployment, and other subjects closely or remotely related to it. Furthermore, the law provides that transportation shall not be furnished to any person to proceed to any point where a strike is in progress and that an employee shall be notified when a strike is in progress. This provision places upon each postmaster the burden of ascertaining where strikes have been declared, and might draw the whole post-office system into industrial conflict. An additional duty not covered by the bill, but essential if any degree of efficiency is to be attained, would include the keeping of records.

In an interesting interview in the New York *Sun* of July 12, 1914, Congressman MacDonald is quoted as saying:

The post-offices offer easy and immediate means of inter-communication. The importance of this may be illustrated by a parallel. A theater has tickets to sell. They are for sale at a number of different offices, all of which are trying to dispose of the same tickets. It is necessary, obviously, that there shall be prompt and ready communication between the various offices in order that the same seats may not be sold twice and for other reasons. It is much the same way with a system of labor exchanges. Some people are applying for employment, others are anxious to hire labor. Ready and immediate means of intercommunication among the exchanges is necessary. The post-offices already have such means at their disposal.

This is the crux of the whole situation. Assuming that the postmasters are qualified and able and that the equipment will stand the strain without extra provision or cost, labor cannot be handled as if it were theatre tickets or crops.

What will happen is this: A certain position posted as open in Elgin, Illinois, let us say, is not filled in twenty-four hours; this information is sent to the central-zone office and the next day is posted in perhaps 1000 other post-offices. But hungry men and women looking for jobs do not wait to be placed like theater tickets. Some will write, others will telegraph, but many will leave for the spot without notifying anyone or any post-office. Furthermore, employers who have found help, especially farmers in remote districts, cannot be depended upon to notify the central office that they have found some one. The result from such a system would be that in times of unemployment each applicant for workers would be inundated with applicants of all kinds and degrees of efficiency and adaptability for which he would hold the government responsible. In times of scarcity of employees, irate employers would hold the government responsible for the lack of labor, and, before long, charges of favoritism and "pull" would permeate the entire department, for the demand for labor when crops are spoiling or orders are unfilled comes very close to every employer's pocket-book. Any attempt to handle labor on a wholesale plan in a loose, haphazard way, without adopting every safeguard known to science and economics will result in disaster for the experiment and for the government, and will delay any real progress. The direction of labor to employment is the most delicate and intricate problem before the government, and its very independence, individuality, fluidity, and will of its own to go when and where it pleases, caution us to move slowly in this matter.

Aside from these considerations, we must face this question: Shall this government, contrary to the experience and practice of all other governments, adopt the policy of charging its citizens a fee for the privilege of filling out an application for work? The fee as outlined in the law carries with it no guarantee of a position, or even of information, but covers only the service of posting such information. Why should the man looking for work pay for information when weather reports and crop reports are furnished free to business men? Furthermore, many states prohibit a registration fee and compel private agencies to return all fees when no position is secured. What would be the effect of such state regulations upon a postmaster who accepted fees from persons who received no positions?

Repugnant as is the idea of a fee service, and aside from constitutional questions involved, its adoption would mean that the government would not be able to compete with private agencies. Since the bill is silent on the third point of the regulation of the interstate business of private agencies, there would still be no way of stopping their characteristic abuses, and the immigrant would still be helpless in the hands of the padrone, and the laborer in the hands of the general labor agent.

The bill also appears to be administratively impossible. The expenditure of such a sum as $2,000,000 the first year on so dubious a scheme would invite waste, extravagance, and failure. Those familiar with employment agencies agree that the person in charge must be familiar with the employment agency business, be able to devise and keep an accurate system of records and maintain neutrality in industrial disputes. A three-headed commission appointed by two department heads would face some very interesting questions:

Would a postmaster efficient in post-office work but a failure in employment work be retained or dismissed, and which duties should have priority? Would the record of doing good employment work justify shabby post-office work? What voice would the commission have in making appointments or in fixing examinations? Under whose jurisdiction would employment clerks be placed— the employment commissioner's or the postmaster's? The proposed law is quite specific on the subject. It says:

the entire national employment-bureau service shall be under the direct administration of the National Employment Bureau Commission subject to the supervision of the Secretary of Labor, and the postmasters of such post-offices are hereby constituted labor-exchange agents.

What effect does the Postmaster-General think this will have upon the efficiency of the present post-office system?

If such a scheme is feasible at all, it would be well to limit the experiment to a very small territory. But before such a bill is reported it would be better to have public hearings and conferences in which department heads, postmasters, employers, employees, and representatives of unions could be heard upon the practicability of such a scheme. The post-offices themselves do offer certain facilities for such work, but to what extent postmasters can *administer* any part of the work raises nice questions of economics, policy, and administration, demanding the fullest consideration.

The third proposal has been made informally and tentatively by members of the Commission on Industrial Relations. It proposes the establishment of a central bureau which will utilize existing state bureaus and grant them subsidies to make them more efficient. This last proposal is preeminently a recognition of the states'-rights theory rather than a plan for an effective bureau of distribution. Any plan that contemplates knitting into a system the present state employment bureaus is doomed to failure for the cardinal reason that the state is not a natural unit for the distribution of labor or for the administration of free labor offices. The system adopted by this country will ultimately be the municipal bureau for local work, and the Federal bureau for inter-city and inter-state

work. The advantages of this combination will
become increasingly apparent from the analysis
of the state bureau work which follows. Furthermore, to subsidize existing bureaus would mean
the establishment of another pork barrel in
Washington, another bargain counter between
representatives, who will follow a policy of state
loyalty, regardless of their state's needs in the
matter of apportionment.

It may be argued that "it is undesirable to
supplant state and local machinery, however
ineffective that may be." This is carrying the
states'-rights policy very far indeed. When states
pass laws creating bureaus and *make no appropriations whatever* so that nothing can be done even
in great reserve-labor cities like Baltimore, is the
nation to fold its hands and say that this is the
concern of these states and not of the nation?
The same question faced the formulators of the
Inter-State Commerce law, of the new Trade
Commission law, and of the Reserve Board law.
Distribution of labor is in the same condition of
fluidity from state to state as is commerce and
trade, and any loose federation of existing agencies without Federal control will result only in
greater chaos than already exists. The principle of supervision and regulation is a sound-
er method of development and control than
money grants to political offices; and a highly
centralized authority is the only sure constructive method.

In the absence of any comprehensive Federal plan, states and cities have both undertaken to solve the problem of unemployment. Twenty states have authorized the establishment of public offices. One other state, California, passed a bill providing for them in 1913, but it was vetoed by the governor because the appropriation was inadequate. Of these twenty states, four have failed to establish effective offices as required:

Maryland has had an office in operation under a mandatory provision, but since only $10,000 was appropriated for two years for the entire Bureau of Statistics, and no funds set aside for employment work, the office is reported as "entirely inactive."

Nebraska has been unable to take up this work under a similar mandatory provision for the same reason. The appropriation for the Bureau of Statistics is but $9680 for two years, with no separate fund for employment work. With no specific appropriation whatever, the Bureau placed 647 persons in 1911-12, saving nearly over $2000 to the wage-earners.

Montana stipulates that it is the duty of common councils to provide for the establishment of free public offices to be conducted upon the most approved plans and to provide for the expense, and that the annual report of the Commissioner of Agriculture and Labor and Industry shall contain a detailed report of the work. Three municipal offices have been established under this law, but no reports have been made and it has been impossible to obtain any satisfactory record of activity from the "common councils."

South Dakota has adopted a unique law constituting each register of deeds an employment agent, and requiring him to receive applications and keep an employment book. Most of the law is devoted to the form of record to be kept, but he is required to forward a daily advice sheet to the State Bureau of Information, which is to communicate by postal card with the persons registering for work and help. The registers of deeds are required to pay the expense in their offices while the State Bureau of Information carries the expense of distribution. The following report from a state officer is of interest:

The Bureau of Information in this state has been established as provided by law but has not worked to any satisfaction whatever. Has been mainly a joke. One county I visited recently has had just one entry in its books and that was application for a job of wheeling smoke out of the court house. Of course, it is not regarded so lightly in all cases, but I think no register of deeds has evidenced any sincere desire to make it valuable. There is the germ of a good theory in it, but it is complicated and has hardly been considered practical. I confess I rather like the idea myself, but admit we have not gotten anywhere with it.

There remain sixteen states, or 33 per cent. of the total, that have made appropriations for this work and can therefore be regarded as having made serious attempts to organize the labor market. These include Connecticut, Colorado, Illinois, Indiana, Kansas, Kentucky, Massachusetts, Michigan, Minnesota, Missouri, New York, Ohio, Oklahoma, Rhode Island, West Virginia, and Wisconsin. Such important industrial states as California, New Jersey, Pennsylvania, and Iowa have taken no action in this matter.

Certain fundamental principles have come to be recognized as essential to the successful organization of public employment offices, and we can somewhat gauge their efficiency by applying these tests to each office. These may be grouped under: (1) powers, (2) appropriations, (3) appointment of officers, (4) range of facilities, (5) methods, (6) clearing house or coöperative features, (7) value as compared with other agencies, and (8) neutrality in labor disputes.

(1) State offices are organized generally as a part of an existing Department of Labor, or Bureau of Statistics, or corresponding office, either by the creation of a bureau under a deputy, or by the appointment of a superintendent or director. This plan of organization has both advantages and disadvantages. Such a bureau has placed at its disposal the usual facilities of an established department, in the way of system, records, and equipment. On the other hand, it is very often apparent from the laws that an already over-burdened official has to add a new and highly

specialized branch of work with no increase in either staff or appropriation. Even when a special officer is appointed, he is often given other duties. This practice more than any other has prevented state offices from becoming effective. Six states authorize the commission to appoint superintendents of public offices, with assistants; one state authorizes him to appoint a manager; three states provide for a director, one of which places him directly under the governor rather than under a Commission of Labor and requires him to report separately; four states place the responsibility upon the Commissioner, authorizing him to secure such assistance as he needs, and one state makes no mention of any assistants.

The powers of these officials vary greatly, and in general the law is very ambiguous as to either the duties or the methods of conducting such bureaus. Where appropriations are made, the official in charge is usually authorized to employ assistants and open offices, to get in touch with employers, to advertise when necessary, and in general to use diligence. How much of this power can be translated into action depends primarily upon the appropriation.

(2) The appropriation is, therefore, the real test of the efficiency of the law, though not by any means the sole one; some of the state systems having the largest appropriation have not the best management. So far as the records were obtainable, but eight states have made adequate

appropriation. These are Illinois, New York, Massachusetts, Ohio, Wisconsin, Colorado, Indiana, and Connecticut.

Considering the magnitude and importance of the subject, these appropriations are not large, but they have enabled the states to make a creditable showing. The largest appropriation is that of Illinois which is $54,235 for the year ending July 1, 1915. The state maintains eight bureaus, of which three are in Chicago. The work of the Illinois bureaus has not been considered of the first grade, owing to the influence of politics, the system of records used, etc., and it furnishes an illustration of the fact that the appropriation alone will not make state bureaus efficient. In this case the question may well be raised as to whether the very methods in use have not been the means of securing this unusually large appropriation.

New York has the next largest appropriation, of from $40,000 to $45,000. If the future of this Bureau is to be judged by its past, this winter will see little change from last year. The bill was passed last winter; the appropriation was available October 1st. Yet on January 1st, nearly a year from the date of the passage of the bill, no offices had been opened, no assistants had been appointed to help the director, no advisory committees had been selected, and the whole situation was involved in political juggling and civil-service red tape. Eight cities which the state is authorized to assist were deprived of this help at a time when it was urgently needed.

Massachusetts is third with an appropriation of $36,350. The report of the director may be of interest to those interested in the administration of offices. It states:

1. There are four State Free Employment Offices at the present time administered by an aggregate of thirty-two persons, exclusive of the Director of the Bureau of Statistics, whose duties include numerous directing and supervising functions as the head of the department. Each of the several offices is carried on by an administrative and clerical force as follows:

Boston Office: 1 superintendent; 1 assistant superintendent; 5 men clerks; 6 women clerks; 1 woman stenographer; 1 male messenger; 2 male laborers; and a scrubwoman.

Springfield Office: 1 superintendent; 1 male clerk; 2 women clerks; 1 woman stenographer; and a male laborer.

Fall River Office: 1 superintendent; 1 male laborer.

Worcester Office: 1 superintendent; 1 male clerk; 1 woman clerk; 1 woman stenographer; and a scrubwoman.

In addition to the above administrative and clerical staff employed on the premises of the several offices, approximately one-half of the time of a statistical clerk in the Bureau of Statistics is devoted to checking up and tabulating the daily and monthly reports made by the superintendents. Her salary is $1020 a year, one-half of which is paid from the appropriation for the Free Employment Offices, being charged to the accounts of the several offices as follows: $204 to the Boston Office and $102 to each of the other offices. This clerk is included in the total number of persons on the pay-rolls of the Free Employment Offices given at the beginning of this section.

2. All appointments in the Free Employment Office service, including superintendents, are made subject to the rules and regulations of the Civil Service, except laborers (that is, persons who do ordinary cleaning and so-called janitor work), who are exempt.

3. The total appropriation for the maintenance of the Free Employment Offices for the fiscal year ending November 30, 1914, was $36,350. This appropriation is made by the Legislature in a single lump sum, being based, however, upon detailed estimates prepared by the Director of the Bureau, and when made allotted to the several offices in accordance with the preliminary estimates. There are no overhead charges, every dollar of expense being charged to the office against which the expense is incurred, or, in the few cases where this is not possible, the aggregate is prorated in such proportionate amounts as seem fair. For example, as it is not practicable to reduce to an exact figure for each office, except at too great an expense for time-keeping, the salary which is paid the clerk who keeps the statistical records for the several offices, this amount, $510, is prorated to the four offices roughly on the basis of the business done; that is, $204 being charged to the cost of the Boston Office, and $102 to the cost of each of the other three offices; total $510. Similarly the cost of printing the annual report, which might be regarded as an overhead charge, is prorated.

All supplies, including postage, stationery, forms, and other job printing, are supplied to the several offices only on requisition by the superintendents, and the proportionate cost of each consignment, if it is a kind of supply which has been purchased in bulk, is computed and charged to the expenditure cost of maintaining the office which makes the requisition. An account of all stock on hand is taken near the close of each fiscal year and taken into account in estimating the probable expenses of the next year.

Any system of departmental accounting should reduce overhead charges to a minimum and distribute as much as possible of the aggregate expense to the various functions or branches of the work being administered; and while there are a few items in the general administration of the Massachusetts offices which might, as above indicated, be properly regarded as an overhead charge, they are so few that, as explained, they are prorated, so that our books show nothing as an overhead charge, every dollar of expenditure being charged up to the account of one or the other of the four offices. In this way and by the adoption of a uniform, standard classification of expenses, I am able to know as closely as it is possible to determine the exact cost of our offices from year to year.

Ohio is fourth with an appropriation of $16,200 for salaries. Adding the rental of the offices now furnished by the various cities, equipment, janitor service, etc., the cost of running these agencies is not far from $25,000. There are five offices, located at Cincinnati, Cleveland, Columbus, Dayton, and Toledo.

Wisconsin is fifth, with four agencies, appropriating $1800 for a supervisor and $5220 to the Milwaukee agency, $1800 to the Superior agency, and $720 each to the Oshkosh and La Crosse agencies, making a total of $10,260. In addition, however, the local governments pay the charges for telephone, light, heat, janitor service, etc., so that the amount expended is approximately $12,000.

Colorado is sixth with an appropriation of $11,300, $8800 of which is for salaries and $2500 for running expenses. There are four offices, located at Colorado Springs, Denver (two offices), and Pueblo. Indiana is seventh with an appropriation of $11,000, $9000 of which is used for the five agencies located at Evansville, Fort Wayne, Indianapolis, South Bend, Terre Haute, and $2000 for the Indianapolis office. Connecticut is eighth, with five offices, and the salaries and expenses of each may not exceed $2000, making a total of about $10,000. Michigan is ninth with an expenditure of $8287.27 out of an annual appropriation of $40,000 for the whole Department of Labor.

Beyond these nine states, it is an open question whether the appropriations are sufficient to enable state offices to do more than meet the minimum demand made upon them. They can certainly do little toward *organizing* the labor market. Oklahoma, with three agencies, has an appropriation of about $4100, with another $500 from the contingent fund, making $4600 in all; Rhode Island,

with one office, is second with an appropriation of
$4000; Kansas is third with a $3200 appropriation; while Kentucky appropriates $2000, and
West Virginia $500.

We now come to the states that make no appropriations but give a lump sum to the Department
of Labor or to other corresponding state bureaus.
Of these, Minnesota has $10,000 for two years
and Nebraska $9680 for two years. Missouri
with three offices uses about $3500 a year in its
employment agency work, although the constant
interchange of work and lack of any specific appropriation make this an inaccurate estimate. It
is impossible in these states to estimate the cost of
employment work, as the employees carry so many
other responsibilities and perform other duties.

(3) How far an appropriation will go and how
great will be the returns from it depend largely
upon whether the employment offices are in or out
of politics. Excepting in four states, they may be
in or out at the pleasure of the governor and his
appointees.

Massachusetts, New York, Ohio, and Wisconsin are the only states that require that all
officers, including superintendents and managers
of employment offices shall be in the classified list.
The New York provision is noteworthy and is the
most specific.

The bureau of employment shall be under the
immediate charge of a director who shall have recog-

nized executive and managerial ability, technical and scientific knowledge upon the subject of unemployment and administration of public and private agencies for remedying the same. The civil service examination for the position of director shall be such as to test whether candidates have the above qualifications. As a part of such examination each candidate shall be required to submit a detailed plan of organization and administration of employment offices such as are contemplated by this article.

Illinois includes all but the superintendent and assistant superintendent and an occasional clerk. Governor Dunne has just removed the heads of some of the public employment offices in Illinois and has appointed others as the first step in efficiently organizing the Illinois state labor market. The law has been in effect fifteen years. Minnesota specifies that the manager must possess qualifications satisfactory to the board of examiners, but such important states as Indiana, Colorado, Connecticut, etc., have not taken these offices out of politics.

The number of really efficient state employment offices, considering the three most important factors,—powers, appropriations, and non-political appointments—narrows down to practically three —Massachusetts, Ohio, and Wisconsin (New York is as yet an unknown quantity) with which the Federal government might with some degree of assurance begin its work of coöperation in the expectation that these state agencies would constitute an efficient link in a national system, and would not be corrupted by promises of Federal aid.

(4)   An analysis of the range of activity of these state bureaus shows a number of interesting things: First, their work is limited very largely to unskilled workmen.   In some states women as well as men use them, especially servants; in others chiefly men.   Skilled workmen evidently prefer the private agency, newspaper advertisements, and other organizations.   How much effort states have made to obtain this business could not be ascertained, but the placing of skilled workmen is much more expensive and in many cases it could not be undertaken with the given appropriations.   In but three states, Ohio, Wisconsin, and Massachusetts, are provisions made for children. The provisions of the New York law, not yet in operation, are of interest as representing the most progressive legislation on this subject in the country:

Applicants for employment who are between the ages of fourteen and eighteen shall register upon special forms provided by the commissioner of labor. Such applicants upon securing their employment certificates as required by law, may be permitted to register at a public or other recognized school and when forms containing such applications are transmitted to a public employment office they shall be treated as equivalent to personal registration.   The superintendent of each public employment office shall coöperate with the school principals in endeavoring to secure suitable positions for children who are leaving the schools to begin work. To this end he shall transmit to the school principals a sufficient number of application forms to enable all pupils to register who desire to do so; and such principals shall acquaint the teachers and pupils with the purpose of the public employment office in placing juveniles. The advisory committees shall appoint special committees on juvenile employment which shall include employers, workmen, and persons possessing experience or knowledge of education, or of other conditions affecting juveniles. It shall be the duty of these special committees to give advice with regard to the management of the public employment offices to which they are attached in regard to juvenile applicants for employment. Such committees may take steps either by themselves or in coöperation with other bodies or persons to give information, advice, and assistance to boys and girls and their parents with respect to the choice of employment and other matters bearing thereon.

There are two notable departures in the matter of placing professional workers, namely, the teachers' agencies run by Massachusetts and Minnesota under the management of the state boards of education. These are both comparatively recent experiments, Massachusetts having created its teachers' registry in 1911 and Minnesota in 1913. In both states a registration fee is charged, $2 in Massachusetts and $3 in Minnesota, but no further payment is required. The chief

features of these two registries are: first, their
function of establishing standards of qualification
and certification for the applicants they register,
thus giving them potentially at least a powerful
influence over the teaching standards throughout
their states; secondly, their lack of aggressive
work in the interests of employees; and thirdly,
the disclaiming of responsibility for results.
Names of teachers and information concerning
them are sent only at the request of employers.
The Minnesota law specifically says, "no responsibility is incurred by this bureau." The registries
are, in short, information bureaus, evidently established not only with the object of regularizing
the methods by which teachers secure engagements, but also with the broader object of increasing the efficiency of schools and standardizing
preparation for teaching. These facts do not
make these two agencies less significant as illustrating the various powerful influences which government bureaus may exert.

(5) The general methods of operation as
authorized by law vary greatly. Twelve states
stipulate that no fees shall be charged and penalize
officials for accepting fees. This is the most
common prescription. Nine states provide that
records shall be kept, although most of them are
indefinite as to the manner and kind and detail.
Four provide that these records shall be confidential and that no person refusing to give the information requested shall for this reason be denied the

facilities of the office. Seven states require that weekly reports be made to a central office and three of these provide that they shall be exchanged among the different offices *within the state*. One provides for the publishing of a bulletin. Six require that notices of the office be posted. Two states make provisions for separate quarters for women and two for separate quarters for boys. The methods authorized for facilitating the placement of employees are advertising, which is specifically authorized in six states, and getting in touch with employers, which is authorized in four states. Four states make an application unfilled and not renewed void after thirty days. One state gives the preference in placement to residents. One state stipulates that information shall be sent to applicants by mail. Four states provide that if employers do not notify the bureau within ten days that they have received help, they may forfeit the right to use the bureau.

It will be noted that the aim of many of these provisions is to provide against possible abuses against or by the officers while others make some attempt to insure business methods and procedure. They are designed rather to protect a business than to build up and administer one, although most offices are still in the stage of building. There are some notable exceptions. In Massachusetts a vocational counsellor is provided, an employee is in charge of the handicapped, and another especially looks after the high-grade work. The school committees in Boston are required to maintain registers and to coöperate with the public offices. The New York law provides for a separate department for men and women with separate entrances and requires the bureau to coöperate with school principals to secure positions for children leaving school. The director is authorized to advertise, but the amount so used may not exceed 5 per cent. of the total appropriation. The law provides for coöperation between the various state offices, and for the sending of lists of vacancies to newspapers and other agencies and for the publishing of a labor market bulletin. *Private agencies are required to keep such registers as will give the same information supplied by public agencies, which registers may be inspected and shall be furnished when required by the public agency officials.* This is a pioneer effort to obtain completé standard data for an entire political division. In Wisconsin the machinery for attaining the same object exists in the requirement that all agencies shall keep registers or records in a form approved by the Industrial Commission, and that any commissioner or deputy of the commission may examine these records or registers. The New York law also provides for advisory committees for each branch office and for the already mentioned juvenile department, which is made a special feature of the law, following the precedent set by the Industrial Commission of

Wisconsin. An interesting provision governing
these New York committees is that at the request
of the majority of employers and employees on
such committees, voting must be conducted so that
there will be an equal number representing each
side even in the absence of some members. The
New York law represents the nearest approach
to model legislation, but it has not yet borne the
test of operation. Ohio has an excellent provision
authorizing the Industrial Commission to investigate both the causes and extent of unemployment
and to devise remedies for and means to prevent
unemployment and to collect and publish the data.

(6) The most discouraging thing about the
present state offices is the utter lack of any sense
of national responsibility, shown by the absence
of coöperative and clearing-house provisions, certainly one of the most important requirements.
Only seven states require that branch offices
report weekly to a central office, and but five provide for the *regular* exchange of reports among
offices. Three states provide for publishing a
labor bulletin, but no state is clear in its mandatory provisions as to *what it is important to publish.*
In other words, each official is left a large measure
of initiative and discretion both as to the time of
publishing and as to the details to be published.
Since many officials are not men of business or
labor experience, much of the information issued
is of little practical value; in other cases it consists
largely of statistical sheets. One or two states are

publishing such data and bulletins without specific sanction of law.

We have been unable to find any state that provides for interstate information or distribution, so that there is little systematic communication between the various state bureaus. The fact that city offices in several different states do coöperate to some extent directly with each other is a further evidence that the city and not the state is the best unit in a national system of distribution.

(7) One of the arguments used to secure the establishment of state bureaus has been that they would compete with private agencies and probably make them unnecessary. It has been very difficult to ascertain the effect of the establishment of public agencies upon the general labor market or upon private agencies, fo- this has not seemed of much importance to the officials in charge. Even where the public agency is charged with the enforcement of laws regulating private agencies, the answer to inquiries has been largely to the effect that the result is unknown. Each official has been more or less interested in making a record for his bureau, and its *relative importance* and general effect on the labor market have more or less escaped his notice.

To illustrate: Colorado reports that 30,787 persons were placed in two years and that two employment agencies were driven out of business. The total number placed in the state and the per cent. of the total placement by state and by

private agencies is unknown, as is also the number
of new private agencies started and those operating
without licenses or evading the law through subter-
fuges. The reports of all the states are in general
similar, showing the volume of business but
indicating little or no relation to the whole labor
market. There are some interesting exceptions:
Illinois reported in July, 1914, that 367 licensed
private agencies were in operation, an increase of
38 over the previous year, with 8 state offices
in full operation. There were 12 revocations
of licenses. Massachusetts, through regulations
by the Boston police board, limits the number
of private agencies, and a new business can be
started only by the purchase of an existing license.
Missouri reports that there are 33 licensed and
99 unlicensed private agencies in the state,
making it difficult for the state public bureaus
to flourish. The New York public bureau
meets this situation by providing for full and
similar reports by all private agencies as well
as by public offices, so that the full state of the
labor market may be known, but it has no way
of ascertaining the effect of the enforcement of the
private employment agency law except by the
courtesy of the cities charged with its enforcement.

From the meagre data obtained it appears that
private agencies flourish and even increase with
the establishment of public offices. So evident
has this seemed to the municipal agencies of
Washington that a state law has been passed

under the initiative which prohibits any agent from accepting a fee. This law which has recently been upheld by the courts puts the government in entire control of the state's labor market.

(8) The greatest single element in delaying the extension of public offices has been the fear of their partisan use in strikes. Four states have guarded against this by providing that records shall be confidential, and that any person refusing to give information requested shall not be discriminated against in the use of the bureau. On the direct subject of neutrality during labor disputes only two states have spoken decisively. The New York law provides that notices of strikes shall be posted after communication with the employers involved, and that any applicant for a vacancy in such an establishment shall be notified of any strike in progress, and of the conditions, and that no person shall suffer at the hands of the agency if he refuses to accept such position on account of a strike or for lower wages than the current rate. Wisconsin has a similar provision. In effect, however, most public agencies follow this rule and without authority of the law notify applicants about strikes; and complaints against them for sending out workmen as strikebreakers are very rare.

From an analysis of the available reports, a brief summary of the principles governing public agencies shows that with the exception of from three to five (two of which combine with cities

in expense and administration), the state bureaus
come under the following indictment: the powers
are limited, the business handled is largely unskilled, and little provision is made for the
women and for children with their first working
papers. Their influence upon the general labor
market and their place in it are inconsiderable
as compared with that of private agencies. Their
statistics are more or less unreliable and are
frequently padded; for instance, their records of
placements do not show whether they were permanent or transient, or, if the latter, what was the
length of the job, and how many times the same
person was placed. In most offices every person
sent to a position is counted as placed. The
appropriations are insufficient and the appointments political. The state is not apparently
a rational unit for public office work and has
not in one instance performed a constant useful interstate function in distribution. The methods are indefinite, unstandardized, the cost of
placement per head is high and there are as
many kinds of bureaus as there are managers,
since the laws leave the organization of such
bureaus largely to the heads appointed. No
attempt has been made to organize the general
labor market. There is little coöperation and
little exchange of information. With the exceptions above noted it can be truthfully said that they
secure several thousands of jobs a year at little
cost to the applicant, and at high cost to the

government.   There is no corresponding data to
show their relative efficiency, and their importance
and necessity in relation to the whole labor market.
For instance it is assumed in the reports that
every man placed represents a saving of an employment agency fee.   On the other hand it has been
found that registered men have often paid at
private agencies fees which in many instances
were not returned.

This widespread failure of the states to measure
up to their opportunities has been one of the chief
reasons for the establishment of municipal offices,
a reason second only to the fact that unemployment concentrates in cities and especially in reserve labor cities, of which there are about eighteen
of the first importance.   While most of these
municipal bureaus are comparatively recent, many
of them having been begun in 1913 and 1914, the
idea of municipal responsibility apparently ante-
dates the idea of state responsibility as is shown
by the fact that the New York City Corporation
in 1834 provided that a place be appointed in
every market for persons who wanted employment
to meet those who wanted to hire them.   Certain
hours were set for men to come and certain others
for women.   This may have been the first public
employment office.   It apparently was only for
servants.   Seattle, again, dates its municipal
bureau from 1896.

Before taking up the city offices it is of interest

to note the success of the two systems of combined
state and city employment offices now in operation in Ohio and Wisconsin, *constituting two of the
five efficient* bureaus included under state bureaus.
The Milwaukee, Wis., and Cleveland, Ohio,
offices are among the most efficient of the public
employment exchanges in the country. Both are
under the general supervision and direction of the
respective State Industrial Commissions. The
state accordingly makes all staff appointments
from regularly established civil service eligible
lists, pays all salaries, outlines the broad policies
to be followed, prepares the form of records to be
kept, facilitates the exchange of reports, and is
always consulted before any change is made. In
Milwaukee, the state pays the salaries of the six
employees—four in the men's department, including an interpreter, and two in the women's department—and pays for all printed matter, while the
city assumes the rental of both offices, and expenses
for office supplies, light, heat, janitor services,
telephone, and occasionally for stationery. In
Cleveland, the salaries of four employees are
paid by the state, while the City Immigration
Office registers all non-English-speaking applicants.
The superintendent of this office, who is an experienced social worker, is also the city commissioner
of employment (an office created under a recent
charter amendment) and was appointed to both
offices as the result of a special civil service
examination. The state also provides office sta-

tionery and printed matter and allows a small sum
for advertising purposes.   The city has set aside
a large office in the City Hall and provides light,
heat, janitor and telephone service.   As the work
of this office has largely increased in usefulness
and efficiency during the last six months, and as
most of the placement work is of direct benefit to
the city, those interested in the work contemplate
asking the city council for a special appropriation
to pay the salaries of two additional clerks and
one interpreter.

Both in Milwaukee and Cleveland, fitness is the
first requisite in all placement work, and special
cards are made out for the applicants having
special qualifications.   In Cleveland, each is
rated according to ability, experience, and general
appearance, and references are requested.   In
Milwaukee, special arrangements have been made
with the county poor officer and the Associated
Charities by means of which all applicants for
relief are referred to the public employment
office and are told to report there daily until work
is obtained.   The superintendent of the employment office then stamps and signs a special card
each day the applicant appears at his office.   When
relief is again requested, the applicant must show
his card and if he has not appeared fairly regularly
at the employment office and has no valid excuse
for not appearing, he does not obtain relief.   In
this way, both the county and private philanthropies reserve their funds for the worthy cases.

22

The Cleveland office has not as yet appointed
an advisory committee, but in Milwaukee the
usefulness of this advisory body has been considerably developed. On this committee appear
five representatives of employers, five of organized
labor, five county officials, and five city officials
(members of the board of aldermen). The committee meets once a month in the public employment office for an hour or two and the superintendent or members of the staff present for discussion any problems of policy or of additional small
financial needs. After a general discussion, the
superintendent is advised to experiment along
certain lines. Any proposed change, with the
recommendation of the advisory committee, is
referred to the State Industrial Commission,
which usually authorizes the experiment. Although no friction has at any time been reported,
the final decision always rests with the state
authorities. In both cities, the local superintendents also enforce the state laws regulating the
activities of private employment agencies and
they have obtained excellent results. Nearly all
of the applicants for work have at some time or
other applied to the private agencies for employment, and when registering at the public office
(an absolute requirement in these two cities) are
therefore usually asked about their experiences.
Much valuable evidence is obtained upon which
charges have later been preferred and licenses
revoked by the Industrial Commissions. Through

this close coöperation between state and city, all of the state's employment work is coördinated and the records are standardized, and local interest and support are secured. It is evident that one of the dangers of a state-city system would be that the city agency might be a very local office, connected with the state only in that it receives state aid. It is interesting to note that in Milwaukee the scope of the territory covered is constantly increasing. Much use is made of the long distance telephone, and in addition to this the office has the coöperation of several country banks.

Of the city bureaus reporting, at least five were created under separate ordinances. These offices are usually created directly under the mayor or in Departments of Public Safety and provide for salaries and expenses. In one city, Portland, the mayor appoints an unpaid board of control of three members to supervise the work, including representatives of trade unions, manufacturers' associations, and the common council.

Among the other city bureaus a few were established in the winter to meet an unusual demand and then discontinued in the spring. One was created temporarily to check the exploitations among private agencies. Unlike the state public bureaus, nine-tenths of the city bureaus have been organized not to deal intelligently with the local problem of unemployment the year around and to study the local causes and needs, to inaugurate city planning and really become the effective

center of all work in the city, but on the more
temporary basis of meeting a particularly critical
situation. Few of them, therefore, have any considerable degree of method or efficiency; and few
have sufficient appropriation to enable them to
operate effectively.

It is significant of the very indefinite conception
of municipal agencies in America that in those
cities in which they have been established or are
now being agitated they have been referred to very
varied authorities. Sometimes it is the Department of Social Welfare, sometimes the Department
of Public Health and Safety, the Civil Service
Commission, the Commissioner of Licenses, the
Commissioner of Charities and Correction, or the
Municipal Market Commission. One city is now
contemplating a city bureau under the city
matron. In these varying procedures one fact
stands out—the emergency or relief aspect of
municipal agencies has seemed to be more
influential than any other in their establishment.
Municipal bureaus conducted by the city charities
departments are a distinct and rather more common type. In Denver, Colo., the superintendent
of the Municipal Lodging House is also superintendent of the free employment bureau, and
employment has been generally secured for
common laborers and for the handicapped, at
wages ranging from ten to twenty-five cents per
hour and board. This employment work has
been "an excellent side line of assistance" in the

city's relief work.   The cost of this work has been
nominal since one man operates both departments.
In New York City there is, beside the city employment bureau with its branches, a bureau conducted by the Department of Charities, dealing
with persons needing relief as well as work.

In those cases in which a series of municipal
agencies has been established in one state, as in
Washington and Montana, their work has been
correlated by no clearing-house exchange;   each
city has worked independently both in finding
jobs, and in keeping the unemployed away from
the city.   In but a few cases have municipal
agencies gradually expanded their work over a
larger area.   As a rule, there is very little advertising of a municipal employment agency either in
the city itself or in rural districts or towns throughout the state.   The theory is, of course, that such
advertising is likely to create the illusion in out-
lying districts that workers are needed in the city;
whereas the bureaus are interested in demonstrat-
ing that the city is already overcrowded with
workers.   Those situated on the highways, so to
speak, have persistently defined their point of
view concerning the casual or seasonal or migrating
workman.   The Chicago bureau this winter devised a census of the unemployed, one of its express purposes being to exclude any but resident
Chicagoans from the city's labor market facilities.

With one exception, the services of the municipal
agencies reporting are free.   Marquette, Michigan,

under its Department of Public Health and Safety, operates a bureau in charge of the market master, and charges "the same fees as private agencies" for finding positions. The Seattle office *may* charge an applicant twenty-five cents, but the secretary of the Civil Service Commission has never availed himself of this permissive power.

With comparatively few municipal agencies in the country, operating on different bases, and in very different kinds of communities having very different points of view, it is impossible to classify them on any uniform basis as to their methods of operation and their efficiency. In many cases there are no reports, and it is impossible to tell what records are kept. A few estimate the cost of finding work per person, Los Angeles reporting an average cost of $32\frac{1}{2}$ cents, and Seattle, Wash., somewhat over eight cents, although the latter estimate does not include overhead charges, office rent, and equipment, and other incidental expenses which are, in this case, borne by the Civil Service Commission. Some report the number of positions filled in a year, or in a month, sometimes for men and for women separately. Berkeley, Cal., for instance, reports that it averages one hundred a month. In Kansas City, Mo., the bureau under the supervision of the Board of Public Welfare was established to eliminate vagrancy, and took over the work of a philanthropic employment society, the Helping Hand Institute. It has now developed an effective employment bureau, reporting 31,146 positions filled in a little less than three years. The figures as to both cost and numbers vary greatly; without a knowledge of the *kinds* of labor placed, or of the system of records used, they are not significant. It is of especial importance to know what classes of labor are placed. One bureau definitely reports that "the best class of laborers are not registered," and this seems to illustrate the general tendency. Three city bureaus, Portland, Ore., and Spokane and Tacoma, Wash., are authorized to inspect and regulate local private employment bureaus,—a most significant point in any analysis of the powers and functions of municipal bureaus.

It is of interest to set forth here certain of the provisions governing New York City's new municipal bureau. Those bearing upon coöperation with other agencies, clearing-house functions, and specialization of work according to trades are especially important. Sections 3 and 4 of the establishing ordinance provide:

There shall be kept in the principal office of said Bureau, and in each and every branch office thereof, such system of records as may be necessary properly to record and classify, according to trade or profession: (1) all applicants for positions; (2) all positions to be filled as reported to said Bureau; (3) all persons sent to those seeking employees; (4) all such persons who secure employment, and (5) such other records as the Commissioner of Licenses deems necessary. A report

of the transactions of each branch office shall be transmitted each day to the principal office of the Public
Employment Bureau in the Borough of Manhattan.

The Public Employment Bureau shall, in as far as
it is feasible, coöperate with such employment bureaus
or intelligence offices as now exist, or which may hereafter be established and conducted by the United
States or the State of New York.

The bureau is under the supervision of the Department of Licenses. It is maintained out of the
general taxes, and its services are free "to all
competent, reliable, and temperate persons." All
appointments of the office staff are made from
the classified Civil Service. There are to be nine
departments for handling all classes of workmen
in the building and metal trades, mercantile,
professional, technical, industrial, domestic, hotel,
investment, institution, agricultural, skilled and
unskilled, male and female help, and general
laborers. There are separate entrances for men
and boys, and for women and girls. It is to be
the policy of the bureau to require references from
former employers or other responsible persons.

With the growing realization that public employment exchanges are essential to organization of
the labor market, greater care is being taken in
the drafting and enactment of legislation creating such agencies. In Virginia, for instance, the
state legislature amended the charters of the
cities of Richmond and Norfolk, enabling them
to establish local municipal employment bureaus.

An examination of the ordinance already enacted in Richmond and the one now pending before the Norfolk Common Council, indicates: (1) that these bureaus are known as Public Employment Bureaus, and are empowered to furnish information concerning the condition of the labor market at no cost either to employer or employee; (2) that unpaid Commissions (representing, in Norfolk, labor, industry, and the public) are charged with its general direction; (3) that such Commissions are to meet regularly and make rules for the management of the bureau; (4) that salaries are to be fixed by the City Council; (5) that adequate, specified records are to be kept; (6) that the Bureau coöperate with all other agencies, and (7) that the local administrative department supply stationery, equipment, etc.   The extension of similar legislative provisions in all ordinances creating municipal bureaus would enable them gradually to become constructive permanent agencies for the study and relief of unemployment.

Besides the employment bureaus definitely and separately conducted by municipalities, employment work is sometimes done by other municipal agencies, notably the Municipal Lodging House. This is of course quite in line with the work of the municipal bureaus the management of which is referred to the city charities department. It is a part of a general relief program. Up to this time, where it has been undertaken at all it has been done in a desultory

way.   This is inevitable so long as municipal lodging-houses are regarded as distinctly emergency
measures, for the purpose of providing shelter, and
are therefore quite unrelated to other agencies
in the community. Municipal lodging-houses
have been very informal and uncertain bureaus
for furnishing temporary work of distinctly limited
kinds.   Whenever they could, they have given
men and women a few days' work around the
lodging-house premises.   In a lodging-house like
New York City's, opportunities at this work
within the lodging-house plant may be very
considerable.   Besides the work involved in the
heating, lighting, motor service, or small repairs,
all the operations that belong in every night's
procedure, such as the bathing and feeding of the
lodgers, the receiving, fumigating, filing, and
distributing of their clothing, etc., involve a large
force.   But municipal lodging-houses have had no
facilities for learning of opportunities throughout
the city, and no one on their staff to do this work.
In the New York City lodging-house this winter
an experiment is being tried by which those of the
lodgers that are able to work may be helped
to employment.   There is to be a social-service
department, including an employment secretary,
whose business it will be to look out for employment opportunities, and attend to the details of
placement, or else put those seeking work into
relation with other agencies that may help him.
There is also to be developed an industrial de-

partment for providing "temporary work and vocational training as a test, and as a step to independence." In other words, the temporary work heretofore only desultorily furnished is to be organized under an industrial manager with the following workers: a foreman painter, foreman carpenter, foreman tailor, foreman cobbler, a plumber, a plasterer, barber, locksmith, electrician, an institutional gang foreman, a street-cleaning gang foreman, woodyard foreman, park work foreman, trades gang foreman, laborers' gang foreman, a record clerk, laundryman, washer-mangleman, wringers, counters, dryers, and rack tenders. It has become a truism that the rehabilitation of men and women destitute through unemployment can be brought about only by getting them work. But the few municipal lodging-houses that have been provided in American cities have not been founded or operated upon this basis.

Among employment facilities under municipal control must be mentioned the employment activities of public trade schools. In a few cases, as in the Manhattan Trade School in New York City, the employment work is sufficiently organized to include retaining a secretary for this purpose. It is her task to make a survey of the field, with particular reference to the work offered by the school, to arrange for placement, to do a certain amount of "follow-up" work, and to make readjustments when they are necessary. In Gary, Indiana, the distinctly industrial organization of the public-school system, and the active interest of employers in it, as evinced by their visits and their acceptance of the upper high-school instruction in their trades as partial fulfillment of apprenticeship, while it now includes no organized fee system of finding jobs, points a significant possible connection between the public-school system and the placement of child-workers. In these cases the initiative is taken by the educational system. The instances in which state bureaus take the initiative have already been noted in connection with Wisconsin, Ohio, New York, and Massachusetts.

There is another very influential part of the labor market which has never been considered in its relation to the efficiency, stability, or regularity of that market—namely, the civil service commissions and also the less organized form of job peddling by aldermen or councilmen. These are, however, government labor offices and agents and no labor market can be organized without considering their relative influence and position. Their activities cover both skilled and unskilled occupations.

The civil service laws are of comparatively recent origin. The first Federal act was passed in 1883, as a result of an attack on the spoils system after a disappointed office seeker shot President Garfield. A state law was enacted in New York in the same year. Since then eight other states—California, Colorado, Connecticut, Illinois, Massachusetts, New Jersey, Ohio, and Wisconsin—have passed similar laws. There are similar provisions in the constitutions of New York, Colorado, and Ohio. These laws show some variation in the kinds of positions which are put under civil service rules and can be filled only by appointment from eligible lists secured as the result of competitive or non-competitive examinations. Usually the highest positions in the service and also the lowest are exempted. The laws also vary as to whether all public positions in state, cities, and counties, or only those in the state service, are included. The extent to which employment is affected by these rules is indicated by the statement in the 1912 report of the United States Civil Service Commission, which says: "Of the whole number of public employees in the United States—federal, state, county, municipal, and village—not far from 600,000, or nearly two-thirds of the entire number, are withdrawn from the spoils system and appointed upon a merit basis, under laws intended to regulate and improve the public service."

These laws usually prescribe that only citizens of the United States are eligible. The municipal ordinances frequently lay down the additional qualification of residence. In Milwaukee, for instance, positions in the city service may be held only by citizens of the United States who have been residents of Milwaukee for three years. In

New Orleans they are limited to registered voters
of the city who voted at the last general election.
In Dayton, Ohio, even casual laborers must be
electors of the city.   In Butte only resident voters
of the city may be appointed to official positions
or employed by the city on day's wages.   In
Detroit all applicants for work as laborers must be
residents.   These examples illustrate the variation in municipal provisions.

The civil service bureau is consequently the rank-
ing governmental labor office in the country and has
the selection of employees and positions.   There
has been so little knowledge of the effect of civil
service on the labor market that there is little available data.   It is clear, however, that any solution
of the unemployment problem will involve careful
consideration of the constant "wire-pulling" to
secure places, of the system of promotions by
which the inefficients at the bottom of the list are
carried to the top, especially as temporary help,
of the manipulation of reserve lists, of the dovetailing of work for extra and temporary help, of
the effect of civil service lists upon related industries, and especially upon the efficiency of men
carried for long periods on such lists.   The guidance of children into industry will be paralleled
by the guidance of workers into civil service,
including more adequate examinations prepared
by experts and training in public schools, looking
toward equipment for such positions.

One serious difficulty in attempting to organize

the labor market, whether under civil service rules or without them, is the opposition of those interests that have hitherto exercised a powerful influence on appointments, particularly to unskilled labor positions. This opposition takes the form of reduction of appropriations, blocking of work, postponement of action on proposed measures, and other frequent means of delay. In one city an appropriation was reduced by about $2000 because unskilled laborers were put in the civil service class, thereby depriving the councilmen of patronage. Another city opened a free public office in an attempt to relieve unemployment, only to discover that men sent out by it to positions for snow removal could not get jobs with the card of the city unless the alderman of the district approved and his card was given precedence by the contractor. In the effort to keep this work in the control of the local politicians, a resolution was introduced before the Board of Aldermen that stated that the men were floating laborers, non-citizens, and non-residents, drawn to the city by the publicity given in the newspapers to provisions for relief of the unemployed; and it was urged that no men be employed except residents of the city, and that they be employed in the district where they lived—in other words, in the district where the leader would vouch for them. The attempt to mask political control by considerations of residence is often the last resort of the district leader. This situation illustrates another of the

difficulties in the way of a thorough organization
of the labor market.

*A survey of governmental agencies in the United
States leads to these conclusions: so far as public
agencies exist at all, they have failed to organize the
labor market. There are a number of reasons for
this, but all the reasons proceed from one source:
lack of a general realization of the need or the scope
or the possibilities of public agencies, and failure
to understand that only a nation-wide system can
deal with conditions in labor and industry not
bounded by city or state lines. The Federal attempt
to distribute immigrant labor proved a failure even
with its limited object, and is only now experimenting
on a somewhat broader principle. The state agencies
have in general been political bureaucracies rather
than public utilities. They have secured no coöperation between states, and in most cases they have not
made even their intra-state operations uniform or
state wide. They have not taken into account or
regulated private agencies, nor have they become
clearing houses for the employment activities of the
state. In short, they have signally failed to organize
the labor market even so far as this can be done within
state limits. Municipal bureaus are of late development, and are as yet very miscellaneous both as to
their foundation purpose and their scope. With a
few notable exceptions they have been largely local
attempts to deal with an urgent local need. In a few
places they are already conceived to be a municipal
experiment in organizing the labor market; in many*

other places they are still regarded simply as a local relief agency, a division of the city's charities. Their position in municipal functions is greatly in need of clarification, and their relation to the whole labor market of the nation needs to be defined and established.

It is plain, however, that the potential function of the municipal agency to organize the labor market is far greater than that of the state. The state is not an industrial unit. The labor reserve city and the industrial community large or small are, on the other hand, logical distribution centers. The adoption of the city unit would mean, therefore, more direct and immediate connection between the logical centres, and a simpler administrative framework for organizing the national market. The present need is for greater uniformity in the powers and scope of city bureaus, and an adequate Federal policy to secure and maintain the necessary connections among them.

23

CHAPTER XI

IT is apparent that the government has not obtained control of the labor market by competition nor has it added materially to its national organization. The question naturally arises: what else has the government done to abolish these abuses and to protect the unemployed.

The legislative history of unemployment shows that regulation has been confined almost exclusively to the labor market, and has attempted to remedy only those flagrant evils that had already grown to considerable proportions. It represents for the most part a reactive, and not a constructive, public opinion. In some instances it has upset rather than steadied the labor market. With a few notable exceptions hereinafter to be noted, there is no indication that such considerations as the general distribution of labor, the regularization of industry, or inquiry into the causes of unemployment have been taken into account to any considerable extent in such legislation. There are no national regulations, the matter having been left wholly to the states and cities; the regulations there are consist largely of local attempts to deal with a national problem having important interstate aspects.

There are insurmountable difficulties in the way of the effectiveness of such local regulations. For instance, New York City is the principal center of distribution for immigrant labor throughout the United States, and no municipal or state regulation can be devised to protect a laborer stranded in Oklahoma or Montana through the fault of a New York employment agent. This is true in a corresponding degree of Chicago, which is the distribution center of the central west, as well as of St. Louis, New Orleans, and Minneapolis. These and other cities are reserve labor centers and are the common labor markets of the nation. Because of this concentration of labor, unemployment is erroneously regarded as a municipal problem. Not only are there many local problems to settle for the workers within the city, but from these centers are distributed most casual and seasonal laborers, and to them come for training and positions the youth of the country, many of whom are later redistributed to small communities. At the close of the season, many of the laborers return to these centers to spend their savings or to get odd jobs until the next season opens.

The most common form of regulation is of private employment agencies. There are apparently two methods followed by the twenty-three states which have adopted some form of regula-

tion since Massachusetts enacted the first law in
1848 requiring all agencies for laborers and
domestics to have a license, price $1, and impos-
ing a $10 penalty for failure to comply: (1)
State laws by which administration and enforcement are placed in the hands of state authorities.
The states in this class are twelve in number and
include: California, Colorado, Connecticut, Illinois, Indiana, Kansas, Michigan, Missouri, Ohio,
Oklahoma, Virginia, and Wisconsin. (2) State
laws prescribing regulations but leaving the
administration to cities or counties. Nine states
have such laws, including Idaho, Louisiana, Maine,
Massachusetts, New Hampshire, New Jersey,
New York, Pennsylvania, and Utah. Of the
latter, however, Idaho leaves it to the county
authorities, while Utah permits both cities and
counties to enforce the law. Utah and Massachusetts also permit cities to enact supplemental
regulations. One other state, Minnesota, maintains an apparently equal authority in inspection
and enforcement as between the state and cities
although the license fees are paid to the various
cities. Iowa, while giving city and town governments the power to regulate and license agencies,
has passed state regulations and gives the enforcement of these to state authorities.

Of the remaining states, Tennessee, Montana,
Kentucky, and West Virginia require licenses but
make no regulations whatever; Rhode Island
empowers town councils to license "suitable

persons"; and Alabama, North Carolina, Florida, Georgia, Mississippi, and South Carolina have emigration laws prohibiting agents from sending persons out of the state or inducing them to leave, without a license. In these southern states, the license fees for such agents are prohibitive, being usually $500 for each county in which the agent operates. The Alabama law has been declared unconstitutional. There are no regulations in these states for intra-state business. Arizona has but one regulation. This prohibits any employer or his agents or employees from receiving fees or commissions for giving employment. Nevada has a similar provision, but also prohibits false representations by agents. Washington prohibits fraudulent statements and misrepresentations and the acceptance of any fee whatsoever for employment service. Such important states as Nebraska, Texas, Vermont, and Delaware have passed no legislation whatever.

There are, therefore, but twenty-three states, or 45 per cent. of all the states, that can be said to have laws which regulate private employment agencies with any degree of success. As certain minimum standards have come to be recognized in the successful conduct of public employment offices, equally important fundamental principles have come to be recognized as indispensable to the proper regulation of that part of the labor market represented by private agencies. These include the following:

(1) Jurisdiction of the law to include every agency conducted for profit.

(2) Employment business as a public utility.

(3) Fees, refunds and advance or registration fees.

(4) Business methods and records.

(5) Fraud and misrepresentation.

(6) Protection of women.

(7) Neutrality in labor contracts.

(8) Enforcement provisions, including appropriations.

(1) As to the jurisdiction of the law there are two important phases: first, what classes of agencies are included, and secondly, what territory. Fifteen states or 65 per cent. have the broadest possible definitions, intended to include every agent that charges a fee for profit. In these states only employers, trade unions finding employment for members, and charitable organizations are excluded. Of the others, New Hampshire limits the operation of the law to domestics and laborers; Connecticut, Indiana, and Maine exempt teachers' agencies, and New York, New Jersey, and Pennsylvania exempt teachers' agencies and also professional agencies conducted by institutions such as educational bodies. Massachusetts divides the agencies into two classes, mercantile and general labor, and has a separate law regulating teachers' agencies.

There is no sound reason for the exclusion of teachers' and professional agencies. They may occupy better offices and their clients may be better dressed and better educated, but it has not been demonstrated that they are not in need of regulation. On the contrary, it has long been known that their registration fees are exorbitant and the placement charges disproportionate to the investment and service rendered. Such information as is available shows that only about 10 per cent. of those who pay registration fees of from $2 to $5 receive positions. Teachers' agencies have one unique and generally unrecognized advantage over other agencies—they gather in the employed, as well as the unemployed.

As to the territory covered, the laws of the twenty-three states being considered are applicable to all localities within the state, with these exceptions: The New York law applies to all cities, but domestic and commercial agencies are exempted in third-class cities. The Pennsylvania law applies only to cities of the first class, all others being without protection.

(2) In the twenty-three states that have passed laws, private agencies are clearly held to be public business. Seventy-five per cent. of them require licenses and bonds, while a number of states specify in detail what records shall be kept and what they shall contain, and 87 per cent. authorize inspection. Fifty-six per cent. prohibit agencies in saloons or on premises where liquor is sold, and a very few states include living rooms and lodging places in this prohibition. Wisconsin and New York also require em-

ployment agents to furnish reports regularly or upon request.

That the regulation of employment agencies comes under the police power of the state, is universally conceded. Statutes requiring agents to obtain licenses, procurable only under certain conditions, are held not to be in conflict with the constitutional right to carry on a lawful business without legislative interference. A recent case[1] expresses the prevailing view that as such legislation has for its object the promotion of public health, safety, morals, convenience, and general welfare, and also tends to prevent fraud and immorality, it is within the police power of the legislature.[2] The constitutionality of the law previously mentioned, recently passed in Washington State, under the operation of the initiative, which prohibits the charging of any fee whatever for the service of furnishing employment or information concerning employment, and does not exempt existing business, has been sustained.

(3) In the matter of the regulation of fees, the essential matters covered by legislation are the

[1] People *ex rel.* Armstrong *v.* the Warden of the City Prison of New York (183 N. Y. 223, 1905).

[2] Certain statutes have, however, been held unconstitutional on account of certain provisions they contain. The most frequent example is a provision limiting the fee that may be charged for services in procuring employment. Provisions to this effect are sustained in eighteen states, yet in California a similar provision was held unconstitutional, as an infringement on the right to contract (*Ex parte* Dickey, 144 Cal. 234, 1914).

amount, length of time an agent may retain fees, receipts, and division of fees with representatives of employers. Little attempt has been made to limit the amount which employers may be charged.

In the matter of employees' fees, nine states regulate the placement fee or total fee including registration fees. There is a tendency to let the agent charge what he can get when he actually furnishes a position. Colorado has the lowest placement fees, limited to $1 for general laborers and $2 for professional workers. Connecticut, Indiana, New Jersey, and New York limit the fee to 10 per cent. of the first month's wages, and Utah limits it to 8 per cent. New York and New Jersey limit it, for professional workers, to the first week's wages or 5 per cent. of the year's salary. Pennsylvania limits the charge for temporary work to 10 per cent. of the first month's wages.

Three states—Massachusetts, Minnesota, and Utah—prohibit the acceptance of advance registration or filing fees before the agent has anything to offer or has rendered any service. Wisconsin requires permission from the Industrial Commission before a registration fee can be charged. It is the absence of such a provision which makes it possible in most states to start an agency with no capital or equipment and to keep fees, even when no service is rendered. Of the states permitting a registration fee, twelve compel the return of the full fee when no position is secured. Iowa and

Virginia permit the retention of a $1 filing fee; Illinois permits the agent to deduct from the $2 advance fee the amount actually expended in seeking employment for the applicant. Michigan and Pennsylvania permit the retention of 50 cents, and in Massachusetts the agent can keep one-sixth of the fee if the workman is discharged within ten days. The other states are not specific upon this point. It is significant, however, that 78 per cent. of the twenty-three states have dealt with fees for employees.

The permission to charge advance fees is of great importance when considered in connection with the length of time an agent may retain such fees, especially when collected from migratory workers. An analysis of the prevailing refund provisions leaves the impression that they were drawn to create as much delay and hardship as possible for the worker. In Massachusetts and Utah, two of the three states where no advance fees are permitted, and in Kansas, refunds of placement fees are returnable upon demand. Wisconsin, Idaho, Louisiana, Minnesota, and New Hampshire are silent upon the matter of refunds. In New York and New Jersey the fee is returnable within three days when no work is furnished. In California, in addition to this, if the worker has been sent beyond the city and is discharged within one week through no fault of his own, he is entitled to a return of the full fee and his transportation.

Outside these states, the burden rests heavily

upon the worker. In Connecticut, Missouri, Ohio, and Oklahoma, if no work is furnished or accepted, the agent may retain the fee one month and then return it on demand. In Iowa, the time is a matter of agreement between the parties and can be "a reasonable time" if no such agreement is made, but the failure to make an agreement and furnish the employee with a copy is a violation of law. In Colorado the agent may retain the fee five days. In Pennsylvania the agent may retain the fee one month and the law enforcement officer may then determine what is a reasonable time thereafter for its return. Michigan permits the agent to retain the full fee one month and then to keep 50 cents of it. Illinois permits the registration fee to be retained from thirty to sixty days, less the amount spent in obtaining work for the applicant, but the placement fee must be returned within three days if work is not found. It then caps the climax by stipulating that if a person is sent to a place where no work exists he must still wait five days though he may receive his transportation in addition. This has led to the practice of assigning fees by one agent to another when the employee gets a position through another agency. Maine stipulates that the fee shall be returned within six days if no contract with the agent has been broken. Connecticut provides that if a person accepts a position he loses his whole fee notwithstanding that "acceptance" may mean accepting the position in the agency and afterward finding conditions wholly misrepresented. The New York and New Jersey laws are peculiar in one respect. If an employee fails to remain in a position one week three-fifths of the fee is returnable within four days, but if he is discharged through no fault of his own he is entitled to three-fifths of his fee, *time not stated*. As if these safeguards were not enough for the agency, some states require the demand to be made within thirty or sixty days or the fee is forfeited—a difficult condition when imposed upon laborers stranded throughout the country who often do not know the name or address of the agency and must "beat" their way back to it.

When agencies are permitted to charge advance fees of any amount they can get, and keep them for a month or more, there can be only one other question of moment to the applicant for work. How can he get his fee back? On demand or within thirty days means very little if the agent disputes the claim or refuses to return the money. Only five states, Illinois, Maine, New Jersey, New York, and Pennsylvania provide a definite system of hearings by the licensing officer, whose word is final and who can revoke the license for failure to comply with the law. Nine other states also give the enforcing authority power to revoke a license, usually specifying that a hearing must be held, and also authorize the officer to bring suit on the bond; and Utah leaves it to the injured person to sue. The other states make no provisions. Those familiar with the law's delay and cost know that the percentage of the unemployed who can afford to go to court to recover a small fee is very small—a fact which makes the agent willing to risk the outcome in nine cases out of ten. According to the data supplied for 1913 by one state which permits the acceptance of an advance fee and a retention of a $1 filing fee, there were 40,446 applicants of whom 21,239 were found positions *but only 667 fees were reported as refunded.*

It is apparent from this summary that the regulation of fees has never been based upon any study of the amount of the investment or of the cost of operating such agencies. The safeguards of delay thrown about the agent to give him time to make an effort on behalf of the applicant and to verify reports do not provide corresponding safeguards for the transients, the men placed through other agencies and no longer in need of the services of the agent, or for those dissatisfied with his services. Many of the laws have been forced through the legislature by means of stories of exploitation and by appeals to prejudice. The result is that higher fees prevail in cities than in small towns, in spite of the greater volume of business in the cities; and high fees are common in lines where fluctuations are great and vacancies correspondingly frequent, with low fees in other lines where fluctuations are small. It is evident that as yet scientific rate-making based upon the volume and cost of the business and upon the rate of profit is unknown.

The subject of fee-splitting between agents and employers and their representatives in charge of hiring or promoting laborers is prohibited in various forms in a number of states including Arizona, New Hampshire, Pennsylvania, Utah, Minnesota, Nevada, California, Wisconsin, New York, and New Jersey. These provisions have become necessary to prevent the exploitation of workers who frequently have to pay such representatives in order to keep their jobs or to be advanced to better jobs. In some states workmen as well as employers are penalized.

The same lack of standard is found in the amount exacted for license fees and bonds as in employment fees. They range all the way from $2 in one state to $150 for a general license in another state. The average is $25. Seven states make a distinction between cities of various sizes while others have a flat rate for all. The bonds vary from $250 to $2000, and it is doubtful if this amount has ever been based upon an investigation of the volume of business. The insurance company fixes the premium according to the risk; the legislator fixes the bond, completely ignoring the workingman's risks! The bond is of especial importance in connection with the protection of the workmen, as so many states provide no redress but an action for damages for the recovery of fees upon the bond.

(4)   In an attempt to protect the unemployed, various standards have been set in business methods.   Seventeen states now require the keeping of registers while fifteen require that receipts shall be given to those that pay fees; and two that full particulars as to name and address of employer shall be given to each applicant sent out.   The posting of the law and of the license is quite generally required and some states have found it necessary to compel agents to designate on all advertising matter and all official papers the fact that they conduct an employment agency.   To many, these regulations may seem to be superfluous, but the character of the employment agency business is such, and the responsibility and range of the business are so great that some such regulations seem imperative if certain phases of the work are ever to be dignified by the term *business*. It is quite generally acknowledged now, even by agents who most vigorously opposed these regulations, that their educational value has been very great and that they have done more than any other one thing to put the employment agency upon a business basis.

(5)   Owing to the origin of these laws, we expect to find and do find that the provisions against fraud, misrepresentation, and false and misleading promises are strong, definite, and adequate. Fifteen of the twenty-three states prohibit such misrepresentation, while ten of them forbid sending a person out to any position for which the

agent has not received a *bona fide* order. Two states not included in the twenty-three, Washington and Nevada, have strong provisions against fraud. In Colorado a written order for an employee is required. When an agent has sent men out to a place where no work exists, they can recover their fee and transportation expenses in California, Illinois, Michigan, New Jersey, and New York.

California, Illinois, New Jersey, New York, and Pennsylvania endeavor to prevent fraud by providing that a copy of the employment contract be given whenever one or more persons are sent as contract laborers outside the city or on theatrical engagements. Each man must be given a statement, in a language he can understand, containing the name and address of the employer, the nature of the work, wages, destination, cost of transportation, and duration of work.

Eight states require that the agent must be a person of good moral character and provide means for ascertaining this by investigations, affidavits, and hearings. The remainder of the states open the door to any one with the price of a license, though they sometimes provide additional safeguards for its revocation, as for "good cause shown." In addition to these specific laws, many states have general statutes or penal laws which are effective. Typical of these is the provision in the penal law of New York which makes any false statements in regard to employment a mis-

demeanor enforceable directly by the district
attorney's office and not through the Department
of Licenses which enforces the employment agency
law.

(6)   It has been generally recognized that the
dangers attending the employment of women call
for special legislation on both physical and moral
grounds.   This feeling is reflected in the many
laws regulating hours and conditions of women's
work in factories and stores.   The unemployed
woman is also exposed to danger and temptations.
Fourteen states specifically prohibit sending a
woman or a minor to a house of prostitution or to
any immoral place.   Missouri imposes a fine of
$100 to $1000 and imprisonment for sixty days to
a year for this offense.   Some of these provisions
include sending a woman to work in a place where
liquor is sold, and forbid agents to allow persons
of bad character, prostitutes, gamblers or intoxicated persons to frequent the agency.   There are
general statutes which protect women to some
degree, but as women not as workers.   Less than
30 per cent. of the states have recognized this
danger and erected legal safeguards.   The extent
to which employment agents shall make investigations of positions offered before sending women to
them is a debatable question.   Some states meet
this by providing that the conditions should
be such as could be ascertained upon reasonable inquiry.   If the situation in New Jersey,
which has the strongest provisions on record, is

24

typical, the present provisions are largely a failure. The Commission of Immigration of New Jersey, which made its report to Governor Fielder in 1914, stated that in its investigations of employment agencies in the state, it found that nineteen out of twenty-nine agencies were willing to procure girls to work as servants in disorderly houses and for immoral purposes. The provisions forbidding the conducting of agencies in rooms used for living purposes or where liquor is sold were also disregarded. Seventy-two per cent. of the licensed agencies inspected were violating this provision of the law. Three were being operated in saloons, two of which ran dance halls in the rear, and many other agencies were located in tenement house kitchens and bedrooms.

(7) No problem in the organization of the labor market is more pressing to-day than the question whether an employment agent shall act simply as a medium for bringing employer and employee together, and then leave them to make their own arrangement, or whether he shall assist in the making of the contract, and therefore be held responsible for it. The prevailing custom allows the agent a considerable degree of participation. There is, however, a growing tendency to limit the agent's duty to merely furnishing the exchange where such contracts may be made, without his being a party to them or in any way influencing them. The impossibility of holding the "go-between" responsible for the acts of the

principals, the dissatisfaction resulting from the agent's interference, and the failures in adjustment due to the agent's manipulation or inaccurate statement of the orders they have received, support the growing belief that they should act as agents only.

The "personal service" practice is most strongly intrenched in the domestic service agencies. The provision in several states that references be furnished makes possible much fraud and misrepresentation, and in some places has given rise to a traffic in references. This would be eliminated if the agreement were made entirely between the prospective employer and employee. It is a doubtful question to what extent references handled and filed by agencies actually protect homes, which was the purpose for which the laws were first passed. Under the present methods there are certainly evils on both sides. Agents unquestionably decide now where and under what conditions employees shall work; they are brokers in character and wages alike, and they frequently misrepresent and misunderstand both, and are imposed upon as to both.

Four states prohibit agents from taking or enticing employees from positions in which they have been placed, with a view to furnishing them with other work. In two of these states, the provisions seem to have had their origin in labor troubles. Indiana forbids an agent to assist in having one employee discharged, to make a

vacancy for another on his list. New Jersey and
New York forbid inducing a domestic servant to
leave her position. Maine forbids inducing an
employee to leave with a view to providing other
employment through the agency.

There is a growing belief that every man sent
out to a position should be informed of the conditions of the work and that a strike is one of the
essential matters upon which he should be informed, and that he should then decide, without
influence or inducement, to accept or reject this
offer. But two states provide that all applicants
for work shall be notified when a strike is in progress before being sent out. Probably no other
misrepresentation has led to so much hardship
on the part of employees who have found themselves stranded and penniless under such conditions. Certainly this deception has brought
general labor agencies into disrepute. Where
general provisions against misrepresentation have
been invoked, silence upon the matter of a strike
has not been generally held to constitute a ground
for complaint.

Beyond these minimum requirements, public
opinion is fast advancing. Six states prohibit
agencies from placing children in violation of law,
thus securing their coöperation in the enforcement
of child-labor laws. The limitation of the number
of agencies to the population, to prevent "cut-
throat competition," is being proposed. Two
states have found this competition so menacing

that they have passed laws prohibiting agents from inducing or compelling any person to enter such agency by force or by taking possession of his property.

(8)   Public spirited American citizens who have labored hard to secure the passage of good laws have a way of "going to sleep" when the laws are safely on the statute books.   The most ironclad law is weak unless it is in the hands of a good officer with a sufficient appropriation.   Whatever enthusiasm may have been aroused by the way in which some statutes have dealt with this problem on the statute books may therefore be chilled when the enforcement of these laws is analyzed.   Many persons still cling to the mistaken theory that the issuance of a license is a regulative rather than a revenue measure.

In the matter of appropriations, not one law carries a definite appropriation so the enforcing officer may know what he has to spend and can plan his work intelligently.   Illinois comes nearest to this by providing for a chief inspector at a salary of $3600 per year who must give a $5000 bond, and one inspector for every fifty licensed agents at a salary of $1500.   Three states, California, Indiana, and Missouri provide that all fees and fines shall constitute a fund for enforcing the law.

Where the law is left to cities to enforce, the amount with them is optional and there is therefore a great variety of results.   In New York City about $50,000 a year is appropriated, in the other cities of the state practically nothing. In Boston the appropriation to the licensing board is adequate; in other cities of other states like Philadelphia the law is a dead letter, one inspector on part-time grappling with the situation.

Where state departments enforce the laws, the general appropriation bills carry small appropriations, but only too often the enforcing officer has been expected to make his already overburdened appropriation cover the additional work. The surest way to nullify these laws is to kill the appropriation, a trick not unknown to private employment agents and their supporters.

Almost as important as an appropriation is the fixing of responsibility for enforcement. Twelve of the states meet this issue squarely by placing the enforcement in the hands of the state labor department or commissioner or bureau of statistics with powers of investigation, revocation of licenses, and institution of court proceedings for violation. Two states,—California and Illinois—give the commissioner power to make arrests, while others provide hearings. The enforcement in these states is fairly uniform. Two states divide the responsibility between state and cities. In the other nine states where the matter is left to the cities or counties, there is no uniform enforcement even in cities of the same state. In New York one city makes provision and enforces the law; the others do not. Speaking of conditions in

Buffalo, a port and a very important employment center, the State Commission of Immigration in 1909 said:

An investigator of the commission who visited the employment bureaus at Buffalo found that only 2 of 17 kept their registers according to law. Fourteen made no entry in the last four columns, namely: (1) names of applicants for help, (2) in what capacity, (3) place of residence, (4) fees. One agency, which in November secured positions for 63 men and women, had no entry whatsoever in the register. The investigator was given the names and addresses of 10 unlicensed employment offices. He found the employment agency law in various languages to be unknown in Buffalo and that vicinity. Only English placards adorn the walls, and the foreign applicants are ignorant of the law. Other violations were reported, such as sending applicants to places where there was no bona fide order for labor and placing girls in disorderly houses.

The report of the Immigration Commission in 1914, in New Jersey, where municipalities enforce the law, shows that 69, or 37 per cent., were operating without a license. Of 51 licensed agencies investigated, 32 had the license posted as required by law; 34 were located in living rooms, which is prohibited; only 20 kept their books properly, only 15 issued adequate receipts, and in but 24 instances was the law posted as required. These are the simplest provisions to enforce, as violations are much more easily proved than are fraud and misrepresentation; yet they are largely ignored.

These illustrations are typical and can be duplicated in every other state where there is no fixed responsibility for enforcement. With no inspectors, a few voluntary license fees will be gathered in, but it will be cheaper to do business without a license and the risk of an occasional fine is too remote to lead agents to fear the law. Many of these laws do not contemplate any preventive work as they provide for action only on complaint.

It has not been possible to make a study of the actual effect of these laws upon the labor market. It is clear, however, that they have caused no widespread reduction in the number of agencies. In Massachusetts, the Licensing Board limits the number of agencies, each new agency being compelled to await a vacancy in the list. Boston is therefore free from "cutthroat competition" and its evils. In New York City, notwithstanding that 182 licenses were revoked from 1904–14, the number has increased, except during the past year among theatrical agencies which have found a way to evade the law. In Indiana, on the contrary, the reports show that of the nineteen licensed agencies in 1910, eight went out of business in Indianapolis, the license of one of these having been revoked.

It practically narrows down to this, that in thirteen states of the union and in a few large cities, so far as state laws go, the unemployed are protected because there is machinery for enforcing the law. In all others, except where the laws are modified by strictly local regulations, they are at the mercy of the middlemen. Undoubtedly the laws have operated to prevent the more open frauds and graver abuses, but many are the agents who still take chances on the law, and with big returns for small risks in many cases.

There are other protective laws which have very vitally affected the labor market, especially those dealing with unskilled immigrant labor. These are the so-called peonage laws. The Florida law is typical of the state laws enacted in many Southern states:

Any person in this state who shall contract with another to perform any labor or service and who shall, by reason of such contract and with the intent to injure and defraud, obtain or procure money or other thing of value as a credit or advances from the person so contracted with and who shall without just cause, fail or refuse to perform such labor or service or fail or refuse to pay for the money or other thing of value so received upon demand, shall be guilty of a misdemeanor and upon conviction thereof shall be punished by a fine not exceeding five hundred dollars or by imprisonment for a period not exceeding six months.

Under such provisions immigrants, to whom fare has been advanced or supplies given on credit, have been held in bondage and compelled to work out their indebtedness. The Maine law is typical of provisions in Northern states. It provides as follows:

Whoever enters into an agreement to labor for another in any lumbering operation or in driving logs, and in consideration thereof receives any advance of goods, money, or transportation, and unreasonably, and with intent to defraud, fails to enter into such employment as agreed, and labor for a sufficient time to reimburse his employer for said advance, and expenses of transportation, shall be punished by a fine of not exceeding ten dollars, or by imprisonment not exceeding thirty days.

Judges of municipal courts and trial justices shall have jurisdiction of the offense described in this act.

Before this law was passed, employers could have resorted to civil action, but they considered this too costly, and not calculated to have the same moral effect on other woodsmen as a fine or imprisonment. There have been disputes as to the justice of this law, but not so much concerning its theory as the manner in which it has worked out. This law affects mainly men working in the lumber camps, who are now principally immigrants, shipped through Boston labor agents who misrepresent the conditions in the camps. The men, rebelling at the situation they find, leave the camps, against the will of the lumbermen, who have advanced transportation and supplies.

Similar statutes are in force in Alabama, Arkansas, Florida, Georgia, Louisiana, Minnesota,

Mississippi, New Mexico, North Dakota, and South Carolina. Some of these statutes have been declared unconstitutional. In 1905, in the charge to the Grand Jury, in the Arkansas case, it was stated that:

Peonage, within the meaning of this law, is the holding of any person to do service or labor for the purpose of paying or liquidating an indebtedness due from the laborer or employe to the employer, when such employe desires to leave or quit the employment before the debt is paid off. It is wholly immaterial whether the contract whereby the laborer is to work out an indebtedness due from him to the employer is entered into voluntarily or not. The laws of the United States declare all such contracts null and void, and they cannot be enforced.

In Bailey *v.* Alabama (219 U. S. 219), it was held:

That so far as the refusal without just cause to perform the labor called for in a written contract of employment under which the employee has obtained money which was not refunded, or property which was not paid for, is made prima facie evidence of an intent to default by Ala. Code 1896, Sec. 4730, as amended by Gen. Acts 1903, p. 345, and Gen. Acts 1907, 9, 636, and therefore punishable as a criminal offence, such legislation offends against the prohibition of the thirteenth amendment to the Federal Constitution against involuntary servitude, except as punishment for crime, and against the provisions forbidding peonage, found in R. S. sec. 1990 and 5526, enacted to secure the enforcement of such amendment, especially since, under the local practice, the accused may not for the purpose of rebutting the statutory presumption, testify as to his uncommunicated motives, purposes, or intentions.

The ease with which such laws can be used to oppress the victims of unscrupulous employment agents is apparent.

The Federal law prohibits peonage in the following terms:

The holding of any person to service or labor under the system known as peonage is abolished and forever prohibited in the Territory of New Mexico, or in any other Territory or State of the United States; and all acts, laws, resolutions, orders, regulations, or usages of the Territory of New Mexico, or of any other Territory or State, which have heretofore established, maintained, or enforced, or by virtue of which any attempt shall hereafter be made to establish, maintain, or enforce, directly or indirectly, the voluntary or involuntary service or labor of any persons as peons, in liquidation of any debt or obligation, or otherwise, are declared null and void. (Comp. Stat.)

Every person who holds, arrests, returns, or causes to be held, arrested, or returned, or in any manner aids in the arrest or return of any person to a condition of peonage, shall be punished by a fine of not less than one thousand nor more than five thousand dollars, or by imprisonment for not less than one year nor more than five years, or by both. (Comp. Stat.)

Whoever kidnaps or carries away any other person,

with the intent that such other person be sold into involuntary servitude, or held as a slave; or who entices, persuades, or induces any other person to go on board any vessel or to any other place with the intent that he may be made or held as a slave, or sent out of the country to be so made or held; or who in any way knowingly aids in causing any other person to be held, sold, or carried away to be held or sold as a slave, shall be fined not more than five thousand dollars, or imprisoned not more than five years, or both.

Whoever holds, arrests, returns, or causes to be held, arrested, or returned, or in any manner aids in the arrest or return of any person to a condition of peonage, shall be fined not more than five thousand dollars, or imprisoned not more than five years, or both.

Whoever shall knowingly and willfully bring into the United States or any place subject to the jurisdiction thereof, any person inveigled or forcibly kidnapped in any other country, with intent to hold such person so inveigled or kidnapped in confinement or to any involuntary servitude; or whoever shall knowingly or willfully sell, or cause to be sold, into any condition of involuntary servitude, any other person for any term whatever, or whoever shall knowingly and willfully hold to involuntary servitude any person so brought or sold, shall be fined not more than five thousand dollars and imprisoned not more than five years.   (Acts of 1908-9.)

In 1904 and the years following, the Federal government vigorously enforced the law with respect to immigrants in the Southern states. An extremely flagrant case was found in Arkansas. An immigrant was arrested as a vagrant, convicted before a justice of the peace, and sentenced to pay a fine of $10 and costs. To this was added, illegally, the expenses and mileage of the constable who came to arrest him, and the expenses and mileage of both constable and prisoner on the way to the convict farm where the prisoner was taken to work out his indebtedness. The lessee of the farm paid the county only 25 per cent. of the fine and justice's costs, and held the prisoner to work out both the legal and illegal expenses at 75 cents a day. Eighty prisoners were kept in a barn of moderate size, with no special arrangement for ventilation or sanitation. On Saturday nights they were locked in and kept there until Monday morning. While at work they were guarded by trusties armed with shotguns. Some of the prisoners were whipped and otherwise illtreated. A substantial verdict was obtained by one of the prisoners against the proprietor of the farm.

The Immigration Commission reported that the chief causes of the abuses known as peonage—holding to enforced labor under undesirable conditions—are the systems of making advances to laborers, the operation of contract labor laws, and the misrepresentations made to laborers by unscrupulous employment agents. Cases of involuntary servitude were found in all states investigated except Oklahoma and Connecticut. In the

Southern cases, it was shown in nearly every instance that the laborers who were held in peonage had been sent from New York City, the victims of gross misrepresentations made by labor agents there as to the conditions under which they were to work, and in many instances they were totally unfitted for the work to which they were going.

In addition to the regulation of private agencies and the protection of employers by peonage laws, some states have passed legislation which indirectly affects unemployment. Both New York and California have passed laws establishing state departments or commissions of immigration, a part of whose function is the protection and distribution of the unemployed. These states have also adopted regulations for the minimum sanitary requirements in camps, including clean sleeping places with adequate air space, separate kitchens, sanitary garbage receptacles and toilets, and an adequate and uncontaminated supply of water in the camps conducted by the padroni or otherwise. Such regulations have much to do with maintaining the steadiness of the labor market.

In a period when home rule is the popular legislative cry, we turn hopefully to the cities to see what they, of their own initiative, have done to protect the unemployed. We find that few cities have considered this as a local matter requiring regulation. Where ordinances have been passed, they usually cover merely the license tax, bond, and the fee that may be charged; sometimes they give power of revocation to the police department or to the licensing authority, and prescribe a penalty for misrepresentation. The general tendency, however, is either to rely altogether on the state law, no matter how inadequate it may be, or else to ignore the whole problem. One city with over 35,000 inhabitants is a good example of this latter attitude. The mayor reports that they have never found it necessary to pass any legislation regulating private agencies as the labor problem there has proved negligible, owing to the very small percentage of foreigners in the population.

On account of the number and menace of many colored agencies in Washington and in line with the movement to make that city a national model for the country, there has been enacted a very excellent law, enforceable by the Commissioners of the District of Columbia. This law provides for a bond and for a license and that the applicant shall be a person of good general character; for the posting of the license and law, and that no agency may be conducted in living apartments or on premises where liquor is sold. Registers and receipts are required and a copy of the labor contract must be given to the employee. The provisions against fraud and misrepresentation are adequate and prohibit among other things sending employees to employers who have not

applied to the agency. Women may not be sent
as servants, inmates, or performers to immoral
or gambling places nor are disreputable persons
permitted to frequent the agencies. Ample provision is made for prompt hearings and revocation
of licenses and court proceedings. The enforcement of the law places the least possible burden
upon the unemployed, and conditions have been
much improved under the aggressive action of the
commissioners and interested civic organizations.

The rules of the Licensing Board of Boston are
a good example of careful, efficient municipal
regulation. In addition to the provisions of the
state law regulating private agencies, the city
Board has made the following rules: Every
licensed intelligence office keeper must post upon
the premises, his license, the fee for which is $50,
and two copies of the rule limiting the amount of
the fee and must also post a suitable sign on the
outside door; he must keep a record of names and
addresses of applicants placed in positions and
employers to whom workmen are sent, and also
of all sums of money received for such services.
The fee is limited to one week's wages, except that
if the applicant is discharged within six weeks,
the office is not entitled to keep over one day's
wages for each week or part of week the workman
has been employed; and if a person who is provided
with employment leaves it within three weeks, the
agent must refund to him within four days of
demand, three-fifths of the fee he has paid. The

agent must also refund all fees and transportation to applicants sent to a place where there is no vacancy of the kind applied for, or if the employment is not as specified by the license. These rules are enforced by the police. Licenses may be revoked for violation of statutes or rules or for any other cause deemed sufficient by the Board. It is stated that the Board has had no report for some years of any infraction of its rules or of the law.

Other typical city provisions are as follows:

Keokuk, Iowa, requires employment agencies to take out a license at a fee of $500, payable in advance. Upon violation of any of the city council's provisions, the license is revoked and a fine of $5 to $100, or imprisonment for not over 30 days is imposed. The St. Paul and Minneapolis ordinances simply reënact the state law, providing for licenses at $150, $100, and $75, for general, male, and female agencies; a bond of $2000 for a general or a male office and $1000 for female; a record of terms of employment, to be kept in a book for that purpose, and duplicate copies for workmen and employer; and also the prohibition against accepting any fee unless the agent has a *bona fide* order for the applicant's services; the ordinances add a fine of $100 or imprisonment until the fine is paid, or not over 90 days. In Providence the agencies are regulated under a state law authorizing cities to license agencies, and a city ordinance prescribing local regulations;

any one wishing to open an intelligence office
applies to the city clerk, who refers the application
for investigation to the inspectors' office in the
Police Department.   The license fee is $20, and
a sign bearing the word "licensed" must be conspicuously posted; a record must be kept showing
names and addresses of all applicants.   The fee
is limited to $1, and must be refunded within
6 days if no work is obtained.   Agencies are not
permitted to induce employees to leave other
employment.   The enforcement of the law is in
the hands of the Chief of Police.   No penalty for
misconduct is provided except revocation of the
license.   In Lowell, Massachusetts, the Licensing
Commission grants licenses and may revoke them
after a hearing upon a complaint; if a crime has
been committed, the police authorities are notified.
The Commission reports that it has not been necessary to revoke a license or to prosecute an agency.

On the other hand some cities have passed
ordinances which handicap the unemployed and
place a premium on law breaking when enough
American born workmen cannot be found for the
jobs.   These are charter provisions or ordinances
prohibiting the employment of aliens upon public
works or by the city government, and prohibiting their getting licenses as venders, hucksters,
peddlers, hackmen, junk dealers and many other
of the callings open to men with only a small
amount of capital.   Typical cities are Philadelphia
where contractors on public works can employ

only citizens, and only citizens can get licenses as bankers, peddlers, etc., of fish, vegetables, fruit, general produce, wood, coal, or wares and merchandise of any kind; and Portland, Oregon, where all civil service officeholders must be citizens, preference must be given to citizens on public works, and where only a citizen can get a liquor license. In Quincy, Illinois, the employment of aliens in any capacity is forbidden. The unskilled laborer going around the country seeking employment often finds himself shut out from work by such laws as that in Detroit, requiring that all applicants for work as laborers must be residents of the city, or that in Butte, which provides that only resident voters may be employed by the city at day's wages.

With the failure of the states to regulate or successfully compete with private agencies, with the cities neglectful and indifferent, one turns confidently to the Federal government, only to find that no direct attempt has been made to deal with the interstate abuses resulting from the enormous distribution of labor that takes place from coast to coast. A bill is now pending before the Labor Committee of the House which provides for the licensing and regulation of all agents that do an interstate business and who send persons from one state to another. There is considerable sentiment in favor of this and its enactment into law seems not unlikely.

The greatest activity on the part of the Federal government has been in regard to the employment of seamen. The law provides for the appointment of shipping commissioners to superintend the engagement and discharge of seamen, and also requires that in the foreign trade shipping articles be made by the master before the voyage begins, stating the nature and duration of the voyage, the port at which it is to terminate, the number of the crew, wages, provisions, etc. This agreement is to be signed in the presence of the shipping commissioner. The law also prohibits retaining a sailor's clothing or demanding or receiving pay from a seaman for providing him with employment. The violation of these provisions has been made a misdemeanor, with a penalty of not over $500 fine or not over six months, or both, attached. Another provision of this Federal law, which stipulates that the only advance a sailor can get is an amount not over one month's wages advanced to an original creditor for a debt for board and lodging, has had an effect different from what was contemplated. It was meant to safeguard the sailor, but it really protects the boarding-house keeper by making it safe for him to trust the sailor. If the sailor wishes to leave money with his wife and children, his only resource is to get in debt to the boarding-house keeper and then give him an assignment to cover the debt and the amount for his family, which the keeper pays over to them.

The Collector of the Port in New York, supplementing the regulations in force at Ellis Island, has issued a series of dock regulations which protect arriving unemployed aliens by prohibiting hotel and boarding-house representatives from having any business relations with steamship agents or paying them any commissions or gratuities, and requiring them to conduct patrons to their destination without unnecessary expense and without delays on false pretexts. Hotels must have inclusive charges posted, are allowed to require advance payment for only one day, must give rebates for service paid for but not used, and must give correct advice and protect patrons from imposition and coercion. Aliens with complaints to make must be directed to make them to the collector, and disputes arising on the piers must be referred to some government official. The violation of any of these rules results in cancellation of the dock permit and the withdrawal of all privileges from the offending hotel or boarding-house.

It must be apparent to those who have followed the description of the intricate interstate activities of employment agents that these half-developed, inadequate, unenforced, and often unenforceable state and city laws provide only a minimum of protection, that they reach but few of the unemployed, who often do not know of their existence, and that the nation has shown but little comprehension of the task before it and little resourcefulness in meeting it.

We need uniform state laws, enforceable by state authorities, the extension of these laws to all states, and the regulation of interstate business. We need in every case provision for inspectors, and adequate appropriations. No law dealing with unemployment can be enforced which deals with complaints only and does no preventive work. The initial burden and cost are now too great to the worker and society pays the ultimate cost in loss of production and efficiency. Furthermore, without adequate regulations to cover the field of competition, no governmental agency can hope to succeed.

CHAPTER XII

HOW AMERICA RELIEVES UNEMPLOYMENT

WE have shown how America markets its labor. It remains to show what America does to meet unemployment when the labor market furnishes no answer. What does it do when workers, destitute through unemployment, have no food and no shelter, no means, in short, of preserving their employability. What does it do for those normally capable workers who, because of the hardships of an unemployed period have temporarily lost their working power so that, when perhaps they do get a temporary job at shovelling snow, they fall beside their shovels after an hour's work. What does it do for that predominant type of the American underemployed, the seasonal worker, who after a summer of fruit picking, for example, beats his way back to the city quite "broke" because the season was a poor one, the weather too stormy, or the conditions of ripeness too variable.

Never having analyzed the causes and factors of unemployment, America has naturally enough devised remedies only for those aspects of it wherein there is a menace to law and order, or inconvenience to a community because of large numbers of unemployed, or suffering so sharp that it cannot be disregarded. The preceding analysis of the present labor market has shown that there has been little general conception of the relation of the labor market to unemployment. Yet unemployment as a labor market problem has been a good deal better understood than unemployment as an industrial and as a social problem. This explains why a new labor bureau is usually the first measure proposed by way of remedy when any community becomes really convinced that the unemployment in its midst has reached an "actionable" degree. The confusion caused by the spasmodic multiplication of unrelated bureaus becomes a fertile source of the very difficulties the bureaus were designed to meet. They do not increase or steady the volume of work; they do not improve the equipment of the worker; they do not safeguard the individual worker or enable him to maintain his employability when he is out of work. Any real solution of unemployment must meet all of these points, as well as the problems of distribution and adjustment which properly belong to the labor market.

It is the purpose of the present chapter to set forth first those practical emergency measures that have already been instituted or tried in America with the direct and conscious purpose of remedying unemployment; and, secondly, the more numerous proposed measures which, while not yet confirmed by experiment, suggest both a new point of view in regard to unemployment, and further possibilities in the way of practical remedy. The second group includes efforts of two kinds: practical measures to serve either temporarily or permanently; and various forms of propaganda. Although these perhaps owe their origin to present emergencies, they cannot help resulting in a more fundamental understanding of unemployment, and an increase in permanent as well as in emergency measures for dealing with it.

Of the practical measures already tried, to some degree in this country, we may consider first the efforts to create work when the supply of work in the industrial field is plainly inadequate. This has been done sometimes by charities and philanthropies, sometimes by cities, sometimes by industries.

Among those begun by charities and philanthropies are such enterprises as sewing rooms for women, and woodyards for men. As has been noted,[1] sewing rooms have long been conducted by certain of the larger churches, and in critical times of unemployment they have been instituted as a purely emergency measure by such organizations as the Conference on Unemployment Among Women, the Vacation War Relief Work Committee of New York, the Brooklyn Bureau of Charities, the Emergency Aid Committee of Philadelphia, and the Buffalo War Relief Committee. The sewing rooms provide the women with warm

[1] See page 271.

shelter for the day—which is not an unimportant detail since most of them have unheated rooms at home, and some of them live in "Homes for Working Women" which expressly stipulate that they are not to be at home during the day; they provide them with lunch and pay them from 50 cents to $1.25 for their day's work. An effort is usually made to secure the work from hospitals and other institutions, and thus avoid entering the regular market. The sewing room now being conducted by the Vacation Committee of New York is making articles for the Red Cross; that conducted by the Brooklyn Bureau of Charities is making articles to be sold only to those wishing to send them to the Belgium Relief Fund. The following account of the chairman of the Buffalo Work Room Committee is suggestive:

Our first idea in opening the five rooms which we started to-day was, as I said, to meet a need of which we were perfectly conscious and the places in those workrooms were really filled in advance by the women whose needs we knew. Of course, we were conscious that it was a drop in the bucket but we were not prepared for the great need among a very different class of women, which came to light after the papers announced the fact that the Red Cross would give employment to some of Buffalo's unemployed. The constant stream of sewing women of the better class, women who were not dependent, women who came for work and not for charity and for whom we felt every effort must be made to keep them out of the dependent class, has raised a situation which we hardly know how to meet. Much of this unemployment, we feel is just a case of maladjustment. There are women who are capable of getting positions as seamstresses by the day and we feel there is sufficient demand for such women in Buffalo to lessen our list. In the Social Service Building we are, therefore, opening next week a sixth work-room for afternoon work, the work being entirely for hospital supplies, bandages, etc. Positions in this room will be given to women only while we try to place them in permanent work. We are also giving out the equivalent of two days' work each day in bundles of hospital shirts to women who can do the work at home. Our six workrooms, therefore, will care for twenty-seven women a day, few enough in face of serious need. We are not offering permanent positions to any one, simply work by the day.

You ask about the wages and the occupations represented among the women. The afternoon workroom is filled almost entirely with unemployed women from the shops, seamstresses, and dressmakers. The other women are chiefly working heads of families, women with children, all of whom know enough about sewing to run a sewing machine. They are from all nationalities, Italian, Polish, English, Irish, and Sicilian.

We are offering $1.50 a day for an eight-hour day. We have been criticized a little for this as it restricts the number of women we can employ, but we insist upon the point as it has taken years of education to get the Buffalo public educated to the idea of a $1.50 wage and we do not feel that we should take advantage of this emergency to undermine the principle. We have practically no young girls in our employ who would be receiving a less wage in a shop or workroom. All of the women sent out from these organizations are given $1.50 a day for other work. The money has come easily. People are very much interested in the idea, and although we have not yet enough for the whole six months, we are starting in with the confidence that it will come.

The four settlements in Buffalo which are carrying workrooms are supported by four prominent churches and we have thrown the responsibility on these churches for raising the money for the support of those workrooms. The papers have given us good notices and the idea, as I say, has taken hold in Buffalo.

Workroom blanks . . . are filled out by whoever is responsible for the workroom, the estimate at the end being mailed to me at the end of each week, so that a record can be kept. We have had in our mind in our estimate of expense and the number of garments which can be made, the surgical night shirt. We will, of course, vary our output, some weeks making larger and more expensive garments, trying only to keep an average.

Some churches in connection with their sewing-room run a small shop which the church members are expected to patronize. Usually women are admitted to sewing-rooms entirely on the basis of their need, and not at all on the basis of sewing ability or previous occupation. In New York the Vacation Committee runs the sewing-room in connection with an employment bureau, and admits to the sewing-room only those registered in the bureau. In other sewing-rooms there is no selective principle whatever. Often a large percentage of the women are domestic servants suddenly dismissed in seasons of general retrenchment, and quite without resources. Sometimes they are stenographers and office assistants. There is usually no relation between the amount of work done and the daily wage, and no organization whatever on any efficiency basis. A woman may take a week at seventy-five cents a day to make a garment that will sell for seventy-five cents. In some cases sewing-rooms begun with the purpose of tiding normal workers over a period of unemployment by the creation of work have become permanent measures for looking after the handicapped of a community on other than a frankly charitable basis. Often their service to the normal unemployed has consisted to no small degree in restoring them to working conditions by supplying good food and by giving them a recess from the ceaseless job hunting, with the exposure and hardship it entails in freezing weather. It does not appear that sewing-rooms, established for unemployed women, have been self-supporting.

In this they differ in some instances from the artificial work supplied for unemployed men in woodyards and like enterprises. These are usually conducted either by charitable societies or relief organizations as tests of the worthiness of applicants, and for the purpose of making able-bodied men earn a part or all of the relief given; or by cities, especially reserve labor centers through which seasonal and casual workers regularly pass or in which they spend the winter. Private organizations or missions often use them in connection with lodging-houses. For instance, the price of lodging is twenty cents a night at a number of lodging-houses or missions throughout the country. The man without the price works in the woodyard for two hours the next morning to pay for his board. He earns, that is to say, ten cents an hour for the two most valuable hours of his day, a rate not half that paid to the ordinary unskilled laborer working a few blocks away. Such woodyards are not infrequent throughout the country.

Woodyards and kindred enterprises operated by the larger charitable societies vary greatly in the amounts paid. In Oakland, California, a municipal woodyard is run in connection with a lodging-house and a free employment bureau. The woodyard is especially designed for transients, and a bed or a meal is given in return for an hour's labor. The city of Tacoma reports, for the winter of 1913–14: "When men came from surrounding places jobless and penniless, the city established a wheelbarrow brigade and gave them work at $1 a day, the money to go for food to relieve the immediate necessities."

In some cases in which large numbers of unemployed men have stimulated cities to create relief work, the work, while being in a sense artificial, has had some connection with regular city work. Such, for instance, was the Duluth rock pile, operated by the city of Duluth in connection with the Associated Charities. The idea was to provide work enough for each man to enable him to get food, shelter, and anything else he needed to put him on the road to a steady job. In January, 1911, work was begun at demolishing a huge wall of rock intercepting the growth of Duluth's main thoroughfare. The skilled work, the blasting and drilling, was done by regular employees of the city. The preparation of the rock for the crusher was left to the unemployed men. Every man engaged had to have an intention to return to his regular employment at the first opportunity. If he plainly had this intention, upon presenting his case to the Associated Charities, he was put to work on the quarry, at a wage of $1.20 a day, paid in meal tickets, employment office fees, or whatever else the man needed. The quarry was in operation two winters, not being started in the winter of 1913 because there was so little involuntary unemployment. The first year each man averaged three days, the second year somewhat longer. In both years a considerable percentage of the men returned to their regular employment.

St. Louis provides a few hours' work on the public streets and pays for it by a lodging and three cheap meals. It also provides public employment on a rock pile or in similar work at wages slightly less than the market rate. Kansas City provides work for the unemployed in its quarries at $1 a day and permits them to earn so much as $3 a day if they are fast workers. They may work only every third day, however.

Des Moines, Iowa, for two years operated a municipal farm by farming "a piece of cemetery ground not yet converted to that use." The income of the first year is reported to have been greatly modified by the initial expenses; that for the second year to have been good. As a departure from the common "poor farm" maintained by cities and counties for defectives or delinquents of one kind or another, the Des Moines experiment is suggestive.

A number of cities in the winter furnish work at shovelling snow for a considerable number of their unemployed. In New York City in the winter of 1913–14, men of all trades and professions and of all conditions of life applied for this work. The difficulty was that many of those that applied for a snow shovel had not had anything to eat for days and were too weak to shovel snow; also, they were far too thinly clad, the great majority of them being quite literally "on their uppers." This situation was so marked that a high city official, watching the gangs being mustered, urged the sending of health inspectors along with each gang.

These, while they do not form a complete history, are illustrative of the attempts American

26

cities have made to relieve unemployment temporarily by creating work. In general, these attempts are evidently directed toward the transient, or the migratory laborer. Some of them are semi-punitive; Utah City, for instance, reports "transients going through our city or rather stopping off here, if they have no visible means of support are given a term and worked on our streets." None of the measures mentioned pretends to conform to the normal conditions of industry or to operate under regular industrial standards as to wage and efficiency. One city, which is now agitating relief work for the unemployed in the war crisis, called the attention of its council to the fact that last winter when work at rock removal was furnished the unemployed the rock had been simply carted to one section of the city in the winter and—back in the spring.

Providing unemployed men with public work that is *not* artificial, that can be assigned with due observance of all the necessary discriminations, and supervised according to the normal standards, is practically unknown in America and must be discussed among proposed remedies rather than previous experiments. It has been approximated here and there in the past, notably in Los Angeles and in San Francisco. Los Angeles in 1913–14 used emergency funds for public improvements designed to give work to the unemployed. San Francisco, in the winter of 1913–14, put 1000 unemployed men at work on government reservations near the city, after the expenditure of $5000 for that purpose had been authorized at Washington. Two thousand others were put to work on boulevards and other public improvements. The reason that public works under normal standards have not been used more than they have to draw off the forces of the unemployed is undoubtedly that it would involve careful classification of the employable and unemployable, and a record of the trades and training and previous efficiency of the applicants—and these studies of the unemployed as a preliminary to remedying unemployment are not comprehended in the conception of unemployment thus far generally developed in America.

In some cities certain public officials have on their own responsibility dealt with unemployment. The attempt has consisted usually in regularizing their own work as in the case of street departments, making whatever adjustments were necessary to keep their men at work. For instance, in New York, the Park Department announced to four hundred of its employees a curtailment of hours and wages in order that an otherwise necessary laying off of one hundred of them might be avoided. In a few cases the action of officials affects unemployed men outside the particular department. A notable instance of this in times when unemployment is marked is the practice of certain coroners in saving jury work only for the deserving unemployed, assuring them at least a part of a day's work. This plan has been successfully followed in Chicago and elsewhere in Illinois.

The seasonal trades have been pointed out as one of the greatest factors in unemployment. We have not learned of any instances in America where the dovetailing of seasonal industries has really been brought about by industry. The burden of making connections regularly several times a year still falls upon the workman. Here and there a training school has taught its pupils millinery and lamp-shade making because when the millinery trade is at its worst the lamp-shade trade is at its best, and because the same kind of faculty and skill is required by both. Here and there also a separate industry has devised a side line,—a shoe plant, for instance, swinging over to Christmas cards—to tide over its own dull season by such an adjustment. But such arrangements within a single industry are very different from an accommodation policy among several separate industries.

It would be difficult to make any general statements as to what individual adjustments isolated *single* industries may have made at various times throughout the country, thereby increasing or maintaining the supply of work. Before the present crisis one large automobile company arranged to have its slack season fall in the summer, instead of in the winter as it traditionally had, in order that harvest work might fill the gap. At the same time the company reduced the working hours from nine to eight in order to permit the employment of 4000 additional men, established a minimum wage and a clearing house policy by which a man is moved from department to department until he finds the work he can do and likes to do. The policy behind all these measures is increasing the firm's employment capacity and stability *permanently*. Movements of this kind are not to be confused with the purely emergency adjustments within industries which the war crisis has produced.

Nowhere does the result of America's failure to classify the unemployed show more than in the nature of the provisions made for the shelter either of natives in a community, homeless through unemployment, or of migrating workmen passing through a town on the way to or on the hunt for a job. In Germany it is recognized that unemployed men passing from one job to another and without funds are neither vagrants nor subjects for poor relief. Germany has therefore a system of *Herbergen*, shelter stations, a half day's walk apart. The traveler on the way to a job has a chance to work a half day and walk the other half, presents at each his records, and has the time of entering and leaving registered in a pass book which he presents at the next station. In America where distances are vastly greater, and the transportation problem much more considerable, and where the migrating worker is at least as essential as he is in Germany, the sheltering of the unemployed has received no organized attention, and very little attention of any kind. The unemployed man in America is likely to avoid the few shelters that do exist as long as he can; he will rather go to the back room of a saloon, or he will creep under the platforms of warehouses by the river when the policeman is around the corner, or will sneak into the ovens of the brick kiln on the outskirts of town, when the heat has gone off sufficiently to make them at all endurable, or into the "side door pullman" in the freight yard, or into a dozen other places suitable only for the cautious.

A few weeks ago the newspapers of one of the largest cities in the country announced that a proposition for a municipal lodging-house would for the first time be agitated in councils. This belated interest in the matter of housing the unemployed indicates the situation all over the country. The municipal lodging-house is an "advanced" feature found in a very few cities of this country. And in practically none of these few is it found with adequate facilities or with the kind of management that indicates any constructive intention. For some curious reason a municipal lodging-house is likely to be a discarded city jail—or some other outgrown building rigged up as a makeshift, and intended to remain so.

In Chicago in which there are hundreds of thousands of unemployed men and women every winter and which is a natural station for the casual laborer going to the east or to the west, there is a municipal lodging-house or "emergency home." It accommodates 250 and can be made to accommodate 500 more of the 4000 homeless destitute unemployed men to be found in Chicago, by a conservative estimate, on every winter night. The lodging-house is not well known, would not be easily found, and is not advertised. It is on a dark and old street, and the building is a makeshift which thirty-five years ago was a police station, later a store room for city wagons. Men often sit up on the stairs all night—and perhaps are as comfortable as those that are herded together, the foul with the clean, the sick with the well, in the inadequate sleeping quarters. There is no provision for women. Where do the homeless unemployed women in Chicago and elsewhere sleep?[1]

In the nation's capital the experience of an investigator[2] of lodging places for the unemployed throughout the country was as follows:

I asked of the first policeman I met where I could get a free bed, and he looked at me seemingly in surprise and said, "A free bed?" then continued, "Go to the Union Mission." I asked, "Do they charge for a bed there?" and he replied, "Yes, ten or fifteen cents." "But I haven't even that to-night," I answered.

[1] Chicago has recently increased the capacity of its emergency shelters.

[2] Edwin A. Brown, Denver, Colo., *Broke*, Chicago, Browne & Howell Co., 1913.

Then he seemed to remember that Washington had a municipal lodging-house, and told me I would find it on Twelfth Street, next to the police station. I asked two other policemen with similar results, and started in search of my desired object. I looked down Pennsylvania Avenue, a blaze of lights, and for one mile I could see and read guiding signs of theaters, breweries, hotels, and cafés.

Presently I came to Twelfth Street, dark and gloomy, but there was no sign as in Chicago to guide homeless man or woman, boy or girl. There was a three-cornered box over the door, intended for a light, but it was not illuminated. Through smoke-dimmed windows there came a feeble light by which I could just discern the words, "Municipal Lodging House," and on the door the inscription, "To the Office."

Before entering I stepped back into the street and looked up at the building. It was an old three-story brick building with no sign of a fire-escape. I entered and found myself in a low and very narrow passage-way. I applied to the "office" through a small window-door for my bed.

When I stepped to the window and asked for a bed, I received no word of welcome from a woman seated at her desk, her demeanor being decidedly unwelcome. Abruptly a man's voice asked from within, "Are you willing to work for it?" I replied earnestly that I was. The woman then snatched up a pen and asked: "Were you ever here before? Where were you born? Where do you live? What is your business?"

My answer apparently being satisfactory, she thrust me a bed check, and said something about a light and something else which I did not understand, and slammed the door in my face. I stepped along

and found myself in a woodyard among piles of wood,
saws, sawbucks, and sawdust.   I tried several doors
and finally found one that admitted me.   A narrow
flight of stairs led me to a bathroom, where a number
of men were already trying to get a bath.   There
were two attendants, one who was working for his
bed and breakfast, and the other, I judged, a paid
attendant.   I was told to go into a closet and strip,
and to hang on a hook all of my clothes except my
shoes and stockings and hat.   Having done this,
I stepped out into the bathroom.   It was heated by
a stove, which emitted no heat, however, as the fire
was almost dead.   There were two bathtubs, and
six of us were standing nude in that cold room waiting
each for his turn.   The boy working for his bed made
a pretense with a mop of cleaning the tubs after each
bather, but left them nasty and unsanitary.   I got
into about six inches of water, and hurriedly took a
bath, because of the others waiting.   I did not want
to wash my head, so omitted that, but just as I got
out of the tub the Superintendent came in and said,
"You haven't washed your head."   I immediately
and meekly complied.

Shivering with the cold, I got out, was given a towel
to dry myself, and then a little old cotton nightshirt
with no buttons on it.   Several of us being ready, we
were led by the Superintendent up another flight of
narrow stairs, through another long hall, and up two
more series of steps to a small dormitory.   I would
have suffered with the cold if I had not seized an
extra blanket from an unoccupied bed, and I slept
very little.

I heard a man say to the one next to him, "Do you
think this place will be pulled to-night?" and the

other answered, "Why, no; what makes you think so?" The first one said: "They pulled the Union Mission one night for vags, but I don't think they will pull this place, because it's a city lodging-house." Comforted by that thought, they both fell asleep.

During the night a frail boy, with no clothing except the thin nightshirt, went to the toilet, down the long cold halls and stairways, into the still more cold woodyard. When he returned he had a chill and as he lay down I heard him groan. I said, "What is the matter, boy?" and he replied, "I have such a pain in my side."

Just at daylight we were called, went down into a cheerless room, and were given our clothes, then on down the cramped dining-room, with scarcely any fire, where we were huddled together, thirty of us, whites and blacks. Here we waited one hour for breakfast, and then we were driven out into the woodyard for some reason we could not find out, and waited another half hour until breakfast was called. During that long wait almost the entire conversation was about work and where it could be found.

We went in to breakfast and sat down to a stew of turnips and carrots, in which there was a little meat. In mine there were three pieces of meat about as big as the end of one's thumb. There was some colored sweetened water called "coffee," and some bread.

Having finished breakfast, and while we were waiting to be assigned to our work, the door between our room and the inner room was left open for a moment and we saw the Superintendent seated at a well appointed table with flowers upon it, a colored man waiting upon him. One of the boys looking in said, "Oh, gee, look at the beefsteak!" and then another boy looked at me, and said, "You see how Washington treats the out-of-work, and this place is self-supporting or more than half-supporting." And then a boy who had come early and worked his two hours for that bed and that breakfast, gave us a cheerful good-bye and started off to walk seven miles to begin work on a farm, a place he had secured the day before.

We waited to be assigned to our work. I wanted to saw wood; the wood looked so clean and inviting, and, too, I had sawed wood when I was a boy on the farm, and knew how; but I was not allowed to do so, and was given the task of making the beds.

Some of the men scrubbed, and some swept the floors and stairs; some worked about the dining-room; others sawed wood.

While waiting in the woodyard for breakfast, I jokingly said, as we looked at the wood: "What's the matter with getting out of here? Then we won't have to work." And one replied: "We can't; we are locked in." To prove if this was true I stepped to the door and found it as he said. We were locked in and could not have escaped in case of fire or accident if we had tried.

There is a sign, sometimes seen to-day in the dance halls of our Western camps, "Don't shoot the pianist, he is doing the best he can," and so with the Superintendent of Washington's Municipal Lodging House, under the conditions he may be doing the best he can. Work is always a grand thing. The floors and stairs were clean, also our food and dishes. He impressed me as being the right man in the right kind of place. But the Washington Federal Lodging House is only a suggestion of such an institution. As the house now stands it is the lodger, the workless man and boy, who keeps the floors and stairs and windows clean. They do it willingly, but they should be treated fairly for their labors. No one should be allowed to go to bed hungry. He should be given a clean, warm bed to sleep in, and a good wholesome breakfast, and all he can eat. He should be given a pleasant welcome, an encouraging word, and a cheerful farewell,—it means so much, and costs nothing.

In Boston the unemployed man applying for shelter at the municipal lodging-house fares no better. He is given no supper, his bed is woven wire covered with a blanket, and no matter what his state of health he saws wood several hours *before breakfast.* In January, 1915, Boston, however, made a significant contribution to municipal provisions for sheltering the homeless by opening a shelter for unemployed women. In one of the smaller Pennsylvania cities every able-bodied man that receives shelter in the municipal building must work the next day for two and a half hours on the streets.

For the work the city furnishes him a substantial breakfast and afterwards requests that he leave the town or obtain work. Should any refuse to work, we send him to jail as a vagrant for thirty days and his diet consists of bread and water. The city, besides getting value received from the tramps, has been able to rid the municipality very largely of their presence. The problem of the tramp will always be a serious one in the country, but this year it is more serious on account of the men who are out of honest employment.

There are several other municipal lodging-houses in the country like Washington's; there are at least two others of a different and better order. These are the municipal lodging-houses of Denver and New York City. In the latter, a man gives his record at the office, is given decent food in a large clean dining-room, is taken to the disrobing room, and his clothing—in a separate tray—taken to the disinfecting room. He is taken to the bathroom, where there are thirty shower baths, and required to take advantage of the soap and germicide provided. Then he is taken to the physician's room for examination. The perceptibly diseased man is given a specially marked night-robe, taken to the isolation ward, and given treatment. All are given clean night-robes. The beds are of painted iron, in two decks, with wire springs, hair mattresses, and clean lining. There is an attendant in the dormitory all night long. Breakfast consists of oatmeal and hot coffee, for which no wood sawing is required. The building accommodates one thousand men and fifty women, is fire-proof, and is ventilated by a modern forced-air system. In short, after a night spent in New York City's municipal lodging-house, an unemployed man is in much better condition to hunt for and to hold a job than he was when he entered it. The only difficulty is that its capacity is wholly inadequate for New York City, even with the annex on the pier.

The New York State Commissioner of Excise, in reporting on the conditions of the homeless in

New York City in 1914, made the following recommendations:

If the various estimates are true, that there are between fifty thousand and one hundred thousand homeless men out of employment in the city of New York, there is here a vast economic waste. If these men have no other way of securing sustenance except the piece of bread and the coffee given at one o'clock in the morning in the bread line, or the chance of getting into the limited accommodation of the municipal lodging-house, how can these men be put into condition to secure employment or to render service if the opportunity was offered. If a man has to sit up until one o'clock to get a lunch, and then walk the street until morning, he is not in condition to look for work or perform it if secured. Thus the question is presented, if the state would not be justified, from an economic standpoint, to try and stop this waste, which is now being carried on.

The Committee of Fifty, of which the Hon. Seth Low of New York City was President, appointed to investigate conditions, substantially reports that the saloon performs a double office. "It is meeting the physical craving for intoxicating liquor, but it is also meeting the thirst for fellowship, for amusement, and for recreation. Not only is the saloon performing such a service, but it has, or has had, the field practically to itself; in a word, it has had handed over to it by the community, the monopoly of the social life of the majority of the American wage-earners."

This Committee further states: "As yet, adequate substitutes for the social benefits which thousands of people actually derive daily from the saloons have not yet been developed. It is to this problem that the experience, the wisdom, and the wealth of those interested in social progress must now be directed."

There can be no question that this is a most fertile field for philanthropic endeavor. Generally speaking, on every corner, and on every street, are found hospitable saloons in which the ordinary wayfarer can find warmth, comfort, telephones, newspapers, etc.

If additional clubs could be established, furnishing reading-rooms, billiard-tables, lunch-rooms, lodging-rooms, etc., and carefully managed, they ought to be self-supporting, and if started first in the very poorest sections of the big cities of the state, they would not only furnish a substitute for the saloon, but, in a way, furnish a resting-place and lodging-house for the very poor and homeless.

The Social Service Bureau, newly begun at the New York municipal lodging-house, aims not only, in the way previously mentioned, to find work for the men, but also to direct the whole organization of the municipal lodging-house toward rehabilitation. The idea is that when a man reaches the lodging-house he shall not only have found a much-needed temporary shelter but may at once begin to get upon his feet. He may avail himself of certain "house privileges" which will bring him nearer to work: he will find a file of the newspaper advertisements for the day, and will find other advertisements posted on a blackboard. He will find paper and ink and a free mail box by means of which he may send his answer. Blacking and brushes, combs, scissors, whisk brooms, a barber, a cobbler, and a tailor shop, and an opportunity to have his clothes washed, will enable him to put himself into as good shape as his equipment will permit. If he is in evident need of immediate relief, he will receive it; otherwise he will be assigned for examination to determine whether he should be sent to a hospital or a home, should be kept at the lodging-house for observation and a work test, or should be consigned to the employment division. Supplying a man with tools or clothes, giving him medical care, looking after his family or dependents for a short time, often mean restoring his employability and putting him in the way of a job. These things are a part of the work of the Social Service Bureau in the New York lodging-house. It follows the general principle of the Bellevue Hospital Social Service Committee.

The Borough of Brooklyn has no municipal lodging-house. Yet Brooklyn is a city of considerable distances and of many unemployed. The New York State Commissioner of Excise says in his 1914 report: "The homeless man who finds himself on the east side of the bridge must walk a long distance to avail himself of the Manhattan shelter." He then surveys the possibilities open to the homeless unemployed in Brooklyn. They are: to be taken before a magistrate and committed to the almshouse, to sleep in chairs in the rear of the barrooms of cheap saloons or five-cent whisky resorts; and, if driven out of these to go to the police station to be arrested as vagrants. "We have no homeless over here" said a Brooklyn charity worker; "we send them all to Manhattan!" Rather, they are left to go—to Manhattan or anywhere else they can think of; the burden is entirely upon them. Yet the lodging-house in Manhattan has no room for them even if they manage to reach it.

It is readily seen that a survey of the municipal lodging-houses of this country is soon made. They are for the most part badly equipped, at best inadequate. They are completely decentralized, with no connection with employment facilities or relief agencies, and no common recognition of the real nature of the situation with which they deal. As an *organized* institution for shelter, they do not compare with the saloon—or, on the other hand, with the police station. What other shelters are open to homeless unemployed men and women? The organized charitable societies of cities and towns do not ordinarily maintain shelters, and are open only from nine until five, so that applicants for shelter by night have no access to them. If there is no municipal lodging-house, there are just two other possibilities—missions or philanthropic or semi-philanthropic "homes" of one kind or another, and the bull-pen of the city jail.

Most of the cities of the country leave the hous-

27

ing of the unemployed men to "Galilee" or "Whoso-
ever will," etc., missions, which charge from ten to
twenty-five cents a night, or when money is lacking,
as it usually is, take payment in labor at the price
of ten cents an hour. It takes several hours at this
rate to pay for value received, and these hours are
the hours most valuable to the worker—the early
morning hours in which he should be seeking work.

The following is Mr. E. A. Brown's[1] report of a
mission where, in his disguise as an unemployed
man, he found shelter for a night in Kansas City:

Kansas City had the "Helping Hand" institution,
to which I have referred,—an ostensibly "religious"
institution, backed up in its operations by the co-
operation of the city authorities.

I went first to their religious service where I heard
an exceptionally able address on the features of
Christ's humanitarianism, and on the wonderful
merit which there was in the application of the
"square-deal" principle between man and man, individually and collectively.

The house was filled with a large number of men
whose broken appearance told only too plainly that
the world was not dealing kindly and "squarely"
with them. When the speaker had ended his address,
the men were asked to come forward and thereby
signify that they had accepted the teachings of Christ
as they were interpreted by the preacher. Not a man
stepped forward.

[1] *Broke*, E. A. Brown, Brown and Howell Company, Chicago,
1913.

That night, as a destitute workingman, at this same place I asked for a bed. I was told I could have one but was expected to do two hours' work for it.

"I am perfectly willing to do so," I replied.

The office was caged in by a heavy iron wire as though to be protected from thieves. The man at the desk said: "Well, leave me your hat and when you have done your work in the morning you will get it."

I humbly handed him my hat, and numbering it he threw it on a pile of many others. He was obviously holding my hat as a ransom, fearing to trust to my honor.

I was given a bed check corresponding to the number of my hat, and told to go upstairs. A man sat at a desk on which an old, smoky kerosene lamp was burning. He showed me into a room in which one hundred and sixteen men were sleeping. He did not turn up the light, even for a moment, so that I might see the kind of bed I was getting into. He explained this by saying he feared to awaken the dead-tired, half-starved individuals on the bunks. As a result I was afraid to get into my bed at all, but lay down on the outside of the covering and stayed there all night. Not a word had been said about supper or a bath.

The odor of the hundred unwashed bodies was nauseating. There was the usual consumptive and asthmatic coughing, and expectoration upon the floor; there were no cuspidors, and the air was stifling.

Not far from me I heard a young man moaning, and every few moments he would exclaim, "Oh, my God! Oh, my God!" I went to him and asked:

"What is the matter?"

"Oh, I am suffering from inflammatory rheumatism," he groaned.

I felt of his arms and hands, and found them burning hot and swollen hard from his elbows to his finger tips.

"Can't I go out and get something for you?" I anxiously asked.

"I don't know what to tell you to get. I need a doctor."

I called an attendant. The sufferer asked if he could get a doctor from the city hall across the street.

"No, not until nine o'clock to-morrow morning," was the answer.

The man had two rags about twelve inches long and three inches wide. All night long, at intervals of every twenty or thirty minutes, he went to the water faucet, wet these rags, and bound them upon his arms.

On arising in the morning we went downstairs and waited an hour for our breakfast. We could see our hats piled up behind the iron bars.

When the long wait was over, we were given a breakfast consisting of dry bread, stewed prunes, and some liquid stuff called coffee, without milk or sugar. What a hungry man would eat at that table, if he had been able to stomach it, wouldn't amount to a value of over three cents a meal. While we ate we were supposed to refresh ourselves spiritually by reading the religious mottoes on the wall. "Come unto Me all ye that labor and are heavy laden and I will give you rest," "Blessed are the Merciful," "He came to preach deliverance to the captive," and "When did you write Mother last?"

After the so-called breakfast I was sent to work in the long, poorly ventilated room, in which the hun-

dred and sixteen men, unwashed, diseased, and foul,
had slept the previous night. I worked two long hours
making beds and cleaning floors, in payment of the
three-cent meal I could not eat, and the bed I dared
not get into. The Mission people valued our meal
at ten cents, and our beds at ten cents, and we were
paying for it at labor at ten cents an hour, while at
every other place in the city employers and the
municipality were paying twenty and twenty-five
cents an hour for common labor.

The boys who had paid ten cents for their bed sat
out in the office, and stood a chance of getting a job
at twenty or twenty-five cents an hour at the labor
bureau, but the boys whose hats were held as a ransom
had no such opportunity.

In the room where I was at work a young boy was
dressing himself. He looked up at a coat and hat
which hung by the door, and asked me, with an
innocent look:

"Whose hat is that?"

"I don't know."

After a moment's thought, he said:

"I've got a job this morning if I can get there, but
I can't stay here for two hours and get it."

The other possibility is the city jail. The bull-
pens of these hardly need to be described here.
They are the most sardonic comment that exists on
America's conception of unemployment as an
industrial problem. In most of the cities and
towns of this country a destitute unemployed man
that at nightfall asks the policeman on the corner
where he can find shelter will be referred to the

city jail where he will be locked in for the night with the drunks and the insane of the community. Perhaps he will not get a chance to ask the policeman; the policeman may address him first. And in the morning the man is arraigned as a vagrant and told by the judge, if it is his first offense, that sentence will be suspended, if he will move on at once—to take the same hazards in the next town.

There are not always even jails. For women there is, everywhere, practically no free shelter at all. In general these lodging-houses are to all practical purposes a modification of police stations, involving a good deal of the policing principle: "We try to make them feel that they are here on suffrance," writes the head of one lodging-house in speaking of the unemployed it shelters. American cities that adopt this conception of lodging-houses for the unemployed certainly need enlightenment as to where freedom from sentimentality ends and a gross and brutal stupidity begins. Very generally it is the destitution of the inmates that municipal lodging-houses take into account, not the fact of their unemployment.

The whole present system of emergency shelter was devised for hoboes and tramps. The provision, such as that existing in the New York lodging-house, that a man can be arrested as a vagrant if he returns more than three times in any one month, really exemplifies the foundation policy of even the best form of shelter for the destitute. Provisions to guard against vagrancy may always be necessary.   But nothing in America is more significant of our failure to recognize the nature of unemployment and to change our policies and measures with changing conditions than the survival of a police method to deal with an industrial problem.

Certain private funds have in various places established cheap lodging-houses especially designed for the unemployed, such as the Mills Hotels in New York, and the Rufus D. Dawes Memorial Hotel for the Unemployed in Chicago. These, for a trifling sum, save a man's self-respect, and preserve his employability.   The difficulty is, of course, that he often does not have the trifling sum, or does not have it for very long.

A very interesting provision for the shelter of the unemployed is found in the Gypsy Smith Tabernacle in Portland.   The building was put at the disposal of the unemployed as a result of a conference between the unemployed themselves, organized into the Unemployed League of Portland, and the Civic League of that city.   The house is run by the unemployed themselves.   There is an executive committee, a kitchen and floor department.   There are beds for about 400 men and blankets for 600 more, but several hundred more than this are lodged in the Tabernacle every night.   Some of the men, cobblers and barbers for instance, ply their trades for the inmates, without pay.   There is an employment department in charge of an agent who daily visits city

and county officials, and all large employers of
labor in Portland, asking for work for the men.
The city has appropriated $2500 to keep the Taber-
nacle running. In Seattle, a number of casual
laborers under a leader who was also a casual
laborer, established in the winter of 1913–14 the
"Hotel de Gink" now the Hotel Liberty. The
men that succeeded in getting jobs put their
earnings into a common fund for the maintenance
of the "hotel." The significant feature of the
work was the securing of contracts for ground
clearing from the city. The Central Council
of Social Agencies of Seattle interested itself in
the project, and this winter the Hotel Liberty has
an appropriation of $2000 from the county. A
Hotel de Gink, to be operated on similar principles, has recently been opened in New York.

States and cities and private foundations have
instituted other emergency measures for supplying
temporary shelter which may affect unemployment. But these again are not *designed* for the
unemployed, but rather for those who for some
definite reason or other are temporarily or permanently unfit not only for work but for society.
Vagrant farms and penal or inebriate colonies are
not to be quoted even among emergency measures
as remedies for unemployment, although it is
true enough that the unemployed may easily
drift into them. Once in a while, however, the
principle of operation of one of these farms for
"down and outs" may be so broad as to make it

have a bearing upon unemployed men needing a temporary lift. One of these is the municipal farm of San Diego, supported by an annual appropriation of $16,000. It covers 6000 acres and can accommodate thirty men in comfort and decency. Anybody that applies is taken in, provided there is room, no records are kept, and the main requirement is simply that everybody shall contribute his share of the work. The "rounder" and the unemployed man are on exactly the same footing. Each man is kept ten days and then dismissed. He is given time, in short, to recover himself physically and to regain his courage. The work is new, and still in process of organization in various ways. Such experiments do not make any distinction between the helplessness due to unemployment and that due to very different causes. They are merged in the general problem of emergency relief. However, such experiments are few. The idea of diverting unemployed and underemployed men and women to the land undoubtedly offers a fertile field for experiment. But at present those that benefit by "back to the land" schemes usually qualify for them quite specifically, by a court sentence, or by inebriety for instance. Here and there, but not often, the foundation principle of a private "farm" suggests the breadth of application of the San Diego Farm. There is, for instance, one in New Jersey maintained by a philanthropist, at which no questions are asked upon entrance, and in which there is just one rule—that a man shall improve while he is there.

Such then have been the nature and extent of efforts made in America to provide work and shelter in emergencies. There have been besides these a number of miscellaneous measures specifically designed for the relief of unemployment. Among these is the bread-line temporarily maintained by a newspaper in New York City in the winter of 1913–14, and recently opened for 1914–15. Sixty thousand loaves of bread were distributed in two months. Those that saw the men, women, and children in that line needed no further proof that unemployment was the cause of most of the tragic need there shown. In Chicago the McDowell bread-line made the same revelation, and was a not unimportant factor in bringing about the Chicago Commission on Unemployment. Within three months of one year over 12,000 were helped in the bread-line, almost all of them unemployed men. Some of them were given sufficient clothing to go to work in the ice fields.

In the winter of 1913–14 Chicago maintained a municipal grocery store, not intended to be permanent but merely to bridge over a precarious period. It sold goods at cost, to unemployed persons only. It does not seem to have been successful, the average daily sale having been only $9.11. The reason for this may have been the difficulty in maintaining a rigid system of investigating customers as to actual unemployment. The experiment is, however, very significant as showing municipal cognizance of unemployment as a distinct community problem if not an industrial one.

The above illustrate the emergency measures already definitely tried in America. A year ago they would have formed a complete history of our methods or projects for relief. But now that the war has caught up America's unemployment problem, hitherto almost unrecognized, has clarified its outlines, crystallized its significances, and brought its menace sharply home, America is writing an additional chapter into its history of unemployment measures. It shows two tendencies—first a definite increase in immediate practical adjustments and devices, and secondly an organized interest on the part of citizens and organizations official, semi-official, or private in the unemployment situation in the locality they represent, and often also in unemployment as an industrial problem of national scope. From all the suggestions of remedy produced by this crisis, there cannot help resulting not only a better understanding of unemployment as an industrial and social as well as a relief problem, but also more stable, reasoned, and scientific ways of dealing with it.

The most significant thing in the emergency measures of the present time is the realization they show that work does not exist but must be made. On the part of cities, the first spontaneous impulse toward retrenchment has been reversed by a movement to open up public works and to make what financial adjustments are necessary in the way of issuing bonds, negotiating loans, or transferring funds in order to do so. The opening up of public works with distinct reference to supplying work for the unemployed is undoubtedly a matter needing careful administration, and different methods in different communities. Each city's credit, for instance, is certainly an individual situation. The need of repairs and of permanent improvements is, again, a varying equation in different places. But it is hard to see why public work done by the unemployed *needs* to cost more, or to be less well done, than when in the regular course of the city's routine; and why the same discrimination as to employable and unemployable workmen cannot be exercised in this case as it normally is in any other. The care of the destitute unemployable is, as this study has maintained from the beginning, a separate matter; and failure to keep it so will lead to confusion wherever it occurs.

The fact that stands out is that cities all over the country, the old and conservative as well as those newer and more friendly to experiment, are turning their governmental functions to the remedying of the present employment.

Behind these movements there is in many cases

marked courage and conviction on the part of mayors and other officials. When, in order to meet unemployment, a mayor insists that the city shall borrow and pay by taxation, and shall authorize the use of sinking funds for the purchase of new bonds, he has often a hot fight to face in council. The mayor of one of our largest cities, upon the laying off of some 450 repair men in one day, went at once to the council and asked for an appropriation of $50,000 to employ them, steadily meeting every objection with the calm statement: "Every consideration of public policy demands that the money should be provided." Later the same mayor pressed for a permanent loan of $11,300,000, over $4,000,000 of it to be *immediately* available for public works. This was sometime ago. It must be added, however, that though the city has appropriated $50,000 for relief, it is still debating as to just how much money it has that *could* be used for providing public works for the unemployed. A conviction of responsibility is not peculiar to the powerful cities; from a small middle Western city comes word of another mayor staunch in his realization of the necessity for immediate action. When reminded that even if the loan he sought for immediate public improvements could be negotiated it would be illegal to expend public money not already appropriated, he simply maintained "The way to resume is to resume." In working out their financial situation to meet the present need, the cities show a striking individuality and independence of their neighbors' policies. In one, the city manager plans to sell $100,000 in 5½ per cent. bonds over the counter, the proceeds to be used in waterworks' extension, and the bonds to be offered directly to small investors in amounts of $25, $50, and $100. In another, the mayor is drafting a piece of emergency legislation to present to the next legislature, providing for an appropriation of $250,000 for the reclamation of swamp lands, the work to be done by the unemployed. Another is submitting a $75,000 emergency bond issue to provide for protection against landslides and for other city work. A number are pressing upon councils the levying of an extra half-mill tax to provide funds for instituting public works for the unemployed. Not an unimportant element in the situation is the fact that in all the cases cited, and others, the work itself seems to be in no sense artificial; the plan simply acts to make necessary work coincide with the present need. In one case at least the appropriation for public work for the unemployed was expressly guarded by the condition that the improvements *must* be permanent.

In several cities, at least, civil service heads are planning to keep all their street men on their lists, and to carry on into the winter so long as the weather will permit, work that is usually arbitrarily stopped at the end of the summer season. In one city the secretary of the civil

service board has started an "eligible list" of
men with families. Only those with families are
to be hired, and no one is to be employed steadily
throughout the winter. This general rule is
being followed in a number of places.

In a few cases cities have, as a preliminary to
the proposed opening of public works set out to
secure a census of their unemployed, by means of
a registration office and through the mail. The
object is to secure not only the number of the
unemployed, but a statement of their trades,
their capabilities, the number of their dependents,
and, it must be admitted, a guarantee that they
are residents. For the purpose of making a
survey of all the possibilities of work both public
and private, and other provision for the unemployed, in a number of cities official bodies
are conferring with the heads of various public
and semi-public departments and companies and
with labor leaders. In one city, for instance, the
city has appointed a joint committee of five from
each chamber of the city council to confer with
the charitable organizations of the city and to
organize a conference which one hundred representative citizens are invited to attend. In a
Southern city the city council in special session
has named a committee to "inquire into the
existing facilities both private and municipal
and to devise ways of meeting the situation."
All these arrangements for getting information
are hopeful because they admit the need of

information. In one large seaport city an official proposes the use of the police in the routine reporting of the employment conditions in their precincts. In a large inland city an employment expert, again, urges the use of police stations as employment bureaus and submits that the experiment would "socialize the police." Our sole experiment in the use of the police as agents to ascertain the amount of unemployment was not a fortunate one, and the American interpretation of police power and personnel would have to be greatly changed in order that any such use of it could be profitably made. But this does not alter the significance of the intention that appears in these suggestions. *In general, the attitude of many American cities in dealing with the unemployment now present and impending marks an epoch in the very slow development of a general understanding of unemployment.*

The war period has brought forth a number of adjustments within industries. These, as they have been put into practice, have been not so much policies as short cuts to one end—avoiding turning off men at a time when unemployment is already critical. Instead of definitely laying off a considerable part of their force, some industries have instituted a shorter working day and a wage reduction for all; others have kept their full force and are working their plants every other week; others have instituted a working week of from 2½ to 5 days instead of 6; others are working two shifts, a half day each. These attempts within individual industries to maintain an employment level are important in the evidence they give of an assumption of responsibility for planning work with reference to standards of employment. Such expedients as short time, while very effective in a general crisis, are of course purely emergency measures and can hardly be accepted as permanent possibilities of remedy, if they are to be arbitrarily exercised.

An interesting attempt to create work is under way among business men in a western city. They have formed an Employment Company, to create work, chiefly in street grading, and to distribute it through the city employment bureau. Any profits are to be contributed to the city charities for relief work, and any losses are to be borne by the company. In one city where the mayor is supervising city contracts with a view to finding work for the unemployed a Committee of the Chamber of Commerce has undertaken the same work with reference to private contracts.

In a few instances loan funds are in operation. In one city there is a fund of $25,000 from which any man can borrow who can give proof of having been employed in the city during the preceding year. A loan fund for the unemployed is a recent emergency measure tried by the Business Men's Association of a New England city. The money has been raised by pledges. The idea is not a purely charitable one, but is a proposition to tide deserving men over a period of unemployment resulting from business depression, under conditions involving no appeal to charity. Every appeal for a loan is investigated, and referred to a committee. The man gives his note and is to pay the money back when he secures employment. In a Southern city, there has just been projected a "Salaried Employees' Loan Association" the members of which are pledged to contribute to a loan fund for worthy unemployed residents.

A few of the larger unions, notably the typographical and the cigarmakers regularly pay unemployment or traveller's benefits. But quite aside from this organized relief system, a number of unions have in the present crisis proposed various measures: In the effort to maintain work, they have asked their members not to insist upon working full time, and to accept wage reductions for the sake of keeping greater numbers at work. Several local unions in connection with their relief work are requiring all their steadily employed men to take one day off every month, that day's work to be given to the unemployed. "The unions of the city will take care of their members if the general public will relieve the unorganized," said the President of the Building Trades Council in Milwaukee recently. This Council recommended that every union establish a commissary where the necessities of life could be secured by its members. With a like object the Milwaukee Trades Council calls for the appropriation of city and county funds to provide buildings where vegetables and perishable goods bought in carloads may be stored and sold at the lowest possible price. The activities of labor unions in looking after their own unemployed are not new and recent, although their efforts of the present are in one sense distinctly emergency measures. But they suggest a more organized attitude on the part of union labor toward the general problem of unemployment than has ever before been evidenced in the country, and are significant in showing the power and facilities of trade unions to administer remedial measures.

These measures merely illustrate the present tendency to devise remedies and to furnish immediate relief. These and other measures now being proposed have hardly as yet been tried. Certainly they have not been proved. But they are very significant in showing the state of public opinion prevailing among many different groups of citizens.

A great many of the emergency measures proposed or under way now have been due directly or indirectly to the trade unions, acting both locally and collectively. In some instances it was they that questioned a city's retrenchment policy and set the tide the other way. They have urgently addressed public officials, members of common councils, county boards, etc., asking for immediate action, pointing out the need of work, not of charity, and presenting their registra-

tion of the unemployed to back their statements
of the situation. They have conferred with
commissioners and governors and comptrollers,
and have demanded of the public a general and
popular movement to meet the present crisis,
"something like the plan of the Sane Fourth
Commission," to use the definition of the Milwaukee Trades Council. They have organized
mass meetings and arranged conferences with
different civic organizations. And in at least
one city they have ascertained the number of
unemployed men that had formerly worked for
city contractors, have demanded a statement
of the number of contracts held up, and have
thus been able to carry on their campaign on
the basis of facts. They have suggested to
private industries methods of maintaining and
regularizing employment, such as the shortening
of working hours, short weeks, etc., and the
suggestions have sometimes been adopted.

There are throughout the country a number of
special committees or organizations giving especial
attention to the present unemployment. Significant among bodies especially created for this
purpose are the New York Committee on Unemployment, appointed by the Mayor, consisting
of nearly one hundred representative citizens and
students of social and labor problems, and charged
with the task of devising practicable means
of creating work and administering relief. The
Chicago Commission or "Mayor's Commission

on Unemployment" was, unlike the New York Committee, established by law, is of longer standing, and issued its first report in March, 1914. Chicago now has also a Municipal Market Commission which has already issued preliminary recommendations. A number of other cities in the country have unemployment committees or commissions at work. Sometimes these are appointed by the mayors as in New York and Chicago; sometimes they are joint committees of various charitable and civic organizations, including sometimes the council; sometimes they are citizens' committees entirely; sometimes they are subcommittees in chambers of commerce.

The following letter, sent out by the Board of Commerce in one city to all industries employing more than one hundred men, well illustrates the possibilities open to such organizations in the effort to deal with unemployment.

The Board of Commerce of the city having within its membership, among others, representatives of practically every large manufacturing company in the city, believes that some plan should be undertaken by a committee of its members to at least partially solve the problem of the unemployed in our city.

It will probably be admitted, by all who have considered the question, that any plan consisting solely in giving aid, or even in loaning money, would be impracticable, if for no other reason than because of the amount required to materially assist the large number of unemployed. Any plan involving direct aid only, is also open to numerous objections that readily occur to anyone giving thought to this subject. The fact is that no form of assistance is so beneficial or so far reaching as furnishing opportunities for work. The solution of the problem must be undertaken by organized industry, and not by charity under any name or form.

Should a fund of even $100,000 be distributed, either in the form of gifts or loans, it would be of small benefit compared with the benefits arising from, say, one-quarter of the unemployed being given employment at an average wage of $12.00 per week. Such employment would result in the distribution, each month, of a very much larger sum in wages.

It is the desire of this committee that the various employers of labor, represented by membership in the Board of Commerce, should give, through one of their own executives, extraordinary and unusual attention to their own labor problems. It may be that, when such attention is given, a partial solution of the difficulty may be found in the employment of a large number of men fewer hours, rather than a small number of men longer hours; or in the employment of more men than already employed by giving work to some employees one week, for illustration, and to other employees the following week, where the nature of the work permits this to be done. It may be that contemplated extensions of plant can be undertaken at this period, when the work can probably be more economically done, or that an added volume of business can be taken on for a smaller margin of profit, or even at cost, in order to give employment. It may be that the various purchasing departments can buy more supplies, material, and products made in the city, thus giving additional employment to working men in the city.

Many companies will be able to evolve some definite plan of a helpful character for the benefit of their own unemployed.

In some instances, perhaps, the employer has no solution of the problem, and the company is unable to do anything more than is now being done for its own unemployed. In that event, the committee believes that it would be beneficial, if the executive of such company having direct charge, will make an investigation of the individual wants of its idle employees, and will give a letter to such men as request it, stating that the individual has been an employee of the company, has been out of work for a stated time, that the company is unable to do anything for him, but believes that his circumstances now entitle him to assistance. The employee can then go to the committeee at its headquarters in the Board of Commerce, with such a letter and his name will be registered, and he will be furnished with a card stating that he is a resident, is now out of work, and, in the opinion of the company formerly employing him is entitled to assistance.

The committee may be able to assist him in finding employment either with some other company or in some public work. It is probably true that other employers of labor—the condition of whose industry warrants a larger number of men being employed than now employed—would prefer to employ such a man than to add to their force from those who apply for employment without such a recommendation.

The committee desires to emphasize the necessity of the labor situation in each particular institution receiving the personal attention of some executive of that institution, because it is apparent that this plan of mutual help will be of small benefit to anyone unless each company does its best, and unless the circumstances of each employee given a letter is ascertained by enquiry conducted by his own employer.

It may be that there will arise out of this plan some necessity of giving direct assistance. If such cases arise, the committee, after considering the circumstance in each case, may confer with one of the organizations already in existence to do this work, or it may be that the committee will be called upon to give direct assistance in some cases, and if so, arrangements will be made for some assistance of this nature.

The employee receiving a letter should, in so far as possible, be identified by his own signature accompanying the letter.

The success of the plan will, of course, depend largely upon the nature and extent of the coöperation of the employers of labor, and it is hoped that whenever any employee is recommended to the assistance of others, careful enquiry into his wants will be made by the executive of the company having the matter in charge.

All these various committees are rendering valuable service in three ways: in educating public opinion; in stimulating official bodies to action; in initiating enterprises themselves. Their efforts are stimulating a better conception of the nature of unemployment as an industrial as well as a social problem, and have produced the kind of

comprehension in which a preventive policy finds
a hopefully fertile soil.

For the concerted public action and the legislation necessary for any remedial policy, there is
not yet a sufficient backing of public information
concerning unemployment. The recent investigations of the Commission on Industrial Relations
are an example of the kind of study of existing
conditions that must be made in order to obtain
a basis for intelligent action. The Commission
held hearings during the last year in twelve
industrial centers, from New York to San Francisco, and heard over five hundred witnesses,
representing all shades of opinion, and composed
of employers, working men, public officials, and
citizens. Every witness who discussed the question of unemployment regarded it as one of the
most important problems with which this country
must deal. The testimony showed the extremely
fluctuating and casual nature of the work of such
groups of men as longshoremen, harvest hands,
lumber-camp workers, men in the packing industry,
and workers in the clothing trades, and brought
out the imperative need for organizing the labor
market on a modern business basis, in order to
adjust the supply and demand of labor, and
reduce idleness to a minimum. The Commission
made a study of employment agencies, to find out
the character of their work and the methods of
reorganization necessary to put them on an
efficient basis. The recommendations of the

Commission, soon to be published, should give
direction to public interest for the relief of unemployment.

Other instances of Federal interest, and of recognition of the need for emergency measures at
the present time are the establishment of employment bureaus for honorably discharged soldiers,
under the auspices of the War Department, and
the opening of immigration stations, as at Ellis
Island, for the housing of the unemployed.   But
the vast possibilities of drawing off the unemployed in various sections of the country by road
work and other urgent Federal projects are as yet
undeveloped.

*From this statement it is clear that American
remedies for unemployment have up to this time
consisted of emergency measures conceived and
operated to meet the most obvious and most dangerous
effects of unemployment, and having little or no
influence over its causes.   In addition to measures
designed to remove such causes of unemployment
as seasonal and casual work, lack of industrial
training, etc., it is probable that there will always
be necessary certain emergency measures.   With
the exception of unemployment benefits paid by a
very few unions, America has no such provisions
whatever.   The working out of both fundamental
remedies and of methods of dealing with inevitable
emergencies is the foremost industrial problem of
this country.*

But in the present crisis, the problem of unemploy-

ment here cannot be dealt with on a long-time basis. There is a general and urgent need not merely for adjustment, but for relief.   Hundreds of thousands of unemployed men and women are in desperate need of food, lodging, and work.   They must be supplied or made, by whatever emergency operations, whatever sacrifice of routine procedure, are necessary. There is no time, for instance, to wait until legislatures pass bills permitting or compelling cities to build municipal lodging-houses; emergency lodging-houses must be fitted up at once in buildings that already exist.   The problem of supplying work, food, and shelter to unemployed men and women willing to work directly confronts communities, industries, and governmental bodies.   There is needed in every community a commission or central committee to correlate and standardize and hasten the work of these three forces, without too much committee routine and subservience to existing organized philanthropies.

CHAPTER XIII

UNEMPLOYMENT INSURANCE

IN unemployment, as in sickness, accident, death, fire, and all the other hazards of life, an attempt has long been made to devise some system of insurance that would distribute over a long period of months or years the loss that is concentrated at some particular point, or that falls most heavily upon some particular trade or group of workmen. Individual efforts to save a fund to meet such a crisis, which have always been inadequate, especially for long periods, have been in a number of countries supplemented by the collective efforts of trade unions and friendly societies, and later by assistance from the community. Even those who hold the individual responsible for his own welfare know that when men or women cannot obtain work where they are, and cannot get to where it may be waiting for them, it is the community that must, in the end, help them to keep alive or must bury them, if they freeze or starve.

The community's participation in assistance against unemployment, in the form of unemployment insurance, has been put into operation on two different principles—voluntary and compulsory.

444

In the former, the state makes a contribution of a certain percentage to funds for unemployment benefits voluntarily set aside by workmen, either as individuals or as members of a trade union. In the latter, the payment of the premiums toward an unemployment fund is made obligatory upon all workmen and employers in certain trades. As in voluntary insurance, the state contributes a certain percentage of the fund so raised. The first plan is generally known as the Ghent system, because it first attracted general attention by its successful working in that city. The second plan is that recently put into operation in Great Britain.

Until 1900, the city of Ghent was in the position in which most cities are still—with a considerable degree of unemployment, helped by only the municipal, trade, or philanthropic employment bureaus in operation, with no means of financial assistance to the unemployed except very small trade-union benefits and philanthropic contributions, and with the city's charities and labor colonies as the last resource. Under these conditions, investigations were made by Ghent and other Belgian cities in the effort to devise some joint plan against unemployment. In December, 1898, the city council of Ghent appointed a committee, composed of six city officials, six manufacturers, six workmen, and five economists, to work out some effective means of relief. The committee recommended a system by which the city should pay a subsidy, consisting of 60 per cent. of the amount paid out in unemployment benefits both to unions which paid unemployment insurance to their members, and also, in order to provide for workmen not members of unions, to workmen making similar payments to a savings fund to be established for that purpose. In other words, if a workman insured himself against unemployment either by paying dues to his union toward unemployment benefits or by putting deposits in a savings fund, the city would make a contribution toward his provision. The opportunities were open to all trades equally. The work was begun in 1901, with a fund of $1930 voted by the council for the first year. The subsidy was never to amount to over one franc a day to any one person, or 50 francs in the course of a year. Later this limit was extended to 60 francs; and a provision was added that a person who had drawn the full benefit one year might not claim benefits for the following two years. In the twelve years during which the plan has been in actual operation the number of insured workmen has doubled; at present about 20,000 men and women workers are insured—substantially the entire working force of the city. Unemployment among trade-union members fell from 27 per thousand in 1900 to from 12 to 16 in 1913, and the number of recipients of public aid has been reduced about one-half—from nearly 6000 to slightly over 3000. About $200,000 has been paid out in benefits during these twelve years.

This system is administered through the municipal labor exchange, in the management of which the unions and the employers have equal representation. Any workman desiring to claim the benefit reports at the labor exchange that he is unemployed, and it endeavors to find work for him; not until he has failed to obtain work through it is he eligible for the benefit.

Certain features of the Ghent system have led to its adoption in many other places. The trade unions form an easy means of grouping those that claim assistance and of checking the validity of the claim. The system is, of course, favored by unionists, as it tends to strengthen their position. It has been adopted in various forms, in practically all the cities and some of the provinces of Belgium, in 25 cities in Holland, 20 in France, 10 in Germany, 3 in Italy, and 2 in Switzerland. A similar principle underlies the Belgian national provision for unemployment begun in 1908 by the appropriation of 200,000 francs for contributions to the unemployment and savings funds established by the communes, and also the French, Danish, and Norwegian national unemployment insurance system. In Sweden a law based on the same general principle is being prepared by a commission.

France was the first country to adopt as a national measure the Ghent system of contributing to provisions for voluntary unemployment insurance. The movement for trade-union insurance against unemployment developed so slowly in France that after several investigations had been made, the superior council of labor appointed a permanent committee in 1902 to determine what part the state should play in maintaining such funds. The committee, after a year's study, recommended that local funds should receive contributions from the municipalities in which they were located, and also from incorporated bodies, such as councils, chambers of commerce, and employers' associations, and that funds of more than local scope, to which workmen of an entire district or Department belonged, should be assisted by the Department or by the state. "In a general way," the recommendation reads, "the superior council of labor is of the opinion that the state should intervene in behalf of the creation and development of institutions for the relief of unemployment either by means of subvention or by other methods." In 1905 an appropriation of 110,000 francs was made for subsidies to funds whose members belonged to the same or similar trades, whether such funds were founded by trade unions, mutual aid associations, or other societies. The law granting the subsidy contains the interesting provision that each fund receiving a subsidy must provide the free service of an employment exchange to unemployed persons. In cities with over 20,000 inhabitants, separate funds were to be organized for separate trades; only in the smaller cities (under 20,000) could members of various trades unite in forming one fund. This provision has been changed to allow the formation of one fund for several trades in cities with 50,000 inhabitants. The commission believed that societies organized on trade lines rather than on charitable lines would be more able to control wisely the giving of relief, and that under the administration of such societies the risks would be more easily defined. Local organizations are entitled to receive 20 per cent. of their payments, and federated organizations, representing three or more Departments, receive 30 per cent. The state now grants an annual subsidy of 100,000 francs for its contribution to these funds. The number of insured workmen has risen from 33,682 in 1905 to 49,595 in 1912, and 51 towns and 12 Departments now provide subsidies for unemployment insurance funds. The full amount appropriated for this purpose by the state and by the local authorities has never been used; about half of the national subsidy has not been called for. The idea of unemployment insurance has not appealed to French workmen as forcibly as to Belgian or Norwegian, and only seven-tenths of one per cent. in 1000 of the workmen in industry and commerce are so insured.

A similar plan, following the general lines of the Ghent system, was put into operation in Norway through the unions, in 1906. It provided for the payment by the state to recognized unemployment funds of a subsidy amounting to one-

29

fourth, since altered to one-third, of the annual expenditure of the fund for unemployment benefits; two-thirds of the amount thus paid by the state is assessed against the commune in which the beneficiaries last resided for six consecutive months at any time during the preceding five years. Only benefits paid to citizens of Norway or to persons who have resided in Norway may thus be repaid to the societies. An unemployment fund must admit workmen at the same trade, even though they are not members of the union; but the union may charge them 10 to 15 per cent. of the amount of dues as their share of the cost of administration. The unemployment fund is kept entirely separate from the union treasury, and is used only for unemployment benefits. The remarkable strength of organized labor in Norway and the national system of communal employment offices have contributed materially to the successful operation of this unemployment insurance law. Unorganized workmen, however, have not participated in the benefits under this law, and are still unprotected against unemployment; and only 27,000, or about one-half of the union members, are so insured.

Each unemployment fund makes the necessary payments of benefits to its members, and is reimbursed by the state for one-third of the amount. Two-thirds of the state contribution is repaid to the state by the communes. The associations are required to render accounts regularly to the local authorities, who in turn report to the central supervising bureau. The amount of benefits paid in 1912 was $39,091.

A similar law was also put into effect in Denmark in 1907; it provided that a commune that made direct cash contributions to a fund for the resident poor might be reimbursed by the state for one-third of the amount so paid out. In Copenhagen in 1904–5, at about the time the law was passed, 1409 persons had been paid unemployment benefits by the city. Trade unions in Denmark have actively aided their unemployed members for many years by special funds for unemployment relief, traveling funds, etc. In 1907 a national law was passed providing for state aid to unemployment societies, which were defined as societies of workmen engaged in similar occupations; the society can have no other purpose. Membership in these societies is limited to paid workmen whose economic condition entitles them to receive state aid under the sickness insurance act. Any qualified workmen, however, can be admitted to these unemployment societies. This provision takes the administration of benefits out of the hands of unions. A society receives from the state one-half of its total income. The 1907 law also provided for additional state contributions equivalent to the amount contributed by the commune, but in 1914 the state's contribution was restricted to one-half; and the commune in which a recipient of benefit lives may contribute to the payment of his dues to the society, but not in excess of one-sixth of his dues—in recognition of the fact that it is better for the commune to help him to continue to be a participating member than to have him become dependent upon it for relief. No aid is given until the workman has been a member for one year. He is entitled to receive aid for seventy days in a year; but a member who has received the maximum aid for three years is given no further aid until he has been a paying member for another year. Fifty-two trade unions representing 120,300 workmen, or about 60 per cent. of the country's wage-earners, have established unemployment societies, separate from the unions, according to this law. One fund for non-union workmen has a membership of 613. Denmark is the one country in which unskilled and casual labor have been reached by unemployment insurance measures. 39,000 of such workmen have been organized into an unskilled laborers' union. The dues for unemployment insurance in this union amount to $2.75 a year, and the benefits to from 27 cents to 40 cents a day for 70 days. Unskilled women workers have also formed an independent union with 3000 members. Their premium is $1.40 a year, and their benefit 27 cents a day for 50 days. Benefits paid in 1912 amounted to $459,810, of which the workmen paid 53.8 per cent., the state 31.9 per cent., and the communes 14.3 per cent.

The societies are supervised by an inspector of

unemployment. The absence of a system of labor bureaus hampered the work of these societies; and the employment bureaus maintained by trade unions were finally transferred to the employment societies organized in the same trades. The good results of this law are due partly to the fact that Danish workmen already knew the value of similar provisions in the sickness-insurance act.

Germany, notwithstanding considerable agitation, has as yet made no national provision for unemployment insurance. Some trades unions, especially among the book printers, maintain unemployment benefits, and certain cities, following the general plan of the Ghent system, subsidize them in various ways. Berlin, Freiburg im Baden, Offenbach, Stuttgart, and Feuerbach contribute both to the funds of industrial societies and to those of individuals. Erlangen, Schwaebisch-Gmünd, Mannheim, and a number of cities in Alsace-Lorraine pay them only to industrial societies. Cologne, Kaiserslautern, and Schwaebisch-Gmünd also pay what are called public voluntary unemployment insurance funds.

Holland provided in 1912 for the payment of a subsidy to aid unemployment funds, and several cantons in Switzerland make contributions, varying from 40 to 60 per cent., to workmen's unemployment benefit funds.

Certain features are common to all these forms of the Ghent system. They usually provide that a member may not draw benefits till he has paid premiums for a certain time, until he has been unemployed for a number of days, usually a week, and unless he is not able to obtain other work; some systems disqualify him for refusing work outside his own trade. The amount of premium the workman must pay differs, as does the amount of the state's contribution, and the number of days in one year for which benefit may be received is carefully stated.

The Ghent system has both defenders and critics. Its supporters point to the ease with which it can be administered through existing agencies, to the fact that claims go through the hands of officials cognizant of all features of the labor market in the trade in which the applicant works, and to the encouragement of individual thrift and initiative that results from the system of helping only those who are willing to help themselves. Its critics maintain that it helps only those who are *able* to help themselves, and that it leaves unaided those who most need assistance; and they are inclined to consider the reduction in the number of unemployed as due, not to the insurance features of the plan, but rather to the establishment of labor exchanges to provide men with work. The situation in France shows the real rock on which unemployment insurance founders: the necessity for an extensive system of efficient labor agencies to make the law a success. Furthermore, these laws have at no time provided satisfactorily for non-union men; even those systems that contain provisions for subsidizing these workmen as individuals, or for admitting them to unemployment societies, have failed to attract non-union men to any proportionate extent. The Ghent system works best in a country where labor organization has been greatly developed—such as Denmark, where even unskilled men and women are partly organized. It can be operated successfully only by means of coöperation, which, in turn, depends on confidence and trust—and also on experience. In Denmark workmen had had twenty years of experience with sickness insurance.

The provisions and workings of the British unemployment insurance act are here described in some detail, since it constitutes by far the most considerable experiment of this nature ever undertaken. The description of the act is mainly as given in the blue book containing the First Report of the Proceedings under the Act.

The history of unemployment in England is known to all students of economics—and, indeed, to all readers of the press. For years a slackening in industry had been apparent, which had resulted in an increasing amount of unemployment and consequently in a corresponding increase in the number of those who, being constantly undernourished and depressed, became less and less capable of being employed. To cope with the needs of the unemployed, the Unemployed Workmen Act was passed, under which relief works of various kinds were begun by local governments throughout the United Kingdom. These public works had a rather unsatisfactory result; the work usually cost more than if it had been done in the regular course of trade, and the men for whose relief it was specially designed—the workman "ordinarily in employment, temporarily unemployed"—did not get it. It was almost monopolized by the casual laborer, whose situation it only emphasized. The Poor Law Commission, in its report in 1909, admitted frankly the failure of previous attempts to meet the situation and recommended a system of unemployment insurance, to which the state was to contribute, and which was to be administered through trade unions, after the plan in operation in Ghent. The result was the enactment of a compulsory unemployment insurance act, covering seven trades, and the extension of the labor exchanges to cover the entire country.

The National Insurance Act was passed in December, 1911, and went into effect on July 15, 1912. The trades in which insurance is compulsory are: building, construction of works, shipbuilding, engineering, construction of vehicles, iron founding, and saw-milling in connection with or of a kind usually done in connection with one of the other insured trades. The reason for choosing these particular trades is twofold: they are subject to periods of unemployment, and yet the wages paid in them are high enough to enable

the men to pay the premiums.   In shipbuilding,
engineering, and the metal trades the amount of
unemployment in 1909 was 13 per cent.   In these
trades both employers and workmen pay compulsory contributions at the rate of 2½ d. for
each period of employment up to one week (with
reduced rates for workmen below eighteen and for
periods of employment of two days or less), and
the state contributes to the fund one-third of the
total receipts from employers and workmen.   The
contributions are collected in the form of stamps,
on sale at post-offices, which the employer af-
fixes to the workman's unemployment card or
book.   He puts on a stamp of the value of their
joint contribution and deducts the workman's
share from his wages.   During a period of employment the employer keeps the workman's book, but
must return it, without any marks, when the workman leaves his employ.

The benefit provided by the plan is an allowance
of 7 s. for each week of unemployment after the first
week—the "waiting week," as it is called—up to a
maximum of fifteen weeks in any twelve months,
and subject to the further limit that no workman
can have more than one week's benefit for every
five full contributions paid by him.   No benefit
is paid to persons under seventeen years of age,
and a reduced benefit is paid to workmen between
seventeen and eighteen.   The benefits are payable
in two ways: either to the individual workman
through a labor exchange, or other local office of

the fund, or, under certain provisions, to the association of which the workman is a member. To be entitled to receive the benefit, the workman must prove that he has been employed as a workman in an insured trade in each of not less than twenty-seven separate calendar weeks in the preceding five years; that he has made application for benefit in the prescribed manner, and has been continuously unemployed since the date of his application; that he is capable of work but unable to find suitable employment; and that he has not exhausted his right to benefit. When the act went into effect, each employee in the insured trades was credited with twenty-five weeks' premium. A workman is disqualified, if his unemployment is due to misconduct or to his having voluntarily left his employment without due cause, for six weeks from the date of his so losing employment. He is also disqualified, if he has lost employment by reason of the stopping of work due to a trade dispute at the place of his employment, for as long as the stoppage continues or until he gets work again elsewhere in an insured trade. The workman in the insured trades may deal with the unemployment fund independently, or may, if he is a member of an association which pays unemployment benefits, obtain his benefit through the association. The question whether a workman is or is not entitled to receive benefit lies, in the case of a workman appealing directly for relief, with an "insurance officer" provided for in the act, subject to an appeal to a court of referees, consisting of an employer, a workman, and an impartial chairman, with a provision for further reference to an umpire chosen by the Crown. In the case of a workman claiming benefit through an association, the association is free to pay what benefit it pleases and under what circumstances it pleases, but it cannot recover from the unemployment fund more than its members would have been entitled to receive if they had claimed benefits individually. Questions of refunds to an association for its payments to members are settled between the Board of Trade and the association, or, in case of need, are referred to the umpire.

The act also endeavors to encourage voluntary insurance, in other trades than the seven in which it is compulsory, by providing that such associations as make payments to their unemployed members may recover a proportion not exceeding one-sixth of such payments from the state. Payments in excess of 12 *s.* a week are excluded. No provision is made in the other trades for the direct voluntary insurance of individual workmen; except in the seven compulsory trades, the state contributes only to those payments in respect to unemployment that are made by associations of workmen.

The administration of the act is carried out for the entire United Kingdom directly by the Board of Trade through a single department, combining the labor exchanges and unemployment insurance.

The central office is in London. The country is divided into eight divisions, each having a divisional office, which is the subordinate controlling center of that district. There are also 1496 local offices of two distinct types called labor exchanges and local agencies. The labor exchanges, of which there are 430, are offices under the direct control of the Board of Trade, with a staff of full-time officers, and are used both for labor exchange and unemployment insurance purposes. The 1066 local agencies deal with areas not covered directly by the exchanges; they are not labor exchanges, and are managed by a local agent who gives only a part of his time to the performance of certain duties connected with unemployment insurance. The offices are so distributed as to bring an office of some kind within five miles of every appreciable body of insured workmen. The divisional offices are at London, with 72 exchanges and 200 local agencies; Glasgow, with 83 exchanges and 232 agencies; Warrington, with 80 exchanges and 46 agencies; Doncaster, with 68 exchanges and 104 agencies; Birmingham, with 43 exchanges and 57 agencies; Bristol, with 28 exchanges and 180 agencies; Cardiff, with 33 exchanges and 108 agencies, and Dublin, with 23 exchanges and 139 agencies.

At any local office a workman can obtain his unemployment book, good for a year; when he is employed, his employer has custody of it; and when his employment ceases and he claims the benefit, he must deposit his book at a local office, and must sign the unemployed register daily during working hours. The local office forwards the claim to its division office, and also notifies the applicant's last employer, who has the opportunity to object to the claim, if he desires. The divisional office investigates the case and reports its decision to the local office, which then, if authorized, pays the benefit week by week, up to the limit allowed by the act.

The report of the first year's operation of the act, after six months of payment of benefits, permits certain conclusions, at least, to be drawn. Unemployment books were issued to 2,508,939 workmen; and 559,021 claims for benefit were made in the six months, 415,788, or about three-fourths, being direct claims, and 143,233, or about one-fourth, being claims for payments made through associations. 105 associations in the insured trades, with an estimated membership of 539,775 have made arrangements for payment of benefits through the association. In the other non-insured trades, 275 associations, with a membership of 1,104,000 have been admitted as satisfying the conditions upon which contributions to unemployment benefits can be secured. 774,494 payments were made in the six months at an expenditure of £236,458. Payments varied from £4800 to over 16,000 workmen at the end of May, to £19,200 to nearly 60,000 at the end of January. About 400,000 workmen in the seven trades are shown to have been out of employment at some time or other during a period of six months. Less than one-fifth of the workmen now insured had previously been insured through voluntary associations. Thirty per cent. of the claims did not mature, as they were made during the "waiting week"; 62 per cent. were paid; 7 per cent. were excluded; and 1 per cent. represented unemployment that continued after the workmen's right to draw benefit was exhausted.

The income now being received from employers and workmen is about £1,800,000 a year; the state's contribution brings the total up to £2,400,-000. The cost for the first year of refunds (payments of workmen not found to be in the insured trades), benefits for six months, and administration amounted to about £700,000.

What the fortune of this plan will be during an average year, or during a year of depression, is yet to be determined. It can, however, be said as the Board of Trade reports, that the initial difficulties of bringing the scheme into operation have been successfully overcome; that so far the scheme has been proved to be "administratively practicable," and to have justified the actuarial calculations on which it was based; that it has increased five or six times the number of workmen protected by insurance against unemployment, and has also tended to encourage voluntary insurance in the other trades; and finally, that a large surplus has already been accumulated toward meeting the need of the next kind of depression.

The greatest disadvantage of the English plan is that it does not help the man who most needs help —the casual laborer. The administration of the act is also criticized as being unduly centralized, and in that claims are not sufficiently verified. Only one in six of employers given as the last employer has made any answer to the notice of the claims sent to them. The difficulty of finding a man work, even through a labor exchange, the impossibility of telling whether he is trying to find suitable work himself, the hardships caused by the line of demarcation as to insured and uninsured trades between two men working side by side, are all pointed to as affording possibilities for deception. Other criticisms are that it bears most heavily upon those who are only intermittently employed; the requirement that a man employed for one "period of employment," which may be for only a few hours, pays one penny premium, and a man employed for two days pays twopence, whereas a man employed steadily is taxed only twopence halfpenny per week, is held to be an unfair discrimination against those least able to bear it and least strong to alter it. It is also pointed out that the act does nothing toward preventing unemployment or securing the regularization of industry, except by the provision that the employer may recover one-third of his contributions in respect to a workman whom he has employed continuously for forty-five weeks in one year. A more serious objection is that the system of charging a flat rate to all contributors and paying a flat rate of benefit to all entitled to receive it gives no chance for the practice, ordinarily found necessary in insurance, of demanding a premium proportionate to the risk involved in each class of cases—*i.e.*, in unemployment insurance, to the risk of unemployment in each insured trade.

The Ghent system and the British plan alike seem to require, as a prerequisite for successful administration, a fairly extensive system of administrative agencies that have previously been tested and found to stand the strain. The Ghent system succeeds in proportion to the strength of the unions; and the British plan reaped the benefit of fifty or sixty years of experience with friendly societies, and of the system of labor exchanges. It has everywhere been found necessary to extend and develop the labor exchanges, in order to make them efficient instruments of, or supplements to, the principle of unemployment insurance. Denmark has recently established an employment bureau in every town and commune, to act in coöperation with the trade-union agencies. France has for the last three years witnessed an agitation in favor of the establishment of municipal bureaus, managed by a bi-partisan council, in all places with over 10,000 inhabitants, and of district agencies to deal with special trades, wherever this appears to be necessary. The suppression of all private agencies is also urged.

European countries have, however, maintained a system of employment offices for many years. Sometimes they are mere bureaus for registering applicants for work and for workers; sometimes they are combined with shelters, lunch-rooms, or little inns. The German system is more extended than that of any other country. It consists, first of all, of free employment offices in all important places, which are entirely or partially maintained by the state or by the city. The bureau in Berlin, for instance, the largest in Germany, is maintained by a voluntary association, but receives a large subsidy from the city. This is divided into departments for men and women and subdivided according to trade or capacity; there are departments for the unskilled, for old men, for young men, and according to trades, for painters, locksmiths, tinsmiths, bookbinders, paper-hangers, roofers, machinists, butchers, bakers, laundresses, undergarment workers, domestic servants, etc. The large bureaus have waiting-rooms for applicants waiting for a call for their services, and many of them operate a simple lunch-counter and provide facilities for reading or playing cards.

The management of the German bureaus includes representatives of all classes concerned. There are special trade committees, composed of employers and employees, in equal numbers, from particular trades; there is also a general committee, made up of prominent citizens, which has charge of the bureau. Some years ago the

30

general committee of the Berlin bureau, for example, contained six city councilmen, two aldermen, three members of the Advisory Council, two professors, one of whom was a member of the Royal Council, three judges in trade disputes, a member of the Royal Statistical Bureau and the Prussian Supreme Council, a chief burgomaster emeritus, a councilor of the Admiralty and a consulting counsel in the Imperial Marine Office, a director of the Imperial Statistical Office, a member of the Privy Council and counsel in the Imperial Ministry of the Interior, and the publisher of the Berlin *Tageblatt.* The trade committee of the bureau was composed of a manufacturer, a hat maker, a factory owner, and a merchant, all representing the employers; and a metal stamper, a molder, a clerk, and a printer, representing the workmen. The presence of men with so great an amount of information and experience on the committee indicates why German employment bureaus are so successful, and contains a suggestion of great value for the development of similar bureaus in the United States. The composition of the committees differ; in some cities only representatives of employers and employees are on it; usually, however, one or more city officials or other persons also serve upon it. The most important feature of these committees is that the representation of employers and employees is always equal in number. As these representatives are elected by the bodies they represent, the bureaus have the confidence of both employers and workingmen. Practically all of these bureaus receive financial support from the municipality, and the German states also give aid either to separate bureaus or to the General Federation into which the bureaus have been organized.

The work of these bureaus is effective, and shows a steady growth. The Berlin bureau secured situations for 30,534 persons in 1902, and for 99,557 in 1906. The Cologne bureau filled 10,055 places in 1896, and 29,164 in 1907. The Frankfort bureau found places for 6492 applicants in 1895, and for 37,896 in 1905. The Munich office filled 25,586 places in 1896, and 53,673 in 1906. In 1906 the offices in one kingdom, Bavaria, placed 117,534 persons in situations. The bureaus fill a large percentage of the applications they receive: in Munich in 1906, 63.7 per cent. of the applications for help and 74.1 per cent. of the applications for work were filled; in Nuremberg, in the same year, the bureau filled 61.2 per cent. of applications for help and 95.2 per cent. of those for work.

Another form of assistance to men out of work in Germany is supplied by the public authorities in the relief stations which give food and shelter for twenty-four hours to destitute or unemployed men, in order to enable them to get about from place to place looking for work. The stations are within walking distance of each other. A man who is sheltered in one of them works half the day, and is dismissed in time to reach the next one that afternoon. Certain benevolent societies or agencies also maintain the so-called hospices, or workingmen's hotels and boarding-houses, and Herbergen, or shelters. In the latter, workmen without money pay for their food and shelter by work the next morning.

The free employment offices in France have been established by virtue of a law passed in 1904 requiring every city of over 10,000 inhabitants to establish a free bureau. Seven years later a grant of $6775 was made, in order to permit the reorganization of bureaus then existing and to encourage the establishment of others. Here, as in Germany, the bureaus are under the control of a commission composed half of employers and half of employees; the mayor names the members from among the councilors and administrators of the organization of employers and workmen. All communes, even those with less than 10,000 inhabitants, may establish bureaus and receive a subsidy from the state. The subsidy is calculated on the following basis: for local employment, 15 per cent. of the expenses of every bureau that has found situations for 25 to 50 persons per month; 20 per cent. for 51 to 100 situations; 25 per cent. for 101 to 200 situations; and 30 per cent. for every bureau that has found situations for more than 200 applicants per month. In 1912, 21,420 persons were placed in situations, through 25 bureaus operating in 22 communes, at a total cost of $9339.25.

The bureaus in France have not reached as high a degree of development as in various other countries.

It is not possible to describe in detail the situation in each foreign country with relation to labor bureaus. Suffice it to say that nearly every European country has some municipal or district free bureaus, subsidized by the community. The Swiss bureaus are interesting on account of the proposal that has been made to combine or federate the cantonal and municipal bureaus into a national federal system, with federal aid. The scope of the English system of labor exchanges has already been made apparent in the discussion of unemployment insurance in Great Britain.

Aside from workmen's compensation acts, America has made its first excursion into the social insurance field in widows' pension laws. In other words, reversing the history of foreign countries, we have given *first* attention to the least conservative form of social insurance, based entirely upon a pension, not a contributory insurance principle. Noting the rapid adoption of widows' pension measures within a few years in a number of states in different parts of the country, and realizing the disaster that might reasonably follow unquestioning acceptance of experiments in old age, sickness and invalidity and unemployment insurance abroad, certain watchful observers in America have counseled discretion. They have urged a closer study of the foreign laboratories in which all these experiments were being made before any further efforts to increase social and lessen individual responsibility for the hazards normally prevailing in life and work should be finally organized in America.

Now in England, and the continental countries generally, the social experiments described above are suspended. The systems are still in operation but it is no longer possible to observe them as normally developing experiments, continuously pointing the possibilities to America, their interested spectator. This may not be an unmixed evil with regard to America's future in social insurance. It will mean that a greater burden of analysis and research will be thrown upon us; we shall not be able so readily to assume that because certain plans are at the very moment working well elsewhere, they may be thoughtlessly transported here. We shall investigate these social insurance provisions with more direct reference to our own industrial and social situation and our own administrative facilities; and we shall adopt them, where we do adopt them, on this basis, and with whatever modifications are necessary to make them applicable to American conditions. The danger of our adopting any one of them swiftly and thoughtlessly on the ground that it is manifestly a success elsewhere is now removed.

Far from meaning that the subject of social insurance is less timely in this country, this simply means that the basis for considering it has changed. The developments of the last few months in America have brought one form of social provision, insurance against unemployment, formerly little conceived, very definitely into general speculation. If consideration of this phase of social insurance takes precedence over old-age insurance or pensions and sickness and invalidity insurance, we shall be reversing further the history of European experience in this regard.

This winter, at least two definite recommendations with regard to unemployment insurance have been made in this country: first, the California Commission on Immigration and Housing has recommended a bureau to issue insurance to seasonal workers. The significance of the proposal lies in its direct recognition of one of the few indisputably established causes of unemployment in America—seasonal work; and its direct recognition that some form of insurance is one of the two immediate possibilities of removing from the worker the burden of a condition inherent in the work. The other possibility is the dovetailing of seasonal trades, the responsibility to be upon the industries, not the workers. Secondly, the Municipal Markets Commission of Chicago in reporting recently on a practical plan for relieving destitution and unemployment recommended the appointment of an advisory committee of ten business and ten labor men to study the problem of unemployment insurance.

These instances are mentioned merely because they show that in some aspects, at least, unemployment insurance is now making its appeal in America not merely as an economic theory, suitable for philosophic discussion by civic and legislative bodies, but as an immediate possibility to meet a recognized crisis in American industry.

It is difficult to forecast what lines proposed social insurance measures will take, and it is therefore of interest to note certain principles which will doubtless inhere in the various proposals. That any preventive legislation will be enacted at a time when a crisis calls for emergency measures is doubtful; but the present exigency will serve to stimulate and unite public opinion upon the need for preventive action and urge citizens in positions of power to consider the possibilities and to formulate measures. The subject of unemployment insurance is little understood here. And although American states and communities will readily understand the general theory of shifting upon society a portion of the risks involved in our present industrial system, and although the idea, as such, is likely enough to win ready sympathy, there is still ignorance upon administrative possibilities and dangers.

At the outset it is advisable to state that no one of the European experiments described seems suitable to be directly transplanted to American soil. When unemployment insurance becomes a part of America's industrial policy, it will be a distinctive system, creating no new features perhaps, but containing such of the foreign policies as combine successfully to meet the peculiar financial and industrial situation of America and the peculiar administrative characteristics of a vast federation of states.

It is further believed that unemployment insurance, although necessary and having a part in any comprehensive industrial policy, is not after all a *primary* remedy for unemployment, and that any conception of it as such a remedy would cloud the real causes; it is rather a secondary adjustment, a *sine qua non*, probably, but nevertheless always dependent for its success upon the success of more primary remedies, as the regularization of industry and the organization of the labor market. It is obvious that reinstatement in work is the only final service to the unemployed.

Upon these premises it will be of interest to summarize rapidly the points in the various foreign systems around which the preliminary American discussions must center, and which must be clearly defined and determined before any American policy can be reached.

If we assume that some form of insurance is desirable and therefore waive the fundamental questions as to whether collective enterprise can profitably be substituted for individual thrift, and whether insurance means throwing upon the thrifty workmen the burden of the unthrifty, the most important general principle relates to the question of compulsion. Is the English system of compulsory insurance better adapted to American temper and American conditions than the voluntary principle illustrated in the Ghent system in operation in various forms in various continental countries? Mr. Gibbon[1] has pointed out that on the one hand only a compulsory system could be counted upon to be an effective check on unemployment, that only a compulsory system could bring about a definite assumption of responsibility on the part of employers for maintaining regularity of work so far as possible, and that only a compulsory principle could insure getting workers early into the system, enrolling them, indeed, so soon as their industrial career began. On the other hand, the better class of workmen have been opposed to the compulsory feature; again, it tempts labor exchanges to give work to the less fit on their lists, since unemployment benefit must be paid the man so long as work is not found by the exchange; if the worker is compelled to pay his insurance, the bureau in return is compelled to assume responsibility for finding him work. The "compulsion" is reciprocal.

Seasonal workers have notoriously low wages. Many men now finish a season of fruit picking with no reserve of cash, because they have lost so much time through bad weather, or bad seasons. Is forced saving the fundamental answer to the

[1] I. G. Gibbon, *Unemployment Insurance*, v. also Appendix IX.

problem they present along with the milliners, canners, the camp laborers, the bookbinders, etc.? A compulsory principle is obviously not practicable in any trade unless the conditions of the trade first measure up to certain minimum standards of wage and of steadiness of employment. The working men and women most in need of insurance are those in the least organized trades, where the most irregular standards prevail, or no standards at all. Compulsory insurance, it is to be feared, would not remedy this. It might very conceivably alter some of the conditions of employment, for instance, by encouraging employers by such provisions as that in the English law allowing them to claim a refund of one-third of the contributions they have made for any man kept continually at work by them for at least forty-five weeks in any one year; but it cannot revolutionize fundamental industrial defects. The proposal of compulsory insurance for seasonal workers as an immediate program merely instances the dangers that will lie in regarding unemployment insurance as a snapshot remedy for unemployment rather than a social scheme practicable only when worked out with infinite care and with the closest attention to all the factors concerned *both industrial and social*. Insurance is not a panacea for unemployment; it is a permanent organized measure designed to prevent its worst effects.

So far as America is concerned, the compulsory feature is likely to be less a matter of general principle than of practical possibility. The compulsory principle will ultimately be the only way to make unemployment insurance meet the unemployment situation. But it seems better to begin not by making insurance compulsory for a few trades, and gradually extending the principle, but by encouraging voluntary insurance very gradually, among skilled and unskilled and seasonal workmen equally, and waiting for the policy to secure a logical support. *As a compulsory measure, it must be preceded by fundamental adjustments within industry.*

The storm center of the American insurance discussion is likely to be the organization and means of administration. Both in the continental systems which depend primarily upon the trade unions, and in the system in England which permits men to be insured in groups through their unions, the intimate relation of trade-union ideals to the insurance principle is recognized. The necessity is also recognized that insurance must not *depend* upon union membership, and the Ghent system at the very outset provided that other organizations Catholic, Liberal, or Socialist should have the same right to serve as the insuring body. In England, also, provision for union men in the seven trades is carefully specified. But in practice, very few non-union men are reached.

Our real difficulty in this country will be in finding a sufficiently comprehensive insurance system to include all workmen that need insurance, from the skilled professional to the casual worker. Will such a system be state or federal insurance or both, or will it be a very flexible composite scheme administered in different ways for different classes of workmen, and utilizing *various* social and industrial bodies, as trade unions, fraternal associations, individual industries, or groups of employers and civic or social organizations of many kinds? This is the crux of the problem in America. The greatest danger will lie in too ready an assumption that there is only one way to insure, and too rigid an application of one principle to the manifold industrial forces in America. The question will certainly be answered rather by experiment than by opinion, or by foreign analogies.

In organizing an insurance system we shall have to bear two things in mind: first, a national policy will have to be secured in some way; our industrial situation is like that of no other country, our labor market covers an immense territory, our industrial force is fluctuating. We have only begun to see that the lack of a national organization of the labor market is in normal periods of industry the source of many of our unemployment difficulties. Among the twenty-four states that have enacted workmen's compensation laws there is no attempt at uniformity. The widows' pension system varies in different states. These facts are in accord with our traditional experience. Besides the economic differences between states there are constitutional difficulties in the way of uniformity. Yet there is throughout the country an increasing sense of the need of nationalization with reference to distinctly social policies. In reference to any aspect of unemployment the need is preëminently clear. Whatever is done in cities or states to steady the labor market and improve the conditions of employment must, if it fulfills these ends in any permanent way, show a recognition of the fact that we need a *national industrial policy*, just as we need a national educational and national banking policy. Advocating a national system with reference to unemployment insurance is a very different thing from advocating federal centralization, federal subsidy, or direct federal control.

Secondly, the effectiveness of a system of unemployment insurance is dependent upon an adequate system of labor exchanges. The choice of agents to administer unemployment insurance must be in direct accord with the facilities these agents develop for distributing labor and finding work.

Representatives of organized labor believe that in America, as on the continent under the Ghent system, the trade unions are the logical bodies to administer unemployment insurance. They do not go upon record as absolutely opposed to state insurance, but they oppose state administration of insurance; they "are opposed to having any of our economic functions changed over to the police power of the state." They point out (1) that the cost of administering an insurance system would be greatly increased if done by the state because of enormous overhead charges; (2) that our entire system of distribution of transportation and the limitation of state lines make state insurance impracticable; (3) that a state system would overlook the needs of the migratory worker, and that an industrial factor, so useful in getting the ice and moving the crops of the country, needs care and attention that cannot be given under the "state rights" idea; (4) that the state could collect the funds and the unions could administer them; (5) that the unions would simply have control of the administrative features, and *that the system would not be limited to union members.*

It is to be feared that in this country, as on the continent, the last clause would in practice amount to little more than the expression of a moral aspiration. Trade unions reach only a comparatively small percentage of skilled workmen, and almost no unskilled workers, because they have never been organized. It would at present be impracticable for unions to operate as insurance agents over the whole industrial field. Administering unemployment insurance through unions might, it is true, become a means of building up and developing unions, a probability which would, however, defer many employers from encouraging or contributing to such a plan. Therefore, if the system were put into operation through unions, it would have to be limited to skilled trades, and to such highly organized of these as the building, printing, and railway employees, as an experiment. The unions already have it in their power to make an independent contribution to insurance experimentation by extending and developing the unemployment benefit system now confined to a few unions.

It is upon this point of administrative agencies that America will need most to study its own field. If Mr. Cyril Jackson's conclusion, "a subsidy to trade unions is therefore not only the easiest but the sole effective method of unemployment insurance," or any other conclusion not based upon the characteristic conditions of America, is forced into American experiments, it can only retard the process of working out our own salvation in unemployment insurance. In one important respect America is very different from any one of the countries in which unemployment insurance has as yet been tried; it has a far greater number of civic organizations that assume social responsibility. This number is increasing from year to year. At present in movements for the relief of unemployment in towns and cities throughout the country such associations are very generally acting as the agency both to stimulate action and to correlate the work being done. The question may well be raised whether the trade union and the "benefit" society are the only possible organi-

zations for administering unemployment insurance.
There is much suggestion in one continental provision by which funds are paid to unemployment
societies *organized specifically for this purpose,* and
approved by the state. It might prove feasible to
have such funds administered directly in connection with public employment exchanges, by officers
or committees appointed for that purpose.

The whole question of finance is important from
two points of view: first, with reference to the
actual amount of subsidy, and the proportion of
the contributions to be made by state or municipality, workmen and employers, and the amount of
benefit; and, secondly, with reference to the actual
administration and supervision of the funds.
No system of unemployment insurance should
be definitely proposed, on the strength of approval
of its general principles, before expert estimates,
financial and actuarial, have been made and submitted in detail. The early difficulties of the
Friendly Societies in England, of the "benefit"
societies in America in the 70's and 80's, and of
insurance and pension schemes in general need
not be repeated in formulating experiments in
unemployment insurance.

All administrative details must be carefully
adapted. We have only recently begun to see the
need of adapting the administration of public
employment bureaus to the varying needs of
different groups—children, immigrants, women,
and workers of different grades. In America

31

the present situation with regard to unskilled labor would wreck any national insurance policy that failed to recognize it as a specialized and powerful factor. Some of the usual provisions in unemployment insurance are that a man is entitled to benefit only if he cannot get work of some kind—outside his trade; that he must report to the office daily or lose his title; and, in England, that his employer is asked to report on the fact of his unemployment. The difficulties involved in these provisions for unskilled labor are obvious.

For the great body of immigrant labor in America they would be greatly intensified. Immigrant men and women are in general prepared for fewer kinds of American work than are Americans, they are less able to find it if they are prepared, and stand less chance of receiving it because of discriminating laws in states and municipalities restricting their right to work at various callings or on certain kinds of work. Their unfamiliarity with the language makes any requirement of daily or frequent reports and examinations fairly impracticable. Their relation to employers is notoriously more remote than that of private citizens, and any dependence upon employers for statements regarding them would hardly be feasible. Immigration will intensify the difficulties of devising an American policy of unemployment insurance. But ultimately no scheme that evades the difficulties of the administration of the scheme for immigrants will cover the field of American industry or be an answer to American industrial problems.

These are a few of the questions that arise in the course of any preliminary survey of unemployment insurance methods now in use abroad, from the point of view of their suggestiveness to America. Not only general questions but also the details of all these different measures need very careful analysis in connection with the conditions they meet abroad and the conditions they would, if adopted, be intended to meet in this country.

The unemployment insurance systems in use in foreign countries are not especially adaptable to this country. They would need careful modification, based upon a thorough study of conditions here, with due reference to city and state limitations and to the great areas over which labor is distributed. The successful administration of unemployment insurance is logically dependent upon an efficient system of public labor exchanges which should precede its adoption, or upon the thorough organization of labor and the willingness of capital to have funds to which it contributes paid out through unions. Neither of these conditions prevails to an extent assuring success by this method. Insurance against unemployment should be begun in America in an experimental way by urging unions to increase out-of-work benefits to members, by having industries adopt a system applying to their own plants, by providing state funds to be administered in connection with public employ-

ment exchanges with committees representing employers, the public, and employees, to safeguard their disposition.   We shall then be ready to formulate a national policy.

CHAPTER XIV

A PROGRAM FOR AMERICA

THERE is no panacea for unemployment, no one sure method for its elimination or prevention, no one prophet who has said the last word on the subject. Many ways and many kinds of people are required to master it. Each one will work in the field and by the methods which interest him most and to a limited degree there will be coöperation. The immediate question before us is, can a policy be formulated which will become a common goal, however varying the roads to it may be. If it can be formulated, how can we best shorten the distance from theory to practice, from purpose to action, from waste to economy, from indirection and misdirection to efficiency, in our attempt to shift the burden from the unemployed individual to the group. Unless we can find a way, we shall continue the desultory and futile methods which have hitherto characterized our action and which satisfy nobody, least of all the unemployed.

In considering the following proposals, we need to keep clearly in mind certain fundamental principles which may be stated as follows:

485

(1) Involuntary unemployment, due to no other cause than lack of work is a problem of industry, and its eradication is the responsibility of industry and of government. All other unemployment is primarily the problem of charity, whether administered by government or philanthropy, and its solution should emanate from a relief point. Labor created for relief purposes is therefore fundamentally relief not industry.

(2) Unemployment is characteristic of good seasons as well as of bad and the "revival of business" will not lessen the necessity for dealing with the matter thoroughly and comprehensively. It will only modify the necessity for relief. The need of distributing a surplus or the unfilled demand for labor will always be before us.

(3) Security of employment is second only in importance to the free opportunity to work and is equally essential to the success of this republic. Women and children should have equal security in employment with men.

(4) Discriminations against alien workmen should be made in the exclusion laws and not in obscure ordinances and state statutes.

(5) The maintenance of a neutral organized labor market is the province of the government. The province of business and labor is to bargain but not to control the market place and its regulations.

(6) The actual unit for the local distribution of labor is the city: for general distribution, the nation; and for rural communities, the agriculture

departments of states and nation. The state is not a practical unit of distribution in any organization of the labor market.

(7) The organization of the labor market and the establishment of new agencies will not *increase* the total amount of work. "Odd jobs" may be increased by special appeals but the function of the agency is that of an exchange. Its prime object is to expedite bringing the person and the job together, reduce cost, check waste, lessen maladjustment, prevent fraud and conserve the resources and skill and integrity of the unemployed.

Any program promulgated at a critical time of unemployment should contain two divisions—a short-time, immediate program which will deal with emergencies and which calls for the volunteer services of many more or less skilled assistants. This is intended for the immediate relief of the involuntary unemployed. The second is a long-time program requiring the services of the highest skilled persons available, and is designed for the prevention of unemployment. The information and experience gained in the execution of the short-time program will be of much value to the long-time program, but the long-time program should be in charge of different people with different interests and capacities. Essentially, the short-time program is executive and remedial while the long-time program is analytical and preventive.

On the immediate relief program the national

government has taken no action. With two months of the hardest winter on record already gone, neither the Department of Labor nor the Commission on Industrial Relations has set forth a program for dealing with this subject. The President still believes unemployment to be a "state of mind," although he has advocated the establishment of a Federal system of employment exchanges, based primarily upon the crop removal needs of next autumn. When his message went to Congress early in December there existed a condition among workingmen in this country which gave him a magnificent opportunity to deal with the one vital human problem pressing for solution in this country—a problem upon which his compatriots are working night and day. That opportunity has been missed. However much spring and summer may conceal the suffering, unemployment in an aggravated form is here to stay for a least another long year, and it is not yet too late to act.

The immediate short-time national program includes, first, the establishment of a system of Federal employment bureaus,[1] to distribute the load. It will not increase the number of jobs but it will distribute the ill-proportioned burden which reserve labor cities are carrying, and will lay the foundation for preventive work.

Secondly, an examination of the order books of industries shows that industry has broken down as the saviour of the present unemployment situation and that the government must come

[1] Appendix I: A Bill to Establish a National System of Labor Exchanges.

to the rescue.¹ Therefore the President should institute the most careful inquiry into (a) government contracts and work already authorized, for which appropriations have been made and which could proceed rapidly if red tape were cut and political juggling laid aside; (b) the amount of new work that could be taken up economically, without too great an increase in appropriation and without "pork barrel" log rolling, which would give employment to men in the south and west at this time of the year; (c) Improvements and work scheduled for the summer that can be done now or held over until next winter.

Thirdly, while industry is prostrate, a movement should be begun for sending settlers to the land, and facilities should be provided for this purpose in the Department of Agriculture or of the Interior to work with the various agencies now struggling either single-handed or self-interestedly with the problem. Doubtless a transportation and colonization fund operated on a loan basis would need to be started in connection with this whole short-time program, but a way should be found through precedent and legal obstacles when men and women are without work or means of subsistence. In connection with the stimulation of agriculture, commerce should be assisted in every possible legitimate way to establish new markets and to organize its present markets more efficiently.

¹ Appendix II, The Federal Government and Unemployment.

Fourthly, there should go out from the President's office an urgent message to stimulate local governments of both cities and states to shoulder their burden uniformly. Many cities that authorized public improvements and issued bonds—some of them so long ago as last September—have not yet started this work. "Peanut" politics at this time may cause the responsible party in power a national disaster in 1916 unless this problem is grappled with now courageously and intelligently. This country needs a "get-together" policy in the form not merely of miscellaneous *talking* together at general conferences, but of coöperation on the part of responsible men in power, who will first formulate and then accept propositions A. B. or C., and then put them through. The preliminary educational work has been accomplished by the disaster of 1914 and 1915, and we are ready for national action now.

The immediate short-time program for cities should include first the appointment of a mayor's committee—the smaller the better for accomplishment—which should take the situation in hand; it should first ascertain what are the city's resources, what public works it can continue, increase, or start,[1] and then urge that they be put into operation at once with care to maintain standards of workmanship and of wages. It is better (if only for the sake of the work) to employ skilled men on part time at standard wages than on full

[1] Appendix III, Suggestions for Municipal Public Works.

time at half the regular wage. Secondly, the committee can ascertain the resources of industries, whether they are carrying as full a force as possible, whether they are giving the maximum of relief to their own dismissed employees, and whether their plants could be adapted to other work, the products of which may be in demand. Sewing-rooms and temporary workshops for war relief supplies started in deserted or half-idle factories under the experienced supervision of the owner would be less wasteful in every way than starting new experiments. Part-time shifts day and night could be operated in such plants. Thirdly, the committee should ascertain whether the average citizen cannot participate in an odd-job campaign, to create additional work. And fourthly, it may find out to what extent relief organizations can and are meeting the situation, what supplemental work is needed, and then promptly meet the need by direct relief given by the city unsparingly whenever necessary.[1]

This is not a program of investigation, and its organization should be simple and direct. Every one of these subjects should be dealt with item by item and something definite accomplished; wherever an industry can be found that is able to do more than it is doing, it should be followed up and the expansion made; wherever an industry can be adapted, it must be; wherever organized private relief has broken down, the load under which it has broken must be taken up. Two

[1] Appendix IV: One Municipal Plan.

principles must prevail in an effective program of this kind; the city committee should be in authority and take precedence; it cannot successfully become the tail to the kite of private philanthropy; its right to raise and distribute funds should not be questioned by organized private relief. There should be coöperation but not restriction; private philanthropy should account to the city government, and not the government to it; and certainly the city should never wait until private philanthropy has proved wholly inadequate. This winter, the taxpayer of yesterday is the unemployed of to-day and he feels that he should be able to turn to his government rather than to strangers not allied with him in the responsibilities of citizenship. Furthermore, the problem is not one that private relief, established to detect vagrancy and deal with the "down and outs," has a sufficiently elastic organization to meet. It has a reputation, acquired justly or unjustly as the case may be, which prevents the self-respecting men and women out of work for the first time from appealing to it. Its procedure is to act upon applications, whereas the present situation calls for volunteers to locate the silent sufferers of unemployment.

There is room for everyone to work in coöperation with such a central committee. Relief organizations, civic committees, churches,[1] and individuals can all contribute whether it be through

[1] Appendix V: Church Program Adopted by Inter-Church Committee of New York City Federation of Churches.

sewing-rooms, loan funds, odd-job compaigns, the provision of food and lodging on a self-respecting basis and with particular reference to the status of the particular men and women concerned, through coöperation with school teachers in efforts to find needy families, and through constant coöperation with all possible existing relief agencies to effect better results and to avoid overlapping of work. The greater the number of workers, the wider the range of activities, and the more numerous the demands for funds, the greater need to coördinate the work through such a central committee.

In this crisis the average citizen up to this time has shouldered the burden. And there is a great deal that the average citizen can do; he can find out exactly who are unemployed in his neighborhood and what is the degree and kind of need, and can report these facts to the central committee. He can contribute or can get others to contribute the use of vacant houses, lofts, rooms, or stores for temporary lodging-places,—especially for distinct groups as, for instance, young working girls entirely dependent on their own resources—or for workrooms; he can see that in his residential district especially there is sufficient publicity for these and other shelters—that they reach all classes of the unemployed and that the policeman on the beat knows to whom to refer applicants. The average citizen can encourage the consistent use of the police, in this connection, as information centers. Hitherto, addressing policemen on this subject has meant arrest for vagrancy in our cities. He can encourage, canvass for, and contribute to local and sectional loan funds for high-grade workmen and women, at a nominal interest. He can study at first hand all the factors of the situation in his particular neighborhood, as well as in the city in general, and coöperate with his neighbors in devising the plans that best meet the particular situation.[1]

The long-time or preventive program has five inter-locking divisions: the obtaining of accurate information, the organization of the labor market, industrial organization looking toward the reduction of seasonal and casual labor, the direction of workers into industry, and some form of insurance which will relieve the unemployed.

1. We need first of all accurate information. The publication of the 1910 census returns on unemployment is recommended so that our statistical data upon this subject may be up to date and not fourteen years old, whereas other industrial data is available for 1910. This requires a special appropriation by Congress.

There should be an assembling of all of the available information not included in the census about employment conditions, conducted with skill, fairness, diligence, and patience, covering the whole field in its many local and national phases. Such a superficial, unscientific, popular

[1] Appendix VI: An Emergency Program for Private Citizens.

clamor for publicity and appropriations as has been carried on by the Commission on Industrial Relations will not meet the need nor serve the ultimate purpose of formulating a comprehensive national program. We need a scientific body of people at work on this matter all the time,—not a political body prodding the subject at different strategic points.

It has been shown that our statistics on unemployment now consist only of incidental and unreliable estimates of the number of people out of work in varying places at varying times. Excepting the returns for skilled labor, compiled by a few unions, there is no index to employment, such as statements of the maximum and minimum employing capacity of industries and the fluctuations between these during the year, the reserve of labor necessary to maintain industries, the causes and the amount of irregular and under-employment.

We therefore need to know, industry by industry, trade by trade, and business by business, these among many other things: the normal and comparative labor capacity of the industry, trade or business; the reserve used, as shown by extras and replacements; the reasons for holding the reserve; the methods of securing or disposing of reserve labor supply; to what extent labor supply is based upon efficiency and to what extent upon other considerations as, for instance, long service, handicaps, etc., and the reasons therefor; the amount of irregular employment and of over-employment as shown by the individual record of each employer with the total amount of wage payment; where reductions or increases in force have been made, the reasons therefor; the number of applications made for work and the waiting list.

Along with this body of data we need to know the amount of unemployment as shown by trades, union reports, house to house census, newspaper advertising, the records of relief organizations for the involuntarily idle only, etc., in order to supplement and verify the records of business organizations.

We should know this not only for industries and workers, but for government business. The government is the largest single employer, and not one inquiry suggested for private industry is inapplicable to the various forms of government business. We can get no true understanding or measure of unemployment until we have complete data. Civil service methods, lists, appointments, reserves, etc., should be included in any preliminary survey of government business.

We are now ready to survey labor market facilities, as to number, location, adaptability to locality, methods, and standards, and to study organizations furnishing work and relief and institutions which perform labor market functions. Such a survey should be followed by a study of the agencies for directing children into industry and of the prevailing forces now at work on their behalf. An analysis of emergency measures, including woodyards, rock piles, laundries, sewing-rooms, arrangements to furnish supplies at cost, etc., in their relation to production and labor distribution is also essential.   A study of the effect of prevailing legislation upon unemployment should precede any further enactment of laws.

Herein is indicated, not covered, the field to be included in the gathering of the urgently needed data. Any permanent program proposed here is presented with full recognition of the fact that it should be varied in accordance with such data when it is available.

Such a comprehensive study would lead to the creation of reliable literature upon the subject, the discovery of causes, the presentation of facts upon prevailing conditions, the crystallizing of public opinion, the formulation of remedies, and the discussion of them, the inception of experiments, and the adoption in times of peace and prosperity of measures of relief rather than war measures during critical periods of unemployment. In the absence of such reliable data and practical constructive plans, the public is thirsting for information, or restless with inaction, or disposed to plunge wildly ahead in ill-considered and ill-organized efforts involving reckless expenditure.

The accumulation and centralizing of this information should be one of the most important functions of the second part of a long-time program, namely the establishment of a system of

32

Federal municipal employment exchanges, *kept out of politics from the beginning*. With the establishment of a Federal clearing-house system, the first step should be to abolish the state agencies that are below standard, strengthen the existing city agencies and create new ones as local centers. Not the least important function of this system of exchanges would be the preliminary work of separating the employables from the unemployables. It cannot be done without the coöperation of private and civic agencies, nor can it be done without the interest and the aid of labor and trade organizations. The burden of finding work for the man willing and able to work should without equivocation, subterfuge or evasion be made solely the responsibility of industry and government. The handicapped, for whatever cause, should be made the joint charge of business, the government, and notably of philanthropy *wherever special personal adjustments and personal service are required*. We now ask industry to bear the burden of the handicapped, with disastrous results to both the individual and the industry, and we ask philanthropy to bear the burden of caring for the man willing and able to work, with equally disastrous results upon his efficiency, integrity, and desire to work. The unemployables should be removed from the ranks of organized industry and equipped at public or private expense to return to it or be cared for as permanent dependents, or put at work in such profitable enterprises as may be created or

selected after a just consideration of the conditions.
The "won't works" require the strong arm of the
law, and service at hard labor in the interests of
the state, rather than the sympathetic efforts of
a church to get them work. The "mendicancy
squad" and the "farm colony" will perform a very
effective service for this class of the unemployed.

The passage of the Federal bill appended here-
with,[1] creating a national system of employment
exchanges, or any similar bill will be ineffective
if unaccompanied by adequate regulation of all
agencies furnishing labor to persons or corporations that are engaged in interstate commerce or
that send persons from one state to another, and
by uniform state and municipal laws for the regulation of private agencies. The regulation of
private employment agencies doing an interstate
business raises grave questions as to constitutionality. In the case[2] of John T. Sheppard, in Georgia,
it was decided by Judge Bleckley that an act
"requiring any person engaged in hiring laborers
in this state for employment beyond the limits
of the state to procure a license and pay therefor
$100, and making it penal to carry on the business
without such license," was constitutional, presumably on the theory that the contract of employment was actually consummated within the

[1] Appendix I: Bill Creating a National System of Employment
Exchanges.

[2] John Sheppard *et al. vs.* the County Commissioners of Senate
(59 Ga. 535, Aug. term, 1877).

geographical limits of the state, thus enabling the state through its police power to regulate such agencies even though the laborers were sent beyond the state limits. If this decision holds, it is doubtful whether sending laborers from one state to another is interstate commerce. A separate bill[1] should therefore be drawn to deal with this subject in order not to imperil the passage and operation of the bill establishing a system of employment agencies.

If the labor market is to be really organized, therefore, all the activities set forth in the following summary must go hand in hand.

1. The establishment of a Federal Employment Bureau to act as a clearing house for the state and municipal bureaus and to handle the reserve labor supply and inter-city and inter-state employment, to begin the classification of employables and unemployables, and to make investigations.

2. The extension of the Federal Division of Information as a national agricultural bureau, and the encouragement of rural organizations to establish efficient centers to coöperate with it; for instance, the formulation by granges and other agricultural organizations of plans for organizing farm labor bureaus and the utilization of existing farm bureaus.

3. The establishment in the Federal Bureau of Education of a teachers' agency for interstate

[1] Appendix VII. Bill providing for the regulation of all employment agencies furnishing labor to persons or corporations engaged in interstate commerce or sending persons from one state to another.

placement and bureaus in state departments of education for the state placement of teachers.

4. The establishment of bureaus of information and vocational guidance at immigrant ports for the direction of immigrants into industry, and to land and business opportunities.

5. The establishment in the Department of the Interior or of Agriculture of a bureau of colonization to handle interstate land problems, to direct settlers to the land, to require the registration of lands offered for sale, and to prevent fraud and exploitation, with the administration of a loan fund for the transportation of settlers.

6. The Federal and state regulation of private agencies according to accepted standards, with reports, to enable the government to know and direct labor distribution.

7. The elimination of the padroni and the substitution of commissariat agents employed by the company or the contractor; the elimination of the boarding boss as a labor agent.

8. The establishment of municipal bureaus to handle local work and to clear through Federal agencies, gradually eliminating state agencies.

9. The establishment of local clearing houses among (1) philanthropic agencies, (2) civic agencies, (3) religious agencies, (4) commercial agencies, with a view to eliminating waste and duplication, lifting the burden from the unemployed, and increasing the efficiency of relief work.

10. The safeguarding of want advertisements in newspapers in order to conserve the resources of the unemployed.

11. The separation of the sale of liquor and the

furnishing of jobs; and the abolition of the political manipulation of private business jobs by political leaders.

The third division of a long-time program through organization of business looking toward the dovetailing of trades, the lengthening of seasons, the diminishing of the number of reservists and the concentration of demands upon a few centers, the better distribution of workmen by one industry to another, should be made a common subject for study, analysis, and experiment by individual industries, by associations of industries, and by government departments; it should be made the subject of conferences by trade congresses, manufacturers' associations, chambers of commerce, etc. The whole subject is still in the hands of the academician, the investigator, and the theorist. Their services have been valuable, but we are ready for action. We are ready to see the railroad, not the padroni, send its casual laborers to the ice field or the lumber camp; to see small winter industries locate near farms so that farm hands can get work in winter, and to see community life developed; to see the orders now concentrated at one period cover the year in advance, as has been done in the Christmas card trade; to have a seasonal industry plan to carry two lines of trade, wherever the machinery can be adapted to more than one, so that it may keep employees throughout the year. We are ready

to see the government plan to do its heavy work
when industries are slack and do its southern
reclamation and afforestation and irrigation work
during the dull seasons; we are ready for some
plan from Cleveland and Buffalo by which the
lake carriers can be transferred directly to winter
employment and kept out of dives and saloons.

The possibilities for the dovetailing of trades,
and for adjustments between two or a number of
industries are really dependent upon necessary adjustments to be worked out first within individual
trades or groups of trades.   In this connection the
work of the Joint Board of Sanitary Control of the
Cloak and Suit Makers in New York City is
interesting in illustrating   the possibilities of
adjustments through the joint efforts of employer
and workmen represented in trade unions.   On
September 2, 1910, a protocol of peace was signed
that covered the cloak, suit, and skirt industry in
New York City.   This agreement was made between organizations of employers and employees,
each of which was supposed to control its members
completely.   The essential points of this peace
arrangement or protocol are permanent peace,
maintained by conciliation and arbitration through
a board of grievances and a board of arbitration;
control of the sanitary conditions in the industry
through a joint board of sanitary control; the
preferential union shop; minimum standards of
wages; a satisfactory system for determining prices
for piece work; and the prohibition of home-work

and subcontracting. Similar protocols, embodying the same general principles, with some modification, have since been adopted in the dress and waist, the kimono and house-dress, the white goods, and the misses' and children's dresses industries in New York City, and in the cloak and suit and the dress and waist industries in Boston. In the extension of these experiments lies the best hope of bringing about a better grade of workmen, making it to the employer's interest to conserve them, and insuring on the part of employers that assumption of responsibility which will be the impelling cause in any general regularization of industry.

In a pamphlet entitled, *A Practical Program for the Prevention of Unemployment in America*, John B. Andrews, Secretary of the American Association for Labor Legislation, has set forth a number of suggestions. Although there is some doubt as to the immediate practicability of some of them, they may be suggestive to employers and are reprinted here as Appendix VII.[1]

In the matter of regularizing and planning government work, there should first of all be some reorganization of civil service laws looking toward the establishment of certain principles related to unemployment as well as to city service: 1. Are such laws applicable to unskilled labor; are the tests proposed adequate, and should alien general workmen be excluded either when the work is done directly by the city or when it is done through

[1] Appendix VIII: The Regularization of Industry; John B. Andrews.

contractors? There seems to be every reason to exclude aliens where the work concerns the *administration of government;* but it is a far cry from this to digging a subway or building a barge canal. 2. A new method of determining civil service examinations might be considered, by which public school records and training will play a larger part, and by which the examinations will be formulated by experts having a knowledge of the subject. 3. A better use of reserve lists is certainly possible, as is a better placement of temporary help. Undoubtedly when several hundred persons take an examination for one vacant position, the waiting list carefully selected by the test should be made available for other employment either within the government service or outside it. Such departments as those of parks and street cleaning continually use extra and temporary help, with the sole consideration of getting the work done, and not with any idea of transferring the individual workman from department to department so that he may work regularly. The whole civil service list system, like that of industry, is based upon getting the work done, with little regard to the under-employment or irregularity of employment of the workman. 4. A study of the civil service employment bureaus, from the point of view of the welfare of the workmen will prove most illuminating.

The fourth section of the preventive program, the *direction* of children into industry belongs essentially to the public school system rather than to the public employment exchanges, although in the actual work of *placement* there should be the closest coöperation between the two. Mr. Meyer Bloomfield has tentatively outlined the functions of a scheme of juvenile education and employment exchanges as follows:

1. To provide boys and girls under eighteen with an opportunity to secure *information* and *advice* as to *training opportunities* and *available situations*.

2. To *list employment opportunities*, after inquiry, and endeavor to secure educational opportunities in part time or other ways for those placed, through school coöperation.

3. To *place such applicants as must secure work* in the most suitable position possible, *special effort* being made to *deal subsequently* with makeshift or temporary placements.

4. To organize a *follow-up system* through paid and volunteer workers visiting

a, employers who may be induced to interest themselves in the progress of those placed with them.

b, those placed by the exchange, in order to encourage their vocational, as well as educational social, and physical growth.

5. To *provide a system of medical or health guidance*, with a staff of physicians to make follow-up studies of young employees in specified occupations in order to determine their effect on health, etc.

6. To *conduct lecture courses* with suitable devices to secure interest on the part of parents, teachers,

children and the public in the problems and ways of
choosing and preparing for a life work.

7. To *study the employment* open to the youth of
the city from the point of view of their requirements
and opportunities, advantages and disadvantages; and
publish the results in simple pamphlet form for the use
of teachers, parents, and the children.

8. To *coöperate with employers* and others in
studies and experiments in more scientific methods of
hiring and advancing employees; organization of a
coöperating employment managers' association.

As a preliminary to the adoption of such a
program, a six months' study of this problem is
recommended in each city for the purpose of
organizing the needed coöperation of the schools,
employers, exchanges, and others.   Advisory committees are recommended as part of the plan of
administration.

In addition to this coöperative work between
boards of education and employment exchanges,
there should be an extension of the law prohibiting
child labor under the age of sixteen, a limitation of
the wholesale entrance of children into industry,
and the development of continuation schools and
part-time schools within the industries themselves,
under the supervision of the public school system,
or in connection with it.

The subject of unemployment insurance in this
country is not yet a matter for *immediate* adoption.
Neither the data necessary for its proper formulation nor the machinery for administration in

the form of auxiliary societies and public exchanges which exist in all countries that have adopted it, exists here as yet.[1] Subsidies on any large scale to trade-union organizations are not practical at this time, although limited experiments may be made where payments can be safeguarded through the establishment of committees, representing all contributors to the fund.

We are ready, however, for the encouragement of the payment of out-of-work benefits by trade unions whose trades are comparatively well organized; for experiments in mutual insurance whereby both employers and employees (and the government voluntarily) contribute to a common fund in such steady employments as common carriers, printing, etc. With the establishment of Federal and municipal exchanges we may also be ready for the experiment of the administration of a public fund in connection therewith, limited to certain trades.

On the other hand, we know far too little of casual and seasonal labor, which needs such a fund most, to estimate the amount of risk, or the assessments to be paid. Furthermore the whole problem of unskilled labor is immensely complicated by the presence in this country of 13,000,000 foreign-born persons and the constant forward and backward flow between countries in seasons, amounting to nearly a million a year in normal times. It is highly essential to safeguard any

[1] Appendix IX: Unemployment Insurance; J. B. Gibbon.

fund from exploitation, and in working out our own checks upon this the experience of other countries will not help us much. To those who believe that unemployment insurance can be administered only through trade unions, the reply is necessarily that casual and seasonal workmen must then first be organized. A similar problem faces us in connection with women's work which is as yet almost wholly unorganized. We should avoid the danger and deception of appropriating or collecting a relief fund and calling it insurance without maintaining the principles of insurance.

If this program seems too remote or too idealistic, it must be remembered that it is to be accomplished not by one swift process but by the sum total of what the average citizen does as a business man, by what the investor does as an employer, by what each of us does in office, in business, in school. It is essential that we should be on the right road, that we should realize the complexity of the efforts needed to reach the goal, and not blind ourselves to the fact that our small individual effort is not the sum total of either the task or its accomplishment.

APPENDIX I

To establish in the Department of Labor a bureau to be known as the National Bureau of Labor Exchanges and for other purposes.

Be it enacted by the Senate and House of Representatives of the United States of America in Congress assembled: That there shall be established in the Department of Labor a bureau to be known as the National Bureau of Labor Exchanges.

SECTION 2. *Commissioner.*—That the bureau shall be under the direction of a Commissioner of Labor Exchanges who shall have technical and scientific knowledge upon the subject of unemployment and the administration of public labor exchanges and recognized capacity to direct investigations of unemployment and public and private agencies for remedying the same and who shall be appointed by the President with the consent of the Senate.

SECTION 3. *Advisory Council.*—That there shall be attached to the national bureau of labor exchanges an advisory council appointed by the Commissioner, to serve without compensation or remuneration except for necessary traveling expenses, composed of three persons representing employers, three persons representing employees, and three persons representing the public. The Commissioner shall act as chairman of the council. It shall be the duty of the advisory council to advise and assist the Commissioner in determining the policies of the Bureau. The tenure of office of any member of the advisory council shall be at his own pleasure unless removed for cause. Vacancies, however caused, shall be filled in the same manner as the original appointments.

SECTION 4. *Appointment of Officers.*—That there shall be in the bureau such deputy commissioners, agents, and other officers as shall be necessary to execute the powers and perform the duties of the bureau. They shall be appointed, and may be removed for cause, and their compensation shall be fixed and raised or decreased from time to time, by the Secretary of Labor, upon the recommendation of the Commissioner and in accordance with the provisions of an Act entitled "An Act to regulate and improve the civil service of the United States," approved January 16, 1883 and amendments thereto.

SECTION 5. *Offices.*—That the Commissioner shall establish and conduct a system of free public labor exchanges with branches at such important industrial or commercial centers as he may determine, and any such offices may be designated by him as district clearing houses. Each office shall be in charge of a deputy commissioner or other officer designated by the Commissioner, who shall be subject to the supervision and direction of the Commissioner. All such offices and branches shall keep uniform records and shall exchange reports showing the demand for and supply of labor in such manner as the Commissioner may direct, and shall solicit business by advertising in newspapers and in any other way that the Commissioner may direct, to facilitate the bringing together of employers and employees.

SECTION 6. *Local Aid.*—That the Commissioner may enter into an agreement with any governmental authority, for such period of time as may be deemed desirable, for the purpose of establishing and maintaining municipal free public labor exchanges, and it shall be lawful for the Commissioner to expend funds and to permit the use of public property for the joint establishment and maintenance of such offices as may be agreed upon.

SECTION 7. *Duties and Powers.*—That the Commissioner shall: (a) coördinate through the central office of the bureau the work of all agencies that collect and furnish information regarding employment; (b) collect and furnish information for the purpose of bringing together all persons seeking employment and employers seeking labor; (c) provide facilities for the direction of workers into industry; (d) administer such funds as may be made available from time to time for the purpose of distributing unemployed persons from one place to another; (e) investigate the circulation of information and statements regarding labor market conditions for the purpose of preventing fraud and improper practices and from time to time present to the proper authorities for action thereon the results of such investigations; (f) investigate the work of all agencies and persons engaged in the business of procuring employment or furnishing information concerning employment and require from them from time to time such reports as he

33

may determine will show the condition of the labor market and will facilitate the distribution of labor; (g) publish and distribute information regarding the true state of the labor market in bulletins and in such other form as he may determine, in English and in such other languages as may be necessary, and (h) investigate the extent and causes of unemployment and make recommendations for the reduction of unemployment and for the prevention of distress from involuntary idleness.

SECTION 8. *Registration of applicants.*—That applicants shall register upon forms prescribed by the Commissioner, and there shall be kept at each office a complete record of all applications for employment and all calls for help, all persons referred to employers, whether positions are secured or not, and if not the reasons therefor, and such other details as may be required. That all persons referred to employers shall always be notified of the existence of an industrial dispute, strike, or lockout at or in connection with the business or place of business of the person or corporation making the request for help. That the Commissioner, deputy commissioners, or other agents or officers shall undertake no responsibility with regard to the character of applicants or the payment of wages or other conditions, beyond supplying such information as may have been obtained.

SECTION 9. *Reports.*—That the Commissioner shall report to the Secretary of Labor annually, or at such other times as the Secretary may elect, concerning the operations of the bureau and the results of all investigations conducted under the provisions of this Act.

SECTION 10. This Act shall take effect immediately.

*Explanatory Notes on Proposed Bill to Establish a
National Bureau of Labor Exchanges*

In re Section 1. Dealing with the most important
of labor problems, that of keeping the workman
employed and providing industry with the help it
needs, the proposed bureau is a coördinate division of
and should be attached to the Federal Department
of Labor.

In re Section 2. The administration of public
labor exchanges, with all its correlated duties, is a
highly technical and specialized undertaking, and its
success will largely depend upon the knowledge
and initiative of its chief executive officer. The
President should therefore be given free rein to make
the best possible selection according to specified
standards, instead of limiting it to the rather uncertain
results of a civil service examination.

In re Section 3. Such an advisory council with
representatives of labor, industry, and the public
should be a vital factor in obtaining the full coöperation of employers and employees and the expert
advice of disinterested students of the problem and
in preserving absolute neutrality in labor disputes.
The members of the council should include unorganized as well as organized employers and employees,
so that all may benefit from the policies adopted.

In re Section 4. The merit system and an elastic
machinery for fixing the salaries of all employees will
prove a decided incentive to sincere and efficient
administration. The power of appointment should
be vested in the chief executive officers in order to
centralize authority and responsibility.

In re Section 5. The broad phraseology of this

section permits the gradual development of a closely welded network of labor exchanges and the establishment of such clearing houses as may be necessary. By keeping uniform records, exchanging reports, and soliciting business, the system will eliminate much of the waste and loss of time between "jobs."

In re Section 6. This general power to coöperate with any governmental authority will largely increase the number of public labor exchanges (all closely affiliated with the central office at Washington, D. C.), the Federal government will be relieved of considerable expense for equipment, and local interest and coöperation in the organization of the labor market will be inspired. Cities, and not states, are the industrial and commercial units of the country. The boundary lines dividing the political sovereignty of the states are not the strategic lines involved in the distribution of labor. The proposed Federal district clearing houses, with jurisdiction over great industrial districts, can exchange information between the different cities, entirely ignoring political state lines, with far better results. Federal aid to, and coöperation with, municipal instead of state employment offices will therefore result in greater efficiency.

In re Section 7. The detailed duties and powers, as specified, are of vital importance for the broad and constructive development of the system: (a) by making the central office the clearing house for all employment work; (b) by actually bringing together employers and employees; (c) by guiding children and immigrants into useful employment; (d) by supervising the distribution of any funds obtained from any source in transporting unemployed persons from place to place; (e) by eliminating misleading infor-

mation as to labor market conditions; (f) by standardizing methods and increasing the efficiency of other
employment offices; (g) by giving wide publicity to
the condition of the labor market; and (h) by making
constructive recommendations for the relief of the
unemployed based upon scientific investigation.

In re Section 8. The records detailed are quite
essential. The notice to applicants for work of the
existence of an industrial dispute will prevent the
sending out of strike-breakers. By leaving to employers and employees the actual settlement of the terms
and conditions of the contract of employment, the
bureau is freed from all responsibility of this nature.

In re Section 9. The reports of the bureau, which
would be of considerable value to many readers,
should be printed and distributed freely.

APPENDIX II

The following suggest measures open to the Federal government to provide for the institution or continuance throughout the country of public works that would engage in large numbers men laid off by private industry. These measures were not devised to relieve unemployment and are not to be so advocated. They have long been recognized as highly expedient and necessary public improvements. They may now be made to coincide with the present nation-wide scarcity of work. Further, they will be effective only if carried on according to all the normal standards and methods and discriminations of industrial efficiency.

Reclamation

1. Extension of irrigation and other reclamation projects by the Federal government for Arizona, New Mexico, Nevada, Utah, Southern Idaho, Central Oregon, Eastern Washington, parts of Montana, Colorado, Wyoming, and Nebraska.

2. Advancement of funds to land clearers by the Federal government, if this is not undertaken by the states.

3. Such immediate revision of the requirements

518

and operation of the hitherto unsuccessful Carey Act, and such effective Federal supervision of its administration by the various states that the act may serve its original purpose of swift reclamation and the establishment of settlers on the land.

4. The utmost practicable coöperation, after investigation, on the part of the Reclamation Service with organizations and private individuals in realizing colonization projects on government land for the relief of unemployment. With the present rates for government land, this provision would have to include some adjustments as to time allowed for payment.

5. Greater publicity for the work of the Reclamation Service in the Department of the Interior. This Service now has open for entry 400 farms, for which water has been provided, located on 24 projects in 16 states.

Rivers and Harbors

1. The appointment of an Emergency Commission on National Waterways composed of engineers and other experts and required to report *at once* which of the many and various provisions of the Rivers and Harbors Bill are beyond the shadow of a doubt necessary, of more than local importance, and entirely outside the "pork-barrel" class. The more debatable proposals and appropriations can be left to the longer deliberations of some such body.

2. The immediate inception of the projects approved.

Particularly important are the flood prevention projects, referring especially to the Ohio and Mississippi Valleys. These projects include such operations as regulating the flow of navigable rivers, keeping them from reaching flood height; encouraging afforestation at headwaters to prevent too rapid run-off; building dams, reservoirs, and dikes, dredging, straightening channels, building spillways, and draining swamps.

Among the river and harbor projects which are now most critical are those referring to the Columbia River at its mouth; the Delaware River between Philadelphia and the sea; the Hudson River, in extension of the Erie Barge Canal; Mobile Bay Channel, from the Gulf of Mexico to the city of Mobile; Boston Harbor, Massachusetts, thirty-five foot channel; Ohio River, locks and dams. Much work is necessary along the course of the Mississippi. The exact extent of the work and the amount and variety of employment it can offer can be known only after there has been an expert report upon what levees are necessary, what lands are subject to overflow, what construction is indicated, etc.

3. Provision for making the Panama Canal machinery available so soon as practicable.

Roads

(Of the 2,225,000 miles of highways in the United States, less than one tenth is improved.)

1. Immediate inception of work on needed public highways all over the country. This is no new proposition, but a hastening of the development of a national road system long recognized to be an important governmental duty. The recent recommendations of the Good Roads Congress should serve as a guide and thus expedite the work. The importance of good roads to a system of national defense has lately

become apparent. Their importance to agriculture and to trade and commerce is incalculable. A team that pulls only two bales of cotton on a bad road can pull six or seven bales on a good one. This one consideration has great influence on the celerity with which new supplies can be put at the disposal of industry. Good roads would do as much as increased credit facilities toward solving our annually recurring problem of moving the crops. In the United States, $40,991,449,000 is invested in agriculture. The magnitude of this investment makes an adequate national road system highly desirable, if not imperative.

2. Federal aid to states and counties in the improvement and construction of rural post roads, and coöperation with the states in the *immediate* undertaking of this work.

3. Federal appropriations for the repair of public roads, especially in such states as Arizona and Nevada where the closing of the copper mines and the absence of other industries leave the unemployed peculiarly without resources.

Public Work

1. The expediting and continuance of necessary Federal buildings already provided for in all parts of the country.

2. The hastening of public work now being urged by business men and citizens in Washington, D. C.

3. The opening of coal fields in Alaska to operators and the building of railroads by the government for the purpose of developing the labor resources of the territory. The furnishing of transportation by the

government to recruit the workmen for these operations from men now idle in similar industries in the United States.

4. Organized assistance to the building trades, as well as to communities, by the institution of a national building loan fund, such as the one recently formally recommended by the American Federation of Labor. Muncipalities or responsible private individuals could borrow from such a fund for the purpose of beginning at once the building of model tenements and cottages. The housing bill recently passed in England, with especial reference to unemployment, offers an analogy.

Trade and Commerce

1. Merchant Marine. Building and equipment of ships in this country, engaging American workmen and using American materials—steel, etc. This is a fitting accompaniment to the building up of a new trade system encouraged by the opening of the Panama Canal, the amendment to the registry acts, and the new Federal reserve system.

2. Immediate encouragement to American manufacture of hitherto imported goods, by greater publicity for information about foreign methods of manufacture in the Consular reports, hereafter to be contained in the new publication of the Department of Commerce.

3. Coöperation with students and research laboratories and factories in working out, with the utmost possible speed, ways of developing good dyestuffs, of which the United States does not know the secret, and drugs, such as aspirin and acetanilide. This country has consistently sent its own coal tar to Germany to be developed.

4. The encouragement of new manufacturing industries by the wide circulation of information already gathered by the Geological Survey concerning the location of valuable deposits of commercial substances.

Agriculture

1. Greater coöperation in the Department of Agriculture with existing public employment agencies other than the existing Federal system with which coöperation has already been arranged. Such coöperation is especially effective in placing men with families at work in the country.

2. Federal farm loans and advances on crops and agricultural products. The postal savings funds and Federal reserve notes suggest possible methods. Passage of a rural credits bill.

3. The employment of skilled workmen by expanding to the greatest possible degree the investigative and research divisions in the department's work through:

The expansion of experiment stations.

An increase in the present facilities for investigating the utilization of reclaimed lands.

More extended studies of soil bacteriology, of grain production, of animal husbandry, of cereals, and further special investigations of orchard and fruit diseases, of chestnut bark disease, and cattle ticks.

These merely illustrate the possibilities.

General

1. An immediate intra-department survey of the possibilities of employing further help with profit

is recommended to every Federal department. It is further recommended that a committee, composed of members of several departments, be charged with stimulating this survey and collecting the results.

2. The use of the unemployed, selected with all necessary care, is proposed for the census work, and for any temporary investigations or inspections that may be necessary.

Military Service

1. A citizen soldiery,[1] requiring the enlistment of all young men for a period of about four months, would have, among other results, an appreciable influence upon unemployment. It would raise the level of the physical capacity of workers throughout the country, and the maintaining of their physical efficiency for years would mean also the maintaining of their industrial employability. Moreover, there would at all times be a certain force withdrawn from the industrial competition. Yet no single worker would be withdrawn for a sufficient length of time to handicap his civil career.

[1] The Britten bill now before Congress provides for the enlistment of 100,000 unemployed men, to prevent their loafing in enforced idleness, and to maintain their employability.

APPENDIX III

PUBLIC WORKS—CITIES AND TOWNS

The possibilities of public work will differ widely in various cities and towns. The first necessity is that a committee representing all the authorities concerned, the mayor, the city council, the board of estimate and apportionment, the public service commission, the city engineer, and the heads of the various city departments, come together and decide definitely: (1) what works already provided for can be hastened; (2) what repair or other work arranged for the summer can be done almost as well in the winter. There should be a careful estimate of how many men these works will employ and for how long a time. This number should be compared with the number of unemployed workmen in the city. After these points have been made clear, the committee may determine what *new projects may be undertaken with ultimate profit to the city and with immediate profit to its workmen.* The difficulties in financial operations, in expediting the technicalities involved in appropriations, or of advertising loans or bond issues may be authoritatively and swiftly dealt with if an official and responsible committee has once certified that the works themselves and the money arrangements necessary to get them under way are compatible with the city's welfare.

The most important matters to be settled are whether the work is to be given by the city directly or through contractors, whether it is to be done purely on an emergency basis, at emergency wages, with selection of candidates rather on the basis of need and of number of dependents than of ability, and with a relay system, or a half-time system, designed to permit the temporary employment of a great many rather than the permanent employment of a few, or whether the work throughout, is to be done, and the workers chosen with reference to normal industrial standards and conditions. Except in a few kinds of distinctly unskilled emergency work, such as rock crushing, stump clearing work, etc., where camps can be established, the work will be successful to the degree in which it conforms to normal standards.

The following illustrate types of work open to cities and towns of various kinds and location:

Sewers—
    Mending or cleaning.
    Extending to new sections of city.
Street Improvement—
    Quarrying, stone crushing, getting blocks ready, sand sifted, etc.
    Mending of asphalt.
    Paving, laying cobbles, etc., when ground not frozen.
    Grading, where weather permits.
    Opening streets.
    Curbing.
    Laying sidewalks.
    Street widening.
    Building of boulevards or concourses.

Water System—
  Construction of mains.
  Extension of high pressure system.
Extension of City Facilities—
  Installation of fire alarms.
  Lamp posts.
  Letter boxes.
  Street signs, etc.
Roads—
  Coöperation with state and county road projects.
Reclamation—
  Draining swamp land on outskirts.
  Land clearing, stumping.
Water-front—
  Building or repairing of wharves or piers.
  Construction of bulkheads.
  Dock repairs.
  Filling in water-front.
Improvements—
  Tearing down condemned or old buildings.
  Taking up abandoned car tracks.
  Tearing down old street bridges.
Repairing City Property—
  Overhauling municipal ferryboats, fireboats.
  Overhauling supplies for these.
Municipal Business Projects—
  Reducing of garbage and waste as municipal business venture (if contract permits).
  Municipal ice house (where possible or desirable).
  Municipal woodyards (where possible or desirable).
  Municipal brickyards (where possible or desirable).

Building Operations—

> Repairing of city institutions, by new cottages, boiler houses, coaling stations, laundries, storehouses, etc. Extensions for jails, hospitals, asylums, morgue, etc.
>
> New courthouse, etc.
>
> Municipal market.
>
> Municipal lodging houses.
>
> New public schools.
>
> New reformatories.
>
> Public baths.
>
> Public comfort stations.
>
> Bridges over railroad tracks.
>
> Model tenements, etc., etc.

Indoor Work—

> Making of uniforms (jails, asylums, etc.).
>
> Making of supplies used in institutions—bandages, pads, etc., for city hospital; basket work, trays, etc., for bakeries and laundry departments; bathing suits used in municipal baths; making of brick tiles, etc.
>
> Indoor painting and cleaning.
>
> Making or repairing equipment for parks, playgrounds, etc.

In addition to the possibilities of employing large numbers of skilled and unskilled workmen in these and other ways, cities may employ a limited number of professional workers on investigations already planned or proposed and intended to be preliminary to legislative or administrative provisions.

In the present crisis, certain municipalities in various parts of the country that have not been able to secure or hasten appropriations by the regular procedure have been able to continue or institute city work by the coöperation of citizens; chambers of commerce, other associations, and individual citizens have advanced the city the money for wages, or a fund has been raised by general subscription. In one case at least street grading work has been done through private capital, working through the city employment bureau.

The choice of workmen is made sometimes by the various city departments, sometimes by contractors, sometimes by a Citizens Relief Committee, sometimes through the city's charitable organizations. Very generally the heads of families and citizens are preferred.

34

APPENDIX IV

ONE MUNICIPAL PLAN—EMERGENCY MEASURES SUGGESTED TO THE CITY COUNCIL OF CLEVELAND

1. That the Mayor appoint a committee of competent men to work out a campaign to increase the demand for labor, along lines that they might see fit.

2. That the proposed municipal improvements be done at the earliest possible date. The installation of grade crossings, the building of street railway extensions, and the construction of city sewers, are three plans of improvement which will probably be started in early spring. The commencement of this work now would greatly reduce the number of unemployed and be no extra expense to the city. Cleveland is the natural labor center of the Western Reserve, and for this reason the condition here will probably affect the balance of the district. By stimulating business here, relief will be brought to surrounding towns in the district.

3. That the employers of labor, if they find it necessary to further curtail their forces, should reduce the number of working hours per man, rather than the number of men employed. This would not be an added expense to their pay rolls, but would decrease the army of unemployed in the city.

4. That employers of labor who do not contemplate decreasing their forces, should decrease the

number of working hours per man, and increase the number of wage earners. In this manner the burden of the industrial depression would be distributed among a greater number of men, and a great deal of the suffering would be eliminated, as this would add at least half as many men to the number of those at present employed without increased expense.

5. That the employers of the city of Cleveland, as far as possible, patronize the State-City Free Labor Exchange at the City Hall, an institution maintained by the state of Ohio in conjunction with the city of Cleveland, where employers and wage earners are brought together without any expense to either. A centralization of the Cleveland labor market would greatly facilitate the employers' securing competent and trustworthy employees, as well as assisting the wage earners searching for employment. In this office information is on file which will enable employers to choose between the worthy and the unworthy.

6. That the city through the Council and the Mayor's Committee father a campaign among business men, and urge them, where it is possible, to "hire another man," and that the Commissioner of Employment receive the proper authority from the Council to communicate with the employers and business organizations in Cleveland, and the surrounding towns, stating the real condition of the working men in Cleveland, urging them to join the "Hire a Man" movement. The Council Committee on Labor and the Commissioner of Employment requested a special appropriation of $300.00 for the expense of this campaign.

7. That the Commissioner of Labor encourage families and small firms to hire help where possible for

all kinds of labor, whether the work is washing and
cleaning for women, or beating rugs and shoveling
snow for men.   In this manner the citizens of Cleveland of moderate means can materially assist in helping to solve the unemployed situation in Cleveland.
One day's labor will enable a man to live and secure
the necessities of life for several days.

8.   That the police assist in culling vagrants from
the unemployed who are really in search of work.
This would greatly aid in giving those work where the
wages would bring the greatest relief.

9.   That the State-City Free Labor Exchange be
given greater support by the City Council, and thus
be able to widen the scope of its work and more intelligently handle the unemployed situation.   While at
the present time the Exchange is working at the
highest rate of efficiency obtainable under the limited
means at its disposal and has accomplished a great
deal, increased support would enable it to make
a systematic study of the trades of the great numbers of men who are thrown out of employment
during the slack seasons of their work, and devise some
means for absorbing them into other lines of occupation.   The Exchange should be enabled to act as a
barometer of labor conditions, and anticipate times of
industrial depression, and arrange to meet these conditions with remedial measures.

10.   That the City Council, instead of offering
charity as a solution of the present depression, should
assist the Commissioner of Employment to meet the
great plea of the workingmen, "We want jobs, not
charity."   The receiving of charity does not tend
to raise the standard of self-respect which every
workingman who is able and willing to work should

have. The Council should expedite all contemplated city work, and place the hiring of labor for city construction work with the State-City Free Labor Exchange.

APPENDIX V

THE CHURCH AND UNEMPLOYMENT—WHAT YOUR
CHURCH MAY DO[1]

Be a "Good Neighbor" Have families or individuals in the church become personally responsible for needy families or individuals, after finding out the need. The need may consist of clothing, food, a doctor's service, medicine, or simply friendship. If those who are in a position to render these services were actually to perform them, it would help greatly to solve the relief problem this winter.

This Will Vitalize the Prayer-Meeting At every church prayer-meeting there should be a period devoted to the "good and welfare of our neighbors," when the question should be asked: "Are any of our neighbors in distress of any kind?" If there are such, immediate steps should be taken to assist them. In the churches in which there are no poor, the question might be: "Are any of you in need of workers of any kind, either for temporary or permanent jobs?" The church should then proceed to bring together the jobless man or woman and the manless or womanless job. This may be done in coöperation with the Public Employment Bureau, corner of Lafayette and Leonard Streets, Manhattan (Telephone, Franklin

[1] Program issued by Inter-Church Employment Committee, New York City.

534

6101). It might also be asked: "Are any ready to furnish clothing or other assistance?" Somebody should be ready to see to it that these gifts are properly taken care of and delivered to those for whom they are intended.

Every week there should be printed an announcement in the church calendar stating specifically that either a special committee or the regular church staff is prepared to serve those **Weekly Call for Work and Workers.** who need help, or those who need work, and to receive applications for workers from possible employers, and offers for general relief from any members of the church.

Observe "Unemployment Sunday," either at the scheduled time, which will be announced later, or when convenient, but as early in the winter as possible. Definite suggestions will be made **"Unemployment Sunday" Should be Featured** for this service in a pamphlet issued by the office of the Inter-Church Unemployment Committee.

Housekeepers may find jobs which are usually postponed until spring. There are cellars and attics to be cleaned, or work to be done in the yard; there are all kinds of repairs about **Find Jobs about the House** the house. All these jobs must be done sometime,—why not do them now, when they will give life and hope to somebody out of work?

Office managers and employers in general may take this opportunity for properly disposing of accumulated papers and material,—for setting up adequate filing systems, and doing many **"Left-over" Jobs in the Office** other things which they know need to be done in order to secure the greatest efficiency in their business enterprises. While this may not bring immediate profit to them, it will prepare them for handling more effectively the business which will undoubtedly come later.

There are repair jobs in the church itself which may be done now. It may be difficult to raise the money **Repair** for this purpose, but, if the work must ulti- **Jobs in** mately be done, an effort should be made **the Church** to secure the necessary funds, as work given to the toilers during this winter will be worth many times as much to them now as during normal seasons, when jobs are more plentiful.

A systematic plan to have members of the church canvass certain neighborhoods, or their personal **Church** friends, for jobs for the needy will be most **Members** effective. In the aggregate, many days of **Getting** work will be found in this way. It will un- **Jobs for** doubtedly be much easier for intelligent, **Others** persuasive persons to secure work for the unemployed than it would be for the unemployed themselves to do so. It doesn't matter what kind of jobs they are,—it will be comparatively easy to find needy persons to do them. There are undoubtedly many families in the suburbs or in country homes who can at this time give special employment.

Set aside a day early in the winter, when it will be generally understood that representatives from the churches in the community are to call **A United** upon the people for the purpose of securing **Appeal to** jobs for the unemployed. Give this matter **the Com-** the utmost publicity, so that the neighbors **munity.** may have been prepared to think about it and thus be ready to talk sympathetically and definitely with the visitors. This day may be observed in practically every church in the community.

Urge employers of labor to continue operations as a *religious* duty. The employer who creates jobs should be regarded as doing religious work. The entire problem of unemployment must be made a problem of applied religion. It is as important this winter as any social or philanthropic work that has ever been done by the Church.

Finding Jobs a Religious Task

Influence employers to give part time work to all rather than full time work to a few. Their own industrial forces and organizations will thus be kept intact, and, while there will undoubtedly be some difficulties in the way of enforcing this rule, it will prevent the demoralization which is inevitable on account of the lack of employment,—families will be held together and it will prevent a breaking down in their social and moral life. Undoubtedly the loyalty of these employees will be greatly strengthened by this evidence of friendship and regard on the part of the employer.

Part Time Better Than No Work

An effort should be made to help workingmen maintain a fair standard of wages. There will be a temptation to ask the jobless man or woman to work for less than their work is worth, simply because they are helpless. There will be large demands for money to be used for charitable purposes during the coming winter. Many of these demands should be heeded but, on the whole, it will be much better for employers of labor to keep their men at work, even at a financial loss, than to give the same amount of money as may be lost by so doing to philanthropic and relief agencies. It is better to reduce the hours of labor if a full work-

Maintain a Fair Standard of Wages

ing day cannot be had, than it is to reduce the wages.
When normal times return, the old standard will then
not have been lowered, and workingmen will not be
compelled to repeat their struggle to secure what they
regard as a living wage.

The church may get in touch with needy people
through the public school. The school-teachers are
usually familiar with the situations in the
homes of their pupils, particularly if their
scholars are poorly nourished or thinly
clad. There is an increasing tendency
this winter to take children out of school and send
them to work, because their fathers have lost their
jobs or have to work on reduced time or lowered wages.
It will be a most worthy charity to give the parents a
small sum of money weekly in lieu of wages,—perhaps not quite as much as a child might earn, but
enough to keep him in school.

Coöperate with School-Teachers

Some groups of churches may establish loan agencies;
all that is required is a sufficient amount of money to
begin operations, and a simple, sensible
plan of administration. A low interest
charge will probably make the enterprise
practically self-supporting. The capital
invested would be returned to those who advanced it,
when the necessity for its use shall have passed by.
To loan money in a businesslike way would be better
than giving it outright to those who are temporarily
embarrassed on account of unemployment, or for some
other reason which will not result in permanent disability.

Loans Better than Gifts

Do not conduct bread-lines, soup-kitchens, give
public dinners, or other public relief enterprises for
the destitute without consulting the authorities on

social and relief work. Much harm may be done by such enterprises. A supreme effort should be made to assist families as such, **The Family** keeping father, mother, and children at **Should be Held to-** home, where together they may eat their **gether** bread with gladness of heart.

It is extremely important that the churches should all coöperate in this work, thus avoiding overlapping and overlooking. There will soon be established in coöperation with the New **Avoid Over-** York Federation of Churches a central **lapping and Overlook-** point in each community which may **ing through** serve as a clearing-house for the churches **Coöperation** in that district. It is understood that not every church is in a position to work effectively in meeting the unemployment and relief conditions in New York, but every church may undoubtedly coöperate with all the other churches in its immediate neighborhood in seeing that the utmost is done in the name of religion to meet local needs.

The churches should coöperate with the recognized public and private charities and relief organizations, both because these organizations may render a valuable service to the churches and **Work with** because the churches may be of inestimable **the Estab- lishedRelief** value in assisting these agencies. The **Agencies** measure of actual coöperation may be determined after the office conference either with these organizations, or with the Inter-Church Unemployment Committee.

The homeless man will undoubtedly present a most perplexing problem to the churches. Demands may be made upon the churches, as in previous years,

for the use of their buildings for temporary lodging-house purposes.   There may be some extremely
Shelter for cold weather during the winter which may
the Home- justify the use of church buildings for this
less Man   purpose, and when it is possible to put
        them to such use, it will undoubtedly be
commendable.   But the question of sanitation is a
most serious one, and should be carefully considered
by those who are responsible for the care of the
church buildings.   It should be remembered that it
is the business of the city to take care of homeless
men.   It might be a good plan for some of the
churches to make arrangements with nearby lodging
houses for the temporary care of homeless men.   An
understanding may be had with the managers of these
lodging-houses, or with one of the recognized relief
agencies of the city, that only the tickets actually
used should be paid for.

In emergency cases of any kind, call up, DAY OR
        NIGHT, after January 1st, the Inter-
Emergency Church Unemployment Committee, 200
Calls   Fifth Avenue, Manhattan (Tel., Gramercy
1552), where full information will be promptly and
cheerfully furnished.

APPENDIX VI

All the measures noted below have been established this winter, or are now being projected with distinct reference to the present crisis. They are appended here not as recommendations, but with the idea that some of them may be suggestive to other communities where relief measures could now be effectively initiated by citizens.

Central Relief Committee where there was no Mayor's Committee.

Emergency free employment bureau, when city had no effective municipal bureau.

Central and district relief stations.

House-to-house and shop-to-shop canvass conducted by volunteer workers

1. To find the unemployed that do not apply for aid.
2. To find odd jobs—and other jobs.
3. To find best medium in community through which to administer relief.

Loan funds, especially for skilled workers

1. Through funds privately subscribed.
2. Through money borrowed from banks at interest, etc.

"Be a good neighbor" or "Big Brother" movements by which individuals have made themselves responsible for unemployed individuals or families.

Work Rooms for Women—Sewing Rooms.

With, or without, employment bureau.

With, or without, selection of applicants according to industrial employability.

Wage rates—vary from 50c. or 75c. daily to $1.50.

Product disposed of variously in various places: given to Red Cross, to Belgian Relief Fund; sold and proceeds given to unemployed; given to hospitals and other institutions; regularly contracted for by factories.

One meal given.

Work Rooms for Men.

Bandages, hospital supplies, etc., made for Red Cross or for native institutions.

Men work from 10 to 3 o'clock and look for work the rest of the day.

Paid 50c. a day.

Each man given only a few days' work.

Efforts made to find them regular jobs.

Clothing, etc., distributed to the most needy.

Private owners offered land to be cleared through municipal employment bureau at specific wage rate.

Some form of manufacture started in unused lofts or idle factories.

Discarded railroad ties and telegraph poles collected for temporary woodyards.

Tools, shovels, etc., donated for emergency work.

Letters and circulars issued to employers of labor urging hiring of one more man.

Systematic appeals made to citizens to buy goods made in the home city.

City newspaper conducted campaign to get men

temporary jobs on farms for the winter, with coopera-
tion of state labor bureau.

Money lent by banks and citizens to Building
Associations to stimulate that business.

Lists of skilled workmen hunting jobs posted at the
various exchanges, real estate, cotton, merchants', etc.

Unemployed given free use of newspaper advertising columns on one day a week.

Arrangements made with leading daily papers to
print details of most needy cases, without names, each
day.

Transportation fund raised to get workers to ice
camps and other works out of city, and to send back
to their home towns workers unable to find work in the
city.

General movement to employ men to clean up
neglected burial plots in cemeteries.

Work furnished unemployed, beginning in February,
by developing flower and vegetable gardens around city.

Meetings of school teachers to organize relief work
conducted through the schools.

Subsidizing of penny lunches in the public schools,
with free tickets for destitute children.

Vacant houses, lent by owners, equipped as temporary shelters for special groups of unemployed, as
young girls.

Furnishing temporary homes for unemployed women by getting them into households where they do
a limited amount of housework for their board and
lodging.

Temporary shelters opened in old laundries, audi-
toriums, etc.

Markets established at which unemployed can buy
provisions on credit.

Credit for unemployed heads of families arranged with local grocers.

Coöperative kitchens established, also bread-lines and soup-kitchens.

"Bundle Days" instituted, by which bundles of clothes, etc., are widely collected for unemployed. Necessary work of fumigating, repairing, washing, etc., given to unemployed men and women. Clothing sold in temporary "shops," at auctions, or given directly to unemployed.

Auction sales—goods collected from wealthy residents, manufacturers, and shop owners, and sold at auction to provide money to give work to the unemployed.

Telephone refunds turned over in lump sum for unemployment relief.

Theater benefits, balls, exhibitions held for unemployed and widely advertised.

APPENDIX VII

A BILL

To regulate certain employment agencies and for other purposes.

Be it enacted by the Senate and House of Representatives of the United States of America in Congress Assembled: That after July 1st, 1915, no person, firm, association, or corporation shall be engaged in the business of procuring or assisting to procure employment for persons outside the State where the business is carried on, and which requires their transportation from one state or territory to another state or territory, or of collecting and furnishing information regarding such employment, without first obtaining from the Commissioner of Labor Exchanges, a license if such business is being operated for profit, or a permit in all other cases.

SECTION 2. That an application for a license or a permit shall be made under oath upon blanks furnished by the Commissioner and shall be in such form and contain such information as he may require. With the application there shall be presented to the Commissioner satisfactory proof by affidavits of the good moral character of the applicant, and in case such applicant is a corporation, of its officers.

SECTION 3. That the Commissioner shall investigate or cause to be investigated the character and responsibility of the applicant and may examine or cause to be examined the premises in which it is proposed to conduct such agency, and the methods and books used in the conduct thereof.

SECTION 4. That a license shall be granted upon the approval of the application, the filing of a bond, in due form, to the People of the United States of America, in the penal sum of one thousand dollars with two or more sufficient sureties or a surety company satisfactory to the Commissioner, conditioned upon the faithful observance by the licensee of the provisions of this Act and all rules and regulations adopted thereunder, and the payment to the Commissioner of a fee of fifty dollars. Such fee shall be paid into the Treasury to the credit of miscellaneous receipts. The license, unless sooner revoked by the Commissioner, shall run to the first day of July next ensuing the date thereof and no longer, and shall be renewable annually on payment of a like fee and on compliance with any rules adopted under this act. Every license shall contain the name of the licensee, the address at which he is authorized to carry on business and the number and date of such license, and shall be in such form and contain such further particulars as the Commissioner may prescribe. Such license shall not authorize the licensee or his agents to transact business or to advertise or hold himself or themselves out as authorized to transact business at any place other than that described in the license, without the written consent of the Commissioner, nor shall the license be transferred or assigned without such consent. A permit shall be granted in like manner as a license and shall be subject to all the provisions relating to the granting of a license but no bond or fee shall be required.

SECTION 5. That such holder of a license or a permit shall not charge or receive a registration fee for filing an application for employment or for help,unless he is permitted to do so by the rules and regulations of the Commissioner. Such holder of a license or a permit shall always give a receipt for money received in which shall be stated the name of the applicant, the amount of the fee, the amount received for transportation or for other purposes, the date, the name or character of the work or situation procured, the name of the intended employer, the wage to be received,and whether or not an industrial dispute, strike, or lockout is in progress, and such other details as the Commissioner may designate.

SECTION 6. That such holder of a license, or a permit shall not send out an applicant for any employment without having first obtained a *bona fide* order therefor in writing, stating the terms and conditions of employment and whether an industrial dispute, strike, or lockout is in progress at or in connection with the business or place of business of the person or corporation making the request for help. Such order shall be kept on file by the licensee and shall at all times be open to the inspection of the Commissioner.

SECTION 7. That the Commissioner shall keep different books wherein shall be entered in alphabetical order all licenses and permits granted, the date of the issuance thereof, and the name or names of the holders thereof, with a statement of the place of business, and such other information as the Commissioner may prescribe. Such records shall be open to public inspection.

SECTION 8. That the Commissioner, on the approval of the Secretary of Labor, shall make necessary rules and regulations to carry out the purposes of this Act: (a) to classify the different types of employment agencies and to make appropriate rules and regulations for the different classes of agencies; (b) to provide for the posting of licenses, permits, rules and regulations, signs, and schedules of rates charged; (c) to prescribe the form of books, registers, contracts, and records to be kept and of the reports and schedules of rates to be filed with the Commissioner; (d) to order the refund of fees and transportation charges to applicants who fail to secure employment; (e) to prevent women and children from being sent by such agencies to places of ill-repute; (f) to prohibit the making, publication, or distribution of any false, inaccurate, or misleading statement regarding employment or the making of any false entry in any record kept; and (g) to prevent fraud, misrepresentation, extortion, the dividing of fees, or other improper or unlawful acts on the part of all such holders of licenses or permits.

SECTION 9. That if a holder of a license or a permit is guilty of fraud or misrepresentation or violates any of the provisions of this act or of the rules and regulations adopted thereunder, the Commissioner may order the immediate return of such fees and transportation charges as may have been advanced, and may revoke the license or permit after giving the holder thereof such notice as the Commissioner may deem sufficient and an opportunity to answer the charges.

SECTION 10. The Commissioner, deputy commissioners, agents, and any other officers designated by him, may enter the place of business of any employment agency subject to, or which he may have reasonable cause to believe is subject to, the provisions of this Act, and inspect the premises, books, registers, or other records of such agency.

SECTION 11. That any violation of the provisions of this act or of the rules and regulations adopted thereunder shall be a misdemeanor and shall be punished by a fine in each case of not more than five hundred dollars or by imprisonment for a term not exceeding one year, or by both such fine and imprisonment.

Explanatory Notes on Proposed Bill to Regulate Employment Agencies Doing an Interstate Business

In re Section 1. All agencies engaged in the business of furnishing information regarding employment opportunities outside the state where the business is carried on should be brought under the supervision of the national bureau of labor exchanges in order to concentrate in one central office all matters affecting the distribution of labor.

In re Section 2. This provides for the filing of an application for a license or a permit and for proof of an applicant's good moral character.

In re Section 3. With this power of investigation, the Commissioner may decline to issue a license or a permit if any objectionable features are found in the applicant's business.

In re Section 4. This section provides for the technical procedure involved in the issuance of a license or a permit, such as the filing of a bond, the payment of a fee, the method of renewal, and what the license certificate should contain. It also limits the assignment of such license or permit, and the transaction of business to the one place described therein, in the discretion of the Commissioner. These provisions apply to all classes of agencies except that those not operating for profit, such as philanthropic and industrial agencies, are not required to file bonds or pay fees.

In re Section 5. The charging of a registration fee is prohibited without specific permission, as the applicant for work is usually unable to pay such a fee until a position is actually secured. By obtaining a receipt containing the details specified, the applicant for work can prove his claim in case of misrepresentation or other fraudulent practices.

In re Section 6. Orders or requests for help should always be in writing, not only for the protection of the applicant for work but also for the employment agent in case of any later misunderstanding.

In re Section 7. This simply authorizes the keeping of registers of all licenses and permits granted, for the information of the public.

In re Section 8. Broad general power is vested in the Commissioner and the Secretary of Labor to formulate and adopt from time to time all necessary rule and regulations to meet and cope with the various problems, difficulties, and temptations of the private employment agency business. Such discretionary power in the executive officer will enable him to establish fair rules according to the varying needs and the local conditions, instead of compelling him to enforce detailed and inflexible provisions of law often working serious hardship if they are specifically included in the original law. The various conditions to be so regulated are mentioned for their suggestive and educational value and include: (a) classifying agencies to formulate different rules for different classes of agencies, as, for instance, the general labor and theatrical agencies; (b) posting laws, documents, etc., to prevent exploitation; (c) keeping certain records to make them uniform, and filing certain reports and schedules to prevent overcharges and to centralize all the interstate employment business; (d) returning fees and transportation charges if a position is not obtained without any fault on the part of the applicant; (e) requiring reasonable investigation by employment agencies of places where women and children are sent to secure positions, to protect health, morals, etc.; (f) prohibiting distribution of misleading information or notation of false entries, to prevent misrepresentation; and (g) providing for the general safeguarding of all persons applying for work or for help.

In re Section 9. The Commissioner is given general authority to order refunds and revoke licenses or permits when laws or rules are violated.

In re Section 10. The Commissioner and his assistants are given general authority to inspect all agencies amenable to the provisions of this act.

In re Section 11. This section specifies the penalties incurred when laws or rules are violated.

APPENDIX VIII

REGULARIZATION OF INDUSTRY[1]

(1) Establishment of an Employment Department. The employer should establish, as part of his organization, an employment department, having at its head an employment manager whose special duty it is to study the problems of unemployment in the individual shop and to devise ways of meeting them. Such a department would aim at:

A. Reduction of the "Turnover" of Labor. By a study of its causes through records of "hiring and firing," reduction could be made in the "turnover" of labor which is at present so excessive that factories frequently hire and discharge 1000 men in a year to keep up a force of 300.

B. Reduction of Fluctuations of Employment inside the Shop. Among the methods that might be used for this purpose are:

(a) Systematic transfer of workers between departments.

(b) Employing all on part time rather than laying off part of the force in definitely seasonal occupations where there would not be much prospect of dismissed workers' being taken on elsewhere.

(c) Arranging working force in groups and

[1] From *A Practical Program for the Prevention of Unemployment in America*, John B. Andrews.

keeping higher groups employed continuously.
Those in lower groups will then be encouraged to
keep out of the industry altogether, or to combine
it with some other occupations to which they can
regularly turn in the dull season.

(d) Keeping before the attention of the rest of
the organization the importance of regularizing
employment.

(e) Keeping in close touch and coöperation with
outside agencies dealing with unemployment problems.

(2) Regulation of Output. The employer should
regulate his output and distribute it as evenly as
possible throughout the year. Methods to this end
are:

A. Record Keeping and Forward Planning.
Yearly curves should be kept, showing production,
sales, and deliveries day by day, week by week,
and month by month; and an effort should be
made each year to level the curve and to smooth out
the "peak load." Production should when possible
be planned at least six months ahead.

B. Building up Slack Season Trade. Special
instruction should be given to sales departments
and to traveling salesmen to urge customers to place
orders for delivery during the slack season. Some
firms threaten delayed delivery on goods at the
height of the season. Special advertising stimu-
lates trade in the slack season. Many firms offer
especially low prices, grant special discounts, make
special cheap lines, or even do business without
a profit simply to keep their organization together
and to supply work for their forces.

C. Keeping a Stock Department and Making

to Stock as Liberally as Possible in the Slack Season. This method keeps many firms busy. It is more difficult in industries where goods are perishable or where style is an important factor as in garment making and shoe making, but even here there are conspicuous examples of its success. Other manufacturers deliberately follow a conservative style policy, or concentrate the making of staple styles in the slack season. The making of goods to stock requires the tying-up of a certain amount of capital, but many employers feel this to be balanced by the gain in contentment among the workers and the increase of efficiency and team spirit in the organization. They have the further advantage of being able to supply goods immediately on order.

D. "Going After" Steady rather than Specula,ive Business. Well organized business with a steady demand and a regular and sure profit can afford to dispense with the irregular and unreliable gains of a speculative business which oftens involves disorganization and irregularity of production.

E. Careful Study of Market Conditions and Adjustment of the Business to Take Advantage of Them. A broad market provides more regular business than a narrow one. Foreign trade supplements domestic trade and orders often arrive from southern and far-western markets when the eastern market is slack. A diversity of customers will usually provide a more regular demand than concentration on one or two large buyers. The retail trade will often take a manufacturer's goods just when the wholesale season has stopped. In the shoe industry the ownership of chains of retail stores has enabled some manufacturers to regularize their business considerably, and a garment manufacturer who owns his own retail store is able to stock that just as soon as his wholesale orders run slack.

F. Developing New Lines and Complementary Industries. A diversity of products will often help to regularize a business. Many manufacturers study their plant, the nature of their material, and the character of the market to see whether they cannot add new lines to supplement those they have and fill in business in the slack seasons. One shoe manufacturer, for example, adds rubber sheeting, rubber heels, tennis shoes, rubber cloth, and rubber tires, and achieves a fairly regular business.

G. Overcoming Weather Conditions. The brick-making industry has been made a regular twelve months' industry instead of a seasonal six months' industry by the introduction of artificial drying. Special refrigerating, heating, or moistening apparatus proves effective in other industries. Even in the building trade the amount of winter work can be increased by provision for covering or enclosing and heating work under construction.

(3) Coöperation with Other Employers. A number of trade abuses have been allowed to develop which lead to unemployment. Many of these could be abolished by collective action of employers. Employers should coöperate to:

A. Prevent Development of Plant and Machinery far beyond Normal Demand. An installation of equipment the capacity of which is far in excess of orders normally to be expected is not only a financial burden but it is a continual inducement toward rush orders and irregular operation. In some industries this unhealthy tendency is counteracted by the distribution of excessive orders among other firms whose business is slack.

B. Prevent Disorganization of Production Due to Cut-Throat Competition. Agreements might in some cases be made to restrict extreme styles and other excessively competitive factors which serve to disorganize production.

C. Prevent Separate Reserve of Labor for Each Plant. Agreements among employers in the same industry to take their labor from a central source and to allow their reserve workers and extras to fill in their spare time with other firms would do much to regularize employment. Where this has been done, as in some employment bureaus operated by associations of manufacturers, the men have been directed without delay from one employer to another and get fairly regular employment. This method is to be especially recommended for the building trades where the labor market is usually completely disorganized and attracts the floating surplus of the district. The best central depot of this kind is of course, the public labor exchange.

APPENDIX IX

UNEMPLOYMENT INSURANCE[1]

Mr. I. G. Gibbon in his book *Unemployment Insurance* sets forth the following conclusions:

1. It is necessary that provision should be made against unemployment.

2. It is preferable that the provision against unemployment should be made through insurance.

3. It is advisable that the community should financially assist the making of provision against unemployment.

4. The assistance to be granted to insurance against unemployment should be so given as genuinely to encourage self-help. The amount provided as assistance should not be more than the provision made by the work people themselves.

5. It seems desirable that part of the assistance given by the community should be paid by the central authority and part by the local authorities, the larger proportion being paid by the former.

6. The scheme of assistance should be under the supervision of a committee which should contain representatives of the governmental authorities, of any other class, employers for instance, granting assistance, and also of the persons assisted.

[1] *Unemployment Insurance*, I. G. Gibbon, London, King, 1911.

7. On the whole, it does not seem expedient that insurance against unemployment should be made compulsory.

8. In any scheme of assisted insurance against unemployment, the fullest use should be made of voluntary associations. Preference should be given to insurance effected through such associations.

9. It is advisable that, side by side with the encouragement of insurance effected through voluntary associations, a scheme should be established, maintained, and assisted by the community in which persons who are not members of voluntary associations which provide insurance against unemployment should be able to be insured.

10. In a provided scheme, the rates of premium should vary according to the risks of unemployment in the trade to which the insured member belongs.

11. It does not seem expedient to require compulsory contributions from employers, at least when the insurance is voluntary.

12. Subsidy should be paid in proportion to benefit.

13. It is advisable to provide that different rates of subsidy may be given to different classes of workmen, or for different kinds of unemployment, or in respect of different forms of provision.

14. The rates of assistance should be fixed by the committee of management, subject to limits which should be set out in the law, and to the approval of the central authority.

15. It is desirable that any scheme of assistance to insurance against unemployment should be worked in close connection with an efficient system of labor exchanges.

16. Preference should be given, so far as possible, to insured persons in work found through public labor exchanges or through other public institutions, always strictly subject to the suitability of the person for the work given to him.

17. Insurance against unemployment is practicable for large numbers of workmen not now insured, including large numbers of unskilled workmen.

18. The total amount received in unemployment pay should be considerably less than the usual wage.

19. Subsidy should be paid in respect of unemployment occurring at any time in the year.

20. Subsidy should not be paid in respect of the first few days of unemployment.

21. A limit should be fixed to the daily amount of subsidy which may be received by any one person and also to the time for which subsidy may be received.

22. Provision should be made that, in proportion as a member exhausts the limit of subsidy, so he must contribute for a longer period before he again becomes entitled to subsidy, or as an alternative restriction, that the period during which he may receive subsidy in the next year shall be shorter.

23. The rate of subsidy should not vary according to the persons dependent on the recipients.

INDEX

Agencies, *see* general labor, domestic service, philanthropic, professional, private, public, etc.

Alabama, emigration laws, 357; peonage law, 378; federal decisions, 379

Aliens, on public works, 143; discrimination in occupations, 144, 387, 486. *See* immigration and immigrants

American Association for Labor Legislation, 297

Andrews, John B., regularization of industry, 504

Apprenticeship, *see* vocational training

Arizona, regulation of private agencies, 357; fee splitting, 366

Arkansas, peonage in, 378, 379, 382

Atwood agencies, 163

Boston, regulation of number of private agencies by police board, 332; appropriation to licensing board, 374; labor agents of, and peonage, 378; municipal regulation of private agencies, 385; municipal lodging-house, 412

Brooklyn, sewing-room of Bureau of Charities, 394, 395; municipal lodging, 416, 417

Brown, E. A., 407, 418

Buffalo, lack of enforcement of provisions regulating private agencies, 375; War Relief Committee, 271, 394, 395

Bureau of Industry and Immigration (New York), Report on camps, 134, 155

Business institutes and colleges, 266

Butte, employment of aliens, 350, 388

California, hop riots in, 15; Commission of Immigration and Housing, 154, 383, 471; civil service laws, 349; regulation of private agencies, 356; refunds of fees, 362; fee splitting, 366; provision against fraud, 368; fund for enforcement, 373; responsibility for enforcement, 374; unemployment insurance and seasonal workers, 471

Camps, *see* labor camps

Canneries, children in, 95

Cattle boats, 174

Charity Organization Society (New York), 286

Chicago, census of unemployed by city bureau, 341; municipal lodging-house, 406; municipal grocery store, 426; the Mayor's commission on unemployment, 426, 437; municipal market commission, 437; recommendation for study of unemployment insurance, 471

Children, effect of unemployment upon, 30; and labor market, 58; number in industry, 60; wages of, 63; hours, 66; opportunity for advance-

POVERTY, U. S. A.

THE HISTORICAL RECORD

An Arno Press/New York Times Collection

Adams, Grace. **Workers on Relief.** 1939.

The Almshouse Experience: Collected Reports. 1821-1827.

Armstrong, Louise V. **We Too Are The People.** 1938.

Bloodworth, Jessie A. and Elizabeth J. Greenwood.
The Personal Side. 1939.

Brunner, Edmund deS. and Irving Lorge.
**Rural Trends in Depression Years: A Survey of
Village-Centered Agricultural Communities, 1930-1936.**
1937.

Calkins, Raymond.
**Substitutes for the Saloon: An Investigation Originally
made for The Committee of Fifty.** 1919.

Cavan, Ruth Shonle and Katherine Howland Ranck.
**The Family and the Depression: A Study of
One Hundred Chicago Families.** 1938.

Chapin, Robert Coit.
**The Standard of Living Among Workingmen's Families
in New York City.** 1909.

**The Charitable Impulse in Eighteenth Century America:
Collected Papers.** 1711-1797.

Children's Aid Society.
Children's Aid Society Annual Reports, 1-10.
February 1854-February 1863.

Conference on the Care of Dependent Children.
**Proceedings of the Conference on the Care
of Dependent Children.** 1909.

Conyngton, Mary.
How to Help: A Manual of Practical Charity. 1909.

Devine, Edward T. **Misery and its Causes.** 1909.

Devine, Edward T. **Principles of Relief.** 1904.

Dix, Dorothea L.
On Behalf of the Insane Poor: Selected Reports. 1843-1852.

Douglas, Paul H.
**Social Security in the United States: An Analysis and
Appraisal of the Federal Social Security Act.** 1936.

Farm Tenancy: Black and White. Two Reports. 1935, 1937.

Feder, Leah Hannah.
**Unemployment Relief in Periods of Depression:
A Study of Measures Adopted in Certain American
Cities, 1857 through 1922.** 1936.

Folks, Homer.
**The Care of Destitute, Neglected, and
Delinquent Children.** 1900.

Guardians of the Poor.
**A Compilation of the Poor Laws of the State of
Pennsylvania from the Year 1700 to 1788, Inclusive.** 1788.

Hart, Hastings, H.
Preventive Treatment of Neglected Children.
(Correction and Prevention, Vol. 4) 1910.

Herring, Harriet L.
**Welfare Work in Mill Villages: The Story of Extra-Mill
Activities in North Carolina.** 1929.

The Jacksonians on the Poor: Collected Pamphlets.
1822-1844.

Karpf, Maurice J.
Jewish Community Organization in the United States.
1938.

Kellor, Frances A.
Out of Work: A Study of Unemployment. 1915.

Kirkpatrick, Ellis Lore.
The Farmer's Standard of Living. 1929.

Komarovsky, Mirra.
The Unemployed Man and His Family: The Effect of Unemployment Upon the Status of the Man in Fifty-Nine Families. 1940.

Leupp, Francis E. **The Indian and His Problem.** 1910.

Lowell, Josephine Shaw.
Public Relief and Private Charity. 1884.

More, Louise Bolard.
Wage Earners' Budgets: A Study of Standards and Cost of Living in New York City. 1907.

New York Association for Improving the Condition of the Poor.
AICP First Annual Reports Investigating Poverty. 1845-1853.

O'Grady, John.
Catholic Charities in the United States: History and Problems. 1930.

Raper, Arthur F.
Preface to Peasantry: A Tale of Two Black Belt Counties. 1936.

Raper, Arthur F. **Tenants of The Almighty.** 1943.

Richmond, Mary E.
What is Social Case Work? An Introductory Description. 1922.

Riis, Jacob A. **The Children of the Poor.** 1892.

Rural Poor in the Great Depression: Three Studies. 1938.

Sedgwick, Theodore.
Public and Private Economy: Part I. 1836.

Smith, Reginald Heber. **Justice and the Poor.** 1919.

Sutherland, Edwin H. and Harvey J. Locke.
Twenty Thousand Homeless Men: A Study of Unemployed Men in the Chicago Shelters. 1936.

Tuckerman, Joseph.
On the Elevation of the Poor: A Selection From His Reports as Minister at Large in Boston. 1874.

Warner, Amos G. **American Charities.** 1894.

Watson, Frank Dekker.
The Charity Organization Movement in the United States: A Study in American Philanthropy. 1922.

Woods, Robert A., et al. **The Poor in Great Cities.** 1895.